Not Behind Lace Curtains

The Hidden World of Evan, Viscount Tredegar

Evan Frederic Morgan

Up Through the Sea.

By the HON. EVAN MORGAN.

If I could lose Thine Image for a while
    I would be glad;
If I could hide from Thee, then would I
    smile
        With eyes less sad,
If I could fly Thine Image for a while.

If from my thoughts I could but drive
    Thee out
        Then might I rest.
If for one moment could completely doubt
    What I know best,
And let allegiance wither in the drought!

Such I can never do, so haunted groan,
    Begging Thee go!
Remorseful, tortured, cringe beneath Thy
    throne,
        Condemned to know
Thou, thou art there and I am not alone!

My conscience like an ever-raging sea
    Beats my heart's shore,
Each breaking wave spreads laden misery,
    Until no more
Hard rocks remain unbattered by Thy plea.

Through the long night cascading billows
    fall,
        Thud upon thud!
Up through my dreams I hear the sea-
    winds call . . .
        Thy dripping Blood,
Plashes upon my heart and turns to gall!

Give me the strength to fly Thee, or to keep
    Thine Image clear,
Unclouded in the crystal where thoughts
    sleep
        Untouched by fear:
Nor, as I have sown, in mercy let me reap!

Give me the strength to shun Thee or to
    love;
        Give me the strength!
Divorce me from Earth's force, let roam
    Thy Dove . . .
        Throughout the length,
The breadth of my poor spirit, God above!

Not Behind Lace Curtains

The Hidden World of Evan, Viscount Tredegar

By

Evan Frederic Morgan

And

William Cross

And Thanks to Robin Bryans (1928-2005)

Bust of Evan, Viscount Tredegar
by Prince Bira of Siam

Introduction

Evan Tredegar in His Bath Tub

Gideon

Nestling snugly in a well proportioned bath tub in a room embroidered with Italian mosaics by Boris Anrep,[1] Evan Tredegar [2] mused upon how wondrous the decorations were in this, his new home of 13, South Audley Street, Mayfair. [3] Pride of place was a plaque of *Gideon* from *Della Robbia.* [4] Such sophistication compared well with the stunning bathroom surrounds of his previous London residence at 40, South Street, Mayfair which had included fabulous wall pictures in grisaille, with a set of priceless panels of *The Loves of Cupid and Psyche* painted about 1780. [5] Oh, how Evan prized the perfection of the master craftsman who had created these wonderfully rich images: a born aesthetic, he appreciated the finer things in life.

Evan's thoughts turned swiftly to how wittily his deceased acquaintance, the novelist Ronnie Firbank [6] described the twice daily plunge into the bath tub as "sublime sanitization for the well brought up English gentleman." [7]

Firbank had immortalised the scene of Evan:

"…Lying amid the dissolving bath crystals while his manservant deftly bathed him, [he fell] into a sort of coma, sweet as a religious trance. Beneath the rhythmic sponge, perfumed with Kiki, [Evan] was St Sebastian, and as the water became cloudier and the crystals evaporated amid the steam, he was Teresa…and he would have been most likely the Blessed Virgin herself but that the bath grew gradually cold." [8]

Emerging slowly, dripping and trembling from the tub, Evan gasped in irate tones to Alfred Arthur Lucker, [9] (his handsome seventeen-year-old valet), about the bitter quarrel with Ronnie Firbank over a very silly book dedication. [10]

Sighing, Evan mused at how all this reflection and contemplation was needless folly, ancient history. Alas, poor, ridiculous Firbank who'd expired abruptly in Rome in 1926; "imagine dying of self-inflicted starvation, from an excess of champagne, brandy and tuberculosis."

Ronnie Firbank, who died in Rome in 1926

Ronnie's last message to his friends from the *Hotel Quirinale*[11] was an indulgent ploy to attain posterity by warning others *not* to visit him on account of the dreadful state of the wallpaper.[12]

"Damn the wit of that blasted Firbank, that rake: that Sherlock Holmes-like figure who'd once dared to call *me* a little fool; *me,* Evan Morgan, at the time an Honourable, the son of a *bona fide* noble Lord and his gracious Lady."

It was now the end of July of 1937: Evan was a noble Lord in his own right, a Peer of the Realm, with the rank of Viscount of the United Kingdom, a "Right trusty and Cousin"[13] to his Monarch, the stammering King George VI, and irresistible to foolish men anywhere they chose to party. Evan adored to party, as did his entire generation of *The Bright Young Things.* He was once ranked a leading figure of that clique, along with his dear friend Noel Coward,[14] "the enormously talented playwright, composer and actor."

Noel was to write and record a song to celebrate one marvellous party they'd attended together in the South of France![15]

Evan had plans to find himself an equally marvellous party that night, after turning up for a charity dinner at the *Savoy Hotel*, his second fund-raising event of the week.[16]

"Eccentric, perverse, unpredictable, arrogant, and outrageous"[17]: Evan Tredegar could switch his personality; one minute a witty companion, an open-handed, generous patron of all good causes, but then suddenly change from the placid Dr Jekyll into the terrifying monster, Mr Hyde.[18]

Hastening Alfred to complete his delicate personal manoeuvrings Evan eyed up the invitation card to a reception and dinner at the *Savoy Hotel* in the heart of the London's Strand.

The *Savoy Hotel* was one of Evan's favourite watering holes:

"Oh, Alfred, my dear, the *Savoy*...so much more amusing than that mausoleum *Claridges,* or the synagogue *Ritz*.."

On that particular evening Evan intended moving speedily to a cabaret night-club in the Capital's deeper, more decadent underworld. He would end the evening hunting for "rough trade"[19] from London's sleazy streets. In the Strand, one spot for an easy pick up of a boy was near Lyon's famous Corner House. [20] Evan "knew the night life of Paris, Rome, Berlin, Vienna and Budapest, 'milord' being well known in the bars, cafes and night clubs."[21]

But before going to the charity reception Evan had a duty to perform. This was to attend at the Houses of Parliament in order to give support to a fellow Oxford man, Mr Alan P Herbert [22] whose Private Members Bill was being moved for its amendments to be read after passage through the House of Lords. [23]

Alfred queried whether His Lordship wished to wear his Peer's robes. It was an abiding memory to the young manservant that just two months before, on 12 May, 1937 at the Coronation of King George VI, he had helped to turn Evan out as a picture of aristocratic perfection in all his Peer's regalia of coronet, cape and crimson robe, "with a ring of sixteen silver-gilt balls raised on sixteen points above a silver-gilt circlet." [24]

Then as recently as 14 July, 1937, Evan (adorning the uniform of a Lieutenant-Colonel in the 1st (Rifles) Battalion, The Monmouthshire Regiment, complete with an array of military medals, ceremonial sword and mounted on horseback) had greeted the King and Queen of Great Britain in the town of Newport, Monmouthshire, on their tour of Evan's homelands in South Wales. [25] Naturally Evan put on another marvellous party for the Royal visit. [26]

Alfred had already been half way around the world with Evan; he knew his Lordship adored dressing-up in the finest of costumes and richest of regalia.

"No need to worry, my dear boy," replied Evan, "The black tails will do nicely tonight."

Lords A Leaping to Change the Divorce Laws

On a warm midsummer evening two weeks before,[27] the House of Lords (the second chamber of the British Houses of Parliament) had sat in session all day and the Peers were in the end to sit until twenty minutes to midnight, an unusually late hour for their Lordships. The lengthy debate was full of excitement, with impassioned speeches, in order to conclude the Committee stage of the Private Members Bill on the issue of divorce reform.

The controversial change in the law, to extend the grounds for divorce beyond adultery to desertion and cruelty, was proposed and sponsored by a colourful character, Mr Alan Patrick Herbert, MP. Author and satirist, Herbert sat as the Independent member of the House of Commons for Oxford University. [28] A few years earlier he'd rocked the establishment with his humorous novel *Holy Deadlock*,[29] described by one commentator as a "polemical attack on the divorce laws..." of England [30]

Now Herbert's latest radical measure, painstakingly pushed through Parliament (against the odds as Private Members Bills were usually kicked out early-on) had set man against woman, church against state, lawyer against lawyer.[31] The change, finally supported by some strange bedfellows including the government, became enshrined in *The Matrimonial Causes Act, 1937* – colloquially known as the 'A P Herbert Act'.

Newspaper headlines praised the Lords session as "a debate of fine quality." [32] The House of Lords was (and still is to this day) full of "less rhetoric in their discussions and the arguments .... [with] points.... [always] put more succinctly than in the House of Commons."[33]

Evan, the second Viscount Tredegar who'd started life as the Honourable Evan Frederic Morgan, born in Chelsea in 1893[34] did *not* take part in the Lords proceedings. His own attempt at promoting a Private Members Bill, in May 1935, to end the barbarous use of steel-toothed leg hold gin traps on landed estates failed on its second reading, but by only a narrow margin.[35]

Evan's appearances in Parliament were infrequent, but after speaking with the Marriage Bill's sponsor he slipped quietly into the chamber to listen to the proceedings before rushing off to a social function in Central London where the chit-chat was largely about how Herbert's new divorce law was going to work in practice.

The latest Society divorce was always a high point of the London Season. The author George Orwell[36] once waxed lyrically of how the English were keen on reading all about the nitty-gritty of a good murder case. [37] This was only just ahead of the same macabre and curious folk craving the sordid details of a juicy divorce especially where the wheeling and dealing involved the ingredients that Orwell said makes a good murder, notably "class and sex." [38]

Homosexual Parliamentarians

During the debate on Herbert's Bill a brave but churlish amendment was proposed to make "homosexual perversions" [39] grounds for divorce but the amendment failed. In 1937 homosexuality was illegal in Britain, and to several medical and church authorities the activity was viewed as a perversion. There was some light and intelligence as *Studies in the Psychology of Sex,* the great work by the psychologist Henry Havelock Ellis [40] that was a critique sympathetic to homosexuality, was finally published in Britain in 1935 after being banned for almost forty years as it was considered depraved. [41]

There were a few married homosexuals (and bisexuals) in both Houses of Parliament getting on with their unlawful lives. One of these men was Evan Morgan, the second Viscount Tredegar. It was to take another thirty years until 1967 (almost twenty years *after* Evan's death in 1949) before the British Parliament legalised homosexual practices between consenting adult males over 21.

The existing laws did nothing but encourage blackmailers. Several countries in mainland Europe (including France and Italy) had already liberalised their sex laws well before the UK regarding the minimum legal age for consensual sex. This was one of the reasons why several affluent homosexuals like Harold Acton[42] and Norman Douglas,[43] (both intellectually superior to Evan) lived in exile abroad. Exile was a harsh penalty for some to pay. Whilst Acton's whole life flourished, eventually leaving his magnificent Villa in Florence for an American University, Douglas's last home was "so small that no more than four people could get into it."[44]

Some queers went abroad for freedom of choice whilst others fled in order to escape prosecution and scandal. In the 1930s the fate of William Lygon, 7th Earl Beauchamp,[45] had rattled Evan. A highly successful former governor of New South Wales, this was a man who had carried the Sword of State at King George V's Coronation. Beauchamp's exposure by the establishment forced the Earl to leave Britain for fear of being arrested for offences against his own footmen. [46] He later died in a hotel room in New York in 1938. [47] This example served to remind Evan that *no man* was above the law, that if he was not more careful he too might end up exiled and dying (like Beauchamp, and indeed his old adversary, Ronnie Firbank[48]) far from his native land. [49]

The cover of being married was one safe haven for homosexuals; some wives knew (or they learned in the course of time) about their spouse's *other* side but most wives were oblivious. In the case of Earl Beauchamp's wife it was said that she never quite understood exactly what all the fuss was about.[50]

But most of the men committing adultery were cunning and usually covered up their tracks. If everything was satisfactory in the matrimonial bed the husband's romps with other men (or women) might be kept unmentioned or held safely at a distance.

Wives who knew or suspected their husband of being *queer* or a *pansy* (these words were common parlance in Evan's time) often refused to face a showdown, and with it a scandal.

There was more to marriage (and divorce) than sexual intercourse. Matrimony was about rank, financial security, bringing up a family, (for the titled, it was almost solely about producing a male heir), achieving career goals and many other things, with ambitions often shared between husband and wife.

Evan's homosexuality within his marriage was of no anxiety to him; as we shall see, he lived apart from his first wife. He had no need to be fussed about her financial or social position or about her detection or objection of his own homosexual life style. Their marriage was a mutually agreed sham, *a marriage de convenance.*

Ironically there was more of a danger to Evan's marriage from the new divorce law just passed on account of 'incurable insanity' being added to the grounds for divorce. Evan's state of occasional madness (and the inheritance of neurosis from both his parents) was more fortunately viewed as the natural birth right of a British aristocrat.

Evan Tredegar was an extrovert. He conducted himself in an open manner, parading *all* aspects of his personal life for the world to see. He was gregarious, flirtatious, was often provocative in speech and could be eccentric in his mode of dress. He also flaunted in public his latest, often very much younger, male companion. Some of his boys were like an apparition appearing and disappearing; some lasted weeks, others came, stayed and left, sometimes very suddenly. Evan's elaborate grooming process (particularly if the boy was from his own social class) often took time, flirting, wining and dining them to secure companionship. In between he sought sex from 'rough trade' from the streets, barracks, docks and clubs.

All this was a risky strategy. Most gay men of the era concealed the more obvious, the more damning parts of being gay, from the real world for fear of entrapment or police prosecution. Evan routinely indulged in perilous interludes, obsessions and fantasies, which broke the laws of Parliament where he was one of the nation's legislators. As he was a devout Roman Catholic (a convert by the time he was in his 20's) this way of life also broke the laws of his religion and of God. [51]

But Evan had several advantages besides the pretence of normality within his unusual marital state. He had no guilt or pangs of conscience about his actions, moreover he was protected from being reported (unlike his hero Oscar Wilde who was tried and sentenced to a term of imprisonment in Reading Jail). Evan had relatives and friends in high places and such well-placed angels could intervene to save him in order to shield the Morgan (and collateral) family's good name, and indeed they graciously guarded Evan's back.

Evan's wealth gave him a matchless redress too, preventing his victims from running off to the police with a complaint. He could be generous with gifts of cash and jewellery for services rendered, and to keep mouths tightly shut, whilst blackmailers could be referred to his guardian angels for disposal with a warning that *they* would be arrested, charged and found guilty, with Evan being completely exonerated.

In 1937 Evan was happily living apart from his first wife, the Honourable Lois Sturt, [52] sister of Napier (Naps) Sturt [53] who was another lord-a-leaping the sex laws of the land. Napier George Henry Sturt, the 3rd Lord Alington of Crichel and a widower, was bisexual and liked boys and older men. However, he was also willing to be seduced by girls, famously engaging in a doomed love affair with the darling of the gods, the American actress Tallulah Bankhead. [54] There will be more on Naps and Tallulah later.

Evan and Lois Sturt

Hon Lois Sturt: Actress

Evan and his first wife Lois were public figures. Lois (also a bit of a darling of the gods), was a vivid society dame, an artist and a former actress in feature films including *The Glorious Adventure*[55] (in which she was cast as Nell Gwyn, because of her likeness to the Peter Lely portrait of the mistress of King Charles II [56]). She was also once a performer on the London stage under the famous impresario Charles Cochran. Lois had a ferocious temper. For sheer spite she attempted to divorce Evan in 1933, citing his homosexual conduct as grounds for setting the marriage aside. She had always known about Evan's homosexual tastes: their engagement and arranged marriage, a very grand affair in 1928, was a fraud and one of convenience to allow them both to escape their past sex deeds and offences. In Lois' case her love affairs were legendry with Royal Princes and older married men. [57]

Every aspect of the truth about Evan and Lois was buried in their marital union, hoodwinking the public at large. The commentators of the time in the news media co-operated with the charade.

Popular Engaged Couple

A great many parties are being given for Mr. Evan Morgan and Miss Lois Sturt. To-night they are to dine with Colonel and Mrs. McGrath (Rosita Forbes). Lady Ursula Horne and her husband, Princess Ella Kourakaine, who is one of our fashionable shop-keepers, Mrs. Fitzalan-Howard and the Hon. Charles Rhys, M.P., Mr. Baldwin's private secretary, will also be there.

Evan and Lois : Engagement Parties

Everyone sang the praises of "both bride and bride-groom [as] romantic figures in the young life of today." [58] Both of them had indeed been celebrated throughout the 1920's as members of *The Bright Young Things* brigade. They defied convention with the wedding reception taking place the day *before* the wedding ceremony. Evan had *two best men*, and only changed his mind at the last minute about wearing the costume of a Knight of Malta in favour of ordinary morning dress.

Hon. Lois Sturt & Hon. Evan Morgan with Naps Alington (back left)
and Count John de Salis (one of the two best men).

Next week wedding bells will start ringing once more, the most interesting ceremony from many points of view being that of the Hon. Evan Morgan to the Hon. Lois Sturt. Both are well known in society, Mr. Morgan as a most eligible, *parti*. He is an interesting personality in any case, with a strain of originality which is very noticeable. Miss Sturt is inclined to be unconventional, too, and is keeping the details of her wedding dress very secret. She will have a retinue of child attendants, among whom will be the Countess of Wilton's two little girls and the small daughter of the latter's sister, Mrs. Bulteel, a fourth member of the procession being Miss Pollock. Lady Warrender's boys, John and Simon—who must be getting quite used to acting as pages—Dr. Russell Wilkinson's son, and young Master Stanley complete the list so far. The ceremony will take place at Brompton Oratory next Saturday week, and as the happy pair want to get away for their honeymoon rather early, the reception is to be held on the previous afternoon. This will be at the home of the bride's mother, Lady Alington, and her brother, Lord Alington, will give away the bride.

Interesting Society Wedding:

Evan Morgan and Lois Sturt

Close friends knew the truth, despite their coupling being billed as the wedding of the year, "a singularly brilliant affair"[59] at London's Catholic Brompton Oratory; it was as though it was a movie set or a West End stage play.[60]

"From an early hour crowds besieged the doors, [and broke through] a large number of ushers wearing rosettes in the papal colours of yellow and white..."[61]

Hon. Lois Sturt marries the Hon. Evan Morgan

One report of Lois, the *Golden Bride* [62]who walked up the aisle on the arm of her brother, Naps, describes her extravagant dress:

"The bride wore a golden *lame* frock, appliquéd with golden lilies and trimmed with gold sequins. A panel of old rose point lace trimmed the golden train, which was four yards long. Her veil of pale gold lilies and foliage, and she wore golden slippers and stockings. Her bouquet was of deep crimson Richmond roses. She was attended by four little bridesmaids, dressed in Tudor period frocks of golden tissue – long skirted and high-waisted – with wreaths of gold ivy leaves on their hair, and they too, wore shoes of gold and carried bouquets of deep crimson roses."[63]

The public worshipped them like gods, with reports of crushing to get a much better view.

"Half a dozen policemen had difficulty keeping back the mob of onlookers. The Nuptial Mass lasted an hour and a half, after which the bride and bridegroom were encircled by the crowd as they left the Oratory to get into their car." [64]

After the honeymoon (the couple flew after the ceremony to Paris by aeroplane and later went on to Rome) and a grand European tour, they eventually returned to their separate ways, friends and indulgencies. They maintained a flat in St James's whilst a grand house at 40, South Street, Mayfair was made ready as a permanent residence. [65]

The living accommodation in the flat at St James Square was quite limited. The newly-weds sometimes dined with each other and they sometimes travelled abroad together, but they had their own separate routines and choice of friends and lovers whom they saw and entertained.

Although Lois "didn't in the least mind with whom [Evan] went to bed"[66] (and vice versa) they aimed to stay clear of each others actual displays of adultery and immorality. Evan's friend Henry Maxwell[67] comments that in London both Evan and Lois might return home unexpectedly to find that there was someone new sharing their spouse's bed. The Morgans, like their relations the Alingtons, moved in the set that fostered its own take on original sin. Evan and Lois's brother Naps engaged in constant flings with other men and boys. Naps' adventures were only contained after sustaining a very bad fall down a lift shaft on his honeymoon. [68] Later, an Alington baby daughter[69] gave Lois the real joy of being an aunt; it was to be the closest she ever got to experiencing motherhood.

Evan had no qualms about taking a current boyfriend out and about in public to show him off, as is clear from this description of Evan's fancy costume and that of his young male partner for a 'red and white' party (where attendees were expected to be attired only in something in the colour red or white):

"Evan Morgan was in a scarlet toga, his young gentlemen friend was in a white ski-suit, with a furo shako." [70]

Equally Lois stepped out in style:
"in a Rolls Royce… Lois Sturt - and her lover, a hideous bald headed man…[Captain Freeland]. "[71]

But by the early 1930s the wave of themed parties in *The Bright Young Things* era, described by one commentator as "a reign of terror"[72], was almost consigned to history.[73]

Patrick Balfour[74] describes *The Bright Young Things* as "irresponsible and soulless" [75]and adds that "they live in the glittering scum on the surface of English society." [76] One reviewer puts it well of this era that subjected many socialites to the gossip writer's pen, but marking the scribes themselves as "little insects and parasites" [77]with the "accomplished and disillusioned air of a trainer of performing fleas." [78]

By the end of the 1920s attempts to revive the spirit of *The Bright Young Things* exploits can still be found and also into the early 1930s. One notable party was given (at the home of Evan's friend, the lascivious Canadian dancer Maud Allen) by the wealthy art collector and homosexual Arthur Jeffress. [79] He borrowed the house – with 150 rooms - and mustered three hundred guests for another theme of red and white. Even the food was red and white – with "lobster, radishes, smoked salmon sandwiches and red cigarettes." [80]

Evan as a medieval English Knight   *'Rough Trade'*

On that occasion Evan was in the mood to be playful. His elaborate costume was that of a medieval English knight in a handsome crimson tunic, wig, and helmet. Lois, of whom it was remarked "always a centre of vitality at any party, was in a Hawaiian –looking fringed skirt..." [81]

Lois' ambitious legal action against Evan to divorce him in 1933 (the legal papers on the proceedings claim "for sodomy with two unknown men" [82]), backfired leaving both parties bruised and sour, yet still married. Any new attempt at divorce was deemed unnecessary; a compromise reached suited both parties. By the time the heat was off in her divorce action (which Lois abandoned, ultimately running scared of the bad publicity that might befall her) Evan's father had died; thus Evan became Viscount Tredegar, and Lois became his Viscountess, a glamorous title and one she rather liked. It was of high enough ranking to get her into top West End restaurants and anything similar without a reservation.

By the mid-1930s Lois had drifted away from the limelight and lived as she wished in a large house in Sussex called *Mumpumps*, near Hurst

Green. There she languished with her two chosen male companions, the bald headed army officer Alexander (Tim) Freeland[83] and an eccentric zoologist who ran the reptile house at London Zoo, Ernest Boulenger. [84] Lois also adored her thoroughbred race horses, horse racing and well-bred dogs, Great Danes. She sold Great Dane puppies.

There was a larger litter of her ditched lovers, running concurrently with her brother Naps' sexual lengths and breadths. These included an affair with the bi-sexual "PG", Prince George, Duke of Kent, [85] (an intimate bed friend of Naps) which gave Queen Mary (PG's mother) sleepless nights on account of her youngest son's involvement with a sister and a brother at the same time.

The continuity and form of Evan's marriage to Lois became irrelevant a few weeks after the passing of *The Matrimonial Causes Act, 1937*, since Lois dropped dead on 18 September 1937 in Budapest, Hungary, whilst on a holiday tour of Europe. Her demise was from a combination of heart failure, drug abuse and the consequences of a dependency on alcohol. The Hon. David Herbert[86] (her old lover Reggie Herbert's son) observes that in her final years Lois (who was trying to kick start her film career), "wandered from place to place drinking heavily, and died." [87]

Evan Remarries

Given his freedom by Lois' death, Evan married again two years later, in 1939. His bride was Princess Olga Dolgorouky[88] (a Russian Princess, and a divorcee) and the wedding was in Singapore, just before the outbreak of the Second World War.

But Evan failed to consummate the union. The late Robin Bryans[89] (as we shall see, a writer whose volumes of autobiography feature numerous tales of Evan) is clear about Evan's natural leaning, saying he "could *only* be happy in bed with men."[90]

Olga, a young woman who naturally wished for a semblance of normal marital arrangements and who almost certainly envisaged having children, divorced Evan four years later, in 1943, on the grounds of his sexual incapacity. This was an attack as head-on as Lois' failed divorce action ten years earlier; but whilst Lois' action was held *in camera*, Olga's proceedings were paraded in the public arena with full press coverage that the marriage had been annulled and the stark reason for it ending.[91]

Evan (second from the left) with Princess Olga (third from the right)

The greater sadness was that Olga had all the makings of a very fine Viscountess Tredegar in her confidence, style and charming personality. She scored an immediate impact at Tredegar House (the Morgan family's "stone garland-bedecked, red-brick 17th century country house" [92] seat in South Wales) and on the wider Tredegar Estate, especially with the wives, at a difficult time when Britain was at war. Olga reached out to the wider community and to people in the Morgan family's home town of Newport, South Wales. Her predecessor Lois had not achieved the same warmth of feeling or wisdom in her role or maintained any regular presence as the chatelaine of Tredegar House.

Evan was a mix of the wild, warped hallucinations of characters drawn from fiction like Walter Mitty or Billy Liar criss-crossed with a few rogues from real life. He possessed the mendacity of Frank Harris and the bawdiness of Ronnie Firbank.

Evan's one-time trusted colleague, Frances Stevenson,[93] private secretary (later wife) to Prime Minister David Lloyd George records impressions consistent with this in her diaries calling Evan "a hopeless liar… clever but thoroughly degenerate..." [94]

This was not Evan's view of his inner self. Indeed he considered himself a visionary, a romantic and an artist, a great creative talent, the reincarnation of the poet Percy Bysshe Shelley,[95] or a born disciple of the late Victorian aesthetic, the illustrator of erotica, Aubrey Beardsley.[96]

Evan lamented "that the humanities, or cultural education, were neglected".[97] And he sought devotees, invariably impressionable young *male* devotees.

Evan Morgan's whole life was a performance where he played out his own several parts, "poet, painter, musician, aristocrat, millionaire"[98], and he was unbalanced enough at times to fail to distinguish between fantasy and reality. This was something Olga remarked about in later years:

"My husband, who was an eccentric, used to have 'great flights of fancy' at times and I never knew what was fact or fiction."[99]

Not Behind Lace Curtains

Hon. Evan Morgan

This book is a sequel to the overview of Evan Morgan's life in Aspects *of Evan: The Last Viscount Tredegar* published in 2012.[100] In *Not Behind Lace Curtains* I make a deeper cut into Evan's hidden world, one that aims to clear up a number of assertions about his private life. The narrative delves into Evan's clandestine side. It features some of the people with whom he interacted and the places where he was to be found as a socialite and predatory homosexual. Here it will be seen he indulged in all kinds of living, exposing himself to all kinds of risks, and whilst taking part in public deeds there was always private illegality. I examine Evan's relationships with a handful of his contemporaries, several people who are still to this day well known personalities, whilst others were famous in their own time but are much less well known nowadays. A particular focus is placed on several of Evan's Eton school chums: these life-long friendships were tested by life's cut.

Nothing in the book has been invented to fit scenarios, but some literary licence has been used in extracting material from the many comments and references to Evan made by his friends and contemporaries. Compiling this further narrative about Evan Frederic Morgan has been a challenge. It's been a jigsaw puzzle in which there are still missing parts of the border as well as gaps within the main picture area.

Who *really* knows what goes on behind closed doors? Behind the scenes in one's *own* private space, whether it is a cave, cottage, terraced house, or castle? What is taboo in private? Evan Morgan himself supplied the title *Not Behind Lace Curtains.* In the book certain things might shock or may not be supposed (by some) to ever occur in upper class homes where the drapes (the lace curtains) are a metaphor for the wealth and conformity of the occupants. As Evan puts it: perhaps the reaction from others if something wretched does emerge as having taken place would be: "what, surely not that? Oh! My dear, *Not Behind Lace Curtains!*"

The distinguished diplomat and writer Harold Nicolson, for a while a friend of Evan Morgan, once said that the purpose of "pure biography [is]... to reveal as far as possible the *absolute truth* about the subject."[101]

This book is *not* a straight-forward biography but the underlying sentiments in compiling it are that of a biographer; that it is the ultimate goal is to reveal, expose, divulge as much as one can about the subject. It is *not* meant to condemn Evan or *only* condemn him. If Evan was alive today his liking for boys (providing they were at least aged sixteen and consenting) would be *within the law.*

Evan Morgan: Birdman

In some ways Evan satisfies the type identified by Cyril Connolly (another of Evan's friends, and also a writer) as being in an arrested state of "permanent adolescence" [102]. This, says Connolly, is peculiar to many public school old boys of the upper classes, that he is the worst kind of delinquent and invariably must fail as an adult. Another poignant observation describes Evan as having "an adolescent, impulsive temperament". [103] Evan's boyishness especially comes through in his life long love of animals, which he turned into the reality by keeping a zoo with a collection of wild pets and exotic birds. Birds were Evan's great forte.

In Society circles Evan was a dandy who used frivolity as a medium of expression, for taking serious matters lightly. This became complicated in Evan's case when he discovered religion. However he was bound to be affected – even before he was converted to Roman Catholicism by his mother's religious visions, but which she safely translated into paintings of religious images. These works of Evan's mother are described as "graceful, mythical paintings of angels on wings ...and... angels trying to climb the many steps to heaven." [104] Evan also had a pre-occupation with religion and religious images; he first used his poetry to describe scenes of religious torment, punishment and the failure of love.[105] But he also painted lurid scenes resembling still life pictures on par with a shocking image from a film by Pier Paolo Pasolini or Derek Jarman[106] - uplifted from his extreme range of sexual activities - which manifested themselves "in watercolours of his semen lovers stretched on crosses."[107]

Despite these extremes, Evan could appear naïve too, and much too trusting of the integrity of his pick ups ("trash"[108] as one of his fellow peers observed) and the honesty of house staff attending on him in hotels.

Evan's friend: Cecil Roberts

This is best reflected in a story from the journalist, Cecil Roberts[109] who once called on Evan at the *Hotel Lancaster* in Paris:

Evan was just rising from his bed; his previous night's conquest had left before dawn. Roberts "noticed that Evan... had left on the dressing-table four rings, a Faberge gold cigarette-case studded with emeralds, a Cartier wrist watch with gold bracelet, and tie-clip...made from a Venetian gold ducat." [110]

Roberts was surprised. "Shouldn't you lock them up – it's a great temptation for servants to steal". Roberts was also referring to the dangers arising from his friend's habit of picking up stray youths.

Evan snapped irritably and walked out of the room scowling "Why should they? They're well tipped!" [111]

Evan's own choice of book title and Tales from Robin Bryans

Robin Bryans   **Evan, Viscount Tredegar**
(1928-2005)   *(1893-1949)*

As explained above, the spark that kindled this present account with the title *Not Behind Lace Curtains* is based on Evan's *own choice* for a book title. The text uses *his own testimony*; his admissions as told to, and recorded by, the Irish travel writer, the late Robin Bryans. [112] Evan met Bryans first as a teenage boy in the mid 1940's when Bryans was studying at the time in a Protestant Bible School near Barry, South Wales. [113]

The scene of their meeting was at the home of Evan's cousin Kitty Stewart.[114] Bryans' description of Evan is that he was "one of the most extraordinary men I had so far encountered in my young life." [115] He adored Evan from the moment he saw him and, as we shall see, he and Evan almost certainly became lovers. He remained a disciple of Evan his whole life.

Evan reached out and encouraged the adoration of a number of young men. He remained interested or amused by them whilst they were in the blossom of youth. He was great fun to be with and all received their just reward, for Evan was a generous patron. But then he often ditched them and moved on to the next interest.

Evan was not faithful to anyone. But Bryans' close companionship was retained by Evan, with perks for each of them; Bryans was only aged twenty-one at the end of Evan's life. An early memoir entitled *The Protégé* [116] written by Bryans in 1963 reveals an innocent boy's-eye view of Evan. Bryans was naturally engrossed by the fifty-three-year-old aristocrat's way of life, his large home and colourful (and famous) friends. In turn Evan was attracted to the good looking sixteen-year-old Bryans, a lonely, vulnerable, but intelligent lad living away from home.

Bryans (whose real name was Robert Harbinson[117]) had grown-up in grim Belfast, a City riddled with religious intolerance, with "King Billy for ever on his high horse and rude injunctions with regard to the Pope". [118] The internecine bitterness between the neighbouring Protestants and Catholics was only relieved for the growing boy by brief periods spent on a farm in County Fermanagh. Just before coming to Wales, Bryans was a cabin-boy on a mud-dredger in Belfast Lough. Latterly he had become consumed by religious mania, spending much of his free time distributing gospel pamphlets.[119] He was offered a place at the Barry Bible School in South Wales, being sponsored by members of the Cardiff-based Pethybridge and Wills family who were connected with Cardiff's civic and maritime history, and they in turn had links with Evan's Stewart relations in nearby Barry. [120]

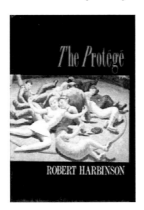

Bryans' early book *The Protégé* follows his quaint journey through late adolescence. After meeting Evan, Robin Bryans became a social

climber; facilitated by Evan's push and patronage he formed links with many infamous political and high society figures,

From first conforming to God and the dictates of his Protestant hosts at the Welsh Bible School and preaching in the gospel tents and caravans, Bryans soon fell hopelessly under the seduction of Evan's half-Catholic, half-satanic spell. Evan's wit, wealth and rich living and that of his friends appealed more to Bryans than bible bashing. A more spectacular and mature set of observations about Evan – including statements in the defence and of his strange obsession for Evan - are in Bryans' later quartet of autobiographies, *The Dust Has Never Settled, Let the petals fall. Checkmate: Memoirs of a Political Prisoner* and *Blackmail and Whitewash.* [121]

Nina Hamnett

Evan's own proposed expose of his life in his own book *Not Behind Lace Curtains* was once well enough underway to have his friend Nina Hamnett, [122] the Welsh artist and illustrator, complete a number of illustrations to support the text.[123] Evan's book was never published; the manuscript is entirely lost, as sadly are Nina's illustrations. If the Irish author Seymour Leslie's comments on Nina's images [for one of his books] are a clue, Nina's work was "bound to shock the old ladies of the lending libraries" [124], as indeed would have the original text of *Not Behind Lace Curtains.*

The books by Robin Bryans perhaps contain the nearest surviving fragments that would have appeared in Evan's own narrative. Bryans' four books of autobiography have left behind something of a trail of establishment bashing generally, (for which Bryans became well known in the 1980s and 1990s and which is mentioned in several publications[125]) but he largely defends and exonerates Evan's legacy, albeit many of the stories comprise the flotsam and jetsam of Evan (and Bryans') life together, and some parts of it do sicken and shock.

It is hard to find copies of the later Bryans titles in the public domain. He died in 2005. None of his books from the 1990s had a wide circulation, they are not to be found on the Internet for sale or undiscovered in the catalogues of main book-sellers. The publishing company *Honeyford Press* was Bryans himself and an enquiry to the literary executive of the Bryans Estate has brought no response. [126]

The use made of a selection of Bryans' words (for the purposes of review and to test the accuracy of the often lurid claims made about Evan) have been extracted from the editions of the books held by the British Library under the Legal Deposit Scheme. I have uplifted *only* the kernel of what in effect amounts to *samples* of the key events and activities revealed about Evan, and people with whom he connected or circumstances reflecting Evan Morgan's life and times.

The ubiquitous coverage given to Evan by Bryans in *his* autobiographies dwarfs everyone and everything he mentioned. Despite the fact that the long narratives are uneven, portray an often unsatisfactory account of Evan's chronology with the constant repetition and restatement of several Evan stories and usually *without laying down concrete sources*, the great wads of detail do fill in many of the gaps in Evan's life story and timeline. Readers must make up their own minds. My appraisal of the Bryans books has reached various outcomes and conclusions revealing truths, half-truths and untruths in the claims and statements made. From this there is still much of note to discover about the public and private face of Evan Frederic Morgan, 2nd Viscount Tredegar, beyond *Aspects of Evan*, with details not ever previously revealed. Here is the hidden world of Evan Morgan. There are some surprising angles to his human side, his occult side, his sexual proclivities, the secret, bizarre and sometimes wicked side of a complicated man who was the product of a very dysfunctional family, an aristocratic family, the Morgan family of Tredegar House, Newport, South Wales. These passages expose the sort of things that you would not believe go on behind lace curtains.

William Cross, FSA Scot, Newport, South Wales 1 May 2013

Chapter 1

The beginning of the Morgan family's decline

Courtenay Charles Evan Morgan
Third Lord Tredegar

Alec Waugh[127] (brother of the more famous Evelyn) informs us that when the Great War broke out in August 1914, ex-public school men were granted commissions in the army and navy.[128] The Hon. Evan Morgan's father, Courtenay Charles Evan Morgan, [129] Third Lord Tredegar of Tredegar House, Newport, South Wales offered his steam yacht *Liberty*[130] to the British Admiralty; he kitted the vessel out as his own expense as a hospital ship and threw himself in as its skipper. [131]

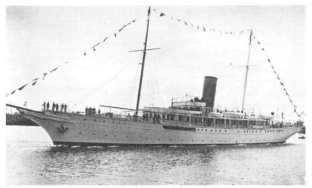

Courtenay's Steam Yacht Liberty

Keeping his distance from any such similar display of patriotism, the twenty-one-year-old Evan Frederic Morgan (the Tredegar heir in waiting) snubbed his father and dismissed talk about his own military enlistment.

To add to Courtenay's growing impatience with his only son, the heir in waiting also refused to reside at Ruperra Castle. By convention this turreted mock castle was the home of the Tredegar heir until his succession, when in glory he would transfer to the family's show piece mansion, the 500-year-old Tredegar House [132] as the next Lord Tredegar. Instead of serving King and Country or obeying his father's wishes, and to be on hand to substitute for his father whilst away doing war service, Evan made his way frantically to the sanctuary of Oxford. Here he had secured a University place at Christ Church College. Evan kept his head down until sufficiently agitated by Courtenay (Evan was certainly not pricked by conscience or desire) to join the Welsh Guards in 1915.

Evan Frederic Morgan

Evan never actually *served* in the army in the Great War, but he was measured up for his plush new Welsh Guards uniform, giving rise to him being mocked by his friend, the Society portrait painter Augustus John,[133] who thought Evan the wrong shape and far too thin to wear a uniform at all effectively[134]. The only occasion Evan actually wore this military costume in these early years was for a photograph to be taken for the newspapers. [135] Courtenay, Evan's father, went along with the whole charade.

2nd Lieutenant the Hon. Evan Frederic Morgan of the Welsh Guards was even a contributor to a collection of war poems *Soldier Poets: Songs of Fighting Men.* [136]

Evan and Courtenay in their Uniforms

Moreover, this was both to prevent any talk of the Tredegar heir being thought yellow-bellied and also to reduce the risk of him being sent the dreaded white feathers, the symbol of cowardice. In South Wales, the wounded and crippled men who had fought the Boers in South Africa were still a plentiful sight aboard Newport trams and in Newport streets, parks and public houses. Newport, Monmouthshire (now Gwent) was the seat of the Morgan family, at Tredegar Park with its red brick mansion, Tredegar House.

Tredegar House: Seat of the Morgan Family

The wealthy Morgan family's reputation for their menfolk was of them being soldiers, fighting men, through battles fought long before the Great War. Their meritorious record was imbedded in living Welsh memory. Evan's grandfather, Colonel Freddie[137] and great uncle Godfrey Morgan [138] were brave veterans of the battles of Alma and Inkerman in the more distant Crimean War. In the 1850s Godfrey sealed his life's fame when he rode his brave horse *Sir Briggs* at the Battle of Balaclava with the gallant 600 in the Charge of the Light Brigade, with both horse and rider surviving to enable Godfrey to tell the tale at dinners and anniversaries for almost the next sixty years. [139]

Godfrey Morgan at the Charge of the Light Brigade[140]

Unlike his Morgan forebears, Evan was *not* cut out for the military, for combat or fighting. Instead he took after his mother's Scottish family, the Carnegies of Southesk, in the Highlands of Scotland [141] who possessed a more liberal, cultured, literary bend than the Morgans. Evan was seen as being the sensitive, artistic type, with no head for money, agriculture or business; he was a poet (like his romantic, adventurous maternal grandfather, James Carnegie, 9th Earl of Southesk), and a painter and someone who loved animals. This broke the manly mould of Morgan men, whose traditions were steeped in national politics, land development and estate management. They reared good healthy animal stock, especially cattle and pigs, bred dogs, and killed off vermin like foxes and otters by ruthlessly hunting them down with hounds. Evan followed after his mother, Katharine;[142] in fact they were devoted to each other in the early years of Evan's life, "bound perhaps by their mutual feeling [of compassion] for wild creatures."[143]

Grave and Memorial to Sir Briggs

In Memory of Sir Briggs Favourite charger. He carried his master the
Hon. Godfrey Morgan, Captain 17th Lancers boldly and well at the Battle
of Alma, in the first line of the Light Cavalry Charge of Balaclava and the
Battle of Inkerman, 1854. He died at Tredegar Park February 6th 1874.
Age 28 years.

There was no shortage of money to spend because the Morgans were
millionaires. Courtenay and Katharine indulged themselves in the
modern fads: everything to aid their daily living was laid on by gangs of
house and personal servants. This privileged life was about to change,
with politicians like David Lloyd George determined to claw back on the
aristocracy's power base, i.e. their estates and succession, by imposing
land taxes and claiming heavy death duties.

James Carnegie, 9ᵗʰ Earl of Southesk, Evan's adventurous grandfather, in Canada

As he reached his majority Evan was a spendthrift; he easily spent his £2000 a quarter allowance whilst also incurring a regular bank overdraft. [144] He suffered from chronically bad health, rogue genes, as he was afflicted by congenital lung disease which often required medical input and long stays abroad in warmer climes than Britain. Throughout his life Evan was at the mercy of doctors and new fangled treatments for consumption and pulmonary disease.

Behind the lace curtains of London's town houses, in the country estates of the British gentry, all the way up to the gossip in the Royal Palaces, the Tredegar heir was marked out as being molly-coddled by his mother; a physical weakling, to which was added that "a Lord he may be, but he is almost certainly not a gentleman". [145] Moreover they whispered that he was lacking in moral fibre; rumours were rife about Evan being a follower of decadent art (and bohemian artists), a hedonistic pleasure seeker and a dandy with some extreme tastes. All this masked the simple truth: the Honourable Evan Frederic Morgan was a homosexual.

The consensus of opinion was that Evan's time to come as Lord Tredegar was destined to be one of depravity, rashness, extravagance, pleasure and eventual insolvency, with the result being gloom and doom for the Morgan line. Evan's tenure would surely be the beginning of the end of the Morgan family's decline and lead to its inevitable demise. This prediction proved to be true; the male line became extinct, triggered first by Evan's death in 1949 (after succeeding his father in 1934 and despite Evan's two childless marriages) followed by his last two male collaterals dying off, namely his elderly uncle Frederic George in 1954 and in 1962 his cousin John[146] (whom Evan delighted in calling *Pinhead* [147]). As we shall see, this was history repeating itself as the original Morgan male line had failed less than 200 years previously, in 1792.

The rise and fall of the Morgan millionaires of South Wales, once dubbed "the Kings of South Wales", [148] is a tale of how one great landed family can gain enormous wealth under the steady management of one or more generation but then in time can just disappear at the hands of the bad management of the later lines.

Morgan Men and Morgan History

Ruperra Castle, c1920, but now a ruin

The Morgans of Ruperra Castle[149] and Tredegar House [150] were at the forefront in the life and history of South Wales for hundreds of years. Their real history goes back to the ancient Celts and Princes of Wales. They were rich, powerful and influential. Historically, they were first and foremost landowners - in possession of large estates in South East Wales of 40,000 acres and property interests in the East End of London and in some other English counties. They had two large Welsh houses to maintain at Tredegar House and Ruperra Castle, a town house in London, [151] a large Home Farm with a great number of servants and hundreds of tenants who worked numerous small farmsteads.

After umpteen generations, the Morgan name was in serious danger of disappearing completely. When John Morgan of Dderw died on 25 June 1792 his elder sister Jane became the last heiress of Tredegar. This failure by the male line required an urgent reconstitution of the family name with Charles Gould, the husband of heiress Jane Morgan,[152] assuming the surname and forms of Morgan which brought with it Jane's Morgan money and a baronetcy from King George III (Gould was the King's Judge Advocate General).

In the generations that followed, a peerage was added to the family titles in 1859 "on the [Lord] Derby Ministry recommendation". [153] The three successive baronets of the Gould-Morgan family merger, all respectively named Sir Charles Morgan, (great-grandfather, grandfather and father of Godfrey of Balaclava fame), saw the family's fortunes rise in the glorious Industrial age of the 19th century.[154] Their tremendous wealth came from coal mining, the railways and their expansion of the town of Newport with its re-creation as a revamped port with expansive docks facilities able to take large ships bringing in imports and moving out exports from and to places all over the world.

For three hundred years Morgan men sat in Parliament as diehard anti-Catholic Tory Members of Parliament, representing their outpost seats in Wales of Brecon and the family homeland in Monmouthshire. The heir to the family titles, by obligation to his heritage, sat in Parliament. These were the days of election by the freeholders of the parliamentary seats of county and borough, and usually (but not always) it was a foregone conclusion that the lord of the manor would be elected by securing advantage over any opponent with a few hundred or more bribed, imbibed or at least sweetened electors.

The third baronet, Charles (Sir Charles Morgan Robinson Morgan[155]) was the father of Godfrey of Balaclava fame. Godfrey's uncles George[156] and Octavius,[157] his elder brother Charles[158] (who died young, and in disgrace, in 1854) and his younger brother Freddie all met this obligation to sit in the House of Commons. By the time Freddie was ready to pass the baton on to his eldest son Courtenay (Evan's father) the first irreparable weak link emerged. Whilst that link was to fragment even further with Evan, the inner rot begun with Courtenay himself who had no desire to be a Member of Parliament. [159] He put no effort into his nomination as a Conservative candidate and lost the contest in the subsequent election campaign. There was another gripe about Courtenay from the old Morgan lags, in that he was far too extravagant, spending money on yachts and world travels. Indeed, before he was married, Courtenay's claim to fame was that he had been around the world, including visiting *every* British colony. Godfrey and Freddie had always been frugal, albeit they tried to be fair, good and decent landlords. They were judged by outsiders as having met this goal very well.

The first two sons of Sir Charles Morgan Robinson Morgan, the first Baron Tredegar, had already caused some collateral damage to the Morgan family's genealogical blue print. The heir apparent, Charles Rodney Morgan, was a black sheep who chose pleasure instead of responsibility and died relatively young whilst his younger sibling Godfrey of Balaclava fame, who was beloved in Newport as Godfrey the Good, never married.

The afore-mentioned Sir Charles' eldest son and heir, the wayward Charles Rodney Morgan, led a degenerate and chequered life hunting down the two Morgan no-go areas: women who were Roman Catholic and women who were whores. There was no respite for the family's concerns; Charles was an excessive womaniser and gambler who burnt the proverbial candle at both ends. Add to this drunkenness, sexual deviation, dalliances with French aristocrats and bastard children, he was exiled to Marseilles, Bouches-du-Rhone, France where he died aged 25, [160] officially of a fever but his demise was said to have been from the pox or some kind of venereal disease. [161]

The survival of the Morgan dynasty then fell on Charles Rodney and Godfrey's next brother Freddie (Frederic Courtenay Morgan) who was married and had two sons, then Courtenay and another named Frederic.[162] (There were five sons of the first Lord Tredegar, albeit the two younger ones were disabled [163]), To add to the dismay Frederic Courtenay Morgan died before his brother Godfrey, leaving Courtenay, and his son Evan (born at Chelsea, London in 1893) as respectively the heir and next heir. Godfrey had become the second Lord Tredegar in 1875 and on Godfrey's death in 1913 Courtenay became the 3rd Lord Tredegar with Evan the 4th in 1934. As Evan died without producing an heir, his uncle Frederic (Courtenay's younger brother) became the 5th Lord Tredegar in 1949 and Frederic's son John (Evan's cousin, whom he abhorred) became the 6th and last Lord Tredegar in 1954. John died with no son or other male collateral line in 1962.]

Besides this, in 1926 Courtenay was created a Viscount;[164] this title passed to Evan in 1934 and became extinct on Evan's death in 1949, leaving the baronetcy (of 1792) and barony of Tredegar (of 1859) to be handed down the line.

The Morgan Women

Rosamond Mundy: The First Lady Tredegar

A key component to the success of any family like the Morgans was in choosing the right woman as a wife and partner to strengthen the head of the dynasty, one who was expected to be an excellent hostess and have the ability to help her husband run a large country estate. She also had to produce children, so she needed to have a good womb. She had to be firm and confident in her dealings with staff skills and moral standing as a leader in the community, someone the estate and town's people looked up to and admired and respected – and in a sense feared - much the same as her husband.

The line of Morgan women from the heiress Jane Morgan (from 1792 onwards) has a mixed batch of incumbent Lady Morgans and Lady Tredegars. [165] Most notable of these was Rosamond Mundy, [166] the first Lady Tredegar from 1859, who produced five sons and six daughters to help continue the family line. In the generations since, to the present day, only Rosamond's daughters keep the Gould-Morgan blood flowing through their still surviving descendants. The male line finally died out in 1962 when Evan's cousin, John Morgan the sixth and last Lord Tredegar, although married with step daughters, left no male heir.

From 1913 Evan's mother, Katharine Agnes Blanche Carnegie, was the 2nd Lady Tredegar. Since Godfrey was a bachelor there had been no Lady Tredegar for the thirty years between Rosamond's death in 1883 and Godfrey's death in 1913. Evan had two wives, but no children. After the high profile and splendid calibre of Rosamond, she was a very hard act to follow. Each of the later four Lady Tredegars[167] brought their own style and enthusiasm (or lack of) to the role. Katharine was only outstanding for being difficult, stubborn and uncooperative towards Courtenay although she did produce the Morgan male heir in Evan. Isolated, lonely, and often physically sick, Katharine's descent into a state of mental decline over the next few decades was a sad reflection on the great pressure on a woman not cut out for marriage, children, and a life helping to run a large home and reaching out to the wider community as the lady of the manor.

Katharine, 2nd Lady Tredegar: Evan's mother[168]

Just before Courtenay inherited the family titles, there was a last desperate attempt to repair his marriage to Katharine. They had married in 1890 more as a part of a business deal between the Morgans and the Carnegies than about love[169] However, despite two children from their union, (Evan and Gwyneth) Katharine had no wish to play further happy families with Courtenay; she hated and despised him as much as she loathed Wales. Courtenay was seen by Katharine as sulky, selfish and dull. The match had been disastrous, in part as Katharine was dwarfed by the overbearing Morgan women who surrounded Godfrey of Balaclava and Freddie, Courtenay's father. Courtenay was bullied by his male and female relatives and Katharine thought he was not his own man at times.

After Freddie's death in 1909, and in an effort to coax Katharine to live in Wales, Courtenay spent large sums on upgrading Ruperra Castle. Katharine continued to put off any move there because she preferred London. Even when Courtenay succeeded to the title of Lord Tredegar, Katharine had no wish to live with her husband at Tredegar House. Accordingly, in 1914 Katharine took a separate home for herself, called *Honeywood House* on the Surrey-Sussex Borders at Rowhook, near Dorking. She lived there until a few months before her death in 1949 which, in turn, was only a few months after Evan's death.

Divorce would have been unthinkable as it would have cost the Morgans dearly in undoing generous marriage settlements but Courtenay found Katharine a strain from the early part of their marriage. Unloved by his wife and away in the army for long spells he took up with other women, which irked Katharine, (indeed it hurt her at times) but she could hardly protest too much, since the Morgan coffers largely sustained her comfortable life-style.

As the Great War loomed Courtenay was minus a society hostess and wife, and except for some showing of her public face in the dying days of the London season, the Lord and Lady Tredegar lived apart and met up only very occasionally. The last Court of 1914, before war engulfed everything, saw Courtenay and Katharine's only other child, their daughter, the Honourable. Gwyneth Ericka Morgan (born 1895) being presented to the King and Queen. Katharine also stood back from this event, with Gwyneth's maternal grandmother Susan arranging for her relative in law 'Bee' Herbert (Countess of Pembroke[170]) to present Gwyneth at Court. Gwyneth was a troubled soul: dubbed *A Beautiful Nuisance*, she was physically attractive but of a highly strung nervous temperament (a condition shared with her parents). She ultimately rejected the expectations of a life (as a Peer's daughter who might generally appeal to a suitable young man in the gentry or in one of the professions) not necessary in a secure or exceptional union but a state of dignified obscurity in a marriage with children. Instead Gwyneth met a desperate end within ten years, her body being fished from the River Thames in 1925. [171]

That year, 1914, saw Gwyneth in her only moment of glory. It was Evan's coming of age but, like his sister, he was not a good, robust or healthy prospect for marriage and procreating the next Tredegar heir, especially since he was a homosexual. This fact had been known in wider than just family circles, which accounts also for the accusations and scorn of Evan not being a gentleman; this label had attached itself to him at least from his schooldays when in 1910 he had been removed from one of England's famous public schools, Eton College, "under a cloud".[172]

Chapter 2

Getting Evan Out of Scrapes

Evan's Departure from Eton College "Under a Cloud"

Robin Bryans[173] informs us in *Let the petals fall* (which is based on Evan's own statements and admissions) that the Hon. Evan Morgan left Eton College "under a cloud". [174] This choice of words is a stock phrase for when there's been a cover-up or a compromise. Where someone leaves a place in this way it usually means they are at least suspected of doing something bad.

So what was the something bad that blew over Evan's terminal escapades at Eton? It was almost certainly a case of *flagrante delicto* involving the worst deed that could be done at the school, viz, committing buggery or engaging in a lewd sexual act with another boy or master.

Harold Macmillan: Was he the other boy?

The names of the participants are not given by Bryans. However, in Eton's hall of fame there is at least one notable recorded precedent in close proximity to the time of Evan's breach. No less a figure than Harold Macmillan,[175] sometime Tory Prime Minister of Britain, was expelled from the school for alleged buggery.[176] If Macmillan's school dates are carefully examined it can be seen he was only a year younger than Evan and they were certainly at Eton for part of the same time. It makes one wonder if *Super Mac* (Macmillan's later nickname) was the other boy? This assertion is not so ridiculous as it is further enhanced by the fact that Harold Macmillan's mother later chose Dilwyn, the brother of a homosexual cleric named Ronnie Knox,[177] to tutor her son. [178] The baton on mentoring and befriending the seventeen-year-old Harold shortly fell thereafter upon the said Ronnie Knox, who was always treated as a Macmillan family friend, with his strong attachment to *Super Mac* lasting till death.[179]

Macmillan's own testimony of their relationship says "Among my tutors was Ronald Knox, who afterwards became one of my closest friends. He had a profound influence upon me, both then and afterwards." [180]

The journalist Malcolm Muggeridge[181] also "chose to disclose that [Macmillan] was the [old] Etonian schoolboy beloved of Ronnie

51

Knox…"[182] with stories told of their simultaneous use of an adjoining double bath-tub installed at Knox's private quarters at Oxford. [183]

Robin Bryans suggests that closeness existed three ways: "Evan Tredegar's old Etonian friends included Harold Macmillan and both shared the affection of Father Ronnie Knox, the Catholic Chaplain at Oxford." [184] Knox was a regular attendee at Tredegar House in the 1930s at the height of Evan's decadent weekend parties which were a regular feature of the Evan years from 1934 until the start of the Second World War. Desmond Leslie, [185] Evan's godson, cites Knox in his memories of Evan's house parties as the inventor of *In the Manner of the Word*, a parlour game that Evan insisted on playing every evening. [186]

Among Eton's other former high ranking politicians of the 1860s and 1870s Lord Rosebery[187] and George Curzon[188] (later a Marquess) were more than familiar with the practise of sodomy and both were charmed there as young boys by the resident pederasts. Evan's second cousin Charles (Chat) Williamson [189] (later a Catholic priest) was Reggie Brett's [190] prized lover at Eton, as well as Chat being on general offer to the same pederasts as Rosebery and Curzon. [191] The said Reginald Brett became the 2nd Viscount Esher and enjoyed a pivotal role in the service of Queen Victoria and later monarchs at Windsor Castle as a Mr Fixer. [192]

Three decades after the 1860s and 1870s outpourings of pederasty at Eton, what was it that appeared on Evan's indictment sheet to provoke matters and for it all to be papered over and erased and no longer dare speak its name? Any fall-out was avoided by his departure being precipitated with no necessity for anyone to fall on a sword.

Evan may have been as guilty as sin and of sinning. There may have been a shadow of doubt, or an argument giving him the benefit of the doubt. But it takes two to commit buggery. One commentary records "both the granter and the recipient of such favours were regarded as equally culpable." [193] The offence was not mitigated by consent; it was still against the rules and the law of the land. Often this kind of situation may be accompanied by ambiguity as to the real facts, or the degree of culpability involved and the integrity of any corroboration. But if one is caught with one's trousers down there is no defence.

Evan's gay cousin 'Chat' Williamson,
later a Catholic priest

It all had to be swept under the carpet to avoid a scandal. Similar shades of grey cloud are on record in Eton's history with the mysterious departure from the school in the 1870s (just around Chat Williamson's time there) of the known pederasts Oscar Browning and William Cory Johnson.[194]

Whether in 1910 Evan stood accused or was the victim - just whatever event or series of events was involved in the fracas is unfathomable. Eton College Archives have no accessible record of exactly *why* Evan left the school. But they do have a record (a sparse one) of when he started there and when he left, and advise that this ran "from 1907 Summer [to] 1910 Lent"[195] and that he was in Mr MD Hill's house.[196]

So what did Evan tell Robin Bryans about the foreclosure to his Eton school years? The testimony in *Let the petals fall* offers insinuations (as opposed to concrete evidence) that Evan was caught up in dangerous sex rites with another chum also called Bryans. (NB there is an old family blood link connecting these two friends of Evan with this same surname.)

This other boy was James Lonsdale Bryans.[197] Another participant in the sex games was Lord George Rodney, with Robin Bryans describing the trio of Evan, Lonsdale Bryans and Rodney as "homosexual Eton pals".[198] A fourth boy, Peter Spencer, known also as Peter Churchill (his father was the first Viscount Churchill[199]) is included in the close coterie, as is reflected in this statement:

"Although George Rodney and Peter Churchill had belonged to a group at Eton centred around Evan Tredegar and Lonsdale Bryans, neither of them had been in the same house."[200]

In fact not just the same house: this author's research suggests they were in slightly different time zones.

George Bridges Harley Guest Rodney, [201] the 8th Baron Rodney, had inherited his title in 1909 aged 18. He must have been enrolled at Eton well before this time.

Rodney's noteworthy claim to fame is as Britain's (indeed the world's) first Boy Scout. He was, it is claimed, "...the first youth to sign the register at the original scout camp in 1907 on Brownsea Island ...organized by Robert Baden-Powell"[202] at the founding of the Boy Scout movement near Poole, Dorset in the first week of August 1907. A formidable biography of Baden-Powell makes no bones about the character who was the founder of the Boys Scout Movement, a man whose repressed homosexuality, like that of Lord Kitchener "fired his career."[203]

Rodney's mother, Lady Corisande,[204] also helped to stage Baden-Powell's "boys own" great adventure at Brownsea Island at which her four sons, George, James,[205] Simon [206] and William all attended.[207] These boys constantly appear at Morgan family gatherings, albeit William was killed in the Great War. [208] As we shall see later, Corisande Rodney was in fact the mistress of Evan's father, Courtenay Morgan.

Whatever horse-play occurred behind the scenes between the attendees at Brownsea Island, the experience had a profound effect on all the Rodney boys. They continued in the Scout movement and mourned many of their fellow Brownsea Island Scouts killed in The Great War.

There was an immediate impact arising from George Rodney's homosexual experience at Eton public school. His next brother, James who went first to Eton, was hurriedly moved on to Harrrow. According to Robin Bryans the next boy Simon "had bitterly resented not being allowed to go to Eton College [along with his closest chums from prep school]. That prohibition had been imposed by his formidable grandmother, Lady [Cornelia] Wimborne [209]…she knew that her grandson George had been found by his housemaster attending Evan Tredegar's homosexual exploits and black mass dabbling at Eton."[210] Simon was accordingly sent to Repton, Derbyshire and the youngest Rodney, William, went to Oundle School, Northamptonshire; as Bryans adds, "far from the fleshpots of King Henry VII's foundation at Eton on the Thames."

The reference to George Rodney's grandmother overlaps also with Peter Churchill since Lady Cornelia Wimbourne was another member of the Spencer Churchill family. Peter's father (a descendant of the 4th Duke of Marlborough) was a cousin of Cornelia (a descendent of the 7th Duke of Marlborough).

From the Evan-Rodney–Lonsdale Bryans dates, it is entirely conceivable that Lord George Rodney was present during Evan's initial time at Eton. The second Rodney boy, James, ages exactly with Evan, as does Evan's regular sparring partner, James Lonsdale Bryans.[211] They were both well placed to be caught up in Evan's sexual and occult web from its beginning.

James Lonsdale Bryans

James Lonsdale Bryans became Evan's disciple early on in his boyhood. It is likely that Evan first met him at Eton, although he could have been a fellow pupil at Evan's preparatory school in Brighton, where Evan only just escaped kidnapping. [212] James Lonsdale Bryans was two months older than Evan, the son of Herbert William Bryans, a fine artist who specialized in stained glass windows for churches. [213] After attending Eton and Balliol College, Oxford, James went to work for his father for several years. James Lonsdale Bryans led a remarkable life, often high profile, usually in the fast lane, but as in Evan's case the myths and truths were always blurred. There will be more about this story later.

Lonsdale Bryans is well established by Robin Bryans as an Evan devotee at Eton and in later years, when the two of them were inseparable, socializing and taking early holidays together in Paris, North Africa and Germany in the 1920s and 1930s. However, the jury is still out on exactly how much effect Evan's proclivities had on James

Henry Bertie Rodney, the second of the Rodney boys, or indeed whether he was involved at all in Evan's sideshows before moving schools.

Lord George Rodney and Peter Spencer Churchill's Age differences with Evan

It has to be said that in 1910 James' older brother Lord George Rodney was aged nineteen, two years older than Evan and almost certainly not directly implicated in Evan's ultimate showdown with the school.

Nor can it be true that Peter Churchill was still participating in any of this malarkey at the school as a pupil during the years 1909-10.

Churchill was three years older than Evan; he had begun at Eton in 1905 so he would have certainly have seen Evan arrive at the school and this may have revived an old friendship, as they first met in 1901. However in 1910 (when Evan had been enrolled three years) Churchill was then aged twenty so he must surely have left the scene, albeit he was often at Windsor Castle (where his father was a Courtier), which is in close enough proximity to Eton College to arrange a flying visit.

Evan fell under young Churchill's spell during their first meeting in 1901, and this is when he was initiated into a life of sexual deviance, by Peter.

The Honourable Peter Churchill

Peter Spencer Churchill, a godson of Queen Victoria, was a Page of Honour at Windsor Castle and in other Royal Palaces. This required him to take part in Court and State ceremonies until he was aged sixteen. The official record shows his service began in 1901 and ended in the middle of King Edward VII's reign in 1907. Viscount Churchill [214] (Peter's father, a cousin of the more famous Winston) was a Lord in Waiting at this time and some of his official duties were fulfilled at Windsor Castle. Peter saw and came to know Evan when after 1901 he was charged as one of Evan's mentors to guide him in the duties of being a Page to the new Prince of Wales (the later King George V).

Hon. Evan Morgan, Royal Page, 1901-2

The eleven-year-old Hon. Victor Alexander Spencer (Peter for short) had already been broken into the pleasures of importuning for the sex trade after spending several years of his very early childhood living with his highly strung mother Verena[215] (who, like Katharine Morgan, was estranged from her husband) in Djenan Kaid Mohammed 'the garden of the prince Mohammed', a Moorish house and small estate Verena owned in North Africa. In his autobiography Peter admits that his own early sex education "was accomplished". [216]

"I had learned to speak Arabic from the Moorish children I played with there. The street of the Ouled Nail ...turned out to be an unexpected gold mine for a kid who was blond and looked Anglo-Saxon. ...It was through trying to supplement my pocket-money that I became the best tout in the street of the Dancing Girls...I never bargained with the tourists as some boys did; I took what they gave me....Sailors on shore-leave were my most profitable customers, and I liked them best."
[217]

Eight-year-old Evan was at the mercy of this older, sex- experienced boy. Peter liked Evan, he soon adored him and after Evan was dead he worshipped him in loving memory. Peter Churchill went on to enjoy a remarkable career; he was a journalist, an actor, served in Spain in the

Civil War, the American Army in the second World War and in his twilight years he lived in Brighton among the decaying vestiges of an old world order.

Robin Bryans (who attended Peter's wake after his cremation) reveals in *The Dust Has Never Settled* that the actresses "Flora Robson and Hermione Baddeley read some of Evan Tredegar's poems at [Peter's] funeral" in 1973. [218]

Back in 1901-2, Evan was first chaperoned by his father at Windsor Castle but then Courtenay left him there to learn the ropes needed for the very exacting ceremonies to come in Wales. At Windsor Castle the angelic Peter Churchill was at his zenith as a Page of Honour – with an elaborate uniform of "scarlet coat and white knee breeches and a real sword with an ivory hilt in the shape of a horse's head". [219] Courtenay (who was newly returned invalided from the Boer War [220]) was in charge of the ceremonial duties that were to fall on troops and horsemen from the Empire due to take part in the Coronation of Edward VII. This was the Coronation that was delayed on account of the new King falling ill. Courtenay found himself at Alexandra Palace (where there was a large space for parading soldiers and horses) with extra rehearsals. [221] As a result Evan spent longer periods unprotected and sleeping-over at Windsor, thus allowing the boys to get still closer. Although Peter had sisters, they were off at boarding school, the same school as Evan's sister Gwyneth. [222] It did not take much for the boys to become fond of each other.

Unknown to Peter, Bryans claims that Evan had already been the subject of sexual abuse at the hands William (Willie) Hampton Pethybridge, a Cardiff City solicitor, Alderman and later the Mayor of Cardiff. [223] The misuse had occurred in South Wales in the Pethybridge home or at Penarth during a summer holiday when Evan and his sister Gwyneth, their Stewart cousins (from Barry, an off shoot of the Carnegies) and other childhood friends, the three Wills children (from Cardiff) all spent days out together on the Pebble Beach at Penarth, (a Victorian seaside resort a few miles from Cardiff) where they enjoyed the waters. The swimming party to Penarth often included Willie Pethybridge, uncle of the Wills children, and he participated in going into the water with the bathers, Evan had not uttered a solitary word about being abused but he was later to reap a kind of revenge upon the wretch in question.

During Evan's tutorage under Peter Churchill, Evan met George Marochetti Jnr, [224] whose father's portrait of Peter had been commissioned by the Royal Household. [225] A close friendship formed later between Evan and George which overlapped into intimacy; George became another young boy mad about Evan.

Evan's mother Katharine and maternal grandmother Susan Southesk (herself a Royal attendant in her time, as was her mother, who was one of the Herberts of a Pembroke[226], Wilton House, Salisbury) ensured that Evan's costume for his Royal duties was exactly as prescribed and that it fitted properly. He completed his ceremonial training with Peter Churchill and after this ended Evan carried out his duties satisfactorily as a Page to the Prince of Wales, in Cardiff. Afterwards he received welcome comments from the Prince and the Court and Peter. The next uniform that Evan donned was at Eton College, leading to the renewal of his contact with Peter Churchill and (after four years) to Evan's exit "under a cloud". In the years that followed the boys were reunited again as grown men.

As for Eton mopping after up Evan's departure, in effect there had been no great flurry over Evan's offences. The detail would probably have been recorded and information retained, but such shameful evidence could still be suppressed.

This model of choice of a private educational establishment for the royals, nobles and aristocracy of England and overseas always survived albeit at least one former pupil whose time there overlaps in part with Evan records that homosexuality was the "general rule" at Eton. [227] A few years later another reliable source puts "the highest percentage of boys at Eton in his day as homosexual." [228]

By simply ignoring the stains and drawing a line under particularly excitable incidents involving sex, Eton believed that it could all just be smoothed over as a phase of adolescence or of life among the upper crust. Eton's headmaster during Evan's time was himself an aristocrat.[229]

Homosexuals at Close Range at the Royal Court

Katharine would have been even more cloistered than she was, not to have noticed the kafuffle over Oscar Wilde and Bosie Douglas in the 1890s. Equally she must have been aware of the gossip about certain men and their predilections. Many such affairs were an open secret in parts of high society. Katharine grew up in the secluded Highlands of Scotland and her mother, Lady Susan Murray, was a lifelong close friend of Princess Louise, Duchess of Argyll;[230] the latter's husband, John Campbell[231] (best known as the Marquess of Lorne and later as the 9th Duke of Argyll), was a homosexual and from 1892-1914 was Governor and Constable of Windsor Castle.[232] It was a well-known fact that Princess Louise and the Duke went their separate ways". [233]

Mothers of vulnerable sons were known to insist their cherished boys stayed clear of the well-known and well-placed paedophiles at Court. Reggie Brett (2nd Viscount Esher) had a reputation as a *Mr Fixer* and abused at least one of his own sons, Maurice Brett,[234] whilst Esher's friend Lewis (Lou Lou) Harcourt's [235] attempted seduction of Edward James[236] (son of Mrs Willie James, a close friend of King Edward VII) almost certainly led to Lou Lou killing himself. [237] He had an eye for girls too: Dora Carrington records in her diaries "Last Thursday the arch-bugger Lou Lou Harcourt came to supper...a terrible long creature..." [238] Lou Lou also made a pass at Reggie Brett's daughter, the painter Dorothy Brett.[239]

Peter Churchill refers in his memoirs to his father's friend Reggie Brett being a ubiquitous presence at Windsor Castle without disclosing any details of contact between them beyond the official ceremonies.

Reggie Brett was not the only example of a remarkable bisexual at Court. Another was Horace Farquhar, the first and last Lord Farquhar, [240] the Master of the Household, and latterly Lord Steward, who was "later posthumously exposed as a crook".[241] Farquhar graced almost every state occasion and knew Evan as a boy from his time training with Peter Churchill. He was an intimate of The Duke of Fife and his two daughters, one of whom, Maud, married Evan's half cousin Lord Charles Carnegie. [242]

Farquhar was given the perfect residence of the White Lodge, Richmond Park, to conduct his secret sexual assignations and these premises were also used as a sleep-over for Edward VII (when he was Prince of Wales) and numerous courtiers. [243] Prince Albert (later King George VI) took over the property with Elizabeth Bowes-Lyon as Duke and Duchess of York; the couple first met at a party given by Farquhar.

Protecting Evan after Eton Debacle

By 1911, and considerably ruffled by the Eton College affair, the outwardly prudish Katharine whisked Evan off to safer residence abroad. There was always the fall-back that the Morgan's London town house of 39 Portman Square was free if Katharine and Evan needed to return to the Capital at any time. Katharine also acquired a lease on 37, Bryanston Square, London as a further safe refuge. This house was latterly opened up by Katharine as a hospital for wounded officers in the Great War.

Katharine's instincts were to keep Evan far away and out of sight. This exodus to the Continent was as much to ensure that Evan was kept well enough away from temptations from past influences. Travel to Paris and down to the Riviera would also benefit Evan's chronically weak chest.

Evan had his own agenda. He had several quiet passions to fill his time and act as decoys to give Katharine an impression of good behaviour. However, once the grip on him was slackened by Katharine, he took his own rooms and travelled, dined and drank excessively and made merry with other young men. His family had always encouraged him in the arts and painting. In the couple of years leading to his coming of age in 1914, Evan was praised for his talents as a young artist with two pictures displayed in an exhibition at the Paris Salon. According to Robin Bryans it was Alice Pethybridge of Cardiff, an accomplished artist, who first taught Evan to draw, adding that "the best dessert service at Tredegar Park had been painted by her before Evan was born." [244]

Evan also bought pictures and drawings, with a fondness for one deceased artist from the 1890s, Aubrey Beardsley. His less than pure reputation appealed to Evan's own search for a muse. He also enjoyed works of art that reflected his loves among his bohemian lifestyle during his pre-war days in London and Paris.

In Paris he was often reunited with Peter Churchill, who was studying at the Sorbonne. [245] Rumour was that Peter was doing a course in Sanskrit. [246] This caused one of the great London hostesses to remark on "Perhaps the most fascinating exchange of languages that I ever heard was a conversation between Augustus John speaking Romany and Victor [Peter's real first name] Churchill speaking Sanskrit; they understood each other with ease and spoke fluently..."[247]

Evan and Peter Churchill, the Occult, and Herbert family links

Evan's interest in the occult began even before he left Eton, the linchpin being his past spiritual and sexual guru, Peter Churchill, who had picked up a fountain of knowledge from the magicians and tricksters who inhabited the temples, kasbars, souks and arcades in the towns of North Africa, where he had grown up.

It is suggested that during Evan's time at Eton the enactment of Black Masses, described by Robin Bryans as "black mass dabbling",[248] revolved around Peter's participation and that Churchill almost certainly led things as the older boy and central figure.

Robin Bryans offers very little detail as to the specific role play, or the hierarchy, or where these ceremonies took place. There is the testimony of George Rodney that "even as a boy Evan had worn Eucharistic garments to celebrate his own version of the Mass" [249] but when prancing around in a deserted church he donned "a black witch's cloak". [250]

The exact nature of these occult rituals, whether the practises performed were Satanist, i.e. devil-worship-inspired, or pagan in nature is unknown. Besides Lonsdale Bryans and George Rodney two others boys, Robin Chester[251] and William (Billy) Whitaker,[252] were among the others candidates persuaded to submit themselves to the will of Peter and Evan as well as to give, or be coerced into giving, a sample of their semen or blood to achieve their right to take part in the service.

Robin Bryans identifies this further early occult thread between Evan and Peter in *Let the petals fall.*

"Before leaving Eton… Evan Tredegar had started his interest in the occult. But in 1910 occult meetings attended by Peter Churchill and his mother [Verena] led to a sex scandal…"[253]

The suggestion here is that Peter was performing occult ceremonies in a churchyard at Canford, Dorset, close to Canford Manor where his Wimborne relatives lived. On one occasion, he had been disturbed by a passer-by who had alerted the police. The matter went no further, although tongues wagged for years afterwards.

Otherwise, given this reference to Verena, the main scandal around her was played out in Paris. There was a well-publicised matrimonial quarrel between the Churchills, as they were never suited. Verena set up home in Paris where she later lived with another woman, a widow, whom she coaxed Peter into marrying. [254] Peter was studying at the Sorbonne at this time whilst his mother grew ever more detached from reality in her lesbianism.

Peter's father had also became attracted to another woman and after many years divorced Verena and remarried. [255]

The bad blood between Verena and her husband Viscount Churchill is described in one account as "a sensational marital feud with the husband, which had involved gun play, the hiring of Arabs to kidnap the children, threats of disinheritance, and the scattering of virtually all their material possessions."[256]

The further trigger was that Peter's mother Verena became attracted to spiritualism and more so by theosophy, roughly defined as "those seeking divine wisdom of the mysteries of being and nature from supernatural power, such as God or spirit things." [257]

Verena had abandoned her husband, marriage and "her fox hunting and socialite friends" [258] to become a disciple of Annie Besant.[259] This led to Verena being cut off by almost everyone, including her own family and at Windsor, so she was living periodically in Paris. Despite this social branding and exile, Verena appears on a fairly regular basis in *The Times Court Circulars* for 1911 onwards, with an address at 44 Grosvenor Gardens, London. Additionally she made a sterling effort to raise funds for soldiers and sailors buffets at London's wartime railway stations and her state of being *persona non grata* did not compromise her two daughters being presented at Court or finding husbands.[260]

Peter was long estranged from his father before his mother's sex somersaults.[261] He eventually lost his mother in the process of her "Alice in Wonderland change."[262]

Peter tried to live the same way as a follower of Besant and was dazzled by the presence of beautiful young Indian boys to seduce, since Besant's work brought into her fold numerous nationalities and age groups who visited or stayed with her. But Peter ultimately turned against living in Paris, following theosophy with Verena to return alone to London where his aunt Gwladys de Grey, Lady Ripon,[263] became his guiding hand. She was a lady (born a Herbert) who, by a remarkable coincidence, was also a Herbert cousin of Evan's maternal grandmother Susan, Countess of Southesk.

Back in London Evan supplied Peter with much-needed male company at *The Café Royal,* as did Augustus John whom Peter closely befriended, describing this relationship as a "unique sense of freedom and warmth". [264] John told Peter that his father, Viscount Churchill, was spreading malicious stories about him and Verena living a decadent life abroad (which indeed they were). John offered to put Peter up but he was forced to return to Paris to support Verena.

Although Verena's hold on Peter returned, his mother even choosing him a show wife, (the woman she was living with, hence the reference in part by Bryans to sex scandal),[265] he broke free to settle down in London. First (arranged by Evan) he stayed with Tony Gandarillas,[266] a mutual friend, a married bisexual who was attached to the Chilian Embassy. "After parties [Tony] loved food, drink, opium, gambling, travel, art and young men." [267] Peter later shared a flat in Chelsea in what became a live-in relationship with one of Gandarillas' later young men, the artist Christopher (Kit) Wood, [268] whom Peter describes as "one of the best of the young English painters, in fact, except for Francis Rose, the only good one of that particular age". [269]

Sir Francis Rose   *Peter Churchill*

Evan also knew Christopher Wood and Francis Rose[270] through his own flirtations around the West End scene with Tony Gandarillas.[271] Wood later became Gandarillas' constant companion, living in Paris and travelling with him to Tunisia, Italy and Greece [272] where Evan and Peter met up with them both again. A combined love of art, sex and drugs held them together in their mutually intense relationships. So intense in Wood's case that he committed suicide by throwing himself under a train in 1930.[273]

Taking up a post in Army Intelligence, Peter was addicted to sex and drugs. There is evidence of his drug taking, with accounts in print by Society gossip Beverley Nichols[274] (who also served in the Army Intelligence Corps) and David Herbert, [275] second son of Reggie, the 15th Earl of Pembroke, both young, homosexual men who were also in Evan's inner crowd.

Thus the scene is set to bring into Evan's story several people to join in the timeline between Evan and Peter, including evidence of a family blood link between them. Moreover various people emerge to provide evidence of the tie-ins with other personalities who feature here and there in Evan's story. Peter Churchill ultimately decided (with rumours of all sorts still flying about him) [276] to leave Britain to live in the USA, but before this he served with distinction in the British army in the Great War, including being mentioned in despatches.

Lady Tredegar's Supervision of Evan fails

After the nightmare of years past in removing Evan from Eton, his mother Katharine was never far away from her precious son. She knew of the closeness between Evan and Peter Churchill and (with the family links) was bound to know Peter's mother Verena, in particular the publicity Verena had received over the scandal in Paris of living with another woman. But Katharine was duped; her supervisory role over Evan was ineffective and Evan often played away with Peter until returning safely into his mother's refuge when anything went wrong or he needed extra funds after spending his allowance.

Funeral of Godfrey the Good

The only important family interruption was when Evan reached supreme importance as the Tredegar heir in waiting after the death of Godfrey Morgan, 2nd Lord Tredegar in 1913 and Courtenay became the 3rd Lord Tredegar.

An image taken at his uncle Godfrey's funeral shows a thin, willowy figure.

Courtenay's Nightmare over Katharine and Evan and mistress Corisande, Lady Rodney

Corisande, Lady Rodney

In 1913 when Katharine became Lady Tredegar she refused to live at Tredegar House with her husband, leaving Courtenay to fall mercilessly on his bossy sister Violet (Mrs Mundy[277]) and a number of his domineering female cousins and one surviving great aunt, Mary Anna (Viscountess Hereford[278]) to act as his society hostesses at house functions. These ladies had also performed these duties in Godfrey's day so were alert and advanced to the task. The encroaching war brought relief to Courtenay's nightmares of not only having to fulfil the busy timetable of house and servants functions, but also being dragooned by his female relatives. One small comfort was that Tredegar House had an excellent house steward in Edward Perrott and an equally good land agent, Mr Innes-Mitchell, who was followed by Mr L Foster Steadman. Courtenay's own personal staff were discreet, dutiful and loyal.

Courtenay liked women as companions and he took mistresses as did his father Freddie, a widower for nearly the last twenty years of his life. At Ruperra Castle Freddie installed his resident lover and friend, Ella K Millar who was twenty two years his junior, [279] and on his death in 1909 he left an annuity to ensure her continuing financial independence.

Long before Katharine's declaration of non-co-operation with Courtenay, forcing him to make his bed with several ladies, one of his longest relationships was with Lady Corisande Rodney (nee Guest), whose marriage was ultimately loveless; she divorced the 7th Lord Rodney in 1901. [280] In the earlier Morgan family history Sarah Brydes Rodney, the daughter of the celebrated Admiral George Brydges Rodney whose defeat of the French had created the Rodney title, was the mother of Rosamond Mundy, the first Lady Tredegar. Courtenay and Corisande were therefore distant cousins.

But back in 1910 a somewhat awkward problem presented itself over Courtenay's mistress. One of Corisande's sons, George, was implicated with Evan in the Eton sex slurs. George is named by Robin Bryans in *The Dust Has Never Settled* and *Let the petals fall* as being a predatory homosexual, and whose particular exploits were shared with another Eton boy, Robin Chester.[281] This boy Chester was so inspired by Rodney's stories of Baden-Powell's Brownsea Island Camp that he later established boy scouting in Shoreditch, in East London. Their meetings at the *Toynbee Hall* were especially supported by Evan, Naps Alington and others in the 1920s and 1930s. Robin Bryans informs on this further:

"Robin Chester had run the Boy Scouts at *Toynbee Hall* in the East End of London for many years with the help of Evan Tredegar's philanthropy, for Evan's family fortune came as much from East End property as South Wales coalfields." [282]

Chester, whom Bryans cites as a procurer of boys for sexual abuse, including candidates to engage for Evan's Black Masses, went on to become a lawyer and played a role in handling the sensitive parts of Evan's final legal affairs.

The profile of Corisande's eldest son Lord Rodney reveals some interesting additional family ties. He went up to Oxford (but before Evan) and served as a Captain in the second Brigade of Dragoons, Royal Scot Greys, in the Great War. He married Lady Marjorie Lowther in 1917, whose father Lancelot (6th Earl of Lonsdale) was (notably) a brother of Verena, Peter Spencer Churchill's mother. After the war Rodney and his wife emigrated to Alberta, Canada where they operated a 1000 acre farm, which was turned into a training ground for the exiled, criminals, stray adventurers, and in some cases homosexual aristocrats.[283]

What Courtenay Knew About Evan

Evan's father Courtenay had been a former pupil at Eton College and would have been alert and aware of where to draw the line between innocent horse play between boys and sexual misconduct. Equally, he'd experienced the all-male environment, routines, ragging, rituals and taunting of army life, and his generation believed in the solemn principle that a gentleman was a gentleman, and that did not extend to gentlemen sleeping with their fellows. Such activity deserved a thrashing. Courtenay knew the army hero Sir Hector Macdonald[284] of Boer War fame who shot himself rather than face a court martial for indecency with young men in Ceylon.

Katharine would have prevented Courtenay tackling Evan other than verbally, and if at all. Would Courtenay have had the confidence to confront Corisande to glean her son's explanations as well as putting Evan under the spotlight? That is doubtful too. There was almost certainly a showdown scene with Evan and his father over the whole Eton debacle and thereafter he left it to Katharine to police the standards of behaviour required from their son in conducting himself. London Society expected Evan to at least behave with some discretion. The lid was held somewhat precariously on this father and son truce until Evan's later outrageous affair with the fantasy writer Ronald Firbank, and an absurd dedication to a book led to Courtenay's further wrath and with it an ultimatum.

Other Morgan Gay Men

Octavius Morgan: An Effeminate Man

In fact Evan being found to be gay (in the modern use of the word to mean homosexual) was not the first time a Morgan or a Morgan collateral had shown these tendencies. Courtenay would have been aware of the reputation of his great-uncle Octavius Morgan, "an effeminate man"[285] whose status as a man's man was a source for some levity among the women of Tredegar House at the time of Courtenay's grandfather, Octavius' brother. Whist dressing for dinner or adjusting their tight Victorian costumes if Octavius was in their midst, the females ignored his presence with a comment from them "Oh, carry on, ladies, it's only Octavius".

Octavius, a Member of Parliament for many years, confined his peccadilloes to his London clubs and with others whose own indiscretions were carefully and successfully hidden away, causing no scandal to fall on any of the families concerned.

Chat Williamson beside his mother Hon. Selina Morgan

Chat Williamson Sees His Mother

It had been a much harder situation to disguise the position of Courtenay's cousin, his Aunt Selina's son, Charles (Chat) Williamson, [286] who lived in Venice for many years with his young teenage male Italian lover. [287] Chat's father, an uncompromising hot-headed Colonel had disowned him, albeit Chat's decision to covert to the Roman Catholic faith was used as the main reason for the severance. Chat was also banned from seeing his mother, Selina. The Morgan women achieved a coup between Freddie's wife Charlotte (also a Williamson) and her sister-in-law Selina, pressurising Courtenay's father Freddie to send money to Chat and a deal was brokered for Chat to see his mother at Tredegar House, unbeknown to the Colonel. [288]

Chat Williamson, Catholic Priest [289]

Chapter 3

Evan's Coming of Age and the War

Evan (left) alongside Gerard Sturt with his mother before the war

Evan shared his coming of age year, 1914, with the Hon. Gerard Sturt,[290] a former fellow old Etonian and the heir to the Alington of Crichel peerage. Gerard is described as having "considerable, if conventional good looks."[291] His track record at Society parties, receptions and state banquets for dressing up and knowing the ropes at grand costumes balls established him as one of the faces of the era: fun loving, but with a serious side too. He was highly eligible in the marriage stakes, a fit sportsman with a promising career ahead in the City or in Parliament as an MP, as well as the successor in due course to his father as ultimately peer, landowner and squire over the large Crichel Estate.

Crichel, in Dorset, was a place well known to Royalty; Bertie, Prince of Wales (later King Edward VII), enjoyed the great shoots and shooting parties there and lavish hospitality whilst Gerard's Aunt Winifred was a lady-in-waiting to Princess Alexandra.[292]

Sadly, the Great War changed everything for Gerard, and at its close he simply could not cope with his horrific war injuries and probably put an end to his suffering by suicide. The Alington second son, the Hon. Napier Sturt (always known as Naps) who was three years younger than Gerard and Evan, had spent his time at Eton College like Evan, engaged in greedy sexual conquests of other boys. The rumour was that the Sturt boys did "not have the same father"[293], to which was added "and one could well believe why"[294] as they were completely different characters. Naps was "a strange Faun, an almost Pan-like creature" [295] who was "naughty, spoilt rotten",[296] The blame for this was put on his mother Lady Feodorovna, "a dark, magnetic, Edwardian beauty who greatly delighted the King" [297] (Edward VII), whereas Gerard was less gentle and often indifferent to his parents; he was treated as the ugly duckling by his mother (compared with Naps) and by his father as more or less a stray.

At the declaration of war Gerard Sturt had no hesitation in immediately taking up his country's call; he left England and fought in the early days of the war as a Captain in the Coldstream Guards as a part of the original British Expeditionary Force and subsequently he fought at Mons. But Captain Sturt was seriously wounded in September 1914 [298] and was completely paralysed from the waist down. He spent the remaining four years of his life a poor, helpless cripple, attending a succession of medical boards and struggling to obtain enough financial support from the army to allow him the dignity of a paid personal male nursing attendant. Even his father's sympathy was strained over the burden of Gerard languishing hopelessly at Crichel. This scene from one wartime Christmas at the Alington seat tells the sad story.

"Lord [Humphrey] Alington complained that... [Gerard's] wheelchair pulled tacks from the carpet and took up room at the dinner table. He stumbled over Gerard's dog and in temper said "You and your dog are nothing but a nuisance in this house..."[299].

It was during a visit to Crichel in 1915 to see his old school chum Gerard (no doubt to raise his morale) that Evan noticed the teenage Lois for the first time; however his amorous eye was more fixed on Naps who was an officer in the Royal Flying Corps. [300]

Evan had tried to seduce Gerard's brother Napier (Naps) and ended up marrying their sister Lois, although he never slept with her in their nine years of marriage. The two families of Morgan and Sturt were to overlap for two decades but by 1940 Evan was the last survivor of the quartet.

Gerard did live briefly in London but, unable to see any quality of life or future (despite being engaged to marry[301]), he almost certainly put an end to his own life on Armistice Day, 1918.[302] The inside story into Gerard's utter misery and depression can be gleaned from his Army file in National Archives, Kew. [303] One poignant after-effect of Gerard's death was that his estate failed to obtain exemption from death duties, since the original gunshot wound he sustained in battle (the official cause of his death) entered his body more than three years before he died. [304]

Gerard's death was a great shock to Evan. Despite all his bravado and frivolousness there were other personal losses in the Great War that affected Evan emotionally and very painfully. The death of several of his cousins who, unlike him, served in army units in the theatres of war and navy posts at sea, had a deep and lasting effect. Among his other contemporaries who died young was Guy Colebrooke, [305] whom Evan briefly caught up with in Rome in 1919. He was another boy, with Peter Churchill, that could be found hanging about in earlier days around Windsor Castle; his father was a long serving Lord in Waiting to several Kings.[306] Guy's mother was a member of the Paget family.[307]

Hon. Guy Colebrooke with his dog in Germany

Good Connections Keep Evan out of the War

*Evan's Royal cousins Princess Maud Duff
and Lord Charles Carnegie*

Evan's wider family got him out of scandals and scrapes several times.
His mother Lady Katharine Carnegie had influential links: her half-
brother Charles was an Earl and her brother Lancelot[308] was an old
school diplomat of substance. Later her half-nephew Lord Carnegie
(who went to Eton with Evan) married Princess Maud Duff of Fife, a
grand-daughter of Edward VII. These high-quality links provided the
security of an armed tank. [309]

Establishment forces amongst the collateral relatives, especially those
at Court, could usually bring about the outcome desired or required by

making arrangements with the agencies of law enforcement. A cover-up was always preferable to ensure the Morgan family's good name was protected from lurid press headlines.

The newspaper proprietors were either friends of Evan's minders or they could be persuaded into holding back or killing a shameful story for their own good or on the grounds of taste or public decency. The last thing anyone in aristocratic circles wanted was a Wilde-Douglas-like shame falling upon their own household.

Evan got away with being overtly dressed – he liked to affect the dress and manner of the poet Percy Bysshe Shelley (to whom he felt spiritually drawn) and enjoyed being the man about town with money to spend. Tradesmen lionised his custom for the contents of his purse. His tastes were as extrovert as his style. He was a patron of the arts and encouraged the latest young poets and artists. This supply line generated some of Evan's conquests. He fell back sometimes on the old chums network; he knew people in high places from his Eton days, some prominent, some covert, who were able to pull off the necessary personal favours on tap. He was not shy to make it worth their while with a generous gratuity. But Evan overstretched his favours, once remarking at a party that "any undergraduate with an allowance of £350 a year is far better off than I am with all my responsibilities." [310]

Oxford Blues

Although Evan gained a coveted place at Christ Church, University of Oxford, he had no intention of studying; his time in higher education was spent in the pursuit of frivolity, fantasy and sexual frolics. He was only brought down to earth at times of inner deflation by the counsels of Thomas Banks Strong,[311] the Dean of the College and Ronnie Knox, an Oxford chaplain who was a long-haul friend of Evan and, like Evan, an Anglican whose faith was turning towards Roman Catholicism under the certain influence of G K Chesterton [312] who was another later Catholic convert. This was coupled with Oxford and London links to GK's friend Hilaire Belloc, [313] the writer and scholar.

Years later Alan Pryce-Jones recalled that he used to meet Belloc and G K Chesterton in Evan's company and he described GK, the creator of the famous fictional detective, Father Brown, as "a vastly obese man with a squeaky voice utterly at odds with his appearance, and a very respectful terror of his wife."

Despite the counsels of such academic, spiritual and literary men, Evan's pastime of attending the rehearsals of the Cathedral Choir school at Christ Church, Oxford had more to do with eyeing up the young choristers.

Evan shared his adult leisure time with several of the more hardworking students at Oxford including his steadier (Carnegie) cousin Raymond Rodakowski [314] and ever faithful Cyril Hughes Hartmann. [315] Raymond's old school chum (along with Robert Graves[316]) at Charterhouse became a close confidante of Evan. These relationships are well described in *Aspects of Evan*. [317]

After others had gone to war, including Raymond Rodakowski (who was killed in action in 1916), Evan had either been sent down or had given up his studies entirely. But he hung about Oxford, taking rooms and breaking open his wallet to win a wider audience, staging fancy dress parties at the *Randolph Hotel* and in between made some excursions to Garsington Manor (home of the hostess Lady Ottoline Morrell[318]), then back to enjoy the high life in London. Evan cultivated several unlikely pairings of himself with others, one of whom was always the artist Augustus John whose weakness was for gipsies and women he could paint and make love to between his brush strokes. However John enjoyed all male company too.

Lady Ottoline Morrell

Evan's Enduring Acquaintance with Augustus John

Augustus John

Robin Bryans tells us that Evan counted the portrait painter Augustus John as one of his longest running and most enduring acquaintances. Each regarded the other as "a drinking companion."[319] Over the years they supped countless toasts to Bacchus together in the bars and cafes in the bohemian quarters of London, Paris and Rome, often experiencing scrapes in these capital cities when their amorous adventures got out of hand whilst under the influence of too much brandy or champagne.

The two unlikely companions enjoyed a high sexual appetite, and although pursuing opposite genders, easily fell back on their natural camaraderie from a worship of wine and filthy stories, propped up by a love of art and sharing in Celtic links with Wales. There are claims that John fathered as many as a hundred illegitimate children. Evan's prowess for taking lovers probably ranks very considerably below this but is still likely to be numbered in dozens, though many of those he seemed devoted to were only for show, so the figure in reality may be much lower.

John was fifteen years older than Evan; they knew each other first from the London scene and would rendezvous around Nancy Cunard's

'Corrupt Coterie'[320] at the *Café Royal* and *Eiffel Tower* (routine meeting places for Evan's crowd) before the Great War. [321]

Evan enjoyed a regular London presence patronising the *Café Royal*. Described by one of his clique as "the chief focus of my initiation into the joys of Life",[322] in this period it was just a café (not a restaurant) and played host to those who simply wanted to meet, talk and drink. Whilst Evan threw his cheque book around supporting the latest group of artists and poets who met there and who thought themselves "London's most brilliant, most independent young people" [323]he was still ranked by them as an outsider of dubious talent.

Left to Right: Epstein, Heseltine, Unknown and Evan

The same gang set up their own spiritual home at *The Eiffel Tower Restaurant* in Percy Street, Soho. An early photograph from 1915, taken outside this cosy retreat which was managed by Rudolf Stulik, a Viennese chef, shows a youthful Evan with three others. The line up is of sculptor Jacob Epstein, [324] and the musician-composer Philip Heseltine [325] on whom Evan had designs at Eton and Oxford. Flaunting his alias of Peter Warlock, a pseudonym he used first in a magazine article, he had an influence on Evan on a par with Peter Churchill, especially given his depth of knowledge about the occult. Also present constantly was a friend of Heseltine, a Scottish musician named Cecil Gray.[326] These two musical figures especially outshone Evan with their creative talent although Evan did have a musical ear; he played the piano competently and composed songs. In his youth he had also received singing lessons from Madame Clara Novello Davies,[327] the mother of the famous songster, Ivor Novello. [328]

The Café Royal

Augustus John's own recount of the *Eiffel Tower* Restaurant is particularly apt to reflect on the names of the additional patrons he lists.

"Evan Morgan and Horace de Vere Cole contribute each in his way an agreeable touch of Byronic reprobation and panache, while Tony Gandarillas, Napier Alington, Peter Spencer [Churchill] and George FitzGeorge provide a *mondain* accent, reminiscent of Monte Carlo and the Jockey Club or worse." [329]

Horace de Vere Cole[330] was a *Café Royal- Eiffel Tower* dweller with a reputation for practical jokes; Evan loathed him as he was a rival for attention. He was not the only one who found Horace tiresome. Natholoe Mamontova Majolier[331] (who married Cecil Gray) describes Cole as "devoid of humour". [332] One of Horace's pranks was to hold up the traffic at Piccadilly Circus whilst he and some friends, disguised as navvies, pretended to dig up and mend the roadway.[333]

George FitzGeorge[334] was of Royal blood, a great-great-grandson of King George III. FitzGeorge was described by Francis Rose as one of Evan's "fatuous, smirking male-flowers."[335]

Evan and Augustus John also briefly overlapped at Garsington, with the writer D H Lawrence [336]observing them long enough to merge much of John's characteristics with a dash of Evan's to create the figure of Carlyon in *Women in Love*.

During the war, Evan welcomed John to his mother's home at *Honeywood House*, Dorking where he sketched a head of Evan and ran off two glorious pictures of Evan's mother Katharine, each he said in about twenty minutes. Katharine took a shine to John, purchasing several of his drawings, at least one of which was still in her possession at her death. As a man who almost never turned down a social invitation, he became a regular evening companion of Katharine for the opera at Covent Garden. Through John, Katharine supported a number of up-and-coming artists including the sculptor Jacob Epstein, whose bronze head of John she purchased.[337] Evan also purchased a magnificent Epstein bronze of the Welsh super-tramp poet WH Davies. [338] This was presented by Evan to the local Museum at Newport where it remains today.

Katharine and Evan merit a smattering of mentions in the letters of Augustus John,[339] with John's renowned biographer Michael Holroyd [340] listing a few albeit incidental references to the Tredegar mother and son.

When Katharine's portrait by Augustus John was unveiled to the public *The Sketch* magazine reported that "Evan Morgan, that puzzling son of hers"[341] was not with her at the exhibition. The date of the quaint remark ties in with Evan's conversion to Roman Catholicism and stammering over becoming a monk. He had newly returned to Britain from America where he had been in retreat in a religious sanctuary at Santa Barbara; his own picture (a photograph by Karl Tausig) had been toasted at an exhibition in New York. [342] This work was described as "a fine head and figure, delightfully posed, full of strength and a masterpiece of artistic work and characterisation".[343]

Holroyd declares that John had by the 1920s "moved into the land of the affluent upper classes"[344] through the company of women like Katharine and men like Evan, Naps Alington and another homosexual Lord, Gerald Berners. [345] These connections opened doors for John. He was fondly regarded by Katharine and the three queer peers, though he was way out of their seduction net. Several people - seeking investment- asked John to introduce them to Evan. One of those in the 1930s seeking the cheque book generosity of "the rich Lord Tredegar" was another of John's drinking companions: the fellow Welshman and *enfant terrible*, Dylan Thomas. [346] From Robin Bryans we learn further that "Dylan Thomas worked as a young reporter for the *South Wales Evening Post* when he started going to Tredegar Park for "sherry and princesses" and so learn't of Evan's life-style in London and Paris with Nina Hamnett [Augustus John] and Lonsdale Bryans." [347]

Nina Hamnett established a reputation as a serious drinker early on in her life, consuming "a great deal of wine and absinthe". Her famous torso (from which she named her memoirs *Laughing Torso*) was carved by the French sculptor Henri Gaudier-Brzeska, [348] the subject of Ken Russell's epic film *Savage Messiah*. Nina's sculpture is in the Victoria and Albert Museum, London. She was also a model for the great Italian painter and sculptor Modigliani[349] who knew Augustus John before her; he supported new art and toasted all the saints and sinners with the clutch of bohemian artists around Nina in Paris during and after the Great War.

Evan often gate-crashed Nina's Parisian company, who were all rarely sober. Madame Vassilieff, one of Nina's artist friends, made two doll look-a-likes of Evan. [350] There were no holds barred on same sex frolics and drug laced capers; Nina had a passionate fling with Princess Violette Murat[351] whose taste was for consuming hashish "several pots of the substance in the form of a compote or jam. A teaspoonful [being] taken at intervals."[352]

Peter Warlock

Back in England to catch up with her drinking pals Nina adored visiting Peter Warlock, likewise a mutual friend with Evan's who had set up a home at Eynsford, near Dartford, in Kent. Warlock's guests were tanked up with vast quantities of beer at the adjoining pub, *The Five Bells*, with even more beer drinking back in Warlock's cottage which he shared with another musician, E J Moeran,[353] although Warlock also liked women.[354] Warlock's antidote the morning after a night of "uproarious wit and effrontery" with the "singing songs …[sea shanties] and drinking beer ...and starting the next day with doses of *Eno's Fruit Salts* and gin." [355]

Nina's description of Warlock could easily apply to Evan also:

"[Peter] was a man who really should have lived in about 1400. At any rate, he did his best to put a real English spirit into life in Kent and he was adored by all the farmers and yokels." [356]

For years Nina and Peter Warlock, like Evan, kept the close company of Augustus John, who considered Warlock an "extraordinary being". [357] Cecil Gray thought Peter hid behind the persona of Warlock with his other self, the "delicate and vulnerable"[358] Peter Heseltine, never able to get a look-in.

When not away socialising abroad, Augustus John roosted in his own artists studio in Chelsea where several of his own exhibitions were staged, with receptions mounted for the literati of London. Afterwards John could be found in various degrees of drunkenness at the all-night parties given in all the nooks and crannies of apartments, boats, gardens and mansions patronised by him and other Chelsea based artists, with their models, patrons and hangers-on, home grown and foreign. Evan's mother Katharine wandered in and out of these orgies once or twice. Evan was only an occasional long-stay visitor to these endless drink and drugs infused romps; he was more likely to be drawn to his own choice of West End nightclubs, hotels or the hidden haunts of homosexuals.

However, on the occasions when he met John, Evan often learned of the existence of new emerging and hopeful young male artists (and frequently about the profile of these fresh young, pretty faces around town) from John's richly embellished story telling. Sometimes this included a comment on their work but Evan dragged out the detail of their age, exact looks, manners and sexual orientation, leading now and then to a sufficient interest from Evan in wanting to meet them: in several cases John acted as his procurer of flesh.

Boris Anrep

After the Great War and into the early 1920s Evan's talent spotting of young artists was interrupted by his flirtation with Rome and the Roman Catholic Church. However, before he was entrenched in this (disappearing from London altogether for months at a time, according to Robin Bryans[359]) he conjoined a campaign blessed by Augustus John for the two of them to take "responsibility for Boris Anrep's circulation in the art world." Boris was a poet and painter from Russia, living in London, who had abandoned his law studies and spent time in Paris. He'd first been seized on by the Bloomsbury sect but then they left him to his own devices. His special gift was in mosaic art. He was married with children and had a capacity to concurrently make sexual advances on a wife, girlfriend, other men's wives and ladies who were total strangers; in a sense he had a resemblance to John and with the same gusto and lack of moral conscience as John.

Anrep was "reputed to be the only man in London capable of standing up to [John] in a fist fight",[360] which makes him a strange choice then for Augustus to help promote his art, suggesting they had feuded (probably over a woman). Moreover, with Boris's macho image, this makes Evan likewise a rather odd-ball enthusiast to give him support and patronage. However John's same masculine appeal to Evan and other gay men was as much about his sexy allure as a prime purveyor of male testosterone and about being in his very lively kind of company.

Evan's backing for Boris Anrep was without strings. He recognised a rare, inherent, creative talent, and indeed this early shoring up was rewarded years later when Evan and his first wife Lois Sturt wanted some expensive mosaic work undertaken for their new home at 40 South Street, Mayfair and later the bathroom at 13 South Audley Street. Boris (by then better established and unwilling to take on new clients) remembered Evan's earlier sponsorship and did not hesitate to agree the commission offered.

Archangel Michael by Boris Anrep

Chapter 4

Evan and Harold Nicolson

Harold Nicolson

One of those whom Evan called upon several times to help him get out of deep and troubled waters over several decades was Harold Nicolson. [361]

The distinguished diplomat, author and politician the Hon. (later Sir) Harold Nicolson shared Evan's sexual preference for men. Evan's exotic taste was for any handsome youth or angelic boy, with no measurement required of their academic qualities or IQ. Those whom Evan ensnared were largely unnamed and unidentifiable now; most hits were of a transitory nature but not entirely anonymous. [362] Harold was fussier about his sexual encounters. He sought "good looking intelligent young men of his own class", and those who possessed some degree of artistic talent. [363]

Both Harold and Evan were equally predatory. They were not looking for love, nor married men, neither were they overly effeminate in their general behaviour although Evan could be theatrical, especially in his dress style, and silly. He could be quite aggressive, especially when drunk. They importuned for self-indulgent experiences of the sexual act without care, sentiment or any commitment. The hazard of contacting a venereal disease was never far away. Nicholson was caught out at least once, not from visiting a male brothel but instead was smitten after spending a weekend in a country house estate with several men (and their lapdog-like secretaries in tow) who were known to sleep with other men. [364] It would be extraordinary if Evan's trawls through the night spots, gutters and beaches of Europe, North Africa and the Far East for sex saved him from the same outcome of suffering a painful sexually transmitted infection at some stage in his life.

Evan and Nicolson's parallel lives

Harold Nicolson was a few years older than Evan. Both were sons of peers[365] and their paths crossed in a sustained way at the Paris Peace Conference in 1919[366] where they were working in the ranks of the supporting staff of diplomats and journalists, as goffers to the Allied delegates and commissions. [367]

Before this Paris interlude they lived parallel lives. Evan had milked his pleasures, far away from the mud, blood and rats of the trenches, at Garsington Manor in Oxfordshire with fellow poets Aldous Huxley, Robert Nichols and Robert Graves, and kept up a supply of new young bodies to exploit with the shebang's at *The Randolph Hotel*.

Evan in Whitehall

Evan took a lease (paid for by the Tredegar coffers) at Boars Hill, near Oxford. Here he invited his camp followers down from London and the latest batch of fanciable undergraduates from the Oxford colleges. As he was limited in going abroad, Evan eased his diseased lungs and his aching loins by visits to the Empire Hotel in Bath.[368] This provided him with access to the town's selection of hot springs, pump rooms and cold springs, as well as establishments that offered bars and smoking rooms.
[369]

In 1917 Evan briefly fluttered a few papers around Whitehall offices in an unpaid position as parliamentary private secretary in jobs in the Ministry of Labour arranged for him by his relatives. He was working for Cabinet Minister William (later Lord) Bridgeman.

Evan was only a mediocre clerk but he later expressed thanks to Bridgeman for his "extreme thoughtfulness and kindness." [370]

It was here within the corridors of power Evan first met Harold Nicolson[371] and learned from gossip that they shared the same sexual proclivities. He realised Harold could be a useful kindred spirit. For his part, Nicolson had heard the sinister gossip about Evan's love of boys, that he dabbled in the occult with questionable characters like Peter Warlock and Peter Churchill and belonged to secret covens who indulged in black magic. Harold didn't particularly like Evan and for the better part of the time gave him as wide a berth as possible.

Indeed Harold, already married to the poet Vita Sackville-West [372](she was a former pupil at Miss Helen Woolf's school in Mayfair with Evan's sister Gwyneth[373]), carefully avoided all the non-combatants of the Great War resembling the lily-livered Evan and his friend Aldous Huxley despite the latter becoming known as a brilliant Oxford student and promising writer. Both Evan and Huxley were largely sitting out the war at Garsington Manor, the Oxfordshire home of Philip and Ottoline Morrell, both of whom were pacifists.

Evan maintained the excuse of not joining up owing to his unfinished studies but Huxley was affected by a bout of near blindness and so was officially exempted wartime service. Huxley was to later use the social milieu gleaned at Garsington's weekend gatherings for his early satirical novels, including *Crome Yellow* which has a farcical character, Ivor Lombard, based on Evan. Naturally Evan adored Huxley's portrait of him, absurd foibles and all.

This is one scene describing Ivor:

"Nature and fortune had vied with one another in heaping on Ivor Lombard all their choicest gifts. He had wealth and he was perfectly independent. He was good looking, possessed an irresistible charm of manner, and was the hero of more amorous successes than he could well remember. His accomplishments were extraordinary for their number and variety.."[374]

Evan's new friend Harold Nicolson snubbed the Morrells at Garsington. His time at Balliol College, Oxford was a handful of years before the rise of the celebrated Ottoline and her MP husband, Philip. He had also received, but had graciously turned down, invitations from members of the intellectual but hideously sycophantic Bloomsbury cult. [375] Nicolson prescribed to the verdict that the Garsington and Bloomsbury sets were inhabited by "Marxists, liberals, pacifists and homosexuals…devoted to surrealism, psychoanalysis and free love." [376] That made him shudder. Even Evan was light weight on qualifying by this membership criteria except for being queer.

Harold Nicolson was of a man of independent mind and was also far too busy serving in diplomatic posts abroad in Madrid and Constantinople, producing with his wife Vita a family of sons (with some still-born). When the war took up speed he participated in high-level meetings and policy groups with government Ministers and senior civil servants. Nicolson was seen as a rising star as bright as Sirius in the British Foreign Office.

Evan Makes a Nuisance of Himself

Evan endeared himself enough to Nicolson's superiors at the Foreign Office to be given some King's Messenger duties,: he acted as a courier taking documents to the British Embassies and Consulates *en route* from London to Algeria. This arose (at his request and insistence) when his health required a few weeks in a warmer climate.

Evan wrote to his old chief William Bridgeman on 3 January 1918 from *La Redoute, Villa Olivage*, Algiers, to thank him for engaging him as a Private Secretary and adding that he was about to "partake of the joys of Arab life. I am at present interviewing small lads as 'boys', since my lack of a servant and knowledge of Arabic forces upon me a guide…"[377]. It was not all fun in "this panacea of warmth" [378]as the doctors are described as "like vultures [they] are already upon me and I am a prisoner to their whims." [379]

Nevertheless North Africa was a favourite spot for Evan to "make twins"[380] with native Arab boys, a proclivity he shared, says Robin Bryans with Peter Churchill and James Lonsdale Bryans. Referring to Peter Churchill (who lived in North Africa and in France some while with his Mother) we learn "having become a lover of Arab youths, Peter disliked returning to [England] ...he soon found out that Evan Tredegar and Lonsdale Bryans also went to North Africa to have sex with Arab boys." [381] A mystery hangs on what Lonsdale Bryans actually did during the Great War; the only clue from Robin Bryans suggests that he was deemed unfit for military duties. In Lonsdale Bryans' own wartime digest *Blind Victory* [382] he says he "originally intended while at Eton and Balliol for a diplomatic career, [but] for reasons of health after the First World War had to abandon taking up this official calling, spending ...time subsequently in extensive world travel combined with a close, and at moments intimate observation of international affairs." [383]

As the Great War ensued, Evan was not content with just being a glorified postman. He made a considerable nuisance of himself in Whitehall over his part in the controversial position taken by the poet Siegfried Sassoon, who had made himself a white flag and stopped fighting in the war.[384] Evan also made a fool of himself especially at No 10 Downing Street in his relentless badgering of Frances Stevenson [385] (the private secretary to David Lloyd George) asking her for favours, showering her with poetry and compliments and invitations to dinner and begging her to put a good word in for any post coming free with the Prime Minister. [386] There are more details about this in *Aspects of Evan*.

On return from North Africa Evan was given a job as a part of the British Press Bureau at the Paris Peace Conference, in the team headed by Sir (later Lord) George Riddell[387] who had been obliged to take him by a Whitehall insider, a friend of Evan's mother, Katharine. [388] So once again, to Nicolson's horror, he was uncomfortably back within Evan's easy reach for a bail-out or a favour.

Chapter 5

Evan's Exploits in Paris After Dark

After the Peace Conference's exhaustingly long office hours some fun was to be had on the social side of the male-dominated symposium with fine dining, cocktail parties and receptions ensuring extra-heavy bouts of socialising between the representatives of the Allied powers. With several countries banning wives from attending, this allowed freedom of association and a catalyst for male-only after-dinner adventures.

Evan's Welsh friend, the larger than life bearded painter Augustus John, was the official artist at the Paris Peace Conference. John had served as a Major in the Canadian army as a war artist and rejoiced in having his skin saved by Max Aitken [389] (Lord Beaverbrook, who was born a Canadian) in several run-ins including knuckle fights, which was John's answer to resolving a dispute. By day he painted several of the important figures attending the Conference, including the legendry T E Lawrence and his friend the Emir Feisal. By night John drank, punched and cajoled his way though the Paris lights, a city he'd visited many times and sometimes resided.

John kept bad hours and the bad company of squalid Parisian Madames and Mademoiselles. Evan preferred the more sophisticated club, cabaret and theatre circuits and the availability of nocturnal one night stands far from the madding crowd. Nicolson's published diaries[390] are a record of the Conference, by day and evening, but contain a very heavy edit about his or anybody else's private romps.[391] Both Evan and Harold had close friends living about Paris, able to provide them perfect safe houses to entertain their evening's male catch.[392]

Evan's manic activities strayed beyond being private; he craved excitement without a leash but he sometimes picked up more than he could handle.

The upper crust were divided between considering homosexuality an illness like the plague, a disability like being born with a stutter or a club foot or a form of madness. Some thought that Evan was tolerably amusing but his kind should be castrated or locked up, (and the key thrown away); others thought he should be shot or should shoot himself (one of that judgement being the King of England). It was cautiously remarked that if those afflicted like Evan, a peer's son, merely confined their relationships to their own class, few people would be any the wiser; moreover there would be little or no aftermath. It was only when the working classes were invited into a warmer, cosier bed outside their class that *they* stirred things up to mutiny and rage.

Evan was not going to settle down to anything as dull and conventional as his own class for adventures. He sought out and liked rough trade and he desired rough handling at times. This meant trawling in bars and quaysides for his very own favourite boys, sailors.

According to Robin Bryans, one of Evan's lingering tales was when things got seriously out of hand in Paris with a group of foreign sailors (whose lure was always an irresistible draw for Evan). Evan had met a trio of matelots and bought them champagne in a quayside bar on the banks of the River Seine. A street brawl ensued, with Evan blamed as the prime instigator of the fury. He'd tried to invite back to his rooms one boy, the prettiest of the bunch, whom he had already tried to embrace. Evan's basic command of French was enough to exclude him from being taken away immediately by the gendarmes. Harold Nicolson's name was offered by Evan to vouch for his coveted position in the British Government's Peace Delegation's main residential headquarters at the *Hotel Majestic*. Diplomatic immunity was claimed by Evan, he then expounded his close personal connections with the British Prime Minister, David Lloyd George. The distortion worked, although Evan received a telling off by his boss, Lord George Riddell. The latter was a curious man, a millionaire publisher in a childless marriage with his cousin, a nurse, he merely told Evan to try to be more careful in future. The sailors were released and escorted back to their ship in a car laid on from the British Embassy.[393] If Evan had had his wish, he would have waved them off, back to sea.

Evan was not always as considerate with his would-be boy lovers. Indeed, he lost interest quickly in some pick ups who wanted to attach themselves to him and his comfortable life style. After Evan had had his fill the boy was paid off and dumped. One story was circulated around London by Guy Allen, an amateur artist friend of Augustus John (with a small studio in Chelsea), that whilst in Paris Guy found a Russian boy "shut out of [Evan's] house. The Russian boy, who was rather drunk and distraught, told Guy that [Evan] seemed to have turned against him for no reason. Guy, who was going in to see [Evan] decided instead to walk home with the Russian boy and try and calm him. They walked along and the Russian boy poured out his heart, saying how terrible it was to have no money and to be dependent for your living on pleasing others and trying to make rich friends." [394]

This is far from being an isolated instance of Evan's rebuff of young men he'd used and in a short time grew weary. Bryans recalls another case of "a medical student who tried to commit suicide when Evan turned against him for no reason." [395]

After the end of the Paris Peace Conference Evan found himself jobless.

A sighting of Evan at the opera back in London by Dora Carrington observes him on the prowl again:

"Evan Morgan, who I saw in an interval. ...eyeing up Ralph [Partridge].."[396]

Evan asked Harold Nicolson to look out for some job for him but nothing emerged. Eventually Nicolson was given a respite from Evan's demands and excesses as the twenty six-year-old Tredegar heir left Europe for his next venture in a Franciscan Seminary in America, where the news broke that Evan (who had converted to Roman Catholicism during the Great War and was confirmed by Cardinal Amette [397] of Paris), was to become a monk. This led in the space of the next few years to a triple feud with his father, Courtenay.

Evan's triple feud with his father Courtenay
Evan renounces his birthright to become a monk

Evan glowed like a lantern, being at the centre of attention when the rumours started that he was to relinquish his birthright claim to the Tredegar Estates and become a monk. To ensure everyone heard the latest posturing, the news was given to friends that Evan could fleece for a favour, guaranteeing coverage in the London and Newport presses. One paper remarked that Evan was "the most paragraphed man of the week."[398]

In South Wales, L. Foster Steadman, agent to Lord Tredegar, treated the reports as a joke. As Courtenay was sailing in the Mediterranean on board his yacht, it was left to Katharine to answer for the family from her Surrey retreat. She said there was not a word of truth in the statement that her son was to become a monk. [399]

Evan incensed his father over his antics. At the time Courtenay was at sea, plagued with worry from bad publicity he'd received over his poor handling of an interview (in public) at the Coal Commission Inquiry into landowners' rights. He was also recovering from the fallout from a scandalous court case involving one of his past mistresses, Mrs Alys Bray who was also known Alys Villiars-Stuart.[400] Courtenay's lawyers, Messrs. Rider, Heaton, Meredith and Mills, added that the story was "unfounded and untrue", [401]emphasising that Evan was a mere guest at the American monastery.

It had all been a further almighty blow that Courtenay's son announced a change of religion. The Morgans were Anglicans; for generations they had always been opposed to the Church of Rome. Second came the *spend, spend, spend* Evan's incredulous utterances that he was going to walk away from any further inheritance. But the third explosion to go off caused Courtenay even greater fury. It concerned a dedication to Evan in a book *The Princess Zoubaroff*[402] by the fantasy writer, and openly homosexual, Ronald Firbank.

Dedication to Evan by Ronald Firbank

"To the Hon. Evan Morgan in Souvenir Amicale of a Previous Incarnation"

Ronald Firbank

Evan first met Ronald Firbank at the *Café Royal* in 1914. They continued to eye each other up at the *Eiffel Tower* restaurant. Both men could be waspish to the point of rudeness, mindless to the point of madness. Firbank, a man of very few words of conversation,[403] took a shine to Evan. It is said he whispered into Evan's ear, "Your name is Rameses", and whisked Evan off to the Egyptian Room at the British Museum in order to see his likeness.

Evan was unquestionably flattered by the attention and liked being seen as a dead ringer for Rameses II, an ancient King of Egypt.

Evan accepted Firbank's adoration. It was not love in the true sense; they almost certainly didn't have a physical relationship with sex, although one description is that Firbank "nursed intense longings"[404] for Evan. It was an affair between aesthetes. There is a contradiction on how friends and biographers see Firbank's sexual conduct. Friends of Ronnie like Gerald Berners believed he "did not wish for intimacy",[405] whilst Miriam J Benkovitz (Firbank's early biographer) suggests that

Firbank waited outside the *Café Royal* each night to pick up his latest freshman.

Firbank was a shy, sly character, a creation of his own. He had a writer's gift for high camp humour and observation which he perpetually recorded in note books he carried around. His gift was in farce and sending up powerful people, but Firbank lived in a fantasy world (it is suggested that he was actually afraid of the sexual act itself, so must have settled for other elements of sex with casual pick ups). Evan lived in a farcical world and practiced disgusting acts.

Firbank was a peculiar fellow, the author of several surreal and satirical books.[406] One anonymous critic records, "Nothing very much happens. There is much innuendo, much winking and leering and a sometimes fatal tendency to 'naughtiness.'" Another adds that "he was a genius for comedy but he also was the oddest of fish." [407]

A central theme of Firbank's writing is mocking sacred institutions, in particular the Roman Catholic Church with its paedophile priests and nuns like dishevelled peacocks. He lampooned the Royal Family and caricatured aristocrats. Firbank's characters were real people whom he turned into fiction. This was a clever trick. The critics said in one breath what a fool, and in another what a genius! [408] He was at his very best on all counts of "delicious malice" [409] against Evan Morgan but more to do with being annoyed than angry.

Firbank was on his own, a recluse, a coterie of one! A misnomer, with red-lacquered fingernails, he belonged to the dandyism of the era of Aubrey Beardsley and the 1890s; "a creature of extravagant moods, who would burst into guffaws in the middle of a solemn public speech, decline to be called by his surname because it gave him 'a sense of galoshes' and, invited out to a magnificent dinner, eat nothing except one green pea". [410]

Evan's recollection of Firbank (years later) contained a coldness, saying that he was "a most speculative and dubious character... and his garish dress... his shirts were too boldly and too broadly striped, his ties too vivid, and his hat worn at too sharp an angle." [411]

The Princess Zoubaroff, the play that contained a dedication to Evan, was a comedy due to be published by Grant Richards in November 1920. Evan agreed but hadn't read the proposed dedication.

A fly-leaf to the original batch contained the dedication in the following terms:

"To the Hon. Evan Morgan in Souvenir Amicale of a Previous Incarnation"

The artist-illustrator Michael Sevier, who had designed the front piece and decoration for the book, sent Evan an advance copy of the play.

Evan later described the "style and dedication [as] that high flowing and beautiful prose of the French 18th Century." [412] Courtenay didn't see it the same way.

The wording of the dedication of *"Souvenir Amicale"* which might be innocently translated to mean no more than *in friendly memory* was blown out of all proportion, with it's connotation appearing to Courtenay as along the same lines as the brutal Marquess of Queensbury's interpretation of his son Bosie's corruption by Oscar Wilde. Evan's name was being scandalously linked to a well known sodomite and the book dedication was in praise of *the love that dare not speak its name.*

Courtenay's Ultimatum to Evan

Courtenay demanded that Evan (who had previously known and consented to the dedication) must ensure that the dedication was removed at once. There would be hell to pay otherwise. For the *first time* as Evan's parent, Courtenay called the tune. The matter would be directed by the family's solicitors, Peacock and Goddard[413] (the same firm who handled the Royal family's tricky domestic affairs). The lawyers would tell Evan exactly what he must say and do to save face. Evan should co-operate or face expulsion from the Morgan family; he would adhere to his father's orders or be cut off or exiled to a meaningless colonial post abroad. Pressurised or not by his Royal cousins Courtenay told Evan further that he would *not* be bailed out of any future compromising situation in his sexual conduct *unless* this matter with Firbank was sorted.

Evan Crawls to Save His Skin

Another first was that Evan was speechless over his father's ultimatum. Courtenay had called all of Evan's bluffs in one move. Katharine refused to support Evan, suggesting she had also been silenced by their powerful relatives. That Royal interference is clearer in Evan's follow-up with the publisher Grant Richards.

On guidance from Peacock and Goddard, Evan told Grant Richards that he "strongly objected to being made the recipient of the dedication", adding that "highly placed personages at St James Palace of whom he was in waiting"[414] were alarmed about the matter.

Richards was paralysed because Firbank was abroad, touring in North Africa. His exact whereabouts there and his travel plans were uncertain. Ronald was the only one who could decide what course was needed as to the future of the publication.[415] Evan's lawyers acted next with objections beyond just the dedication, emphasising "their client's resentment at being associated with the book in any way, especially having regard to its general tone towards the Catholic Church of which he is a member." [416] They further threatened that if the book appeared with the dedication, Evan would "take such steps as he may be advised to protect his interest and to make his views on the subject perfectly clear to the public and his friends." [417]

Grant Richards continued to try to contact Firbank. When he did receive Richards' letter Firbank acted at once: "I wired that on no account would I dedicate a book to a fool & that the first edition must be cancelled...." Firbank later told his mother that it was "a relief not to have a cad's name on the front page" [418] of his play. In the end the initial batch of the book was pulped, with one rogue copy missing.

It was time for Evan to bury his head in the sand, yet he did write to Richards (from Madrid on 2 December 1920) to thank him and thank Firbank for "being so obliging".[419]

Evan's account of the events relating to the dedication - in a letter written twenty years later when his father and Ronald Firbank were both dead – seems at variance in some of the details of the earlier account. In 1940, Evan gave this record to Dicky Buckle, [420] (another young man who was mesmerised by Evan):

"It had long been a standing joke that I should be called "Cardinal Morgan"- it was much about this time that I myself had taken to considering becoming a Roman Catholic and I had been busying myself with ritual and Church practises. Unfortunately this was brought to the notice of my family, precisely by whom I shall never know but was sent post haste to Grant Richards to tell them unless the book was published without the dedication my father would take steps against the author and the publisher. Just about this time I was about to be posted as equerry to Lord Aberdeen, then Viceroy of Ireland,[421] and for some obscure reason it was assumed that this deterrent to my gaining this exalted post, one which I may say I never acquired. The book was published without the dedication. I naturally had a bitter letter from the author and a sarcastic one from the publisher and found myself the victim of a good deal of adverse criticism on the part of the Firbank cult which had already started. Ronald did not speak to me for two years." [422]

Evan's reference to being thought of as "Cardinal Morgan" stems from his generous patronage of the Roman Catholic Church, which began with gifts to his own diocese in Wales, cementing close associations with the Archbishop of Cardiff. From here his wider Catholic contacts spread across cities and countries: Algiers, North Africa, Paris, France, Oxford and London (later extended to Dublin). All of which reached their zenith with Evan's near self-appointment as a Papal Knight at the Vatican between the reigns of Popes Benedict XV and Pius XI, and of being granted titles including Knight of the Order of Malta and Privy Chamberlain of the Cape and Sword.[423]

It is however nonsense to say (as one scribe puts it) that Evan had "rapidly risen in the Vatican owing to his enthusiasm and his quality of mind." [424] Plainly and simply Evan's patronage of the Catholic Church in Wales led to the Archbishop of Cardiff putting forward the wealthy Tredegar heir-apparent as a candidate for Papal Chamberlain. He was a generous patron: it was service otherwise without merit.

Evan's nomination by Francis Mostyn, [425]*Archbishop of Cardiff, backed by Cardinal Gasquet* [426]

Shane Leslie on Evan

Shane Leslie offers a portrait of his fellow Catholic convert in this note:

"His quaint character made Roman excitement when he entered Beda College. As he was already a lay member of the Pope's household he assumed the purple and entered on his studies accompanied by secretary and valet". Evan was easy to caricature and he was once represented running down Victoria station in Papal uniform, to the amazement of a trainload of cocottes and British holidaymakers, to stop the Golden Arrow with the agonized cry: "Secret papers for the Holy Father!"[427]

Evan attended at various Papal ceremonies each year at the Vatican in Rome. This is fully explained in *Aspects of Evan*, as is Evan's short period as a student at Beda College, Rome which, as Eton College, Evan ultimately left "under a cloud". [428]

Beda College records are scanty or destroyed for the period of Evan's attendance, and the door is firmly closed to any in-depth questioning or comment from the present Rector despite a personal visit by the author in 2009 to the current-day site of the College in Rome. An enquiry to the Pontifical Household in the Vatican also brought no response. [429]

Firbank's Attack on Evan in The Flower Beneath the Foot

The Flower Beneath the Foot, published in 1923, was a full-on attack by Ronald Firbank on several people with whom he had long-standing or ongoing gripes, as well as featuring those he simply wanted to lampoon. [430] The character of Hon. Eddy Monteith, son of Lord Intriguer of Intriguer Park is the Hon. Evan Morgan. In the proof copies of *The Flower Beneath the Foot*, Evan was first called *Heaven Organ*, [431] which leaves no doubt about how (and where) Firbank wanted to put the boot (or the foot) in over Evan's earlier tantrums on the dedication to *The Princess Zoubaroff*.

It seems extraordinary that *The Flower Beneath the Foot* was overlooked by Courtenay (and his minders) for legal action (although there was an early whisper of this being considered). The bizarre pen picture of Evan as Eddy and what else it portrays, beside the tameness of the dedication in the earlier play, is splendid revenge by Firbank. But as we shall see Evan and Ronnie did make up their differences.

Evan flips again

Back in the 1920s, when everything quietened down Evan moved from the Firbank put-down to another extreme situation. From one moment announcing his attack of religion and snubbing his family duty (as heir) to annoy his father, then to over-defend his name in the absurd business with Firbank over the silly book dedication.

Evan now flipped a third time returning to his old fetish of trawling for trouble in the occult world. He slipped back to Paris to exploit his friendship with artist and gossip Nina Hamnett, to request that she make arrangements for him to satisfy a deeply held desire to meet the Satanist, Aleister Crowley. [432]

Evan Meets Aleister Crowley

One figure who invariably features in references to Evan's darker side is the occultist, black magic worshipper and Satanist, Aleister Crowley. Also dubbed *The Great Beast* and *The Beast 666*, he was denounced by the press of the day as *The Wickedest Man In The World.* [433]

Crowley didn't impress everyone. Augustus John (who illustrated a number of Crowley's books and sketched *The Great Beast* [434]) said he was not "greatly attracted by him, in spite of his sinister reputation, which some people found irresistible. He held me by a glittering eye as any bore is apt to do, but I was not overawed by his learned mystifications." [435]

Crowley by Augustus John

Crowley had "published many books distinguished for their wild, erotic, blasphemous and disgusting imagery".[436] These books, asserts one observer (writing in the 1970s), were "to the modern reader very tame and unintentionally funny, the product of a mind deranged and immature." [437]

Evan was intrigued by the books in particular as the legend that had already been built around Crowley, whom it was said "organised societies for pagan orgies, had engaged in pro-German propaganda [in the Great War]... published obscene attacks on the King, and had an abbey in Sicily [Italy] where obscene magical and sexual rites were the order of the day..." [438]

Evan eventually met the wizard in Paris through old friend Nina Hamnett, Evan's talented artist and illustrator, originally from Tenby, South Wales. She made her home in Paris for some years; her closeness and loyalty to Evan was more sincere than that of any of his other female friends or relations. Each more than repaid the other's endurance and mutual support.

The first rendezvous of Evan and Crowley is mentioned in Nina's book of memoirs, *Laughing Torso*. [439] Evan was one of those who helped launch her book in 1932, Nina paying tribute also to Harold Nicolson as one of her literary mentors.[440]

According to *Laughing Torso* Evan had heard "the most dreadful stories of [Crowley's] wickedness; [that] Crowley had a temple in Cefalu in Sicily[441] where he was supposed to practise Black Magic there, and one day a baby was said to have disappeared mysteriously. There was also a goat there. This all pointed to Black Magic..." [442]

Crowley usually stayed in Paris at the *Hotel de Blois*, in the Rue Vavin. Nina contacted him and asked if she could bring some friends to see him. He agreed and asked the Hamnett party, of Nina, Evan, James Lonsdale Bryans and Cecil Maitland[443] to "come in one day before dinner and have some cocktails." [444]

Crowley told them he had invented a beautiful new cocktail called *Kubla Khan No 2*. He declined to explain what went into it but proceeded to make it up, using gin, vermouth and the liquids inside two other bottles. One of these "was a small black bottle with an orange label on it, on which was written 'POISON'". [445] He put the mixture together and shook it all up. The "POISON" was laudanum. Only Maitland was affected and Nina observes that "after we left... [Maitland] rushed into the street and in and out of all the cafes, behaving in a most strange manner, accosting everyone he came into contract with." [446]

The incident is reported by Robin Bryans in *Let the petals fall.* Evan thought there was safety in numbers meeting Crowley along with several friends whom he trusted, especially Nina and Lonsdale Bryans. Nina told Evan that Crowley resented people who were rich and was angered by the way they lived but, despite that all being said, Evan and Crowley did meet up again years later, at Tredegar House.

As for Nina, she was to at the centre of a Crowley coup winning *The Great Beast* national and international publicity. Their next encounter was a vicious libel case taken out against Nina and her publishers by Crowley for the way his alleged black magic rituals at the Abbey at Cefalu in the Temple of Thelema, the sex and occult settlement he had set up in Sicily, were covered in *Laughing Torso*. Whilst Crowley lost the libel case and it led to him being declared bankrupt, the large-scale publicity that it attracted in newspapers was a high point for creating a dark and frightening aura around the horrific life style of a very disturbed man. The Crowley cult (which still thrives today) also swelled in number during this period.

Evan's Other Romps

With Mary Butts

Mary Butts[447], was a figure closely associated with Aleister Crowley.[448] She records Evan's name as one of "my friends" in her Journals with an entry that includes references to Evan during a time in Paris in 1927 when (with Butts) he enjoyed frolics at the *Hotel Midi* on the left bank of the Seine in the Montparnasse quarter of the City.[449] The rest of the party included wealthy American artists. [450] A further mutual friend of Butt and Evan in Paris at this time was the novelist Angus Wilson.[451] This is reflected with a sketch in a scrapbook by Wilson and Philippe Jullian. [452]

Butt lists Evan in a group including Naps Alington as "Our Irresponsibles", a euphemism for her gay and bisexuals friends.[453]

Naps Alington

Evan adored entertaining or being in the company of like poles amongst the fraternity of dilettantes and dandies. Paris was the capital for several strays. One writer records that [we] "stayed in the Hotel du Quai Voltaire but could not resist the Ritz ...with its English habitués, Michael Arlen and Evan Morgan, Lord Tredegar..."

Michael Arlen[454] is an interesting addition to the Evan circle. Bulgarian by birth, he was a man who was "always impeccably dressed and groomed and was seen driving around London in a fashionable yellow Rolls Royce and engaging in all kinds of luxurious activities." [455] Another observer of hotel foyers and their bars sweeps in Naps Alington as a kindred spirit of Evan and Arlen, commenting "and then the English dandies dropping in – Evan Morgan, Napier Alington and Michael Arlen". [456]

With Francis Rose in Paris and Germany

An especially long-standing companion of Evan's in Paris was the up and coming artist baronet Sir Francis Cyril Rose. He grew up in Paris in the 1920s[457] with Evan providing part of his sex education. Later as a young man Rose was a frequent Parisian dweller who maintained a flat in the city and was a friend of Gertrude Stein.[458] The irrepressible Stein admired his painting skills and helped her "young protégé" [459] to exhibit his work in Paris. A group around Stein were mutual friends of Rose, including Jean Cocteau [460] as well as Stein's lesbian partner, Alice B Toklas.[461] Rose reached the heights of exhibiting his pictures with Salvador Dali.[462] He also painted portraits of dancers:

"Isadora Duncan, and in 1929 did theatre designs for Diaghilev". Later he designed the costumes and scenery for Lord Berners' ballet *Cupid and Psyche.* [463]

Peter Churchill was likewise an early participant in the same company as Jean Cocteau (who adored English men and boys), long before Rose knew him and Evan. The overlaps with Cocteau were usually sex and drug fuelled sessions; Churchill delighted in telling that when he stayed at the *Hotel Wellcome* in Villefrance (in the south of France) with Cocteau "he smoked opium in such copious quantities that if he left the window open you could smell the fumes far out to sea." [464]

By 1929 Churchill was exiled in the USA. He coaxed the young Hon. David Herbert to run off with him on the promise of work in the theatre and the movies, but Peter (like Evan with several of his boyfriends) soon tired of his catch. Giving no reason, he abandoned Herbert (something he was in the habit of doing in other relationships).[465]

Meanwhile in Europe, Rose was aged twenty and sexually promiscuous; another early lover was fellow painter Christopher Wood. He also describes (in his memoirs) nights of wantonness out with Cocteau.[466]

At the same time Evan's other Eton crony, James Lonsdale Bryans, was in search of a job. His father had died and he was not enthused enough to carry on the family business, making stained glass windows for churches. It was in these years at the end of the 1920s and into the 1930s that Evan spent holidays abroad with Francis Rose and Lonsdale Bryans on the Continent, in France and especially in pre-Nazi Germany, where Rose lived from 1931-34. Rose impressed his two friends by introducing them to the sin spots of Berlin. Sex with boys was on tap. Rose once famously said it was "impossible for a young man to go to the centre of Berlin without being accosted." [467]

Evan's Romp in Berlin 1928

Evan's former helper Harold Nicolson was serving in the British Embassy in Berlin at the tail end of the 1920s.[468] He spent Christmas 1927 there with Eddy Sackville-West, [469] another homosexual personality of the era (and a cousin of Harold's wife Vita).

Eddy's sexual activities overlapped with Evan's but it seems the low life male tarts of Berlin were not entirely to Eddy's taste.[470] He records "A dreadful sense of the third rate hangs over Berlin." [471] But this type of soiled bedfellow was greatly prized by Evan.

As Herr Hitler gradually rose to power, the German capital's tally of displaced refugees and divinely decadent cafes, beer cellars and underground dives, thriving against the grander German hotel society, was a beehive for sex tourists like Eddy and Evan to target, attracted there by the easy pickings of surplus young male bodies.

Eddy Sackville-West records of a revisit to Berlin in 1928 of the wider availability of boys, "…..beautiful boys…. I was dragged at night…from one homosexual bar to another. The behaviour is perfectly open. There are even large dancing places for inverts. And some of the people…." [472]

In her attempt at divorcing Evan in 1933, his wife Lois cites instances of Evan committing sodomy in a *Berlin Hotel* in 1929, the year after they were married.[473] Evan had almost certainly boasted to Lois of his conquests. However since almost all the large Berlin hotels were wired with hidden tape recorders,[474] Evan's performances were probably noted by others too, including the State blackmailers.

Crowley in Berlin

Aleister Crowley lived in Paris until he was expelled from there by the French authorities; a similar expulsion followed in Italy and with it came the closure of his bizarre love *Temple of Thelema* at Cefalu, Sicily. Several women from Britain and elsewhere had gone to Cefalu to be bullied by Crowley, besotted with his allure, magical powers and sexual control.

There was no shortage of followers desiring a taste of Crowley's life-style. Whilst there are no concrete facts to support it (only speculation), Evan's sister Gwyneth Morgan may have given some thought to visiting Sicily (and with it Cefalu) during her Italian Intermezzo of 1923. All that is known about this excursion is that Gwyneth was touring Italy (by car, possibly with a female companion) and was forced home to England on account of contracting dysentery.

By 1931 Crowley was banned from several countries; short of funds (although his books were selling modestly) he can be found living in Germany. He had at the time "an exhibition of his weird paintings in a Berlin gallery." [475]

There is *no* hard evidence that Evan was directly engaged with Crowley after their meeting in Paris, almost a decade before, and partaking of the psychedelic cocktails. There is only an embroidered yarn of Evan effecting a clash between Crowley and the glamorous temptress Marchesa Luisa Casati,[476] in London, otherwise there would seem little scope for them to enjoy closer contact. The Marchesa (whom Evan financially supported) was renowned for her outlandishness, her wild costumes, red hair, and exotic pets; easily someone to daunt even Crowley as she was no pushover.[477] Crowley could not abide assertive women. The novelist Louis Umfreville Wilkinson [478](whom Robin Bryans mentions[479]) who was one of Crowley's executors is reported as saying that whilst *The Great Beast* "was offered initiation into the witch [Wicca] cult as a young man he refused because he didn't want to be bossed around by a woman". [480]

The 1930s decadence of the German capital suited Crowley's deranged tastes. There is the testimony of one of Crowley's paid boarders, Gerald Hamilton, [481] the man made famous by the writer Christopher Isherwood in the Berlin story *Mr Norris Changes Trains*. [482] Hamilton was interviewed by Crowley's biographer, John Symonds, [483] to spills the beans on *The Great Beast's* harsh treatment of his *Scarlet Woman*, Bertha Busch, in a drugs and sex attack he witnessed in Crowley's Berlin flat in 1931. [484]

Meeting in Munich with the Nazis c1931

Evan and James Lonsdale Bryans' insider knowledge of the occult may have made them popular with those in the Francis Rose loop within the German underground occult societies, with a bizarre (richly embellished) tale previously set out in *Aspects of Evan*[485]. This relates to a "Meeting in Munich"[486] in c1931 with a motley collection of homosexual Englishmen and Germans, in a restaurant in Bad Wiesse with several senior members of the Nazi Party[487] including Rudolf Hess. [488] A night of alcohol and drug-laced sex and occult rituals invariably followed or may even have replaced the dining plan.

Rose had right wing political tendencies and was enthralled with the rise of Nazism. He mixed in dangerous circles and this led to him becoming (almost certainly) the lover of Ernst Rohm,[489] co-founder of the Sturmabteilung (SA), the Nazi Party's storm troopers, and later its Commander.

Robin Bryans makes no reference to Evan meeting Ernst Rohm (or any of the others allegedly on a seating plan[490] for the meeting at Hitler's favourite restaurant of *Osteria Bavaria* in Munich in 1931). However Francis Rose is generally credited with "hostessing Ernst Rohm's wild parties for the German Youth Movement."[491]

Ernst Rohm

Rohm was killed on Hitler's orders in 1934 on the *Night of the Long Knives*.[492] Rose was reputed to have been in bed with Ernst Rohm in Munich on the bloody night in question; "he fled through the skylight and over the rooftops" [493] and escaped to England.

Evan and Lonsdale Bryans amongst German Aristocrats

Whilst at Eton, Evan and Lonsdale Bryans had an influential German master with family contacts in South Wales; the same man had links with the German teacher of both Nina Hamnett and Augustus John in their early lives at Tenby. [494]

This same German introduced Evan and Lonsdale Bryans to the *Wednesday Society of Berlin*; unlike its 18th century namesake (which was a club of Liberal intellectuals[495]) this was Pro- Nazi. Through this link emerged an overlapping connection with Pastor Martin Niemoller [496]of the Confessional Church, who was anti- Jewish at first (he had served in the German navy in the Great War) but later opposed the clampdown of Jews and minorities by the Nazis. Niemoller was arrested in 1937, imprisoned and later interned at Dachau concentration camp. Robin Bryans claims that one of "Evan and Lonsdale [Bryans's] peace missions [in the Second World War] consisted partly of a scheme to barter Rudolf Hess, imprisoned in Evan's Monmouthshire, for Niemoller." [497] This sounds incredulous, although it is true that once

Hess had been interrogated by British Intelligence (after he flew to Britain in May 1941) he spent the rest of the war as a prisoner in a military hospital at Maindiff Court, Abergavenny, only fifteen miles from the Morgan seat at Tredegar House.

Claims still fly around that Evan met Hess during this period in South Wales; that matter will be evaluated in a later Chapter.

Robin Bryans explains that Evan and Lonsdale Bryans "liked speaking German at Schloss Deineberg in the Harz Mountains home of Prince and Princess Munster, [498] the latter being a Scottish relation of Lonsdale Bryans…..as was the wife of Baron Herbert von Hindenburg, nephew of Germany's (the Weimer Republic's) president before [Adolf] Hitler" [499]

In the same way that Evan and Lonsdale Bryans had provided occult entertainments to Francis Rose' perverted Nazi clique, the two English guests provided suitable music and song for the keepers of the land of German fairy tale castles. Robin Bryans tells us:

"Evan wrote songs in French, Italian and German and liked to hear Lonsdale Bryans sing them".[500] Bryans usually secured an encore with his version of *Drink to me only with thine eyes*, which he first learned to perform at Eton College.

The wives of the German aristocrats mentioned above were British, daughters of George Hay-Drummond, 12th Earl of Kinnoull,[501] and although the two ladies in question died in 1927 and 1938 respectively there may have been a visit by Evan and Lonsdale Bryans as described in the 1920s and 1930s. [502] It is further claimed that "...these connections earned the trust of Germans opposed to Hitler's National Socialists and in 1940 the secret German resistance sent Lonsdale as their spokesman with peace proposals to Lord Halifax, the Foreign Secretary." [503]

Lonsdale Bryans' work for Lord Halifax during the Second World War will be examined later. Robin Bryans makes no bones about the dual motive behind Lonsdale Bryans' fraternising with the men folk of the Aryan race to work for peace, adding "although Lonsdale Bryans enjoyed the company of German aristocrats in the German Resistance, he like Evan preferred the rough company of sailors picked up in London." [504]

Evan in Far East Tour including Singapore

As set out in the references to Evan's fame on the Island of Bali (see *Aspects of Evan*), he adored visiting this part of the world, for his health and for unrestricted sex. However a trip to the Far East in early 1937 with his secretary, Captain Harry Ware, which took in visits to Java, Borneo and New Guinea appears to have been more for rest and some tourism. He appears with Ware, Lady Marian Cameron[505] and Mrs Myrtle Farquharson[506] on board the Italian liner *Victoria*, enjoying a short visit to Singapore. [507] Evan had stood sponsor the preceding year at an exhibition held in the Lefevre Gallery, London [508] to highlight the work of Viscount Hastings [509](the artist brother of Marian Cameron). Among those whom Evan brought along in his party were H G Wells and Lady Christabel Aberconway, with other guests attending including Somerset Maugham and

two film stars of the era, Miss Flora Robson and the American, Edward G Robinson.

Chapter 6

Some Personalities Baited By Evan
1920-1945

Sir Francis Guy Laking: Tallulah Bankhead's Secretary

Francis 'Fatty' Laking

Yellow Chartreuse, a French liqueur made by monks from distilling alcohol and herbs, was a drink favoured by some of the camp followers of Tallulah Bankhead, [510] an American actress who regularly performed in Britain and who met Evan through Naps Alington's circle. Evan preferred drinking champagne or brandy or both together.

The over-indulgence in this concoction of Chartreuse contributed to the death of a central figure in Tallulah's entourage, her twenty six year old secretary who was a homosexual baronet named Francis (Guy) Laking[511] (nicknamed 'Fatty'). The inquest into his death in 1930 reached a verdict that the frail, overweight Laking (a grandson of the first baronet Laking, a Royal surgeon apothecary to Queen Victoria, and Kings Edward VII and George V) died of natural causes in St George's Hospital, Hyde Park Corner, London after being rushed there when found in a semi-conscious state by a neighbour. [512]

'Fatty' Laking was a constant burden on Bankhead and she tired of bailing him out of scrapes and scandals. He was an unstoppable prankster and exhibitionist, dressing as a woman for one party romp in 1926, then "stripped and attempted to Charleston stark naked." [513] Evleyn Waugh records in his diaries that a very nearly sober Laking once made a pass at his brother, Alec. [514] As well as being genetically doomed (his father, Keeper of the King's Armoury at Windsor Castle and a leading London museum collector was dead at the age of 44, his mother at 50) Laking was fat, had no money, suffered from a pronounced speech impediment (a lisp), and was far from being amorously appealing to conquer by Tallulah's own adored bisexual, Naps Alington. One of Bankhead's many biographers cruelly describes Laking as "the first of her [Tallulah's] freaks: a fat, lisping eunuch who resembled a cretinous Charles Laughton." [515]

Evan first saw Laking when, as a five year old child at Windsor Castle, he came to watch Evan and Peter Churchill at rehearsals for Royal ceremonial functions. Later he often ran into Laking in the West End at theatre at first nights and in Tallulah Bankhead's dangerous inner circle in London, Paris and Italy. One of her pack was marked out by the authorities as being "a friend [almost certainly this was Naps Alington, Evan's future brother in law] whom MI5 described as one of the most prominent sodomites in London". [516]

Evan kept his distance from the ugly, loutish, loud mouthed, drunken Laking despite London Society possessing similar knowledge about their scandalous behaviour pattern and the escapades of both these wretches in seducing boys and men. Like Evan, Laking enjoyed outraging the gallery crowd and "took pleasure in constantly setting friend against friend", [517] the consequence of such mickey-taking being that the joker was often snubbed or sent to Coventry until tongues stopped wagging. Although he had an older sister, Joan, and a doting old governess, Laking was not greatly missed by anyone else, and no-one from the *Bright Young Things* brigade attended his funeral or burial in the family's vault at Old Highgate Cemetery, London. He had one final joke to play at Bankhead's expense: in his Will he left her all his motor cars - except he never even owned a motor car![518]

Music, dancing, drugs, drink and sex always fuelled the parties. Tallulah Bankhead's personal expenses were once officially summarised as "marijuana, booze, cocaine and sex". [519] Evan revelled in the same line in debauchery and vice and he, like Bankhead, could drink like fish; Evan could quite easily out-drink all comers, rendering them first intoxicated and helpless and then polishing off even larger quantities of champagne and brandy himself and concurrently flirting the trousers off any young male that caught his fancy.

Ned Lathom: Another of Evan's Eton Chums Dies Young

The early death of 'Fatty' Laking shocked Evan. Edward (Ned) Lathom[520], 3rd Earl of Lathom, rich, homosexual, married, childless and a consumptive (all just like Evan) is another of Evan's chums who was dead by the age of 34, in 1930. Ned's grandfather, the first Earl, was one of Queen Victoria's Lord Chamberlains. Ned and Evan were at Eton College together.

Since (like Evan) his health was shattered by consumption Ned knew that time was running out for him so he (again like Evan) lived life to the brim. Ned "was one of the reasons why the 1920s could be called gay in both the old and more recent senses of the word" [521] A close friend of Naps Alington (probably his lover[522]) and a pal of Gerald Berners, they all gained a reputation at the same time as "namby-pamby English dilettantes ...frivolous, shocking, naughty, and very daring dandies." [523] The latter was Francis Rose's description of these fellows including Evan, Peter Churchill, George FitzGeorge, Felix Yussupov[524] and Louis Mountbatten. [525] One instance of Ned's mischief was to stage a fancy dress party at the Tower of London, asking guests to "come as the person you most want to sleep with". [526]

Ned loved teasing women. Some said he even married as a bet.[527] He did not turn out regularly at the *Cafe Royal* or *Eiffel Tower* but Nina Hamnett reveals a ridiculous tale in which Lathom appeared at both places one night and insisted in presenting all the women with a toffee apple, something Nina suggests was an absurd thing to try to eat dressed in their fine dresses and costumes. Ned hosted lavish booze and sex-laden first night (theatre) parties at his London home in Mount Street (near Park Lane) and theatrical entertainment at the family's country seat, Blythe Hall, [528]near Ormskirk, Lancashire, with its:

"cut glass pillars on the staircase, electric candles, a bowling alley and a Greek-style swimming pool.[529] Ivor Novello was a frequent house guest. Ned was a promising playwright with his own stage company and was also a generous patron to rising playwrights including Noel Coward and Beverley Nichols. [530] Again, as in Evan's family's fate, the family fortune was eventually lost by excessive spending, taxes, and calling in mortgages.[531]

Ivor Churchill

Ivor

Evan's great love of art ensured he enjoyed the companionship of the era's aesthetics. One of the avid picture collectors (of modern works) in the 1920s was Lord Ivor Spencer Churchill[532], the second son of 'Sunny', the 9th Duke of Marlborough [533] and cousin of Victor (Peter Spencer), Evan's lover in their halcyon days of youth at Windsor, Eton and Paris.

Ivor was a mutual acquaintance of the same group as Harold Nicolson; a quiet but sociable figure who usually had several handsome homosexual friends in tow. [534] Described as being among the most eligible bachelors in London, Ivor and Evan were often seen dining together (black-tied at a nightclub) hoping not to be spotted by any predatory females present. [535] One report remarks "It usually proved impossible for them to sit out the compulsory dancing, and they were soon on their feet man-handled by two of the actresses from the footlights show." [536]

Evan (and his first wife Lois) both knew Ivor socially and they spent several evenings out together with the brightest stars in London. The vast attendance list for one function at the New Burlington Galleries included Ivor, the Morgans, "Maud Allen, Lord Gerald Berners, Winston Churchill, Noel Coward, John Gielgud, Constant Lambert. Harold Nicolson (with his wife Vita Sackville-West), Somerset Maugham, the Sitwells, Lytton Strachey and Edward Marsh." [537]

Robin Bryans claims that Evan played the part of go-between with the Pope in the final closure of the famous divorce of Ivor's parents, 'Sunny', the 9th Duke of Marlborough and American railroad heiress Consuelo Vanderbilt.[538]

Bryans says Evan was "responsible through his representations to the Sovereign Pontiff [the Pope] in Rome in declaring the Protestant marriage of [Sunny] the ...Duke of Marlborough null and void." [539]

It is true that Evan knew 'Sunny'; they were among the joint visitors at Cannes in the 1914 Season. [540] They ran into each other constantly on the London and Paris scene. The basic facts are that the Marlboroughs were married in 1895; he married for money and she married to become a Duchess. It was an unhappy union. But Consuelo produced two sons, "an heir and a spare"[541]; they separated in 1906 and divorced in 1920. In 1921 'Sunny' married Gladys Deacon[542] who had been his mistress. He became obsessed with Roman Catholicism and in 1926 wanted the first marriage declared null and void. Consuelo had also remarried and 'Sunny' asked for her help to have his first marriage annulled in order to validate his second marriage. Consuelo agreed to declare that she was first married against her will (i.e. forced to do it by her ambitious mother). She describes her side of the story in her memoirs *The Glitter & the Gold.* [543]But she was hoodwinked, because "the Vatican Ecclesiastical Court, the Rota, annulled the marriage….because Consuelo had been in love with an American…but was forced by her mother to marry the Duke". [544]

Father C C Martindale[545]

Whilst Bryans insists that Evan talked directly to the Pope about the matter, the truth is that Evan only acted in the plot as an introduction service for 'Sunny' Marlborough to meet Father CC Martindale who was one of the Catholic priests whom Evan knew well at the Church of the Immaculate Conception at Farm Street in London.

Martindale's biographer[546] declares: "The Duke [Sunny] then married Miss Gladys Deacon and shortly afterwards expressed a desire to join the Catholic Church. Through Mr Evan Morgan he was introduced to Martindale at Campion Hall."[547]

This led to Father Martindale exploring representations on 'Sunny's behalf which were eventually referred to the highest Catholic authorities in Britain and ultimately to the Vatican.[548]

Brendan Bracken

Brendan Bracken [549] was Winston's Churchill's wonder boy, his right-hand man during the Second World War. The amazing story of Bracken's rise to fame from delinquent Irish beginnings and the shadows of an Australian hilly-billy life to become rich "with a lovely house in North Street", [550] a notable Cabinet Minister and a Viscount, in part (along with Joseph Stalin) the inspiration for Orwell's *Big Brother* in the novel *1984* (as he was in charge of the wartime propaganda machine within the Ministry of Information), [551]can be gleaned from two considerable biographies. [552] But since Bracken destroyed many of his private papers (he apparently burned all those related Evan[553]), the inner truth remains hidden (not least about his sexuality[554]); in all respects he remains an enigmatic figure.

Robin Bryans tells us that Evan Morgan first knew Brendan in London in the early 1920s and began to appreciate his talents. There are references to Brendan being thought of as "Evan's protégé";[555] this may even have extended to attending one or more of Evan's Black Masses.

Bryans claims that as "Evan got the Roman Pontiff to interfere with the Duke of Marlborough's marriage; Brendan Bracken took Churchill's side, which was the side on which Bracken's bread was buttered, and he quarrelled with Evan." [556]

Bracken was a fetching creature in appearance, six foot tall with a "fiery mane"[557] of wild uncontrolled red hair. Peter Churchill is named as having been the man who introduced them. [558]Evan is credited as Brendan's "springboard into higher society", [559] the route first passing through Sir Sidney Colvin and his wife Francis.[560] Evan knew the Colvins in and out of literary circles (whilst he was studying in archives about his hero, the mystic and poet, John Donne) whilst Brendan endeared himself to the childless Colvins as a son.[561] Bracken had a lot to offer Evan too, including an acquaintance with the Irish poet, W B Yeats, [562] who is later given the designation of being "Evan's Black Mass companion," [563] with many of "Evan's black magic rites... connected with Yeats in the West of Ireland." [564] Bryans later reveals a fall out between Evan and Yeats.[565]

Evan in turn introduced Brendan to intimates including Gavin Henderson, a homosexual (later 2nd Lord Faringdon [566] of Buscot Park, [567] an avid art custodian and collector who was a close friend of the notorious journalist (later an MP), the gay Tom Driberg[568] who was also a disciple of Aleister Crowley[569]), at which point the tongues began wagging that the new kid on the block must be of a similar pansy and a darker persuasion.

Despite once addressing his fellow peers in Parliament as "[Oh] My Dears" (and not 'My Lords') there was more to Gavin Henderson's backbone than Evan's. Faringdon was "a strong pacifist, he reconciled his conscience when Word War II came by joining the Fire Service and giving sterling service during the Blitz in London, Bristol and other large cities."[570]

Robin Bryans offers this quotation of Henderson's saying that: "Evan and Brendan were seldom inclined to have much respect for the literal truth. I suppose they were really birds of a feather – and so extremely well matched." [571]

One of Bracken's biographers examines this more closely. "While there was a clinging rumour to whether Bracken was a secret homosexual …especially in London in the 20s, it probably owed more to Bracken's apparent lack of interest in girls and to the fact that he numbered among his companions a number of noted homosexuals, notably Evan Morgan [who is described as flamboyant and decadent], than to any concrete evidence." It seems, ultimately Bracken spurned Evan in favour of Henderson and in 1927 it was he who accompanied Bracken on tour of Rome, Florence and Venice. Whilst Bracken's life was changed when he was later introduced to Winston Churchill (by The Observer newspaper chief, Liverpool-born James Garvin[572]), Bracken continued to keep in with Henderson, despite their politics being at opposite ends. Bracken became the ultra Conservative, to Henderson's surprising support for the republican cause in the Spanish Civil War and being a life long Fabian.

Robin Bryans comments waspishly "The doings at Tredegar Park of the Tory pansy Viscount Tredegar differed little from their counterpart at Buscot Park in the regime of the Socialist pansy Baron Faringdon." [573]

Others echo this with one Member of Parliament referring to Faringdon as "a pansy pacifist of whose private tendencies it might be slander to speak freely." [574]

Bracken chose Princess Dil de Rohan, [575] a long-standing Society friend of his and Evan, to head the Swiss desk at the Ministry of

Information during the Second World War. A lesbian, married to a homosexual (a French Prince, Carlos de Rohan [576] who was implicated with Francis Rose and the group of right wing Germans centred around Ernst Rohm), Dil (short for Dilkusha) was the daughter of a British army officer stationed in India. She had a close association with the notorious Mercedes de Acosta,[577] a lesbian who once said "I can get any woman from any man". [578] Dil became a minor London hostess; she was famous for her grand parties "of pheasants and salmon" [579] in London at her wining and dining table at Selwyn House, St James, where a favourite pursuit with Evan in command was of evenings spent doing tarot readings. With wartime food restrictions Evan's contacts on the black market provided the food for the table and even extra petrol for car jaunts. [580] Robin Bryans had accompanied Evan to the home of his cousin, Sir Otto Mundy[581] who was, luckily, Deputy Chairman of the Board of Customs and Excise; Bryans suggests this family link brought in favours for him, Evan and members of the Royal family. [582]

Evan and Dil de Rohan stuck together against the odds and shared secrets and lies. Robin Bryans, her "dear sweet Robin", [583]came to know her well and their friendship endured the years long after Evan was dead.

Brendan Bracken also proved well placed in the 1940s for Evan to push his campaign for monies from out of public funds to support Lord Alfred (Bosie) Douglas in his hour of need. Winston Churchill was not Bosie's greatest fan; a libel case against Churchill had resulted in Bosie going to prison. Bracken was an honest broker between Evan and his master Winston but the rules governing the public purse, relating to the Civil List, failed to apply in Bosie's favour, leaving Evan disappointed. [584] Robin Bryans refers to gossip of Bracken being allegedly included in a boy-sex scandal, which is partly contradicted in a reference by Cecil Roberts to a (seemingly unconnected) libel case costing Bracken more than £5000 in lost legal costs. [585]

In the end Bracken shuffled off this mortal coil prematurely, as did Evan. Summed up by Cecil Roberts as "A dynamic, wild, full-blooded fellow who pushed himself up from Irish obscurity",[586] Bracken was dead from cancer by the age of sixty- two.

Naps Alington

Naps and his bride Lady Mary Ashley Cooper

"Napier Alington, an oddly harmonious amalgam of Peter Pan, Harlequin and Pireot, ….although he was very ill with tuberculosis, that compelling charm of his quickened all on whom it shone. The tempo of conversation speeded up when Napier was present and laughter became infectious, as if everyone had a sniff of laughing gas."[587]

It was Gerard Sturt's younger brother Napier (known as Naps) whom Evan had the real hots for, but his attention was not well received. The Alington heir, "good looking, a favourite of the royal family" [588], was three years younger than Evan; he was slim, tall, handsome and could be choosy when he was being bitchy. As well as being, like Evan, an accomplished sex pest at Eton College, he was rich, bisexual, vain, flirty and confident of himself. There was one dip in his pedigree; he shared the inheritance of some very bad health genes. Evan had a diseased chest, Naps was riddled with tuberculosis. These fault lines ultimately contributed to their comparatively early deaths, Evan at aged 55, Naps at aged just 43.

Testimony stands describing Naps Alington as "naughty, spoilt rotten.."[589] This has echoes of a similar remark made about Evan by Aldous Huxley: "I now lunch frequently with Evan [Morgan]... I like him, I think, quite a lot, tho' he is the most fearfully spoilt child." [590]

Evan and Naps, these two keen enjoyers of all things carnal and esoteric were proverbial peas in the pod, two like poles who repelled each other, with Naps doing most of the first repelling! It's not established whether Evan persisted long enough for Naps to notch him up on his score card so that they could both move on to other easier, worthier lovers.

Naps liked older men too, much older than Evan. The novelist Somerset Maugham was twenty years older and their consummation receives the attention of one of Maugham's biographers: "The famously charming, famously charismatic young peer Napier Alington was another of Maugham's conquests... a delicious creature", as Maugham described him after their night together." [591]

One surprising twist in Naps' sexual make up was that he also slept with women. His good looks were admired by Dora Carrington who observes "Naps came in...looking very marvellous, in a complete evening dress of black velvet. He is a very odd character, looks Jewish and Russian, He gave strange accounts of freaks at fairs. He has a passion for them. [He] stayed till 2'oclock getting drunker and drunker. Naps has an appalling cough, I do not think he will live long. But I thought for pure SA [Sex Appeal] he had more than almost any man I have ever met". [592]

In the 1920s Naps went on a trip to America partly on financial business (to learn about banking) and partly a shopping spree to eye up the American market for a sale wife to produce the Crichel heir. This turned quickly into an occult and drugs fuelled frenzy of parties and one night stands During a high on one of these benders he was introduced (by Jeffrey Amhurst, the debonair, genial Viscount Holmesdale[593]) to Tallulah Bankhead, who was smitten by his charms.[594] As one observer puts it: "One sentimental smile from Naps would have charmed the ducks off the pond." [595] Naps' charm was deceptive as another scribe rips into him as a "soft-spoken, blond tubercular, well cultivated, bisexual with sensuous, meaty lips, a distant, antic charm... and a streak of cruelty." [596]

But Tallulah, renowned for her "endlessly caricaturized baritonal gurgle of a voice",[597] was a magnet that could not be resisted. One observer remarked that her verbal tones were "steeped as deep in sex as the human voice could go without drowning". [598] Naps was easily and, equally madly, irrationally smitten by Bankhead and he asked her to marry him. They became deeply enveloped transatlantic lovers. Bankhead soon found good reason to take offers to star on the London theatre scene, where their odd and lively public affair continued. Neither party was faithful (with at least one convincing biography of Miss Bankhead saying that they never slept with each other at all).[599] While others maintain they slept with each other and between the rollicking love bouts with their own sex participated in cocaine induced communal orgies ranking with the excesses of Ancient Rome.

Meanwhile Lois, Naps' sister, was also diving in headfirst into the mad, mad world of 1920s London. She was not just a flapper: she was the flapper of flappers and was soon branded the Alington's family's ultra-troublemaker for her wave of high-jinks antics and choice of lovers.

Lois Sturt

Gerard and Naps Sturt had two sisters and the eldest, Diana was quickly married off in 1908 to the heir to the barony of Brougham and Vaux.[600] Their baby sister, the Hon. Lois Sturt – sixteen years younger than Diana, four years younger than Naps - spent her childhood as a close friend of the Keppels, [601] especially when the Sturts' London town house was at 38 Portman Square. Sonia Keppel[602] (who was the same age as Lois) says in her memoirs that she was teased by the child Lois, whom she nicknamed "the monkey". [603] Coincidentally, the Morgans were neighbours too, at 39 Portman Square. Evan saw her growing up, his mother Lady Katharine and Lady Feodorovna Alington being good friends.

Lois emerged after the Great War as a budding painter with an art studio in Chelsea. She had advanced from the caterpillar stages of artist, one of the original *Chelsea Chicks* [604], with her own studio in proximity to Evan's straight pal, Augustus John and his muses. Another of Evan's acquaintances, Rex Whistler, had a studio here too. The area brought the rich, artists, painters and their models together for sex and scandal.

Lois also had a notion of becoming an actress. In 1919 her picture appeared in the newspapers saying she was to dance at a charity matinee (organised by her mother) at London's Palace Theatre. [605]

Lois' regular place in the pecking order and profile in London Society, like thousands of other girls, was affected by the embargo on Court presentations. Whilst Lois awaited being presented as a debutante, she was already sleeping with older men.

By the time she was twenty Lois had the "unique distinction of having no less than seven portraits of herself by well known artists in the annual show of the National Portrait Society….. including four sketches by the French artist [Etienne] Drian, and studies in oil by Ambrose McEvoy, Oliver Snell and Gerald F Kelly." [606]

Ambrose McEvoy also painted Evan and Naps as young men and he also painted Tallaulah Bankhead a short time before his death.[607] The McEvoy study of Naps is among the few surviving public images of this enigmatic, troubled figure who lived his life to the brim, aware of the thin line between mortality and death. He filled that life with extravagances, travel, drugs, and legions of male and female lovers.

Naps, Lois and Evan

Naps' sister Lois became a household name when she starred as Nell Gwynne in the film *Glorious Adventure* alongside Lady Diana Cooper. As a result of Lois' promising talent, she received invitations from Europe and America to work on further films.

Naps chaperoned his sister about London for a long stretch at receptions, parties and state occasions. Like Naps a rogue gene dictating sexual gluttony filled Lois' bloodstream. She had whirlwind affairs with the Prince of Wales and his brother Prince George, who was equally on bedroom terms with Naps. Lois may also have offered herself to Prince Albert. The longest, most sustained affair that Lois had was with Reggie Herbert, 15th Earl of Pembroke, who was an older, father like figure to Lois. That messy business was ended by Lois' mother's firm request to Reggie to leave her daughter alone. To escape from a series of scandals engulfing her (she was seeing others at same time as Reggie, with less tolerant wives than Bee Herbert) Lois agreed to marry Evan in 1928, at the same time as he was looking for a fixed marriage to detract from his own entrails being strung up in public humiliation.

Marriage was an ideal safe canopy for each of the parties to continue their depraved sex lives. Evan liked extremely young boys, Lois adored older men. Since her stage and film career was waning Lois had ambition to serve as a London County Council representative for Shoreditch, in East London, for she was an excellent speaker.

Lois' brother Naps was a fellow candidate in the same place, but they both finished at the bottom of the poll. Evan was also nurturing political dreams of being an MP and in 1926 he was selected as the prospective candidate for Limehouse [608] as one of the Conservative party's crop of well connected, rich young men who were candidates fighting to make a first name for themselves (with no realistic chance of winning) tackling a working class seat.

Like Lois, Naps Alington married in 1928. He chose two like poles as ushers for his wedding to Lady Mary Ashley-Cooper at St Margaret's Westminster, in November of that year. Evan was one, Hugh Lygon the other. Family onlookers and the many Royal guests including Evan's Carnegie relations were relieved the conspicuously happy wedding went as smoothly as clockwork.

Somerset Maugham

Evan was at Monte Carlo for New Year of 1928. He was staying with Somerset Maugham at his extremely attractive house *Villa Mauresque* at Cap Ferrat. Maugham, with a coterie of other writers, had made the Riviera "their bodily, if not their spiritual home."[609] The bisexual author and playwright had entertained Evan the previous year at Easter. The peaceful and luxurious surroundings and company inspired Evan to compose a poem called *The Poet – A Riddle.* [610]

It is clear from one of Maugham's biographers [611] that the *Villa Mauresque* hosted continuous opportunities for London Society's closeted homosexuals (which, with the law as it stood in Britain before 1967, was largely everyone who was gay or bisexual) many romps, resulting rather incautiously in romantic letters being exchanged between the parties who had shared time together there between the sheets. [612]

Cecil Roberts, who described Evan as "a vivid, bizarre personality",[613] was accompanying Somerset Maugham to Paris in 1933 whilst Evan was installed at the *Hotel Lancaster.* Roberts recalls Evan's generosity: "one night, under a full moon, he took the Contesse Villeneuve, Lady Louis (Edwina) Mountbatten[614] and myself driving through the Bois de Boulogne in a twin-horses landau after dining at the Pre Catalan". [615]

Evan and his Political Mentors in London's East End

In 1926 it was announced that "The Hon. Evan Morgan has left Rome and is settling in London, with the intention of seeking election to the House of Commons." [616]

Evan was later adopted as a Conservative candidate in the Morgan family's East London nerve centre of Stepney, Limehouse, where historically they owned land and property. This part of the grim East End, around Chinatown, was also the scene where Evan's wayward sister Gwyneth played out her final years, a hopeless drug fiend.

Evan's political friends in Limehouse and surrounds included the maverick Lt. Col. John 'Johnnie' Dodge[617] ("a big handsome fellow" [618] who had dug the grave of Rupert Brooke on Skyros in 1915 and who, in 1921, was arrested by the Bolsheviks as a British spy). [619] Dodge was also a nephew by marriage of Courtenay Morgan's mistress, Corisande Rodney, and a cousin of Winston Churchill. [620] He later distinguished himself in the Second World War as one of those involved in the infamous *"Great Escape"* from Stalag Luft III.

The East End had not seen it's like before. Dodge (who was adopted as the Tory candidate for Mile End) installed himself inside the constituency. Between his family contacts and those of Evan they raised the public profile of the area with visits from leading politicians and Royalty. Evan was particularly fond of showing off his "great friend" [621] the Prince of Wales, as well as the equally glamorous brother, Prince George, whose attendance at functions dwarfed the appearance of the Prime Minister, Stanley Baldwin, for winning the public vote. The sporting side of the Royals was in evidence with support and patronage of local boxing clubs, enhanced by a boxing peer, Lord Knebworth, [622] another of the Tory blue eyed boys. He knew Evan more from the London night cabaret circuit than the boxing ring, and from the Turkish baths established under York Hall on Old Ford Road [623]in 1929 which "garnered legendry status; its Turkish and Russian baths" [624] became a favourite haunt of Evan and served as an ideal place for him to pick up rough trade.

Also in the crop of would-be Tory stars who all realised they had no hope of winning in the impoverished East End was William Teeling. [625] Teeling eventually enjoyed a steady political career as an MP; he was an intimate of Jack Macnamara (later Colonel JBJ Macnamara) [626] who, like Evan, had a liking for boys. Teeling had also close connections with the high ranks of the Catholic Church and in the mid 1930s met Adolf Hitler and Rudolf Hess through his social contacts with the German spy Princess Hohenlohe. [627] Evan's links to the Hohenlohe dynasty will be explored later.

Teeling records in his memoirs his time in the East End with Evan:

"Far and away the most active of us all was Evan Morgan who had tremendous courage in taking on the constituency of Limehouse, especially as his father, Lord Tredegar, owned most of the slum property there." [628] [Teeling adds affectionate memories too of Johnnie Dodge [629] Lord Knebworth.[630]]

Evan's erratic health spread its own shadow over his political aspirations.

I was glad to hear yesterday from Mrs. Evan Morgan that her husband is slightly better. He has been in bed some days with acute catarrh, which came on quite suddenly much to his disgust, as he had to miss, not only some very amusing parties, but also some important meetings in the constituency he is fighting in the East End.

Hon. Evan Morgan.

Mr. Evan Morgan is one of the intrepid eight young men who are fighting forlorn hopes for the Conservatives. He told me once that he hardly expected any of them would get in at the first or second attempt; but he hoped they would all be in eventually.

Evan's Health Interrupts His Political Career

In 1929 Evan stood unsuccessfully (against Clement Attlee) and was later adopted as Conservative candidate for Cardiff but gave up the nomination in 1931 in favour of the candidate for the National government being elected.

Voting for 'eaven

The Cunards: Emerald, Nancy and Victor
Nancy and Emerald

The two legendry Cunard women, Nancy and her mother Emerald,[631] were regularly in Evan's close orbit. Nancy was one of several women who thought they could make a wife for Evan, without a ring, sex or strings. Nancy could see through Evan, describing him as "a fantasy who could be most charming and most bitchy".[632]

For her part Nancy was slender and rash, the only child of Emerald, the estranged wife of the Cunard shipping magnate and grandson of the founder of the famous line. Emerald was once described as "blue-eyed and with a deceptively Fragonard daintiness." [633]

In her life-long chase to marry Evan despite his sexuality it was observed that she had "much in common with the willowy youth [as Evan was once dubbed]... including a spirit of rebellion against parental authority." [634]

Nancy's mother was one of the great 20th Century hostesses. She was interested in the extra-curricular activities of her guests but not hearing about their sex lives, of which she could be naïve. Nonetheless she simultaneously engaged in her own carnal affairs, most notably one long romance with the music conductor Sir Thomas Beecham, and another with the writer George Moore, the father figure in Nancy's unbalanced life.

Surveillance of Nancy Cunard by Special Branch

Nancy Cunard was rebellious enough from the 1930s to the 1940s to have a Special Branch file.[635] The astonishing contents of this show she was subjected to regular covert surveillance by the police. Much of this focused on monitoring Nancy's support for black men and their causes for freedom and equality.[636]

One Special Branch report from 1932 refers to observations by a Police Inspector and a Sergeant "in the vicinity of the Cross Keys Public House, Theobalds Road, WC" which describes Nancy as "an associate of Fred Thompson of the Seaman's Minority Movement and R F C Bridgeman of the British Section of the League against Imperialism." Nancy was soon spotted inside the pub "in the company of three Negroes in the public bar of the house. We later saw the same woman in Cromer Street, WC…proceeding towards No 59, the headquarters of the London District Committee of the Communist Party and other extreme organisations, and where a meeting of the Negro Welfare Association was taking place. We produced our warrant cards and questioned her as to her nationality, etc."

At first Nancy would not co-operate, but on the advice of her companion (given in the report as a Gerald Bradley) she produced her passport showing she was a British citizen. Nancy (who was living at the time at the premises of her Hours Press at 15, Rue Guenegaud, Paris 6c) complained to the Commissioner of Police.[637] In justifying their actions the police reported to the Commissioner "The complaint by Miss Nancy Cunard does not deserve serious consideration…. [She] possesses anti-capitalist and anti –imperialist views. She associates with members of the Communist Party, League Against Imperialism, Seamen's Minority

Movement and the Negroes Welfare Association and takes an active interest in subversive propaganda."

The police report description of Nancy is glorious: "Age 36. 5ft 9. Hair fair. Blue eyes. Eyebrows plucked. Thin face and lips. Slim build. Artificial complexion. Dressed in red leather coat, with tight fitting hat to match. Dark grey woollen dress. Flesh coloured silk stockings, with anklet socks. Lizard skin shoes...."

Evan's judgement of not taking Nancy as his wife must seem absolved on the strength of Nancy's extreme political connections and causes. Lois, although a colourful player was no match for Nancy the bold.

Despite Nancy's high profile involvement in subversive activities (or perhaps because of it, if Evan was spying on Nancy for his MI5/6 masters) he accepted an invitation to attend one of Nancy's parties, a charity dance in aid of the Negroes Welfare Association.

The event was watched over by Special Branch. One newspaper report referred to "the dance was held in a sun-ray and bathing establishment [in the basement of a London hotel]... which was taken over for the evening. All the sun lamps were left on, and bathing proceeded side by side with dancing in an atmosphere which was tropically hot. ...It was exotic. Mr Augustus John leaned against the bar, breathing air that was practically solid with smoke and enthusiasm, and surveyed a series of moving pictures..."[638]

In 1938 Nancy headed for Spain where she acted as journalist for eight months, between home in London and Paris, collecting money for the National Committee of Aid for Spain.

Evan joisting with Emerald Cunard

LORD TREDEGAR'S WHITSUNTIDE GUESTS.—Left to right: Count Woronzow-Daschkow, Captain E. Ware, Mr. Rendle Mervill, Captain R. O. Finlay, Sir Geoffrey Archer (former Governor-General of the Sudan), the Marchese Mattei, Mr. M. Yates, Count John de Salis, Lord Tredegar, Mrs. J. B. Dodge, Mrs. Shipman, the Marchesa Mattei, Sir Foster Stedman and Colonel J. B. Dodge.

A bank holiday weekend with Evan[639]

Nancy's mother Emerald expected the parlour talk to be on art, culture, about painting, opera and poetry. She was livid when she encountered an irresponsible, drunken side to Evan which John, Duke of Bedford, records for posterity after he was asked to accompany her on a visit to Tredegar House after Evan became the incumbent lord.

Evan had abandoned his guests to attend another social function, although he had asked some Welsh singers to entertain the party during dinner. The choir "stood outside the dining-room windows, which we had to keep open. In the end, freezing to death in an icy draught, we got up and shut them, leaving the Welsh singers burbling on happily outside.....Lady Cunard was the only one of us who was civil enough to go out and thank them."[640]

Evan eventually returned "from what had obviously been a liquid occasion, and flew into a terrible rage when he discovered that we had shut the windows on his favourite choir." [641] Lady Cunard (who had a reputation for having a sharp tongue which spared neither friend nor foe) considered that Evan had behaved badly and should have stayed behind throughout with his invited guests. There with a stand-up row between Evan and Emerald, "who threatened to leave, although the whole thing was patched up again in the morning". [642] In her last days of life, when Emerald was entombed at *The Dorchester Hotel* in London's Park Lane, dying from cancer, she was visited by Evan and was heartened by his kind attention.

Victor Cunard

Another Cunard whose life and life style crossed with Evan's was Nancy's cousin Victor, [643] who was also a homosexual. Victor was always a humorous, good natured chum to Evan; he became a leading foreign correspondent with *The Times* and lived a good deal of his life in Paris, Rome and Venice where he entertained like minded queers, although it is recorded that he may have proposed marriage to Oscar Wilde's wayward niece Dolly. [644] A mutual friend of the eccentric Romaphile Lord Gerald Berners (who was an Honorary Attaché at the British Embassy in Rome), Victor was also well known to Evan's other regular Rome companion, another homosexual with tastes for youthful good looks and illegal flesh, Cecil Roberts.[645]

Of Victor, Roberts informs us that he was "anti-Mussolini in the Dictator's early days so that pressure was brought on the British Foreign Office to have Victor removed." [646] Roberts was impressed by Victor's restoration of a half-ruined palace, *Vendramin-I-Carmine,* where one of his guests was the twenty-four-year-old Prince Umberto, [647] at the time the heir to the Italian throne and who is said to have had homosexual tendencies. [648] Such was the measure of Rome's close-knit literary and regal gay cell, to which Evan had access on tap as a long-standing pal of Roberts; also as a Papal henchman pimping within the seedier, less religious, side of the Vatican's dwellers as well as diplomats attached to the Holy See.

Harold Nicolson (who had an affair with Victor [649]) wrote an affectionate obituary to him after his death in Venice in 1960. [650]

Ronald Firbank Again

Ronald Firbank

'Firbank could be extremely witty and of a particular quickness' - Nancy Cunard

Victor and Nancy Cunard were friends of Violet Trefusis, [651] an intimate of Harold Nicolson's wife, Vita Sackville West,[652] and her long term correspondent and earlier her eloped lover. Evan is included among the guests that were invited by Violet to her house parties; she especially admired those familiar with the life and writing legacy of the surreal fantasy novelist Ronald Firbank:

"Intellectuals of style welcomed at *I Tatti* [Violet's Italian Villa in Florence]were rarely invited, except for friends like Raymond Mortimer [who had a long affair with Harold Nicolson] or Lord Berners, that composer straight from Firbank. Another Firbankian guest was the eccentric millionaire Evan Morgan (Lord Tredegar)." [653]

No-one Firbank came across was out of harm's way from near malicious caricaturing in his books. Evan was not Firbank's only target for revenge after the dedication incident in 1920. Harold Nicolson and Vita Sackville-West appear, thinly disguised as Harold Chillywater and Victoria Gellbore-Frinton in *The Flower Beneath The Foot*.[654] Such well-drawn a picture of the duo was based on Firbank's attention to observing Harold and Vita when he saw them dining out at the Café Royal. Nicolson, in turn, provides a vivid portrayal of Firbank as Lambert Orme in his excellent book *Some People*.[655]

Gerald Berners & Rex Whistler

Lord Berners

Lord Gerard Berners[656] (also a friend of Harold Nicolson long before Berners inherited his peer's title) certainly was one man who was unselfishly loyal to Ronnie Firbank. Berners organised Firbank's two funerals in 1926, the first being by mistake at Rome's Protestant Cemetery and where briefly Ronnie shared a part of God's Green Acre with the poets John Keats and Percy B Shelley. When Firbank's sister Heather (in London) pointed out that her brother was actually Roman Catholic, this was followed by the more desired internment of the extraordinarily mischievous creator of the pederast Cardinal Pirelli[657] in the Catholic Cemetery at *Campo Verano*. Evan had spent thoughts about Firbank after he was dead, and this is evident when in 1940 he shared his recollections of Firbank with Dicky Buckle. [658] But before this, in Ronnie's lifetime their relationship swerved this way and that over Evan's hard-to-get attitude over a dedication to the book *The Princess Zoubaroff* in 1920, which led to a gaping fall out and harsh words by Firbank. They later made up, especially after the death of Firbank's mother, Lady Harriet Firbank, [659] when Evan offered support. Later Evan visited Firbank's grave at *Campo Verano,* Rome, and perhaps this gesture was made in part to make his final peace.

After his humiliating departure from Beda, College Evan continued to visit Rome each year to fulfil his annual duties (lasting a few weeks). In 1929, despite the oppressive heat of high summer in the Eternal City, Evan fulfilled his annual commitment in ceremonies at the Papal Court. Off-duty he enjoyed sketching with Gerald Berners, who is described by Christabel Aberconway, Evan's friend (and South Street neighbour after his marriage to Lois the year before; she was a noted beauty and erudite hostess) as "an eccentric, and an enchanting one, he composed music, wrote witty stories and poems and painted in almost any style".[660]Gerald had a beautiful house in Rome and one of his guests for the 1929 season was the gifted painter of the Tate Gallery's frescoes, Rex Whistler.[661] The trio relaxed around some of the quaint, quiet local beauty spots outside the city walls, at their easels, breaking the silence with small talk and an occasional nude swim in a nearby lake. [662]

Whistler spent time in Wales too, where he had infamous associations with the family of the 6th Marquess of Anglesey and where he painted his startling nude of the Marquess's daughter's Lady Caroline Paget, a famous beauty.[663] It was a remembrance of another Welsh trip, in 1939 [664] in the presence of Evan, Whistler and Berners, that gave rise to Ettie Desborough's considered observation being recorded that Evan was "quite mad". [665]

H G Wells

Evan and HG Wells

Literary figures such as the science fiction novelist H G Wells[666], (the English Jules Verne), provided a modicum of uprightness over the drearier, or the seemingly risky or more outrageous attendees amongst the average head count at Evan's weekend parties at Tredegar House in the 1930s. With a track record of serial adultery, his affair with the writer Rebecca West, twenty years his junior, was one notch in his non-literary output. Wells was an unlikely social animal to mix with Evan's inner coterie. A heterosexual from humble beginnings, he was by age more of a contemporary of Courtenay, Evan's ultra conservative father, and besides which he gave lectures in Socialism and was a darling of the radical left wing Cambridge apostles. [667] Wells was not hesitant to add his voice in support of writers who had boldly written on homosexual themes and who found themselves in trouble with the primmer sections of the literary world. [668]

Closer scrutiny of Wells' past causes also includes him giving support to Robbie Ross in his hour of need over his tussles with Lord Alfred Douglas when the latter eventually renounced his homosexuality and turned nastily on Ross in the same manner as his father, Lord Queensberry, had turned on Wilde. [669] Unlike the gay members of Evan's human menagerie Wells was a notorious womaniser[670] with a taste for upper crust society women. At Evan's parties he latched himself like a limpet on loose women guests.

Lord Berners, Moura Budberg and H G Wells

Robin Bryans informs that in the 1930s Evan was one of the first supporters to dine with Emerald Cunard and Lady Lavery at the *Quo Vadis* restaurant in Soho "to launch Wells and Moura on London Society." "Moura" was the Russian Maria Ignatievna Budberg, married to a Czech but the energetic lover of several high ranked Soviet citizens and diplomats including the writer, Maxim Gorky. She moved to London in 1933 and became Wells' mistress and close friend until his death. She enjoyed others lovers too, notably Lenin's would-be assassin, spy Bruce Lockhart. [671] Moura was also a possible spy and double agent; she was snooped on regularly by British Intelligence. [672] It was said "she could drink an amazing quantity, mostly gin."[673] She almost certainly stayed over at Tredegar House with Wells.

Wells' presence as a house guest of Evan is cited by a smattering of memoir writers but all saying the same: that is, actually nothing of any substance or that marks the event out with a scintillating anecdote or some achievement or out of the ordinary incident. The exception to this is the story of Wells being maliciously pecked by Evan's macaw, Blue Boy.[674] At first it seems that Evan was only providing a pleasant retreat in his dotage years for Wells (weakened by ill-health through the scourge of diabetes) – this was something of merit he extended to other notables, as with Nina Hamnett, Bosie Douglas and the Marchesa Casati, to whom Evan gave generous financial hand-outs. However, Wells most smartly and shrewdly combined his trips to Tredegar Park with speaking engagements in the Cardiff area. He usually met Evan in London for a pre-lunch to discuss his available weekends and fitted a talk or a lecture tour in Wales at the same time. [675]

The pathway of using Evan's gatherings for the up-and coming was a slender means for the yet unknown and yet unsung who might wish to attach themselves to Evan's entertainment circuses in London, Paris, Surrey and South Wales in order to meet, ingratiate or bed great men and women. But it was some opportunity for importuning, a spur for some risings stars, for introductions and to climb up the literary ladder rubbing shoulders with authors like Wells, the begetter of some classic pieces of 20th Century pulp fiction. Evan adored playing the house host; he held them as his prey, like his menagerie collection, dependent on his whim and for feeding. But Evan was not as chaste as Edith Sitwell, whose afternoon tea parties were as innocent as Church fetes and are well described by another period homosexual, Tom Driberg (who cites Wells as a regular guest) and became his stairway to gay sex and the job market.[676] Evan (and others) capitalised by having friends like Wells, whose books were being turned into films for the new mass media of cinema, attending premieres and reception parties with Hollywood movie stars. [677] Wells travelled across America as a speaker, commanding giant audiences and media attention.

Surprisingly, Wells' several biographers make little or no mention of him visiting Evan in South Wales. But one reviewer of a three volume dip into Wells' life [678] does provide a flurry of words putting the great writer's real charms in perspective:

"Anyone trumpeting his [Wells'] affairs in public is likely to cut a figure of fun. Lovable, unintentionally self-revealing, vulnerable, but also jowly, portly, none too attractive physically, Wells might have been suitably cast in a Feydeau farce, skipping about in a bow-tie minus his trousers. And a dirty old man into the bargain.

This reviewer, David Pryce-Jones[679] (son of Alan), then reveals a glorious Tredegar House anecdote:

"My mother used to tell a story of how Wells had pounced on her. Married only a few months, she was staying at Tredegar, the house of Evan Morgan. Wells, another guest, suggested that she row him out on the lake, where he could correct some proofs. Once out, however, he put his hands on her, whereupon she threatened to throw the proofs overboard. Unwilling to believe that she meant it, he did not stop until his proofs were in the water and he was rowed back in silent rage to dry land." [680]

Another of Wells' visits to Tredegar House is recorded for a weekend including 1 June 1936.[681] At least one photograph in the *South Wales Argus* at the same time records his presence with a large crop of society guests that would all have graced any London bash or town house gathering. [682] There were swimming parties (and legend has it also nude bathing in the lake near Tredegar House) but the reflection by one commentator more than sixty years after Evan's death, that he [Evan] "would frolic naked in the pool ... at weekends with his three best friends ...H G Wells, Aldous Huxley and George Bernard Shaw..." [683] is just a ludicrous assertion. Huxley's association with Evan began many years before he became Viscount Tredegar.[684]

Aldous Huxley's time with Evan was centred on the Great War era and in the 1920s, after which Huxley lived abroad for much of the time. However Aldous' brother Julian has left a memory behind of his visit to Tredegar House:

"Through Aldous I met the eccentric poetaster millionaire Evan Morgan, Lord Tredegar. Once while lecturing in Wales I was invited to dinner at his big house in the Rhondda district. In the drawing-room later while inspecting the Tsarevitch's bed-table, made of a single slab of onyx, I was suddenly roused by a sharp nip. One of Evan's pet macaws was using my leg as a ladder for claws and beak, to climb up to the sofa. Evan had a predilection for exotic creatures. Soon afterwards a groom arrived in haste to say that his pet baboon had escaped from its stall…" [685]

A J Symons

A J Symons[686] who established The First Edition (Book) Club (as a means for others wishing to collect rare and unusual books) initially seems something of an oddball friend for any kind of liaison with Evan. Closer study of Symons reveals he was an intimate friend of the surviving disciples of Oscar Wilde including Robbie Ross and Christopher Millard. He was also (in 1934) the author of *Quest for Corvo*, the biography of Frederick Rolfe whose sexual preference (like Evan) was for adolescent boys. Surprisingly, Evan's Catholic friend Shane Leslie assisted Symons in the task of writing this book, which was universally praised. Edward Marsh declared it "a masterpiece – a mixture of the best thriller and the best biography".[687]

There was a great need for an element of secrecy in Evan's commercial dealings with Symons. In the 1920s Evan was exalting in his new-found religion and, following the debacle with Firbank over publication of *The Princess Zoubaroff*, he was playing it cautiously for once. The acquisitions of the First Edition Club included banned titles, and what we might now term 'dirty or pornographic books'. Symons was an expert on the literature of the eighteen-nineties, and a well placed spotter of "anything that was rare and distinctive in the arts, in books, in wine, food and persons aroused his curiosity".[688] How adorable, then, Evan must have found him, especially as an intermediary in Evan's clandestine search for the lesser known works and more obscene drawings of his gifted dead hero Aubrey Beardsley.[689]

But one commentator actually names Evan in relation to Symons. The whistleblower refers to one of Symons' "steady customers" [690] as "EM" and poses the question "could "EM" have been Evan Morgan, Lord Tredegar?" [691] The material supplied to EM was of a more select type, requiring some cryptic record keeping. Symons was writing a biography of Oscar Wilde and accumulating original and, in some instances, banned and exuberant gay texts. [692] A later intrigue revolves around Symons' exclusive Wine and Food Society[693], and another clique of five members comprising "[Shane] Leslie, Symons, Vyvyan Holland, and two men who attended neither Banquet, Oliver Brett and Evan Morgan."[694]

The eccentric Symons was also a friend of Bosie Douglas, who dubbed him (it seems suggestively sexual) "Ajaccio". [695]

Symonds' Backing for Con-Man Maundy Gregory

Maundy Gregory

Funds from angels behind the scenes kept Symons' enterprises going. One of those who gave his enterprises financial backing, including large support to the First Editions Club, was a ruthless trouble-maker named Maundy Gregory[696] who was regarded as a pest by MI5 during the Great War period:

"We don't like him and don't trust him. We have often refused to employ him because of his character. ...He is difficult to shake off as he is an indefatigable 'Nosey Parker', perpetually on the prowl for something saleable." [697]

Gregory tried shirking out of military enlistment in the Great War by attempting to hog official channels with speculative information he thought useful to the intelligence services. Much of the material was complete chaff.

Gregory blew up his own importance, owning and editing a notorious rag *The Whitehall Gazette*. Official files at National Archives, Kew reveal widespread suspicions over Gregory's integrity in everything he dabbled in throughout his life. In the 1920s Gregory was involved in shady dealings with a London nightclub, *The Ambassadors*. A sighting of Evan is recorded a few weeks after marrying Lois, "supping in the gallery of the Ambassador Club"[698], but there is also a reference to him giving a party at the *Ambassadors* on 26 October 1927. [699] Gregory had a luxury hotel in Surrey called *The Deepdene*, which was in close proximity to Evan's mother's home at *Honeywood House*, near Dorking, in Surrey. The caves nearby may have been a site for Evan's occult activity.

Gregory's friend Symons (an inestimable lover of good food, wine and literature, as well as a collector of *objects de art* but who could not always afford these fads) was taken in by offers funds from Gregory (who was always in the money). Much of this wealth came from embezzlement and blackmail by Gregory, especially of fellow homosexuals too afraid to withhold payment to him or stop favours. AJ Symons was probably a homosexual but kept this secret, masked or unexplored. [700] One lover of boys[701] highlights that Symons' brother (and biographer) calls AJ Symons "disreputable, presumably because he had been in prison twice for homosexual offences." [702]

Cyril Connolly said that A J Symons' chief quality as a writer was "the ability to communicate excitement and enthusiasm, which was enthusiasm which was a part of his own excitement"[703] and that Symons became "a kind of Pied Piper whose music drew an enthralled army of gourmets, book collectors, tycoons, publishers, odd-volumers, all with their guineas ready, in hot pursuit." [704]

Symons acquired obscure titles for his black book of secret customers, those whose interest in the volumes was pleasure seeking, lust and titillation. Maundy Gregory was an accomplice, and Symons' patron and fund manager. Evan drooled at one title, *Don Renato,* by Fr Rolfe, the man who was the subject of Symons' Quest for Corvo. This was obtained for him by the Gregory-Symons team. Gregory had personally tracked down proof copies of the work "in a rat-infested cellar." However Gregory, like Evan and Evan fanciers, was such a stranger to truth that he often exaggerated a story until it became "a myth based on embroidered fact." [705]

A brief description of *Don Renato* with its air of pederasty explains why Evan was drawn to the book for his solitary reading.

"It is in the form of a diary kept by a chaplain to the princely Roman house of Poplicola around 1527-30. Don Renato, the son and heir of Prince Marcantonio is a handsome and precocious boy of fourteen living in semi royal state in a household of chamberlains, chaplains, soldiers, men of letters, craftsmen and innumerable pages. So many entries in the dairy deal with the pages that it might have been kept by a successful preparatory schoolmaster with an eye on his charges' health and sexual development and a belief in swimming, boxing and herbal remedies. The Prince is a true Renaissance despot with a talent and passion for painting, but the general atmosphere of the Palace is "black" and papal." [706]

Given what the great advocate Sir Walter Monckton[707] provoked Sir Russell Wilkinson[708] to remark at Evan's Court Martial in 1943, for breaches of the Official Secrets Acts, that "in short, [Evan] would be more at home in a Papal Palace or Doges Court of the 15th Century than in our time …", Prince Marcantonio could well be Evan's perfect model of himself.

Maundy Gregory and Cash For Honours

The ace crook Maundy Gregory – known as 'Bum Cheeks' at school - also features prominently in the Cash for Honours crisis that fell upon Lloyd George's premiership.

History already tingles and some families with inherited titles still twitch at the mention of the title broking of Maundy Gregory who sold honours for cash in the 1920s, typically £25,000 - £30,000 for a baronetcy, or £10,000 for a plain knighthood.

Several scribes have attempted to unravel the secrets and contradictions of the "mendacious, anti-Semitic, possibly murderous venturer [Gregory] who, for a few years after the Great War, was notorious as the man who arranged the sale of honours by the Lloyd George Government". [709]

In short, Gregory was a wicked conman. Symons does not come out of the unravelling well, one author declaring "when ...[Gregory] met A J A Symons, it was a highly diverting case of instant mutual recognition." [710]

Foreign and Papal Honours

Gerald Hamilton, the inspiration for Isherwood's Mr Norris, owns up to being an ally of Gregory in the procurement of foreign titles:

"My job was to help to secure for his clients foreign [titles and decorations]. One particular foreign decoration was the Order of Christ of Portugal because this Order could be worn with a bright red ribbon which most people mistook for the French Legion of Honour." [711] Hamilton also took the credit for introducing Gregory, in London, to the exiled King George II of Greece whose brother Prince Paul (an umbilical connection of Evan's) became King of Greece in 1947.

It is not beyond credibility that Evan was the receiving side of Gregory's blackmail or acting as a procurer of titles (like Hamilton).

A curious side note concerns a trip by Evan in 1924 to Jerusalem (it seems on Papal business) taking a greeting from the Vatican to Mgr. Barlassina, [712]the Latin Patriarch of Jerusalem, the Beatitude Louis Barlassina:

"A few weeks ago, Mgr. Evan Morgan, an English prelate who is one of the chamberlains to the Pope, was sent from Rome to Jerusalem on a special mission. The precise object of his journey was not disclosed, but he was believed to be the bearer of confidential instructions to the Latin Patriarch." [713]

150

In late December of 1924, a few days after Gwyneth Morgan disappeared, Mgr. Barlassina arrived in London. Evan was not there to welcome him, as he was lying low in Rome in fear of his own life after Gwyneth's removal.

A few years later, in 1934, Benjamin George Pengelly, one of Gregory's henchmen, was sentenced to six months imprisonment after a trial at the Old Bailey for blackmailing the Beatitude Louis Barlassina over honours allegedly given by him to Gregory to pass out to others in exchange for money.

Pengelly wrote three letters to the Patriarch, threatening to print the photographs of two cheques for £500 each which Gregory had paid to the Patriarch.[714]

At this time Evan Morgan, also a Knight Commander of the Equestrian Order of the Holy Sepulchre of Jerusalem, was conveniently out of the country.

Maundy Gregory: A Murderer?

Superintendent Arthur Askew of Scotland Yard, the policeman who was in charge of the honours investigation, was also the leading policeman on the inquiries into the death of Mrs Edith Rosse, [715]a woman with whom Gregory had been living for several years before he was charged with the cash for honours offences and sent to prison. Rosse left Gregory £18,000 in her will.

Some people suspected Gregory of causing Rosse's death. The policeman, Askew, was clear: "I'm convinced that Gregory murdered Mrs Rosse". [716] It was said Gregory had poisoned Mrs Rosse. In fact the pair lived quite separately in the house at Hyde Park Terrace, London. Gregory occupied the top floors and Mrs Rosse the ground floor and basement; they each had their own housekeeper.

Whilst the body of Edith Rosse was later exhumed (after Gregory had left Britain, for exile) and it was closely examined by the famous pathologist Sir Bernard Spilsbury, no poison was found. At an inquest[717] hearing Spilsbury advised that the cause of death could not be determined. Gregory did not attend the inquest and whilst there were requests for him to be summoned from abroad, the Coroner decided that an open verdict was correct in law. He did not think any useful purpose would be served by Gregory being cross-examined. Whether there was interference from on high in this decision is a plausible scenario.

It was later alleged that Gregory had arranged for the grave of Mrs Rosse (in a Thames-side churchyard at Bisham, near Marlow) to be near a part of the River Thames that frequently overflowed so if the body contained any poison, traces of it would be periodically washed away.

Gregory's initial exposure was orchestrated by the Conservative Party with J C Davidson (later Lord Davidson[718]) taking steps (fully approved by Prime Minister Stanley Baldwin) to stop and cover up Gregory's mischief. Moreover:

"to break him [Gregory] financially, and this involved making many enemies among the people - and some people were very well known people indeed – who were his clients and who expected honours in return for their payments to him." [719] But Davidson's plans were altered to covering up the Gregory mess and coaxing the villain to keep his mouth shut, with the promise of an easier life.

Davidson became Chairman of the Conservative Party in 1927. Co-incidentally his running mate as President that same year in the National Union of Conservative and Unionist Associations was Evan's father, Courtenay Charles Evan Morgan, Lord Tredegar. [720] As the year unfolded Courtenay hosted a grand reception at Tredegar House in honour of Stanley Baldwin at the same time as the 55th annual conference of the National Union of Conservative and Unionist associations was held at Cardiff on 6-7 October 1927. [721]

It was far from plain sailing for Gregory on other fronts. The devious blackmailer was being blackmailed himself by bitter rivals, including boys he (and others he knew) had abused.

Gregory pushed his luck again too far in 1933 by offering to arrange a title for a naval man - he was found out by the Prime Minister's Office and a charge followed. [722] He was tried in a court of law for offences relating to him obtaining honours for money and served a short time in prison. [723] He was declared bankrupt in 1933 and later (with Davidson's generous secret patronage and promises of a future funding) Gregory went to live in exile in Paris. When Paris was occupied by the Germans Gregory was picked up and interned. He later died in a Paris hospital in 1941. [724] Gregory took to his grave the answer to whether he was caught up in a mystery surrounding the disappearance (as early as 1920) of a Labour MP, Victor Grayson. It has been suggested that Gregory was involved in the subsequent death of Grayson, as he had found out about the honours scam and was intent on whistle-blowing. Several books make the claim and accuse Gregory but all fail to pin the charge of murder on him but equally they do not wholly convince that Grayson did in fact devise his own disappearance in order to simply live out a new life elsewhere. [725]

The Hetman of the Ukraine

Following the Russian revolution of 1918 Prince Paul Skoropadsky, the Hetman of the Ukraine, lost his throne. The Hetman was given sanctuary in Germany and into the 1920s the Ukrainians found themselves worse off under Communism. Several worldwide organisations were created to restore the Hetman and help support him financially. Maundy Gregory came to international attention by leading (with others) an appeal for funds to halt the spread of Communism and put the Hetman back in power. Using his publication *The Whitehall Gazette* Gregory published articles by the Hetman's London representative Ivan Vladimir Korostovetz. Gregory always planned to cash in on access to these Hetman payments; he used part of the funds to support his lifestyle and siphoned off large amounts to repay blackmailers.

Robin Bryans refers to Gregory's connections in the early 1930s, in London, with the Anglo-Ukrainian Council [726]and this overlaps with several personalities who had a link within Evan's clique. It is suggested by Robin Bryans that Willie Pethybridge, the Cardiff solicitor, acted on behalf of the Council. No supporting evidence has emerged to substantiate Pethybridge's involvement. By the time the next prominent organisation, the Anglo-Ukrainian Committee, was officially announced in 1935[727] Maundy Gregory was exiled in France. But there was an open wound created in 1935 by a case in the High Court of *Tufnell v Skoropadsky*. Robin Bryans offers this background:

"One young man who had spent time in building up money for the Anglo-Ukrainian Council in England was Louis Tufnell who then demanded his fare share of the profits from Gregory. But Gregory refused to pay him and Tufnell sued, not the disgraced Gregory but Prince Skoropadsky, the Hetman himself, who was then living in considerable state in Berlin." [728]

Tufnell was presented with a counter claim by the Hetman's camp suggesting he had been one of those withholding funds and he was eventually forced to withdraw his action.[729] Maundy Gregory was far from the madding crowd at the time of the Tufnell litigation, with his head firmly down with a new profile in France.

It is suggested that Evan owes the title of 'Gentleman Spy' to Maundy Gregory:

"'Gentleman Spy' was an ironic label attached to Evan by Maundy Gregory, when they were both involved in the Anglo-Ukrainian Movement." [730]

No other reference has been found to this accolade or linking Evan beyond his mainly social links with Gregory, and in particular of Evan patronising the *Ambassador Club* and possibly visiting the *Deepdene Hotel* near Dorking. It is suggested by Robin Bryans that the caves near to the *Deepdene* were used by Evan for celebrating Black Masses. [731]

Richard Rumbold

Author of Little Victims: Richard Rumbold

One of Evan's doomed acquaintances was with the writer Richard Rumbold. [732] In 1933, twenty-year-old Rumbold caused a stir with a homosexual novel called *Little Victims*[733] which was a study of modern youth. One critic said it was "remarkable", [734] another that it was "a sadly unpleasant book, clever..but marred", [735] the chief character being a "pervert who hates his own perversion." [736] Albeit fiction, the book attacked the Roman Catholic Church, who damned Rumbold "a wicked man who has written a wicked book". Rumbold's clever, matter of fact writing style (unlike the fantasy world of Ronald Firbank) made his tale of physical and sexual abuse believably based on his own life and others he was closely associated with.

It is unclear where or when Rumbold first met Evan; it may have been at a party, possibly one of Evan's many stay-overs at *The Randolph Hotel*, Oxford. The comparatively wealthy Rumbold did not need patronage, thus he does not fit into the customary target for Evan's encroachment. But another link is to Lord Alfred (Bosie) Douglas who was invited to a literary group, *The English Club*, at Oxford run by Rumbold. Evan may well have been in tow, which would place the meeting at around the time of the publication of *Little Victims* in 1933. [737] Evan and Bosie became friends from 1928 onwards, first on formal terms but later Evan was Bosie's saviour on earth, providing a platform for him at the *Royal Society of Literature*, heading a campaign to secure him a pension, and in his dying days, taking treats of salmon and champagne and a galaxy of beautiful boys to call on and sit with Bosie in his last days at Old Monk's Farm, Lancing (with Edward and Shelia Colman[738]) and at Bosie's flat in Hove. Rumbold was a regular visitor to see Bosie;[739] he may have come across Evan attending there too. [740]

When the twenty-year-old Rumbold finally abandoned Oxford he retained all the physical attributes that Evan admired in a handsome youth. They shared a great deal; both were tubercular[741], homosexual, and had the same alma mater, Christ Church, Oxford. In addition both had a bullying father[742] as well as a mother who went insane; in fact like Evan's sister Gwyneth who suffered a watery grave, Rumbold's mother drowned and his sister Rosemary killed herself. [743]

Father Ronald Knox

After the publication of *Little Victims* Evan's Catholic confessor, Father Ronnie Knox (who was also Rumbold's spiritual adviser), refused to see Rumbold, and would not allow him to take Mass.[744] Evan feared being excommunicated if he spoke up for Rumbold; he therefore publically sided with Knox but privately may have made a more sympathetic approach towards the boy. Rumbold knew Harold Nicolson[745] who suggested that Rumbold should visit London Docklands and the coal mines of South Wales to engage with real people; this may have been where he first met or was reunited with Evan. Rumbold ill-judged the consequences of lashing out at the Catholic church as the enemy of freedom and pleasure, and especially for its stance on homosexuality. Despite Evan's own proclivities, he could not be seen to support him; his attitude (as described by Bryans) was hysterical, on a par with his worst treatment of any boy whom he'd tired and later viciously rejected.

Robin Bryans must have first heard about Rumbold's story from Evan and later he also met him; there was a soiled, troubled history between Evan and Rumbold but the detail was not divulged to Bryans. When Rumbold appeared once at a hotel (where Evan and Bryans were staying), Bryans recalls meeting Rumbold on his own but later, when Evan appeared, both men exploded:

"By the time I encountered Richard at the *Great Western Hotel*... [he] did not appear to be on good terms with Evan... [and] as soon as Evan joined us, Richard fled as though he had seen a ghost. Evan's temper then flared up, exclaiming that Rumbold was a "third rate hack [who] has had to be excommunicated by the Holy Father and now he wants to write another book..." [746]

The heated reaction of both parties suggests that they had indeed had a past fall out and one of them (probably Rumbold) had shunned the other's [Evan's] ardent intentions. Rumbold's diaries show that during the war years (when Evan was licking his wounds after his humiliating Court Martial and divorce by Olga) Rumbold was nearby as a patient in a sanatorium in the Cotswolds. [747]

Cecil Roberts (who always kept his own leeching for boys under full self-control) was in love with Rumbold. In *Sunshine and Shadow*, [748] the fourth volume of his autobiography, Roberts devotes several pages to Rumbold's life and in defence of Rumbold's books. Roberts briefly took him under his wing, with stays at Roberts' ultimate sanctuary, his country home in England of *Pilgrim Cottage* at Henley-on-Thames which Evan also visited. [749] In the end Roberts let him go. When war broke out Rumbold joined the RAF (he was later invalided out) and Roberts went to America as part of the war effort, working for Lord Halifax. Although there was a final brief meeting between Roberts and Rumbold in July 1946, Rumbold later entered a monastery; he wandered around North Africa, Ceylon and Japan seeking spiritual rest in the company of an American woman, Hilda Young, who acted as his secretary. In 1961, he committed suicide in Palermo, Italy by (apparently) throwing himself over a high balcony at the *Hotel des Palmes*. [750] He was aged forty-eight.

Chapter 7

A Mixed Bag

Evan: Rosa Lewis' Darling Boy

Evan was the darling of London restaurant and club owners where he liberally threw his money around. *Boulestins, The Savoy Grill, The Carlton* and *The Ritz* were among his favourite places. He could afford to pay his way and the bills incurred by others – but the many associations and many bills paid have hardly been converted into any particular incidents recorded for posterity beyond the mention of Evan's singular generosity. As a refuge for engaging in carnal pleasures Evan used the *Cavendish Hotel.* Rose Lewis' bohemian establishment of the *Cavendish* in Jermyn Street was Evan's chosen place to "make twins" [751] (a bizarre euphemism for Evan having sex with other men there in an upstairs room).

"Evan always perched his vicious macaw, Blue Boy, in a corner of a room in case any of the navy boys in blue over-played the navy lark with whips or demanded too much money [from Evan]." [752].

The invincible proprietor of the *Cavendish* Rosa Lewis had cooked for the famous. She was a Royal provider of the best and the finest cuisine and remained silent in keeping their sex secrets. Members of the House of Windsor were often to be found on Rosa's premises.

Like Evan she was protected from on high. She enjoyed her standing as being one who was pleased to help "… 'initiate' young men from the best families (who [had] every confidence in her) so that they can sow their wild oats with the minimum of scandal…" [753]

Rosa turned a blind eye to Evan's rascality, even excusing his disastrous affair with Evelyn Waugh's sometime Oxford lover, Alistair Graham. [754] This resulted in Alistair's foreign exile, albeit Evan walked away from burning pyres left by the affair without any whiff of shame, as is described in *Aspects of Evan*.

Evan continued to bring boys back to Rosa's nest. The great cook was well aware of the dangerous side to Evan's choice of lovers, the tender age of some of the rent boys often picked up from the street, but she acted as much as a whorehouse madame in keeping one ear to the floor boards in case there was trouble from Evan's charges. Evan also boasted entertaining his own wing of the Royals at the *Cavendish*.

Robin Bryans sums it up neatly, and covers Evan's popularity as host of prostitutes and Royals:

"Certainly Rose Lewis never tired of talking about who was giving her beloved Evan twins. He may have taken 'rough trade' upstairs but he took members of the Royal Family to the dining rooms." [755]

Evan Takes the Waters for His Diseased Lungs

Evan's diseased lungs were eased by periodic visits to the English seaside resorts with a successful track record of success and in him taking the comfort and relief at hotels stays with special spa baths at Sidmouth and Bournemouth. He was also a user of the English spa towns and the thermal treatments offered in such towns as Bath.

In early February of 1932, while Lois joined her father in law and others for a sea voyage to Ceylon and an absence abroad of two months, [756] Evan left London "for treatment at Bath for a period of one month..." [757] *The Court Circular* later duly marked his return almost exactly to the date. [758]

Evan's Scottish Jaunts

As the Scottish grouse shooting parties prepared to retreat back to London the Court Circular of 16 September 1932 reports that "the Hon. Evan Morgan left London yesterday for a series of visits in Scotland." [759]

Evan's Travelling Companions

References can be found often to Evan and anyone else around him of note when he was staying in a Continental hotel in some glamorous city or other, almost always with a young (indeed a very young) man in tow, whom he would show off as though his companion was some toy dog on a lead.

Besides which Evan often travelled with one or other of his own *live* pets. On this count it's worth repeating an anecdote from *Aspects of Evan*:

Journalist Cecil Roberts, a life-long friend of Evan (after saving his life one night in London after the Great War [760]), relates a story of Evan travelling abroad with some of his pets. Roberts was on a lecture tour of the USA in the 1930s and booking into a hotel in Kansas City when the desk clerk remarked:

"Hey, we had another Britisher here a few days ago. A strange guy. He was travelling with a priest, a red haired youth, a baby panther, two snakes, a mongoose and a couple of bird cages"
Immediately Roberts asked: "Was his name Tredegar?" The clerk replied:

"Sure, that's it, Tredegar. We objected to his animals but he said they all slept with him." [761]

Another tale of this same type is told by Sir John Collings Squire (usually known as JC Squire), [762] a poet and writer who first became involved with Evan when literary editor of the *New Age Magazine*. In the 1930s he was in hot pursuit of Evan (with others), probably about an issue of patronage.

"At Bath we established contact with Evan Morgan, who was at that moment staying in a hotel and whom we found in a vast room of which the windows were sealed and the floor covered with newspapers because he was travelling with a flock of birds." [763]

Peter the Parrot and Blue Boy the Macaw

Peter the parrot was no ordinary bird because it had associations for Evan with his dead sister Gwyneth. It was Gwyneth who had given Peter to Mrs Polly, the landlady of a London pub, *The Volunteer* in Baker Street, frequented by Evan's fellow poets. When Peter's language became too obscene for the non-poet customers the bird got whisked off to Cardiff to a new owner in the Wills-Cory family. [764] When Peter passed on to the afterlife, Evan reported that he had received a message to the effect that the said parrot was happy. This news was relayed by Evan's friend, the prolific writer Winifred Graham [765] (herself the owner of a beloved parrot named *Mr Pollock*), who held regular séances at her Thames-side home at Hampton and on visits to her Cory relations at Llantarnam Abbey in South Wales. [766]

Evan and Blue Boy

Whilst Evan's hyacinthine macaw, *Blue Boy* is best remembered in fact and in legend in Tredegar House, Evan caused quite a sensation in the 1920s when he came across a stall in Thane Market selling birds, including an "an Australian parakeet described as 'witless and uncontrollable.' Evan, perhaps sensing a challenge, bought it. Within a month he walked into a packed *Café Royal* to show off his new party piece. Remarkably he had trained the parakeet to crawl up the inside of his trouser leg and poke its head out of his fly."[767] Tellers of this tale add "the effect on old ladies can be imagined." [768]

Blue Boy was Evan's peculiar. They were an inseparable duo who scared staff and guests alike at Tredegar House's weekend parties. After creating havoc the bird "would sometimes perch himself on a windowsill in the Butler's Pantry and swear ferociously as the footmen attempted to clean the silver." [769] Another infamous tale is of the bird replying to the Archbishop of Cardiff (on a visit to see Evan), with *Blue Boy* offering "a pithy phrase" [770]to the question from the Archbishop asking how he was, with no more than two words telling the cleric exactly where to go. [771]

While there are references to Blue Boy's use of bad language[772] for which he is singled out as "one of the most notorious parrots of the 20th century", [773] the contemporaneous record from Evan's own time *only* reliably records tales of the bird's mischief, including that Evan "allowed himself to be teased by a formidable macaw named Blue Boy, which liked to bestow hammer blows at great speed between his toes, bare in the bathroom." [774] Another guest reports "of Evan's pet macaw.... using my leg as a ladder for claws and beak, to climb up to the sofa.." [775] Evan himself informs us that "this remarkable bird is allowed to go where it will in the house and grounds, makes no effort to escape, is master of an extensive vocabulary and makes friends on sight, especially with young people; [adding] "Blue Boy" imitates human coughing to perfection." [776]

But Evan Shoots Starlings Too

Evan's love of birds was not without blemish. Fourteen-year-old Eric Buchanan was employed in 1934 to help to look after Evan's array of animals in the menagerie at Tredegar Park (housed in the stable block and in outside enclosures). Eric recalls seeing Evan shooting starlings off the rooftops at Tredegar House. [777]

This unusual action may have been necessary to protect the species of more exotic birds owned by Evan. This comprised "a pair of flamingos, three pairs of mating cranes, peacocks and peahens...innumerable starlings of rare breeds and a South American crested magpie .." [778]

The magpie was given house room: " ..this little fellow perches on Lord Tredegar's chair, flies about the room and takes no notice of Sven, Lord Tredegar's Great Dane." [779]

Evan As A Patron of The Arts & Fund Raising

Following his mother's example as a patron and sponsor for identifying up and coming painters and artists, Evan was a *well-kent* figure at galleries and exhibitions. In 1927 he was approached by arts-mad Ivor Spencer Churchill (see Chapter 6) to attend as one of the leading named supporters to encourage new talent at the Young Artists exhibition in the galleries of the Royal Society of British Artists in Suffolk Street, Pall Mall. [780] This was a grand event, with over 600 exhibits, paintings and drawings by British artists under forty years of age. The event was summed up as one in which others could see "how young eyes are looking at the world and how clever young hands are at work recording their impressions of today for posterity". [781] Evan was thrilled. He saw such large gatherings as a chance to catch up with people he knew in social and artistic circles. Aside from exchanging pleasantries with Somerset Maugham again and chit chatting with Edward Marsh (who was for ever looking for ways of raising patronage for the poorer male artists), Lady Emerald Cunard (who brought a large party) and Duff Cooper, it was always a bonus for the opportunity such scrums allowed to Evan to pounce mercilessly on some suitable youth or youths to wine, dine and bed.

When asked, Evan was always a reliable sponsor and purchaser of new works by rising stars. He performed the opening ceremony of the *Robes of Thespis* exhibition at the Alpine Galleries on 6 February 1928. Evan was "immaculately clad in a dark blue suit", [782] sharing the star billing with Mrs Winifred Ashley. The most talked-about exhibits and admired were "the strange masks by Oliver Messel." [783] Oliver [784] was an up and coming young (and pleasantly attractive looking) interior designer. These events provided a way for Evan to meet and possibly ensnare his next sexual prey. There were several men pursuing Messel far more successfully than Evan, the most notable of these being the millionaire art collector Peter Watson [785] who also shared time in Paris and Rome with Evan and Lord Gerald Berners. Watson was later linked with Evan and the male American prostitute Denham Fouts. [786]

To his credit Evan was always ready to raise money for good causes.

One of these at Dudley House, Park Lane was billed as being "in aid of the Reconstruction Appeal for the Hospital for Sick Children, Great Ormond Street, WC1". [787] The literary gathering was headed by a notable historical writer, "Mr Philip Guedalla [who] will speak on 'Biography'". [788] This was to be followed by a "discussion in which the Hon. Harold Nicolson, Mr E F Benson, Viscountess Galway, the Hon. Evan Morgan and others will take part." [789] Evan's Catholic chum Shane Leslie (a cousin of Winston Churchill) chaired the proceedings, whilst Viscountess Esher sold tickets at 10/6d and £1.1s.

Years later Evan took Princess Olga (at the time his wife to be) to a private showing of paintings by Oliver Messel held at the Leicester Galleries, London on 1 December 1938. [790] The Princess was already well known in London Society but particular time was taken by Evan to introduce her (for approval) to Christabel Aberconway, Rafaelle, Duchess of Leinster and Edward Marsh. This trio, who have left behind some wonderful, affectionate anecdotes of Evan in their own memoirs,[791] were in no doubt had their more uncertain view of how Evan's marriage to Olga would pan out successfully or not.

Evan on Radio & Literary Gatherings

Cyril Hughes Hartmann, Evan's trusted Oxford contemporary, was one critic that he asked to assess his poetry. Another judge was Alan Pryce-Jones whose Memoirs contain a delicious slice of how Pryce-Jones (who went to Eton with Evan's cousin John Morgan but, like Evan, despised him) views Evan and his parents.

Some evidence has survived of these men's appraisal of Evan's verse. It appears that the process was reciprocated, as Evan responded to them with his assessment of their own work. For instance we learn from the catalogue at Yale University in the USA among the Alan Pryce - Jones' papers that this contains "Correspondence from Evan Morgan... accompanied by heavily edited copies of Pryce- Jones's poems". [792]

Further afield Evan fell on the support of the members of the Catholic Poetry Society to off-load his verse, but his books were largely given to friends and family, who indulged his whims.

Evan adored taking part in public readings of his own poetry. For several years from 1927 onwards he features in radio broadcasts for the BBC in London, where he was assisted with readings by Dorothy Warren[793] (an artist and niece of Ottoline Morrell) and by the actress Cathleen Nesbitt.[794] Whilst attending at Portland Place to record his pieces he ran into old faces from his Garsington days, like Desmond MacCarthy[795] who had a regular radio feature on literary criticism. [796] During this period Evan befriended the poet Alfred Noyes,[797] (best known for his ballad *The Highwayman*), even performing the duty of best man at Noyes' second wedding.[798] In 1926 Noyes consented to write an enthusiastic foreword to Evan's verse compilation *'The Eel and other poems.'*[799] Among the poems is the *Knights Templars' Cat* which in part echoes the events at the Temple of Thelema where, a few years earlier, Evan's friend Raoul Loveday, [800] an Oxford graduate, had died, allegedly after drinking the blood of a sacrificed cat during one of Crowley's mad rituals. The truth was that the twenty-three-year-old had (against Crowley's advice) actually drunk from a contaminated stream.

Years later Alfred Noyes reflected about being present when Evan sat to be painted by Augustus John. "The portrait which Augustus John painted of Evan Morgan gave a sardonically critical background to the scene of this delectable conversation. One could not help wondering whether the sitter had been conscious that the brilliantly executed portrait was also a keenly satirical criticism." [801]

Evan's health crumbled in the autumn of 1930 when he was diagnosed with meningitis. He was forced to cancel some of his public engagements, lying poleaxed at Tredegar House. The timing was not ideal, as he was the Conservative candidate for Cardiff Central at the forthcoming general election. [802] However, the interval gave him an opportunity to write verse and he slowly recovered, spurred on by an invitation to appear in a public reading of his work with his old ally Harold Nicolson.

By the 1930s Harold Nicolson had given up his promising diplomatic career in favour of creating the famous gardens at Sissinghurst in Kent with his wife Vita.[803] To help finance this new life he lectured to young graduate men thinking about a career in the Foreign Office, [804] gave talks on the wireless, explored journalism (with the Lord Beaverbrook's Press), wrote biographies and essays and signed up for at least one ship's cruise as a guest speaker for the Hellenes Travellers Club but the ship with a cargo of public schoolboys ran aground. [805] Harold appears with Evan at the occasional literary gathering, raising funds for charity and where both were public speakers, often with Shane Leslie. One famous event was with the celebrated literary queen E F (Freddy) Benson in 1932. [806] If Evan had dreams of being a religious poet, Harold had ambitions of being a serious writer, beyond the drain of being a hack or pundit or a gardener.

Socialising With Evan

In the late 1920s Evan and Lois were occasionally together in the evening for drinks, with gossip writers capturing them fleetingly at gatherings for Hollywood film stars in London.

One of these was a party for Douglas Fairbanks and included

"...Lady Cunard...Lord Alington, Mr and Mrs Evan Morgan....and Lady Lavery.."[807]

The report adds "No bottles of champagne were being drunk, only magnums."[808]

The Morgans sometimes accompanied each other to functions, parties and the theatre, then split up and with no regard to the time or even the day for returning home again. They each had their own friends in separate crowds; Lois's new passion was horse racing. Evan frequented nightclubs, often with his female cousin Suki, sister of his beloved Raymond Rodakowski who had married a Carnegie half-cousin. [809] Using Suki as his willing stooge provided an ideal method whereby Evan could happily engage in a dance or two. In fact Evan was a very commanding dancer. One scribe comments: "Mr Morgan is one of the best dancers in London, and performs a *pas seul* that could scarcely be excelled by a Nijinsky or a Lifar." [810]

Evan had a financial interest at stake in *Boulestin's* restaurant in Southampton Street, Covent Garden. As part of the celebrations for his 34th birthday (in 1927) he organised a large dinner party there with more than a hundred people sitting down around six tables, with people from his theatrical, literary, artistic and social orbit. One commentator reported "Mr Morgan monopolised the occasion.... the lights were extinguished for the sweet course, and flaming peaches were served in the accompaniment of cries of enthusiasm".[811] Only Evan Morgan could have pulled off a curious mix of guests of various backgrounds "without making enemies or wounding some susceptibilities", including appearances and mingling by the Princess Royal, Mlle Spinelli (a French actress, whose real name was Fournier), the artist Augustus John, Princess Arthur of Connaught and the actor Ernest Thesiger.[812] The latter is a name repeated at many of Evan's bashes. Christobel

Aberconway once found him "nude to the waist and covered with pearls" [813] at a garden party given by Lord Jowitt. [814]

Evan downsized somewhat for his 35th birthday party at the *Eiffel Tower Restaurant*, with thirty five guests and thirty five bottles of champagne. [815]

The Mask of Treachery
All Greek

As the Second World War loomed in Europe, Evan and Harold Nicolson's names appear together at several diplomatic functions, including a *grande dance* at *Claridges Hotel* on 17 November 1938 attended by King George II, the exiled King of the Hellenes (Greece), under the auspices of the Anglo-Hellenic League, with Prince George (PG), Duke of Kent and Lord Louis Mountbatten. [816] Robin Bryans implies an overlap here with several sinister overtones, between the Royal coterie of PG, Mountbatten and the later exposed traitor Anthony Blunt, which is fully described by the author (the late) John Costello in his book *The Mask of Treachery*. [817] The accuracy (or otherwise) of the strange conspiracy theories outlined by Costello (with input from Robin Bryans under his real name of Robert Harbinson) is also considered by Blunt's biographers, one commenting of Bryans telling "many imaginative stories about a relationship with Blunt and Burgess which he [Bryans] claimed started back to the 1940s".[818] Evan was not directly implicated in that particular game of invention, as he was already dead. However Bryans spells out that it was Evan Morgan who gave advice to the Royal family about art *before* the appointment of Anthony Blunt to the Royal Household, except this is a notion that is often tangled up with the actual reality.[819]

Evan and Prince Paul of Greece

Evan found his own Prince Charming, Prince Paul of Greece. He had already enjoyed the company and coterie of British and Foreign Royal intimates, in particular as the late 1920s and 1930s playboy lifestyle on the ocean waves became Evan's favoured way of keeping his libido satisfied and his lungs clear. Prince Paul of Greece was the younger brother of King George II and in 1938 found a cover of his marriage to avert the world's eyes on his affairs with men. Evan went to Athens for the wedding ceremony but he and Paul spent long holidays at sea together on millionaires' yachts. Prince Paul was a frequent insider at Tredegar House in the war years, too, and succeeded his brother to the restored Greek throne in 1947.

Prince George of Kent

In the earlier days of the 1920s Prince George of Kent (known as PG) mixed with Prince Paul of Greece and Evan and Naps Alington in London's East End. Before PG married, he had affairs with boys, men and women. It is claimed he joined the company of Evan and Peter Churchill indulging "their appetites for drugs and Arab boys." [820]

Bryans muses on the reaction of the Royal Court to PG's drugs habit and carnal affairs: "only one solution presented itself, namely for Prince George to cover up by marrying Bridget Parsons [821] ["an unusual beauty, ivory and honey in colouring, with a small boyish head set on a gracefully long neck" [822]], just as Evan himself in 1928 had married Lois Sturt after the Pope sent Evan back from Rome when the Beda College could stand the scandals no longer." [823]

In the end Bridget Parsons "broke off her liaison with Prince George after discovering he was sleeping with a male relative." [824] The end solution was found in 1934 from the ever-obliging – but banished - Greek Royal family, when PG married Princess Marina of Greece and Denmark. [825] That latter Royal personage led PG a merry dance with her own adultery, one informant remarking that "Marina would sleep with any man in trousers". [826]

The final fate of Marina's husband, PG, was to follow in an air crash in 1942. [827] It was a death that made history as he was the "first member of the Royal Family to be killed in active service for 500 years." [828] It was a death that stunned his contemporaries. The diarist James Lees-Milne records: "This morning while shaving and listening to the news I heard the announcement of the Duke of Kent's death. I felt a sharp shock and could think of nothing else for some time." [829]

The reaction of Lees-Milne (Senior) was less thoughtful. James records "I had a row with Papa after dinner. He expressed idiotic views about the Duke of Kent. Said that he was a worthless fellow and no better than a pansy... I could not tolerate this silly imputation by someone who knew nothing whatever about the prince." [830] It was a death that left many questions unanswered. Some very great state secrets remain untold in respect the death of PG, far beyond the upset caused by some writers who have already offered their own highly over creative pennyworth. [831]

Chapter 8

The seeds of Evan's Interest in the Occult etc

Among Evan Morgan's enduring legacies at his old homestead of Tredegar House, South Wales, is a fine portrait of him by Cathleen Mann.[832] The colourful picture, staring out almost like a little Buddha, is fixed on one of the bathroom walls. It shows Evan wearing the elaborate costume of a Papal Chamberlain and Knight. This privileged designation was an accolade awarded to Evan by Pope Pius XI, in exchange for patronage to two Popes including Pius' predecessor, Benedict XV.

Present day visitors to Tredegar House are told of Evan's early religious conversion to the Roman Catholic faith from 1919, albeit the seeds were planted much earlier by Evan's personal blessed duo of saints, Father Ronnie Knox and Father Cyril Martindale.

Occasionally reference is made to Evan's adventurous time in Rome in the 1920s when he was ferried around the streets of the Eternal City and the wider countryside in his Rolls Royce or was a passenger in Lord

Gerald Berners' plush vehicle of the same make, complete with drinks cabinet and portable altar; [833] in Berners' case, his Rolls Royce "won a prize for elegance from the Italian Automobile Association." [834] This was whilst Evan was enrolled as a student at Beda College, where the more mature men studied for the priesthood and began their life sacrifice. In Evan's case he failed to give up any luxuries, including residing at the classy Hotels *Bellini* or *Minerva*. This deceit masked several years of depravity under the guise of Evan training up for holy orders.

It was his Papal credentials that Evan most cherished. His day of triumph as a Papal Knight was undoubtedly when he welcomed King George V and Queen Mary to the Vatican in Rome during their Majesties' visit to the Pope in 1923; however, things dipped to shame two years later when Evan suffered ignominy after he either abandoned his studies (at Beda College) or was more likely asked to leave. Evan continued his labours as a Chamberlain, which included spending a few weeks each year at the Vatican performing ceremonial duties.

Catholic publications like *The Tablet,* a leading international Catholic news weekly, are brimming with references to Evan's attendance at funding raising events for the Catholic Church and he often made rousing speeches. [835] There was an obvious extra attraction for Evan when he championed The Catholic Young Men's Society Conferences. [836]

Evan may have drifted away at times from his faith in God but, faced with a terminal illness, he died a Catholic in 1949 and his mortal remains lie in a private graveyard in Buckfast Abbey. In Newport, Evan attended Catholic Mass at his local Church of St David's, Maeglas. The parish priest there was Father J Maloney. [837] He was kept a busy man hearing Evan's confessions.

Tredegar House: Voids
Evan The Occultist

Today, on the outdoor tours of the Tredegar House cellars, visitors are told of another curious side to Evan's unrighteousness. It is believed that in one of the House's dark eerie voids[838] lay Evan's famed Magick

Room - the fact of its existence is celebrated in a letter by the notorious Satanist, occult wizard and high priest, Aleister Crowley. Evan may have conducted Black Mass in his Magick Room; he certainly played host in 1943 to Crowley at Tredegar House.

Anecdotes mention Evan's inquisitiveness about the occult, the supernatural, and his zest for taking part in spiritual séances and clairvoyant, palm and card readings; in particular tarot readings, of which Evan had a special set. Some references are made to these subjects in the notes in the Tredegar House Archives based on letters and interviews from the 1970s by Evan's surviving old cronies. [839]

Some of Evan's other worldly influences began early. As a young poet he was touched by his family's Celtic roots and equally excited by old legends and the pagan and saintly qualities of his past ancestors among the Welsh Princes. Ronald Firbank provided Evan with insight into other matters of reincarnation after they met in 1916. Firbank was drawing on his own deeply held belief in this process when he claimed Evan was the reincarnation of King Ramases II of Ancient Egypt. [840]

The autobiographies of Robin Bryans add a more significant track on Evan's darker side, including reference to Evan's own extraordinary promotion of Satanism and the occult.

Bryans declares that Evan's deep involvement with the occult spanned many decades, with the earliest sway coming from Evan's fellow Old Etonians, Peter Churchill and Peter Warlock.

Peter Churchill's manipulation was keystone to Evan's baptism into the dark arts, in raising his knowledge of the spirit world and black magic practices. It must have first happened along the same lines of any child's innocent play or game but afterwards transcended into an outlandishly sinister experience, chillingly played out at dead of night, when as young boys Peter (in his early teens) and Evan (barely eight years old) were living as page boys at Windsor Castle. These indiscretions also continued later as schoolboys at Eton College when they were both were into or passed puberty.

Ancient castles and silent school buildings with labyrinths, dark passages, dungeons and deep cellars, as well as Berkshire and Surrey's adjoining quaint churches and churchyards, provided perfect places for secret rendezvous to hold meetings and coax and coerce other occult followers. Peter Churchill was first touched by demons in his own bizarre experiences growing up in North Africa, with its eclectic spread of castes, cultures and religious differences. Besides this the shadowy Moorish tribal underbelly, with the fear of evil spirits, native curses, superstitions and the endemic exploitation (including sexual abuse) of children, was never far away.

Evan and Peter Warlock

Evan's other occult initiator, Peter Warlock, the composer and musician, an ill-fated contemporary of Evan's during his Eton schooldays and at Oxford University, is highlighted in *Aspects of Evan* as the mentor who planted and enticed the developing, nurturing seeds of Evan's occult curiosity, helping him with the early and proceeding steps into a closer study of black magic and the black arts. Warlock had gained his own knowledge of spirits travelling in Ireland, where he met W B Yeats[841] and lifted himself out of depression with a cocktail of smoking cannabis and reading Yeats' early verse, together with gleaning the written works of Aleister Crowley. Warlock's son declares "it was Aleister Crowley[whom Warlock met among the avant-garde at the *Cafe Royal*] who had the most immediate effect" [842] on the young composer.

   Warlock and Evan were university drop-outs; both had unhappy childhoods, both had doting mothers. Evan worshipped Warlock; he was "good looking, tall and blond". [843] Alcohol and drug fuelled parties (Warlock was a heavy drinker, [844] and occasional drug-user), coupled with the distraction of Evan's mind wrestling with the idea of receiving Warlock's adoration (and at least of them engaging in sexual relations together), meant that Evan's lusting after the colourful schizophrenic Warlock and not the occult was really what created and sustained Evan's attentions. However Evan was spurned, since Warlock liked sex with females, although these relationships were described as uneasy....and suggested "an unresolved homosexual streak in his nature".[845] It didn't help to win Warlock's affection or get any closer into his bed that Evan failed to come up with the sum of £200 to help save Warlock's continuance with *The Sackbut*,[846] a magazine edited by him from 1920-1 but whose financial backer withdrew funding and relieved Warlock of the editorship. Warlock was gifted in his music and compositions, an inspiration for the character Halliday in D H Lawrence's *Women in Love*, but he was dead by his own hand at the age of thirty-six, a hopeless depressive. [847] It is noteworthy that Warlock's son attributes blame on Aleister Crowley for first plunging his father into "the practice of magic, which he [Warlock] pursued for several years, and which eventually destroyed him", [848] citing one of Warlock's own favourite chants of capitulation, *'Don Giovanni, a cenar teco m'invitasti, e son venuto'*, [849] and adding "As in opera, once invoked the supernatural takes over and gains ultimate control." [850]

Evan did find escape, desire and satisfaction in male company through the occult and in mysticism. [851] His admiration for the priest and poet John Donne became as fixed as that of his adoration for Shelley and Satan. He probed black magic in its darker side in books and journals including lapping up Crowley's writings and teachings and ordering in banned titles, from the pederasty of Baron Corvo to the sadism of the Marquis De Sade. He also continued to practise occult rites with Peter Churchill, including celebrating Black Mass during the time they spent together in France. The affects of this leak out as an underlying theme in parts of Evan's own religious verse, in his search for Psyche[852] and in a series of paintings, exhibited in 1920s Paris. [853] It was a subject that pre-occupied his mind; it became an obsession.

Palm reading was one of Evan's fads too. "He studied palmistry from school days at Eton and had read the fortunes of kings and presidents." [854] Robin Bryans' 'simian crease' (that is the palm's line of head and line of heart merged in one strongly-marked line across the hand) was deemed rare by Evan. This boosted Bryans' morale and ensured his willingness to be initiated as Evan's sex slave.

Evan's beliefs were later consolidated by a variety of additional occult practitioners and dabblers in ancient myths and black magic, notably Aleister Crowley, W B Yeats and HG Wells. Alongside Evan's devotion to under-age boy sex was his worship of the Black Masses. It is hard to separate Evan's fondness for taking part in Black Mass ceremonies with his stronger desire for sexual deviation. It is even more difficult to reconcile his participation in the blatantly anti-Christian activities of the Black Mass with his public illusion of being a strict adherent and follower of the Roman Catholic Church. But what exactly was/ is a Black Mass?

The Black Masses

One history of Witchcraft and Black Magic explains that the "great central act of Christian worship is the Mass, a Sacrifice which can be offered to God alone, and the ...the black mass is a sacrifice of mockery, impiety and blasphemy which is offered to the Devil." [855]

In short the Black Mass renounces Jesus Christ in favour of the Devil. It "is to mock the Catholic Holy Mass by performing it, or parts of it backwards, inverting the cross. Stepping or spitting on the cross, stabbing the host [the person being initiated] and other obscene acts. Urine is sometimes substituted for the holy water used to sprinkle the attendees, urine or water is substituted for the wine….black candles are substituted for white ones…."[856]

Stories of Crowley's version of the Black Masses drifted out through the literary circles of New York, London and Paris as early as 1910. This is Crowley's own description of the ceremony:

"The celebrant must be a priest, for the whole idea of the practice is to profane the Sacrament of the Eucharist. Therefore you must believe in the truth of the cult and the efficacy of its ritual. At this "mass," always held in some secret place, preferably in a disused chapel at midnight, the priest appears in canonical robes. But even in his robes there is some sinister change, a perversion of their symbolic sanctity. There is an altar, but the candles are of black wax. The crucifix is fixed the head downwards. The clerk to the priest is a woman and her dress, although it seems to be a church garment, is more like a costume in a prurient revue. It has been altered to make it indecent. The ceremony is a parody of the orthodox Mass, with blasphemous interpolations. The priest must be careful, however, to consecrate the Host in the orthodox manner. The wine has been adulterated with magical drugs like deadly nightshade and vervain but the priest must convert it into the blood of Christ. The dreadful basis of the Mass is that the bread and wine have imprisoned the Deity. Then they are subjected to terrible profanation." [857]

Crowley's reputation was elaborated by such people as the poet Victor Neuberg, [858] the novelist Ronald Firbank and members of the Bloomsbury set. Chelsea parties brought attendance by Crowley himself; there was a fascination and preoccupation with spooky tales, a popularity in palm and card reading and spiritualism from America (where Crowley spent the years of the Great War) and the cult around Anne Besant and Theosophy that (as we have seen) embraced Peter Churchill and Verena, his mother.

The period before the First World War is not too early for Evan to become aware of the works of *The Great Beast* but they never met face to face until Nina Hamnett introduced the two them in Paris in the 1920s.

There is a reference to Crowley's 'Black Masses' from the Irish medium Eileen Garrett[859] whom Crowley called a "pythoness."[860] She actually found the rituals boring, claiming that if "there was 'authority' in Crowley's meetings with Lucifer, I never knew it." [861]

Crowley denies that he was competent to actually perform a Black Mass, making the point that the central figure of the priest had to be "a consecrated priest of a Christian Church......the whole idea of the practise [being] to profane the Sacrament of the Eucharist."[862]

Evan was not a consecrated priest either. The Black Masses performed by Crowley and Evan were of their own bespoke design, relying for their effect for the commission of a variety of invasive sex acts and the humiliation of whatever young male host was the subject of the coven's initiation.

Evan did not confine his abuse and desecration to his local Welshlands. Folklore records as far away as the Island of Bali that "liberated by wealth and motivated...by blasphemy and in a sea of liquor" [863] he was remembered there by the natives for "polluting sacred springs and desecrating temples." [864]

What Robin Bryans Tells Us

Human blood (and *semen*) from the host [the initiate] fuelled the formal procedure in Evan's version of the Black Mass. No women were allowed to be present.

This is Robin Bryans' personal account of the ceremony:

"Human blood was essential for [Evan's] version of the Black Masses, as I learnt when some of Crowley's devotees celebrated, and as a boy of sixteen I had seen how Evan Tredegar brightened up more than house parties and indulged in doings from which women...were banned."[865]

In Evan's cabinet of occult secrets lay his own repertory of sexual pleasures, no doubt along the lines of what W H Auden voiced as being the "rites of symbolic magic" [866] including fellatio, sodomy and mutual masturbation. In Evan's closet of sex secrets he was also a devotee of flagellation.

One of Evan's earliest targets to see out his fantasies was Vernon Charles Wills,[867] son of Charles Wills and Mabel Pethybridge of Cardiff:

"Evan had introduced Vernon Wills to black magic rites in his uncle Canon [Henry] Stewart's ancient church at Porthkerry Woods, when the young Vernon not only drank from a human skull but had been asked to supply the semen for the communion cup."[868]

Bryans elaborates "The ritual as observed by Evan's fellow High priest, Aleister Crowley, made no secret about what went into the unholy communion cup. Many celebrants used a chalice set inside a human skull for their communion cup although various ingredients, apart the essential blood and semen, could be used."[869]

There were variations at these ceremonies. "The ritual of *Tantric Hinduism*[870] requiring milk, dung, urine, meat and blood was widely varied by Aleister Crowley....celebrating his love of female flesh as in *The Five Jewels of the Scared Cow*[871] ...but ...Evan Tredegar gave scant consideration to female urine. [However] Evan and Francis Rose did share Crowley's liking for adding drugs such as laudanum to ensure a good response to those partaking of the skull chalice." [872]

Bryans adds, of his own time observing Evan's Black Mass, thirty years after the entrapment of Vernon Wills:

"Evan liked performing his rites in ancient country churches such as *St Wulfran's*[873] at Ovingdean – hidden in the folds of Sussex…" [874] Bryans adds a note about the close proximity of the site of *St Wulfrans* and *Honeywood House*, but it is almost fifty miles between them.

St Wulfran's is mentioned in the Domesday Book. St Wulfran himself was a man of French origin, the son of a nobleman, who rejected his family's long line of soldiers to become a priest and a missionary. [875]

"Music, with the setting of Biblical texts to Evan's own compositions, was used openly at such places as Buckfast Abbey as well as spiritual exorcising of the dead at St Wulfran's Church at Ovingdean."[876] Bryans suggests that he and Evan often visited St Dunstans, near Ovingdean, a retreat for blind servicemen, where Evan enjoyed listening to Bryans sing.

Rottingdean Black Masses

Another site that Evan shared with his fellow Satanists Aleister Crowley and Peter Churchill was at Rottingdean, a coastal village near Brighton and the place where Robin Bryans later lived. [877]

"Aleister Crowley's own cult celebrated the Black Masses with the *Five Jewels of the Sacred Cow* as in Tantric Hinduism. Peter Churchill and Aleister Crowley [who both lived nearby] loved Rottingdean village and celebrated the Black Mass there with distinguished scholars and royalty."[878]

Baile Glas Church, Dinas Powys

The Welsh church of *Baile Glas* (near Dinas Powys) was another deserted edifice used as a favoured site for Black Mass worship by Evan, and this is almost certainly where Robin Bryans was first initiated in a mock Black Mass which seems to have been conducted solely by Evan. Bryans remembers being given a glass of wine beforehand. "I relaxed since I had little experience with alcohol". [879]

"The Church had long been abandoned as a place of [Christian] worship. ...the church remained intact, complete with pews and hymn-books ... Most of the organ pipes still sounded and Evan fell on this at once." [880]

Curiously, what follows seems more like a Mad Hatters tea party or chimp's picnic than a Black Mass.

"Evan had come equipped with a hamper of cold chicken and ham, puddings, fruit, wine and a bottle of whisky... Evan spread a feast before me while the colony of bats fluttered in and out of the broken church windows festooned with ivy. Years of bird and bat droppings, damp and oil-lamp smoke gave out a grave- like smell of decay even on a warm July night and excited Evan..." [881]

It conjures up a scene described elsewhere where "pederast choirboys with powdered cheeks and carmined lips attend a priest presiding over a ritual enveloped in the smoke of toxic incense." [882]

But the actual description of Evan's conquest in the dirty, deserted and dilapidated church in Wales falls short of outlining what else *exactly* took place between them; him acting as priest and wicked seducer of his sixteen-year -old host in a bizarre satanic sex ritual, but Bryans was a very willing participant in Evan's seduction.

Evan's Instruments of Torture

A more gruesome element to Evan's Black Mass is added by the reference made to the implements of pain and torture that Evan's cousin John Morgan found concealed when clearing out the contents of Evan's bedroom at Tredegar House.

These "instruments of most blood curdling nature... sadistic gear, whips and handcuffs" [883] were almost certainly used in Evan's sex games, including his stay-overs at Rosa Lewis' *Cavendish Hotel*. It is not beyond thinking that these were also a part of Evan's Black Masses, which on Bryans' personal testimony were nothing less than homosexual orgies. [884] Bryans remarks "young men had been willing to follow Evan ...for flagellation as live tableaux of Christ-at-the Pillar." [885] Bryans suggests that one young man had even later "committed suicide after Evan tired of their fun-and games with whips and handcuffs..."

Another observer who visited Tredegar House in the 1930s describes "a glorious house, but the feel and even the smell of decay, of aristocracy in extremis, the sinister and trivial, crucifixes and crocodiles." [886]

Beyond this Bryans makes a particular point of comparing Evan's "homosexual sadism" [887]with the brutality of the myths centred around Evan's friend Felix Yussupov[888] who (with others) killed the mad monk Rasputin, cut off his penis and dumped the mutilated body into the icy Neva river.

Once in 1945, when staying with Evan in a house at Brighton (that Evan rented), the French author and illustrator Philippe Jullian recalled, "[Evan] invited me to spend the weekend in an immense and extremely Edwardian house near Brighton that he used to rent. In his bedroom the jewel-laden Madonna stood near a bed with a baldachin that resembled the high altar in St Peter's. On several tables the Marquis de Sade, who was not then published in paperback, companioned the lives of the saints." [889]

Evan saves ancient skeletons in Ireland

Whilst in Ireland Evan learned that "wicked Protestants"[890] in the Jones family, the one-time owners of Lisgoogle Abbey (once a monastery[891]) on the eastern shore of Lough Erne, a few miles from Enniskillen, had "unceremoniously thrown the remains of many poets of the ancient kingdom of Oriel into the Lough". [892] Evan decided he would retrieve the bones and honour the skulls of his fellow poets and monks "by using them as communion cups when communicating with the dead ...with one cup-skull ...specially decorated [of] Gabrielle D Annunzio[893]... who liked to sleep in a coffin." [894]

John, Duke of Bedford on Evan's Black Magic

John, Duke of Bedford relates this anecdote from a visit made to Tredegar House in the 1930s which provides a flavour of how Evan put on an occult-inspired show for guests.

Evan "was an extraordinary fellow, with altars all over the house and a somewhat terrifying interest in black magic. He told somebody's fortune one night in his bedroom. There were three or four of us sitting in front of a huge fire, with the flames flicking on the four-poster bed. There was an owl flying round the room, and our host had put on some clothes which were supposed to have belonged to some witch in the past, and was holding up the skeleton of a witch's hand. [NB these witch's bones are said elsewhere to belong to Meg Jenkins, a local Welsh girl burnt as a witch in the seventeenth century[895]]. While [Evan] was telling this fortune the temperature of the room fell so much that I was absolutely freezing in front of this enormous fire. It was one of the most eerie experiences I have ever had." [896]

Evan and Aleister Crowley

Do what thou wilt shall be the whole of the law [897]

Robin Bryans makes a number of passing references to how Evan was lured by the occult, and with it the translation and actual manifestation into Black Masses and Black Mass rituals in which he personally took part as a young boy of sixteen in 1944. Bryans sweeps in the name of *The Great Beast,* Aleister Crowley, who was at the time that Bryans is referring to, 1943-4, a recently rekindled contact of Evan's, albeit Crowley was washed out by this time as a serious force; he was also suffering from ill-health, penniless and probably impotent. Even a decade and a half before this Crowley is described unflatteringly as "a most impossible charlatan, looks likes a north-country manufacturer and speaks with a cockney-American accent." [898]

But in other people's eyes Crowley's reputation for evil remained intact. Somerset Maugham remarked that Crowley "was a fake, but not entirely a fake". [899]

G K Chesterton thought he was a good poet. Several writers drew on Crowley for characters in fiction including Maugham and also Dennis Wheatley,[900] most famous for his novel (also made into a terrifying film) *The Devil Rides Out*, and who said of Crowley that he was "intellectually quite wonderful, but I don't believe he could harm a rabbit". [901] The early legends built around the Crowley curse were still thought deadly. [902] Evan believed in Crowley's power. Bryans records that "Aleister Crowley ...long reigned as the high priest of the Black Mass at Tredegar Park".[903]

Some details hinted at by Bryans have to be imagined but many of the elements he mentions shock, as he claims as a matter of passing that several young men were exploited as "host" [initiate] in sex magick rituals performed by Evan and Crowley.

Evan's Victim: Vernon Wills

Evan's corruption of Vernon Wills in a Black Mass rite with its invasive sexual deviations had devastating consequences. Throughout his life Vernon suffered extremes of mood, behaviour and finally mental illness. To divert him his relations (assisted by the Rev Stewart's daughters, in particular Kitty Stewart and his aunt Alice Pethybridge) tried to bring him back into conventional Christian worship. Robin Bryans refers to Vernon stomping around South Wales delivering bible texts through letter boxes.

But Vernon was not safe. He was frequently re-offered to the Crowley set by Evan or the Black Mass disciples of Evan. Vernon's sister Sylvia warned Bryans in 1944 : "don't talk to my brother Vernon, he's demon possessed." [904]

Evan's serial abuse of Vernon begs the question whether this was in some way an act of revenge for what had happened to him at the hands of Vernon's uncle, Willie Pethybridge, as this man Pethybridge had allegedly abused Evan as a young boy!

Since Vernon was born in 1900 he would not have reached puberty until 1911-2 or thereabouts, at which time he was attending a private school at Barry. This dates the event of the first initiation ceremony conducted by Evan, who was nineteen in 1912. Peter Churchill had taught Evan a great deal by this time for him to be able to act as the high priest.

There is a suggestion that the boys [Evan and Vernon] were rumbled. Bryans continues:

"No legal action could be taken against Evan since it was Vernon's 'saved' uncle, Alderman Willie Pethybridge, the Liberal Leader in Cardiff City Hall, who had first buggered Evan." [905]

William Hampton Pethybridge

William (Willie) Hampton Pethybridge[906] receives numerous mentions by Robin Bryans. These references are largely derogatory, although Bryans could only have known Pethybridge at the end of his life (if at all); he died in 1944, the same year that Bryans moved to South Wales. [907] A solicitor by profession [908] Pethybridge was a rising star in local government. He was Lord Mayor of Cardiff in 1924-5 and for many years a City Alderman. As he was unmarried, his sister Alice was his Lady Mayoress. [909]

The overlaps between Pethybridge and other personalities and events in Evan's past include an apparent link with Lord Alfred Douglas[910] and Maundy Gregory[911] but the documentary evidence for this is wholly lacking. [912] A Masonic conspiracy is also suggested by Bryans:

Lord Mayor Pethybridge in Cardiff and Mayor Harry George Handover[913] in Paddington were leading Freemasons and behind the Masonic Temple they had to sort out Maundy Gregory and his homosexual blackmailers and the demands of young men making claims on Maundy's Anglo- Ukrainian Council." [914] It is suggested that when Pethybridge died in 1944 it was Frieda Harris, (associate of Aleister Crowley) wife of Sir Percy Harris, [915] who "rushed to South Wales to ensure that the former Lord Mayor's sisters Alice and Mabel had destroyed all of Maundy Gregory's letters." [916]

Willie's sister, Alice Pethybridge, lived until the 1960s and became a close friend and confidante to Robin Bryans who, at Evan's death, removed a number of personal belongings, pictures and treasures belonging to Evan, out of the reach of the Tredegar family. The ultimate fate of these items is unknown.

Crowley at War

In Robin Bryans' own case of being initiated to the Evan cult he admits to having no feelings of regret about being abused. Cecil Roberts (who knew Evan's private life better than most and shared his love of youth) was shocked to learn from James Lonsdale Bryans that his friend Evan, a devout Roman Catholic, also celebrated Black Mass with Crowley. But did Evan in fact see that much of Crowley in South Wales?

Any real proof of such occult or Black Mass activity over any sustained period by Evan and Crowley at Tredegar House is lacking detail, except for the darker passages in Bryans' books and in the myths that have gone down through the decades, with some of that element played down by leaving out the sexual deviances. Such tales have inevitably being embroidered more deviously for entertaining visitors to Tredegar House than recording history.

A narrative entitled *Beastly Life of a Man Called Crowley* – which summarises *The Great Beast's* activities year on year - contains one reference to Evan for 1941:

"During this period Crowley also writes about his meetings with Lord Tredegar, the head of the British top secret MI8."[917] This is interesting, as before and during 1941 Aleister Crowley was being considered for use by the British Secret Service in the Rudolf Hess affair, but this did not happen in the end. [918] More to follow about this in Chapter 9.

Evan may have been approached by SIS (Secret Intelligence Services) (MI5/6) chums for advice but he was never a part of MI 8.[919] Several books make wacky references to Evan being "installed on the south coast [of England] as a part of the Falcon (Interceptor) Unit with instructions to hunt down any suspicious-looking carrier pigeons." [920] This is further reflected in a book by the usually reliable Nigel West who says that "at one stage early in the war [the military] created a special MI 8 unit to monitor the movements of carrier pigeons. The section consisted of Lord Tredegar and Wing-Commander Walker, both keen falconers, whose birds of prey were sent in pursuit of suspected spy pigeons..." [921]

One further write-up may give the tale some half-truth... "falconry did play a small part in World War II. The RAF used 15 peregrine falcons – officially known as Interceptor Unit No 2 – to patrol the wild reaches of the English Channel. The falcons were trained to down carrier pigeons and they are credited with having a real disrupting effect upon Hitler's cross-channel spy service." [922]

Evan joined the Intelligence unit, MI 14 in November 1942, having first been commissioned as a Second Lieutenant in the Royal Signals Corps in January 1942. [923] He rose to Captain (acting Temporary Major) but was subsequently Court Martialled on 19 April 1943 for offences against the Official Secrets Acts. He was found guilty on two counts of disclosing information, reprimanded and soon afterwards left the army, citing a knee injury as the reason for his departure and retirement. [924] He was allowed to continue in uniform with the Monmouthshire Division of the Home Guard, a body he had been involved in before first going into the Royal Signals Corps. But the evidence suggests very little actual involvement by Evan in the Home Guard in 1943-4. He told his local commander that ill health had forced him to quit. [925]

Crowley At Tredegar House
The Great Beast's Unpublished Diary[926]

This is the complete and extraordinary record from Aleister Crowley's unpublished diary covering *The Great Beast's* preparation and subsequent visit to Tredegar House. Crowley arrived at Tredegar House on Thursday 17 June 1943 and left on Friday 25 June, 1943.

37.2.5. Evan [viscount tredegar] wired So Looking forward to seeing you Let me know time and day. Reply: Newport 2.4o die Thursday unless we meet Col Paeton's (?)brother Aleister.

Wed 16 63 Several minor miracles conspired to facilitate my visit to Evan, and to relieve any anxieties. One major miracle:

[Apotheke: GK] gave me 2-25 Tablets instead of on 22nd! Omen for my visit to Evan 19 Lin K/Water Fire/Pisces.

Thur 17 8. Left Paddington 11.55 AM Hellish crowd. Good porter got me corner. Fool-swine opposite gave his seat to low cow with two loathsome brats. Hell! Arr newport about 3 Taxi to T Park.

T put me in the Oak Room- the best in the house.[927] Before me slept here Jeffreys J (on the Western Circuit) the Marquess of Salisbury-[928] my old patron- and Lord Allenby...

Fri 18 42 A wild wet day. Played "Analogies" at night. Studied T's Tarot book. Very curious & interesting. Chemist T Lewis 6 & 7 Dock St newport 2729.

Sat 19 64 Chess with T (said he played for Oxford & England!) He actually played. [game follows] Frieda[929] came across. Mrs Sutherland[930] Emily Cordelia nee Landers 3/5/97 ? L'pool Taurus asc.

Sun 20 50 Mrs Forester-Walker[931] to lunch: an infantile ignorant cocksure she-marmot. Saw T[redegar]'s Magick room- far greater than I thought- and he did expect me to talk to Frieda bout it! My one idea was to get out before any harm was done!

Mon 21 64 Idea came. PAGAD= ?[PAChD Heb] = 93 = PGVD. Frieda left. She may do a Magus based on the Paris Working.

Tues 22 5 Mrs Sutherland went to London early. Gloves off with Evan! He took symbol for our relations: 57 Sun Air/Air & Air plus SOl

Wed 23 9. Wrote to Cambyses Daguerre Churchill Told T about the- Eye of Horus[932]

Thur 24 4 -

Fri 25 25 Left 12.46 arr abt 4 PM v good train. Ill all day

Sat 26 4 LOV here. Tired. 8 1/2 GB here. Too tired to talk. Started to correct Press Proofs of Tarot.

Sun 27 53 mailed Tarot proofs 1-86 to Eifan {evan Tredegar}.

Evan's Magick Room

What is only true is that there was a single visit by Aleister Crowley to Tredegar House in the summer of 1943.[933] This predates Bryans' move from Belfast to Barry to study, as he arrived thereabouts in the summer of 1944.

An earlier appraisal of Crowley's visit to Tredegar House can be found in *Aspects of Evan*. The curious testimony of another of Evan's guests, a Mr James,[934] can also be gleaned from a wonderful book by the inspirational wizard David Conway that challenges the conventional wisdom about Evan and Crowley. [935]

Closer examination of the detail of Crowley's own record of the visit throws up only one hard fact. Crowley mentions in his diary that Evan had a room at Tredegar House, set aside as a Magick room (NB Magick was spelt this way by Crowley.) This room contained enough occult and black mass equipment to impress and even unnerve Crowley.

"Saw T[redegar]'s Magick room- far greater than I thought- and he did expect me to talk to Frieda about it! My one idea was to get out before any harm was done!"[936]

The Magick room was described by Crowley as "far greater than I thought." [937] Anything further than this can only be imagined as a precise description of the contents is missing.[938] It is inferred that this Magick room was used by Evan to conduct Black Masses.

Some histories referring to *where* Black Masses were held mention participants even using a bedroom in their own house.[939] There are surviving alcoves in the rooms within Tredegar House (including Evan's master bedroom) where a suspicion (and no more than this) has been formed that these were used by Evan as a black magic altar. It is interesting that John, Duke of Bedford, refers to "altars all over the house".[940] These however may not have had such a sinister use, since Evan was consumed by religion in his last years; moreover the building was used for many years as a Catholic School. Such alcoves could equally have been used as Catholic shrines, either created first by Evan[941] or later by the nuns for the display of religious figures e.g. of Christ, the Saints or one of the Madonnas.

From Crowley's reaction to the prospect of taking part in occult discussions generally at the visit to Evan, it seems more likely that *The Great Beast* was looking forward far more sensually to playing a nice game of chess[942] and drinking copious quantities of brandy with his host and fellow guests, than participating in rituals or doing cursing spells.[943]

Although, by 1943, Crowley's sinister, supreme powers might have diminished and his body was a physical wreck, his liking for brandy remained unrestrained.[944]

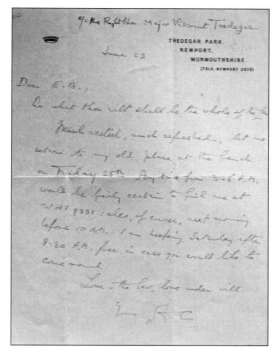

Crowley's letter written at Tredegar House

Other Relics and Citations

It is also suggested that Evan acquired "a piece of the 'true cross', only to misplace it in an all-male Turkish bath." [945]

He also "owned several saints' relics, reflecting his Catholic background [and] had the skeleton of a local Welsh witch (Meg Jenkins[946]) set up in his hallway to greet his guests. "[947] [None of this is recalled in the testimony of those who in the 1970s gave the house Curators their personal memories of Evan's time in Tredegar House, or is recollected in letters from Evan's second wife, Olga or his surviving cousin, Alan Carnegie Stewart, who actually lived in Tredegar House during part of the period.][948] What Bryans tells us is that "Evan loved going to bed with the bones of a woman [said to be Meg Jenkins] and that Evan claimed that Meg Jenkins had been both a *femina saga* [wise woman] and *incanter*, a charmer." [949]

Historical references to Meg Jenkins are otherwise very hard to find.[950] Evan told Bryans that Meg had been "immersed in one of the wells" of Llanover. The Castle of that name and *Llanover House* have an association with Augusta Hall, Lady Llanover, [951] who is recorded as being responsible for a campaign to promote and preserve Welsh national customs including the Welsh language and costume for women (with the traditional black, witch- like pointed hats). [952]

Evan: Adept of Adepts

Other assertions of Evan's occult prowess are noteworthy. Whilst there is evidence that Crowley inscribed and gifted copies of his own books, [953] a book inscription describing Evan Morgan as "the [magical] Adept of Adepts?"[954] remains a curious one. Indeed this is only a snippet from the actual annotation, which does not in fact use the term 'magical'.

John Symonds reveals the detail. Crowley "gave Tredegar a copy of the Book of Thoth fulsomely inscribed:

"To my old and very dear Friend and colleague, Adept of Adepts in the Secret Tradition, Eifon Morgan, heir of the Mysteries of the Round Table, entitled to bear Excalibur, Lord of the Secret Marches about Camelot do I, being the pupil and heir of Merlin, entrust this Book. Aleister Crowley". [955]

Drawing on of all the mortals Alfred, Lord Tennyson *The Great Beast* adds his own signature not one of his hundreds of aliases. [956]

Evan was 'Adept of Adepts in the Secret Traditions'. Crowley himself cites the phrase "adept of adepts" elsewhere which has its roots in magic circles.

"Moreover also is IAF verily 666 by virtue of number; and this is a Mystery of Mysteries; Who knoweth it, he is adept of adepts, and Mighty among Magicians!" Liber Samekh, Section J[957]

Crowley's Death

Crowley lived sometime in lodgings in London before his final years in Hastings, East Sussex, where he died in 1947. It is said that a Black Mass was held at his graveside for his funeral. Since Crowley was cremated that claim begs belief. One account does refer to "an elderly man [stepping] up to what passes for a pulpit in a crematorium...[and] In a deep loud voice of considerable eloquence he began to read A Hymn to Pan",[958] one of Crowley's own works. [959] More bizarre was perhaps the fate of Crowley's ashes "interred beneath a tree in the garden of an old friend in New Jersey. When the man subsequently went to dig them up to take them with him to California, the urn had vanished." [960]

There was no such Black Mass or crisis over Evan's remains at his simple Catholic funeral at Buckfast Abbey two years later. He was, at least, buried a Christian.

Frieda Harris and John Symonds paid a visit to see Evan at *Honeywood House* in the summer of 1948, when *The Great Beast* was remembered with devotion. [961]

Unsourced Claims-Embellishments

In researching the occult and black magic features of Evan's life much intrigues. Is it good enough to postulate that in such circles much cannot ever be *proved*, as everything is shrouded under wraps and mum's the word secrecy? Or does that interpretation mask mendacity and sham?

Some things stand out as not proven. Certain texts that link Evan to the occult stand out as missing key authorities in respect of a variety of statements which are repeated in several formats, in books, articles on the internet etc (set out there as gospel) concerning Evan's occult phase – other fragments too, which appear perfectly plausible, but are not satisfactorily sourced and look contrived.

Several references, for example in respect of Evan's Court Martial for offences against the Official Secrets Acts previously excused as "the aristocrat [meaning Evan] was released and it was whispered that MI5 had intervened in the case" are already discredited by the reproduction of the transcript of Evan's Court Martial in *Aspects of Evan*, based on the official War Office records. Those who still cannot accept this are deceitful if they suggest Evan got off the charges.

Other embellished threads by the same band have done a great deal of harm to the search for truth and in recording historical accuracy about Evan Morgan. These statements have appeared regularly out of thin air with no supporting proof and are presently not verifiable.

This is one example where the authority is missing and an attempt by this author to verify it has been declined by the originators:

"Lord Tredegar belonged to an occult secret society in London called *The Black Circle*, [962]which had the traditional thirteen members of a witch coven. In it the aristocrat was known as the 'Black Monk' and was even painted in the hooded black robe all the members wore for their ceremonies." [963]

Whilst it would not be surprising to find Evan in such a clique the tale is taken to a level of absurdity when it is suggested that, despite the anonymity of the coven, Evan's presence was always known of by his bird-like nose peeking out of a hole in the black hood.

Equally Robin Bryans portrays an alarming array of un-sourced statements that may be similarly embellished, with part of the embellishment coming from Evan who revelled in making up things. Evan was a master at staging charades and playing parlour games; he was capable of choreographing any kind of side show in a sacred place such as a churchyard to entertain and kick convention straight in the teeth.

This is an example:

Bryans draws on a story (which is cited elsewhere, as in the quote below) of Evan conducting incantations to the dead in Rome's Protestant Cemetery, which was a place often visited by him whilst living in Italy in the 1920s. This site, in the shadow of the Pyramid of Cestius (the only Pyramid from Ancient Rome that still stands) near the Porta San Paolo and easily accessible on Rome's city rail network, is where there are fine memorials to the poet John Keats and Evan's great hero, Percy B Shelley.

"While living in Rome it is said that he [Evan] did a necromantic rite in the English Protestant cemetery in the city to conjure up the spirit of the eighteenth-century romantic poet Shell[e]y." [964]

Bryans hits harder still in this coverage by declaring that "Evan astonished onlookers by going into violent convulsions to communicate with the dead poet…" [965]

It seems to this author that Evan performing in this way to a captive audience has a ring of the host's playfulness at Tredegar House party games, albeit these were still intended to shell shock the observer as John, Duke of Bedford's equally horrific anecdote, previously mentioned demonstrates.

In later describing Evan's Black Mass at the Protestant Cemetery Bryans indicates there was even Papal knowledge of Evan's mischief making, which also suggests a public (rather a private, secret, clandestine) event.

"When Evan's black mass adventures in and out of Rome's Protestant Cemetery became too much for his friend the Pope, Evan returned to Wales." [966]

All this may be exaggerated, although it is claimed that among the others that witnessed Evan's performance were by several unnamed diplomats attached to the Holy See. [967] Far more likely is that Evan joined with many other pilgrims who gathered in Rome's Protestant Cemetery in 1922 to pay homage (in their own particular way) at the large scale centenary celebrations (including numerous newspaper articles) to remember Shelley's death on 8 July 1822, drowned off the Italian coast, in his thirtieth year. [968]

Shane Leslie

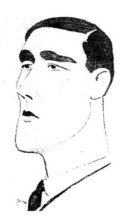

The Pope did take a personal interest in Evan's case. Shane Leslie,[969] one of Evan's Catholic mentors, offers reliable testimony to support this in his biography of Cardinal Gasquet.[970] This English Cardinal offered to take Evan's confessions (and this is referred to in *Aspects of Evan*); it is highly unlikely the Pope was made aware of Evan's prancing about in the Protestant Cemetery. It is more likely that as the advice given by the Pope (Pius XI) was that Evan should marry, it seems more plausible that the Holy Father's essential guidance was based on the knowledge that Evan was known to be chasing live young males about Rome rather than bringing long dead poets back to life again.

Shane Leslie touches on this further "I saw him [Evan] through a matrimonial essay which Pius XI unadvisedly bade him try when his heart was set on the priesthood." [971]

Evan was a convincing liar and there is no doubt his time studying at Beda College, Rome was far from being a calling; it was as great a farce as going to America to enter a monastery in Colorado Springs (since he actually only went their for his health) or his earlier excursions to Christ Church, Oxford, to study and importune other men and boys.

At times, Shane Leslie may have been completely taken in by Evan's sincerity and motives. For someone of Leslie's intellect he sometimes made strange friends: for instance he has literary links to A J A Symons, with authorship of *A Memoir* and tribute to the author in one of the reprints of *The Quest for Corvo*, describing his relationship with Symons as "as close as literary minds could be." [972]

There is no doubt that Evan and Leslie were genuine friends. Leslie was a credible influence for certain good upon Evan and he always provided encouragement. He must also have captured the appropriate tones of righteousness in Evan, or a willingness to repent, since Evan acted as godfather to one of Shane's children, the irrepressible Desmond Leslie, whose claim to fame is for punching the journalist Bernard Levin in the face on live national television. [973]

Shane describes Evan as a "quaint character"[974]... "the last of the romantics... Evan assumed colour against the grey background when everybody became unconventional by looking alike. He is Disraeli's *Lothair,* born after due time and living on Renaissance terms amongst Cardinal and goldfish." [975]

It is rather disappointing that a recent biography of Shane Leslie makes an inadequately short, unimportant reference to Evan. [976] Leslie had a profound influence on Evan's poetry and he wrote an introduction to one of Evan's volumes of verse. Leslie also acted as "godfather to Evan's....wife [Lois Sturt] at her Catholic baptism by Father CC Martindale." [977]

Lois treated the entire ceremony like an audition for a leading part in a theatre production, which of course it was. She "assured the Jesuit priest [Martindale] that she would probably be a bad Catholic, since she did everything badly in her life." [978]

Evan's attempts to communicate with the dead

Turning to the ever-recurring theme of Evan trying to communicate with the dead, there are a few examples of Evan's own strength of inner belief that he could succeed with this, and a more half-hearted assertion of a capability of raising the dead and having the power to exorcise the spirits of the dead. An instance of this will be revealed later, when Evan stayed at Connemara on Ireland's West coast.

Another revealing example of Evan's death watch hangs around what Evan said of his sister Gwyneth Ericka Morgan's demise. He is reported as saying that had he reached her in time he could have saved her life.

Gwyneth Morgan Revisited & Memories of Childhood

Evan's wayward sister Gwyenth's death in 1925 is cited by Robin Bryans as being a particular regret to him. That is unquestionably true. They were close siblings, especially when they were growing up with two dysfunctional parents.

Bryans makes a number of references in *The Dust Has Never Settled* and *Let the petals fall* to Gwyneth, shedding some new light on her childhood, adolescence, early adulthood and her death. There are illuminating pointers to Gwyneth (and Evan's) pastimes as children overlapping with their Stewart relations and connections from Katharine's half-sister Lady Beatrice Carnegie[979] who was married to a clergyman, Rev Henry Holmes Stewart. [980]

Rev Stewart married Evan's parents at Kinnaird Castle in 1890; in fact he acted as personal parson to Evan's illustrious Scottish cousins including the Southesks of Kinnaird Castle, the family of the Earl of Elgin of Broomhall and the Earl of Mansfield of Scone Palace. He hatched, matched and despatched many of them over several decades and generations.

Rev Stewart's Anglican church was latterly at *St Michael and All Angels in Michaeston Le Pit,* a 14th century edifice [981]with the manse house and rectory at Dinas Powys. Leisure time was spent at Barry (near Cardiff) with short holidays (days out) at nearby Penarth. The Morgan children combined with contingents from the Stewarts to enjoy seaside fun with other children who knew the Stewarts, including the Wills family of Cardiff, all playing together on the Pebble Beach at Penarth and swimming in the sea.

"Evan and his only sister Gwyneth loved the company of their Stewart cousins at the Barry rectory and going with the... Wills children to swim at the Pebble Beach which fell so steeply because of the 40ft tide." [982]

But this period contained a gruesome event in Evan's life since it was here as a boy that he was sexually assaulted by a collateral member of the Wills family, Willie Pethybridge who was a Solicitor and local politician and whose sister Mabel Pethybridge married Charles J G Wills, a shop manager in Cardiff.

Mabel and Charles Wills had three children: a boy, Vernon, (previously described as a convert in a Black Mass conducted by Evan) and two girls, Sylvia and Mary. Bryans especially connects Vernon with Evan and Mary with Gwyneth. Vernon was seven years younger than Evan and Mary was eight years younger than Gwyneth.

Mary Wills and Gwyneth

There is a suggestion that James Lonsdale Bryans accompanied Evan to Wales. A relative of his, Canon Lonsdale Bryans, [983] was a kindred spirit of Rev Henry Stewart and "they all met regularly at Lanson House where Charles and Mabel Wills lived...." [984]

In Robin Bryans' references to Gwyneth she does not appear to be quite normal; she is described as "strange" [985] and there are indications of her being in a disturbed state with an early attempt at suicide. Since this occurrence is tied in by Bryans to news breaking of a career decision by Mary Wills (who was very close to Gwyneth) it must be in a time period well beyond their childhood years, given that Mary was eight years junior to Gwyneth. Mary Wills was born in 1903 and her earliest training as a doctor would have been when she was in her 20s or even later. This takes us to the years well *after* the Great War.

"When Mary Wills announced her intention to train as a doctor at the Royal Free Hospital in London in order to join the Egypt General Mission,[986] Gwyneth was inconsolable and one morning at Lanson House, where Gwyneth was staying with Mary Wills, a maid took the hot water jug as usual to Gwyneth's room and got no reply. It was the first of Gwyneth's suicide attempts. "[987]

There follows an extraordinary statement. Bryans declares "The last [suicide attempt] would leave her dead." [988]

The events in Gwyneth's last years are fully described in *A Beautiful Nuisance*. The jury is still out on whether Gwyneth *actually took her own life*. A letter has recently emerged from 1916 which adds interest.[989]

Other new evidence linking Gwyneth to a number of well-known lesbians of the 1920s offers some support for her love of Mary Wills. [990]

A Beautiful Nuisance Revisited

Gwyneth's disappearance in 1924 was a national and international story which appeared in dozens of newspapers.

What did Evan actually do to help find his sister? The answer is nothing. The record (as set out in the book *A Beautiful Nuisance*) indicates that Evan was exiled by instruction and by choice during the long haul of waiting for Gwyneth's corpse to emerge. Between her disappearance in December 1924, and a body (later identified as Gwyneth's) being found in the River Thames in May 1925, Evan hid out the whole time in Rome. Perhaps he knew all along she was dead and so could do nothing for her. Is there more or less belief, then, in Evan's remark that he could have saved her?

Does this new evidence (from Bryans' statement of suicide) give greater credibility to the suggestion (made by a medium consulted by Scotland Yard) at the time of Gwyneth going missing that her body was still in the house (*The Niche*, 3, Lancaster Avenue, Wimbledon) in a cupboard in the hall? Was the body then moved, held for some time and then dumped in the River Thames? It is something we will never, ever know for certain.

After Gwyneth was dead many saw Evan's colossal grief. One of these was his old drinking pal Augustus John who records of seeing him in Rome "in the process of bedecking a shrine he had erected on the wall of his room to the memory of his unfortunate sister Gwyneth." [991]

Evan's Sanity is Saved by Two Women

Two women restored Evan's sanity following the events leading to the declaration of Gwyneth's death. One of these was his Protestant cousin Kitty (Katy) Stewart in Barry. The extraordinary part of this narrative (from Bryans' time frame) is that it was taking place whilst Katy's parents were still alive.

"Katy was more than merely a kissing cousin to Evan since he regarded her modest house as his home. She knew he was a homosexual ....although Katy featured so prominently in Barry's evangelical circle, she nevertheless tolerated Evan's weird tastes in religion and sex. Katie's particular friend had been her cousin Gwyneth, Evan's only sister, and when she died tragically in 1924 at the age of 29 Katie drew close to Evan because of their common grief over the wild Gwyneth." [992]

Does Katy's own outpouring of grief over Gwyneth put her in the dock as being 'the Jezebel' cited by Evan in his long poem *In Pace*, which is reproduced in *A Beautiful Nuisance*?

Bryans draws attention to Evan's depression after Gwyneth's death. The second woman he cites as saving Evan from falling into the abyss is Nina Hamnett.

"Nobody could get Evan out of his depression more quickly than Nina Hamnett, who replaced his sister Gwyneth in his affection." [993]

Two Tales of Evan's Psychic Powers

Evan features in a couple of more lightweight supernatural tales from the explorer Rosita Forbes.[994] During his fancy dress days at Oxford, Rosita was one Evan's own favourite guises. The first anecdote takes place on a sea voyage:

"The tour started late that winter (1937/8). Its only moments of success were on board the big Italian liner from Genoa to Calcutta. Evan Tredegar was on board with 'Porchey' Carnarvon, [995]Cardie Montague and Diana Gibb {Alistair's wife}, also one of the Shaftesbury girls known as Duchess, Lady Alexandra Haig and Barbara Hutton [the Woolworth heiress[996]] with her Danish husband, Count Haugwitz Reventlow. Evan had a crystal which, swinging on a scarlet cord, was supposed to answer questions. One by one, or indiscreetly in special pairs, we consulted it with regard to likely and unlikely futures. It told me that I could get what I wanted if I took enough trouble but would not."[997]

The second anecdote takes place during war time London.

"...by 1943 one only saw a handful of friends working in London. Brenda de Chimay[998] was always a delight. I remember one absurd evening when she and Evan Tredegar dined in our exiguous flat. As a change, being considerably bored with this world, we decided to make contact with another. I don't know which one of us had the energy to let it loose in the production of 'psychic' phenomena. But in a chill, dull, inadequately lit room with my husband and Evan in uniform, Brenda in the tenuous neat black, short of skirt but otherwise providing the maximum of warmth and covering, which was London's night uniform, we raised an extraordinary amount of sound and the wall bristled. Cracks and knocks suggested masons refreshed by beer. But ours was the corner flat; there was nothing beyond it except the blackout." [999]

Séances and a message for Henry Maxwell

In between the Black Masses and attending Catholic Mass, Evan was a devotee of spiritualism. His second wife Olga shared the same interest, once conveying a message (from Evan) to Henry Maxwell, Evan's choice of biographer. [1000]

Maxwell writes, in 1979:

"I think it would be possible but very, very difficult to write a life of Evan. Actually he wanted me to write his life and Olga has often begged me to do so, even saying that at a séance he had 'come through' to remind me of his wishes." [1001]

Maxwell counselled that Evan "rather liked shocking people" and stories of his exploits were tempered "with more than a grain of salt and on a strictly take it or leave it... and don't ask me to explain basis. God help anyone who asked him to 'explain' anything!!" [1002]

Knowing that Evan would erupt if ever challenged or corrected, his house guests and friends tended to keep silent about any of the unpleasant detail that spilled out – even when they disapproved. Evan was their meal ticket but in so doing they covered up Evan's foul deeds, exactly as several modern day sex cases were concealed, including the dreadful Savile case that hit BBC TV in Britain in 2012. [1003]

Maxwell tempers the more seedy elements of Evan's life as being "open to misunderstanding and [would] give quite a wrong impression of that extraordinary man and the life in the house." [1004]

Maxwell was Evan's eraser and a loyal disciple. He was jealous of Robin Bryans who says that Maxwell failed to understand where Bryans fitted in to Evan's life, although he "could see [Bryans] was not Evan's favourite type of sailor picked up in the East end who liked the crack of the whip for the tune of a fiver." [1005]

Bryans claims that Evan was "the greatest love of [the elegant Maxwell's]... life." [1006] Maxwell fostered Evan's close friendships with two of the motor racing Princes of Siam, Prince Birabongse [1007] (an amateur artist who caste a bronze head sculpture of Evan in 1943) and Maxwell's own old Harrow chum, Prince Chula Chakrabongse. [1008] Chula was a friend at Cambridge of the traitor Anthony Blunt and of (Blunt's lover) Peter Montgomery, the brother of Hugh Montgomery [1009] who was sometime a diplomat in Rome at the time of Evan's visits there as a Papal Knight and was implicated in an almost certainly overplayed and exaggerated narrative of homosexual activity at the Vatican involving eminent men, including one man who went on to be Pope. [1010]

Henry Maxwell was not well-off, although he made a living as a writer[1011] and publisher. [1012] He "would hang around Evan Tredegar with expectation of inheriting the *Honeywood House* portion of Evan's vast estate, [to which Bryans adds].. Henry was most attentive to old Lady Tredegar's needs at Honeywood..." [1013]

Evan's Party Frolics

But away from the watchful (though never openly critical) eyes of guests at Tredegar House or Honeywood, Evan was up for accepting invitations to sex parties with indulgent themes where drugs and sexual prancing about with young men and boys were built into the agenda.

"Evan Tredegar perhaps went too far in his fantasies when his passion for fancy dress led him to wear clerical dress at a party given by the disgraced Infante of Spain, Don Luis, Prince of Orleans,[1014] where cocaine was served on silver salvers carried by negro boys and powdered footmen." [1015]

At Tredegar House, one memory recalled by Evan's cousin, Alan Carnegie Stewart (see *A Beautiful Nuisance* and *Aspects of Evan*) is of Evan's collection of handsome young footmen in powdered wigs. [1016]

Evan Encounters a Ghostly Presence in Ireland

Evan is mentioned as once attempting to exorcise a ghost at Renvyle House, in the wilds of Connemara on Ireland's magical West coast. This was at the home of Oliver St John Gogarty, a surgeon, writer, poet, and close friend of William B Yeats, the Irish bard, and occultist. Renvyle had a history of ghostly sightings and Gogarty had experienced an out of the ordinary happening. He records that he was once "woken by ponderous, limping footsteps approaching along the corridor. Lighting a candle, he went to investigate but the moment he left his room the flame was extinguished and he found himself alone in the dark. Suddenly his limbs became very heavy, "as if I were exercising with rubber ropes," as he later put it. Fortunately, nothing further happened that night."

Evan was staying as a guest at Renvyle and agreed to confront the ghost. The tale (in which Evan nearly died) is catalogued by Gogarty in a book *As I Was Going Down Sackville Street*.[1017] The shorter summary of the night's close encounter began when Gogarty told Evan all about his previous experience.

Evan, "on being told that a particular room was haunted, attempted an exorcism", telling his host that "by good fortune I have with me a potent reliquary; come with me and I exorcise the poor ghost". [1018]

"No sooner had he lit three candles and began reciting some prayers than a thick mist filled the room and the unfortunate [Evan] was thrown to the ground. Having been dragged to safety ... he revealed that he had seen the ghost of a pale-faced boy with large luminous eyes, dressed in brown, who was clasping his hands to his throat as if strangling himself. [Evan] concluded that the boy had committed suicide in that room. "

Evan made other visit to Renvyle where often an illustrious Irish literary clique gathered. Among those who witnessed Evan standing face to face with the pale-faced boy ghost was Seymour Leslie (who dubbed Evan the Playboy poet) and who recorded the whole affair in his memoirs, quoting Evan as saying "I went down into the private hell of that poor boy! I've never known such mental agony!" [1019]

In *The Renvyle Letters*[1020] Evan is described by Gogarty as a "family friend".

One of the letters from 1948 (when Evan was in his last year of life) reveals the calibre of Evan's own accompanying followers: "Tredegar is staying at Renvyle, complete with entourage of beautiful young converts". [1021]

There is evidence from the Renvyle letters to show how close Evan came to being rounded up and imprisoned for sex crimes. See Chapter 9. As with other Society cover ups of well-connected homosexuals, Evan Morgan enjoyed nine depraved lives.

Evan's Sex Crimes & Queen Mary's wrath

Bryans says Evan indulged in taking photographs of young boys and men who were completely naked. This practice began in his early days when he and Peter Churchill, along with Lord George Rodney and Robin Chester, were involved in the Boy Scout Movement. There is a comment in the testimony of Simon Rodney (one of George's younger brothers) to Robin Bryans, that (as an adult) Simon's worst fear was that a photograph of him as a boy, taken by Evan, would appear in the public domain. Simon was a partner in a City stockbroking firm; he "was sure Evan had taken indecent photos of him... the embarrassment and blackmail potential had to be stopped at source, and any such prints and negatives destroyed." [1022]

Evan's Party at the End of the War

There were almost certainly pornographic photographs of boys and men in homosexual poses that came to light at a party launched by Evan to celebrate the end of the Second World War.

Queen Mary had heard of Evan's celebrations but without knowing about its theme or the all male requirement for entry. She arrived at the scene and immediately spotted some of the photographs. For his part Evan certainly was unaware of the Queen's presence.

Francis Rose, who had once been the target for a practical joke by Evan on a visit to his Chelsea gallery by Queen Mary, [1023] reveals further details of this all male end of war extravaganza:

"Although the Queen appeared not to be upset by the men in drag who curtsied to her, what shocked her to such an extent that she never recovered were the pornographic photo enlargements on the walls. Her Majesty did not, of course, recognise any of the male genitalia in the photographs but certainly recognised the faces of highly-placed men whom she knew perfectly well and on whose no longer-private parts the royal gaze briefly rested." [1024]

She was furious with Evan. The Queen had the power "to cut him like a surgeon with a scalpel, out of royal society." [1025]

Until this moment Evan had almost redeemed himself of earlier misbehaviour within Royal circles as Bryans comments:

"Evan basked in royal favour; it could be seen by the fact that in response to a request from Queen Mary he [Evan] wrote a miniature book for the Dolls House at Windsor Castle". [1026]

But this latest provocation was too much. Evan had gone too far.

But Bryans leaves no doubt that one of those who had posed for Evan included Her Majesty's own flesh and blood:

"Queen Mary immediately understood much that had previously puzzled her about her own sons, particularly about the former King Edward VIII, when she unintentionally saw Evan's photographs." [1027]

It was not long before Evan was established as being at the centre of a sordid ring of paedophiles and pornographers.

Honeywood House Raided

One of the out sheds at Honeywood House

Evan kept most of his photographic equipment in the out sheds at his mother's home at *Honeywood House.*

Evan's bizarre three-seater toilet
used today as a large flower bed

Robin Bryans reveals more details:

"the homosexual photographs ...brought Evan's downfall. Although the Home Secretary sent the police to clear up Evan's elaborate dark room at *Honeywood House* near Dorking, the law's strong arm failed to know that in Wales Evan had enlisted the expert help of Harry Hinton at 23 Hickman Road in Penarth to develop many of the films involved with the Abergavenny gay trial." [1028]

The Abergavenny case (from 1942) involved a group of men who were tried for homosexual offences following a fifteen-year-boy's complaint of the improper conduct of a cinema manger during fire-watching duties. The Police uncovered "an orgy of perversion ...involving a number of youths, hairdressers, hotel chefs, clerks, widow dressers, and out of work actors." Sentences of one to twelve years imprisonment were dished out to the offenders.[1029]

Evan Remains Protected But Is Warned

Evan was safe, but he was warned by the police over his conduct. He "knew there could be no prosecution over the photographs because the royal family could not have a scandal over his well-known, high-and-mighty guests going into the witness box to explain how they came to disport themselves in Evan's obscene photographs. " [1030]

Dennis Parry

There is no evidence that Evan was directly involved as a participant in the Abergavenny sex scandal. But at the time the convicted boys and men from the Abergavenny case were serving their sentences in Cardiff Prison, a young Englishman named Dennis Parry was on the same wing of the prison serving a sentence for refusing to join the army. Parry was a conscientious objector. [1031]

Parry's presence in South Wales originally came about when he was admitted to the Barry School of Evangelism in January 1942. Robin Bryans later joined Parry at the School in 1944. Parry first shared a room at the school with Ian Richard Kyle Paisley, better known later as the Rev Ian Paisley, a leading Ulster politician and Westminster MP. [1032] Parry was subsequently sentenced by a tribunal to six months imprisonment for his army enlistment failure and his refusal to accept a decision that he should do land work. Somewhere between Parry's arrival in South Wales, completing his prison sentence and subsequent release he met (or came to know of) Evan Morgan, whom he abhorred. Parry gained insight into Evan's double life through his fellow student, Bryans, who bragged of his friendship with the peer.

Robin Bryans cites Parry (who was in his late twenties in the 1940s) as at least being made aware of the existence of Evan's Black Masses. He was also probably told tales by the gay sex offenders from Abergavenny, suggesting some of these men and boys may well have been aware or involved in Evan's sex rituals.

"Dennis Parry could quote from books and newspapers about Lord Tredegar and Aleister Crowley and the weird events at Tredegar Park. Dennis believed that Evan and Aleister Crowley should have gone to prison rather than himself..." [1033] Bryans adds elsewhere that "Dennis... undoubtedly thought Evan a devil..." [1034] Parry's rants about Evan were heard loud enough for the police to closely watch Evan's movements.

Dennis Parry later went to Africa as a missionary, a married man with four children. Whilst serving in the Congo, he, his wife and two of their children were killed by Simba rebels.[1035]

The Revenge of Vernon Wills

It was not Dennis Parry but Vernon Wills who reaped revenge on Evan for being "half-poisoned by partaking in Evan's Black Mass communion cup".[1036] The mad Vernon was also jealous of the part that Robin Bryans was taking up in Evan's life and tried to burn down Tredegar House. Bryans describes how Vernon's accomplice was one of Evan's pet owls…. "the demented Vernon Wills tied a string [onto one of the legs of the bird] with a blazing, oil soaked rag at the end and made it fly into Evan's study."[1037] Luckily the attempt failed.

Evan and Vernon saw each other again briefly at the funeral of the arch-bugger William Hampton Pethybridge.

Alderman William Hampton Pethybridge of Cardiff

Chapter 9

Spying and Espionage

Evan Morgan with a real white rabbit

In April 1943, when Sir Walter Monckton appeared on Evan Morgan's behalf to defend him at a Court Martial for offences against the Official Secrets Acts his noble client, if found guilty, faced a possible prison sentence. Monckton was therefore required to do everything possible to mitigate Evan's serious breaches of the law. The proceedings were held *in camera* and Monckton, like a stage magician, had to pull off the proverbial white rabbit from the hat; in fact it had to be something more remarkable to save Evan from being whisked off to Wormwood Scrubs.

Evan was accused of careless talk after disclosing information about the secret work of MI 14, the department that engaged him during 1942-3, whose main function was to oversee the procurement and the use of carrier pigeons as part of the war effort. This included the dropping of the birds into enemy occupied Northern Europe, mainly over Holland and the Low Countries.

A useful element of intelligence gathering was possible by pigeons carrying messages from Europe back to Britain. Pigeons were also used by air crews who ditched their planes, in order to alert their base of their plight in the hope that a British (rather than an enemy ship) might bring them back home to safety.

Evan was in charge of the branch of MI 14 that superintended the procurement and use of carrier pigeons, for recording where the birds were landed and from where (if any) messages were sent back to Britain. His team was responsible for tagging the birds and arranging with the RAF to drop them by specially adapted parachutes over enemy-occupied Holland and surrounding countries. Special canisters were attached to the birds for messages to be inserted by members of the Resistance in Holland etc, and the birds were then set free to fly back to Britain.

Evan's Court Martial

The particulars of Evan's disclosures against the Official Secrets Acts, made to various people who were not entitled to the information about the work of MI 14, are fully outlined in *Aspects of Evan, the Last Viscount Tredegar* and the book also contains a full transcript of the Court Martial proceedings held *in camera* at Chelsea Barracks on 19 April 1943.

The Myth of Evan Being Held Prisoner in The Tower of London

An assertion[1038] that needs to be clarified. Evan was *not* held in the Tower of London like some ultra special, top security or state prisoner awaiting his Court Martial, where one of his guards was his old pal Dicky Buckle.

Buckle records the facts in his autobiography. He was stationed with the Scots Guards at Chelsea Barracks at the time of Evan's pre-trial, as was Evan. Buckle enjoyed a farewell meal with Evan before leaving for service in Egypt:

"when my marching orders came through, it was in a long dining room of the Mess overlooking Pimlico Road that I ate my last dinner in England for nearly 3 years, seated between Pat Kinnaird, [1039] who had come with gifts of books and money and champagne to bid me goodbye, and Evan Tredegar, who was temporarily with us in barracks..."[1040]

Evan's Reprimand

At the end of his Court Martial, Evan was found guilty on two of the three charges against him and was reprimanded. Monckton asked for mercy for his client on account of his twisted personality, highlighting the Tredegar family doctor Russell Wilkinson's [1041]remarks (given in evidence to the Court) that Evan was a fantasist, someone more at home in a Doge's Palace in 15th Century Venice than his own age and time. To extract further pity from the judges Monckton referred to Evan's dysfunctional family, his life as a child in his parents' loveless relationship and the fact that his own second marriage was precariously close to ending in divorce. For further sympathy, Evan's sister Gwyneth's wretched life and death was also mentioned.

Evan: The Spy Who Was or Never Was?

Monckton made no reference to Evan being a spy or secret service agent, nor did the great advocate mention any count of Evan doing something worthy for King and Country as a peer of the realm or as a private citizen. Surely this was the time to draw deep and refer to such acts, if they happened? Evan's brief period working in MI 14, which ended in a humiliating Court Martial, was ever as far as Evan could say he worked inside the world of Intelligence.

MI 14 was unique but Evan was not assigned to any of the usual well-known departments of state that deal with covert activity, counter terrorism, infiltration, spying, espionage etc, notably MI 5 or MI 6. Indeed, the inevitable lack of trust in political and Society circles over his often dangerous way of life which was protected from on high, with some close friends equally participating in serious immoral and political pastimes, made Evan a target for surveillance by MI 5/6 as he was a vulnerable, usable stooge for spies and blackmailers.

Evan's Importuning of Prime Ministers

In years gone by, Evan attempted to attach importance to himself by getting close to the Prime Ministers of the day, making a plea to them about using his talents in some way.

He wrote to Frances Stevenson, private secretary to David Lloyd George:

"...one day I want to come and work at No 10. [Downing Street] I don't much care what at, but I feel your chief could make some sort of use of me." [1042]

From Evan's fantasy world he saw himself as some great statesman-type figure, popping in and out of Downing Street or being sent for by Buckingham Palace to help resolve a world crisis. Even if it was just wearing the appointed suit, the Eton College tie, a fashionable grey homburg hat and citing a swanky office address in Whitehall, Evan would have been on all accounts in his own mind the Prime Minister in waiting.

David Lloyd George was the first and only Prime Minister to allow himself to be sweet-talked by Evan. Later, beyond the polite and social level of skirmishes with Evan at balls, parties and receptions, he was largely ignored or humoured by other occupants of Downing Street. Frances Stevenson's outrage with Evan over his behaviour towards her, exploiting her to get close to Lloyd George and even offering her marriage, would have been mentioned to her employer and lover Lloyd George, so he was also wary of Evan's grasp.

Frances Stevenson records "The Hon. Evan Morgan... aspires to a position of literary adviser to the government held under the Asquith regime by Mr E Marsh."[1043]

After Lloyd George fell from grace he often met Evan lounging, swimming and playing tennis at parties given by William Randolph Hearst,[1044] the American newspaper proprietor and his mistress Marion Davies[1045] at St Donat's Castle, Glamorganshire, South Wales, a edifice and grounds that hosted several exclusively Welsh events through until the mid 1930s. [1046] Lloyd George learned it was best to promise Evan the earth, to move him on to suitable or unsuitable new pastures. Evan loved telling everyone that Lloyd George expected great things of him.

Stanley Baldwin and the later Tory occupants of No 10 Downing Street (and their hostess wives) did not overly encourage Evan's ambitions, although he was blessed as a Conservative candidate from 1926 and appeared with his father when Courtenay was Conservative Party President; he fought in the 1929 General Election but that was the sum total of his political career. He was also part of a small clutch of men in the Parliamentary Candidate Groups who clocked up several overseas visits but none of these were high level romps or matters of state, or of emissaries sent to deliver a solution at a time of crisis. In later years when Brendan Bracken's relationship with Winston Churchill was observed by Evan, he envied his old friend's power hold over the wartime leader.

Evan's only erstwhile service for his country was in the late years of the Great War when he volunteered to accept elements of what might be loosely termed 'undercover work' but it was all a far cry from the cloak and dagger romance of being a secret service mole.

King's Messenger

During the Great War Evan had a small claim to fame: he delivered documents between British Embassies and Consulates, especially between London and North Africa. This corresponded only to him acting, albeit with merit, as an unpaid King's Messenger, being sanctioned, as Evan was still on the army lists, as extra duties attached to that status. He is more likely to have asked if he could take anything out with his planned time abroad, an absence from the army on half-pay on health grounds. It is unlikely that the authorities asked him first. Evan may have used a huge, bespoke courier satchel with elaborate Royal and personal crests;[1047] he may have adopted elaborate routes, air and ship and submarine being amongst them and he may have been as stealthy as a leopard or a tiger to ensure that the cherished papers got through, but these records were far from being high-risk documents or concerning issues of national security or war. They were more likely to be ordinary, routine, diplomatic communications of a very low-risk type.

Evan, The Honorary Attache

Since the law in Britain prohibited male homosexuality, several gay men of this age and time were able to get their share of uninterrupted homosexual contact by living away (although some by necessity were sent away) from home shores into exile or whilst working at British Embassies abroad. The post of 'honorary attaché' gave several drifters a refuge with little work of any importance or sensitivity; these (usually) young men had relatives pulling strings to get them into sheltered housing abroad. Evan was once quickly despatched and assigned to the role as an Attache in the British Legation at Copenhagen after a run-in with the authorities over one young man's accusations against him of buggery. Like his chum Harold Nicolson, whose own father was a wandering diplomat (and he grew up with diplomats and obliging attaches all around him), Evan also served his country in this capacity. For anyone like Evan in trouble abroad over a boy, the British Embassy invariably had in its ranks of friends an old-Etonian contemporary or a society contact able to intervene to stop any arrest or charge being laid.

Evan the information gatherer

During the unstable political conditions of the 1930s, there were uncertainties galore over the future shape of power and government in Germany, Spain and Italy with the rapid rise of Fascism. Evan, along with many other travellers and journalists, could well have volunteered (or been targeted) to provide assistance or information through any of the British Embassy portals. Invariably Evan would see it as his duty as a British aristocratic who loved his country and whose relatives included Royal half-cousins, some well placed diplomats and also a past ambassador. Evan (with others) was often in a good position, in Britain and whilst living or travelling abroad, to observe and keep an eye and ear open and a nose to the grindstone and to report any irregular goings-on against British citizens or British interests. Time spent on German soil in the years when Nazism was growing and the Weimer Republic crumbling may have been an especially propitious time to be useful. The Secret Intelligence Services had a tag line in asking people travelling around the world to "merely keep ...[their] eyes open for people who might be used later" in the service. [1048]

But whether Evan had or had not been probed to pass on information, and whether any of his utterances were deemed useful or not by the authorities, nothing was of sufficient regularity, quantity or calibre to be thought worth mention by Sir Walter Monckton to save Evan's skin in his hour of need and crisis, when he faced imprisonment for the serious breaches against the Official Secrets Acts.

In the 1930s and 1940s Evan, like others of his ilk, may have been asked to inform on friends and relatives too. It's plausible he was asked, even badgered by those who knew him from the extensive old boys' network, starting with mutual links at Eton College, moving on to Oxford University, then the Welsh Guards and finally from his Whitehall and Parisian past.

This would all have swelled Evan's head. Any of his contemporaries in these places and their handlers could have got Evan to help them prevent or detect a range of possibilities, from mischief to treason. Even Evan might be deemed useful despite (or indeed perhaps on account of) the supreme trail of ignominy he'd left behind in each of these places in his career where he was closely associated.

Evan the 'informer', passing on information about people in his circle, those he was aware of who might act or were already acting against Britain, was much as his Great Uncle Octavius had informed the police authorities (passing on names and tit-bits of gossip he'd overhead in public houses) concerning the revolutionary plans of the Chartists in Newport, one hundred years before, in the 1830 and 1840s. It is said that Octavius burst in tears when death sentences were later passed on the Chartist ring-leaders, including his one-time friend, John Frost. [1049]

217

Evan, Maxwell Knight and Crowley

One of the ace spy-masters of Evan's era was Maxwell Knight, [1050] "a right wing, anti-Semitic homosexual"[1051] and the inspiration for 'M' in the James Bond saga by Ian Fleming. Knight headed B5(b), a branch of MI5 responsible for infiltrating politically subversive groups in Britain.

Other high-ranking spooks included MI5's Guy Liddell [1052] and Stewart Menzies,[1053] the head of MI6. These men and other spy handlers were acquainted with Evan over many years, at least socially, and they had friends in common. Evan also knew some of the more scurrilous MI5/MI6 informers like Gerald Hamilton, Aleister Crowley and the homosexual Tom Driberg (from 1933, the first William Hickey on the *Daily Express*, who infiltrated the British Communist Party, acting for Maxwell Knight[1054]). Out on a limb there was also James Lonsdale Bryans, who had once been very close to Evan but by the years leading to the Second World War they had virtually become strangers. [1055] Their friendship had wavered.

The spy men were all on familiar, pleasant and friendly or at least nodding terms with Evan, and knew his connections including the Royal collaterals. The homosexual as well the straight-laced spies were aware of Evan's proclivities but such a label meant, with Evan's public persona acting the dandy (and often being less than discreet), that he could be a target for blackmail by enemy agents.

There was always the threat hanging over Evan himself that his blissful state of immunity as a pederast could be withdrawn. If anything was wanted from Evan or offered by Evan, a cosy little chat could be assured with this all taking place in private through the innocent backdrop of the spy's subterranean network of society, political, government, and diplomatic receptions, London's restaurants, hotels and gentleman's clubs.

Evan's ego came first in most things. He was assured of being liked by Maxwell Knight since, as well as the two of them being sexually compatible and with an infatuation for the occult, they shared a passion for nature and for the welfare of wild animals. [1056]

There is some book evidence to show that Knight proposed using Evan's buddy Aleister Crowley in an occult-driven escapade dubbed *Operation Mistletoe*[1057] in the Second World War, a mission involving getting Hitler's deputy Rudolf Hess to believe that Churchill wanted peace with Germany but not under Hitler. One exploit, involving a fake horoscope of Hess being prepared (whilst he was still in Hitler's service in Germany and to show him to be the heir in waiting), was led by Ian Fleming who was in Naval Intelligence at the time, but Crowley was dropped in favour of another occultist (a Swiss astrologer[1058]) to do the job. [1059] It was this that sparked the later famed comment that "Hess was completely in the hands of astrologers, eye-diagnosticians and nature-healers!" [1060]

Evan only learned about Crowley the patriot years later, when *The Great Beast* (also suspected also as being a double agent) bragged of what he had done for the war effort.

In one appraisal of the Crowley-Hess affair the entire episode is questioned. "No solid evidence has emerged to prove Crowley participated in a secret service inspired, anti-Nazi ritual as part of any broader plan to entrap Hess. However, the combination of Fleming's, Knight's and Crowley's personalities would not make the possibility of such an event wholly fantastic." [1061] This last quoted biography of Crowley offers a suggestion that upon news breaking of Hess landing in Britain Crowley offered himself to the government: "If it is true that Herr Hess is much influenced by astrology and Magick, my services might be of use..." [1062]

Evan's encounters with Rudolf Hess
The Facts About Hess

Rudolf Hess

Rudolf Walter Richard Hess was born in Alexandria, Egypt, on April 26, 1894, the first son of Fritz Hess, a respected and well-to-do merchant. In 1933 Rudolf Hess rose to the prominence as Deputy Fuhrer of Germany, under Adolf Hitler. A lesser known fact is that Hess often used an alias, 'Alfred Horn', to travel unrecognised throughout Europe, complete with false passport and theatrical disguises.[1063]

On 10 May, 1941 Hess flew a plane into Britain. This story is a legend, with a mountain of material for interested historians. He crash-landed in Scotland, albeit showing his supreme skills as a pilot, he landed within a short distance from his believed target.

The gist of Hess's mission to meet with the Duke of Hamilton (whom he had previously met) was to broker a peace deal between Britain and Germany. It failed. There were grave doubts about Hess's real motives and about his state of mind.

According to a history of the Tower of London, Rudolf Hess was the last state prisoner held there. The Deputy Fuhrer of Nazi Germany was held in the Queen House from 17-21 May, 1941. [1064]

Hess was watched and interrogated and after being held in the Tower of London he was moved on 21 May 1941 to a secret location (known as Camp X) at Mytchett Place, near Aldershot. Within a short time it was clear that Hess was unstable and unreliable and he was classified as a Prisoner of War. [1065] The view that Hess was mentally deranged continued over a much longer period. It was eventually agreed between the British government and medical authorities that Maindiff Court, Abergavenny, South Wales[1066] was a perfect solution to detain Hess. On the morning of 26 June (some accounts say 25 June [1067]) 1942, Hess was transferred there for the remainder of the war. [1068]

The Fiction and the Truth About Evan and Hess

It is claimed that during the Second World War "One of [Evan's] more unusual and notorious house guests [at Tredegar House] was... the Nazi Deputy-Fuhrer Rudolf Hess."[1069]

The same history pranksters who make his claim offer a further assault, saying that Evan dined with Hess at Maindiff Court when his Battalion of the Monmouthshire Home Guard was on duty there.

What an intriguing scenario it is that Hess was allowed a jolly to see Evan Morgan. Alas! nothing sustainable exists in official files or in the public domain linking Evan and Hess albeit some of the excluded files (according to Robin Bryans[1070]) were destroyed by the Secret Intelligence Service and others remain unavailable even today. [1071]

Examination of the collection of war diaries for the period is interesting and even amusing.

One No. 10 Downing Street insider covers the Hess landing in passing:

"The poor Duke of Hamilton feels acutely the slur of being taken for a potential Quisling." [1072]

The same diarist cites another No. 10 insider saying, "if only the parachute had failed to open, he would be a happier and more efficient man" [1073]

Later an additional set of diaries refers to a plan suggesting that the captured German generals be put in with Hess. That same day No. 10 received "a medical report saying that Hess was in need of company" and they were contemplating doing this. It was however stressed: "H is quite cracky as he had been ever since he left Germany, and the generals know this and probably wouldn't say a word in his presence." [1074]

None of any of the folk who trooped through Tredegar House in Evan's time there and who offered testimonials and details of Evan tales (from the evidence held from the 1970s in the Tredegar House files) make any mention of Evan and Hess. The validity of the tale that Evan met Hess at Bad Weisse, near Munich, in 1931, the subject of a BBC Radio Wales programme in which this author took part, is also suspect. All the diarists point out that there was a clamour by government officials and the Secret Intelligence Service to identify persons who had actually met Hess, in order to satisfy them that it was the real man and not (as is still argued by some) a look-alike who had flown into Britain. Evan was never asked to identify the flyer, nor volunteered for the task.

The official record shows that the Hess held in Maindiff Court was allowed out of the Hospital for exercise from his incarceration, but he was closely guarded.

One reliable informant advises that Hess "was allowed to walk in the hills and mountains in the Abergavenny area and even had an RAF staff car at his disposal, which allowed him to go to White Castle. One place that was his favourite area was the Keeper's Pond, situated on the top of the Blorenge." [1075] These are sites around Maindiff Court.

Although Hess's whereabouts were kept secret, there was a leak in the press by the Daily Mail in an article entitled *"The Daily Life of Hess in Prison Camp."* [1076]

Robin Bryans refers to "waiting [at Llanover with village children] to see Rudolf Hess [in a car] going by to Abergavenny secure hospital," suggesting he had become a quaint local attraction. This irritated Hess. According to Bryans he told the Swiss Minister, Walther Thurnheer,[1077] that "he wished to limit the outside exercise because of problems from spectators". [1078]

Evan Morgan was Deputy Lieutenant of the County of Monmouthshire. He could don the uniform of a Major in the Scots Guards so could he pull off a visit to Maindiff Hospital? One suggestion is that Evan's Home Guard Unit may have had a stint at Abergavenny. An historian comments:

"Hess was on occasion guarded by members of the Home guard…in the first few weeks of Hess's time at Maindiff Court, five Home Guard members were attached to the guard in order to show them around the local area…the unit …were not Evan's bunch, but in fact were solely down to the local Auxiliary Unit in the area; mainly the Govilon section." [1079]

On this same point about Evan meeting Hess, one Newport historian who has closely studied the whole story (and written articles about it) takes this view:

"I think it extremely unlikely that Hess ever met Evan Morgan at Maindiff Court or dined at Tredegar House. He was guarded at Maindiff by members of the Pioneer Corps, whilst his personal protection was in the hands of the RAMC. [1080]

A further opportunity to test the whole story presented itself after *Aspects of Evan* was published. An historian, currently writing the later tale about what became of Hess, expressed a serious interest in considering any evidence held. [1081]

The result of a long exchange, including research undertaken in the American Secret Service files within US National Archives in Washington DC, together with the Hess family papers, the Swiss Ambassador's (in London) records and the Red Cross files in Zurich,[1082] by this historian concludes:

"I can now confirm that Hess never met Evan at Abergavenny! During the course of my research I have been enlightened by a source of mine that used to work [in SIS] during WW2, to the existence of an intelligence report by [MI] 5, which deals with the Evan claims. It would appear that he was warned to stop telling tall tales about an interlude with Hess. The Hess files in Zurich do not support the Evan claims; they do mention a military commander meeting with Hess, but after careful research I have established that was not Evan." [1083]

Another worn-weary part of the Evan- Hess hoax asserts "Hess had a family connection with the Tredegar estate as his first wife was buried nearby." [1084]

There is a tombstone in Michaelstone-y-Fedw, near Bassaleg (outside Newport) put up by a Carl Hess in that reads:

"Erected by Carl Hess, of Schleswig, Germany, in memory of his wife, Elizabeth Mackie, who died at Exmouth, Devon, June 13th: 1891, aged 35. In life beloved, in death never forgotten".

Carl Hess was in service in the household of the Bishop of Gloucester and he was steward in the Bishop's palace. Elizabeth Mackie was governess in the household of the same Bishop. In 1890 she met a Carl Hess. They married and went to live in Exmouth but she died from pneumonia 12 months after her marriage. There were no children. Carl Hess later returned to Hamburg, Germany.

This member of the Hess family of Germany is not – as claimed by the same hoaxsters - the father of Rudolf Hess and no member of the Hess family ever worked at Tredegar House. [1085]

Evan and the other Spy Masters

Stewart Menzies, head of MI6, knew Evan in his first two years at Eton, as President of 'Pop ' (the self-electing oligarchy of school prefects). Menzies cut a handsome figure of envy, lust and fear to the younger boys as he dashed around in his "coloured waistcoat, sponge bag trousers, butterfly collars, buttonholes and a blob of sealing wax on his top hat..." [1086] with Evan (three years his junior) firmly under his control. But while Evan was later caught up in adolescent gay shenanigans, Menzies was earning a reputation as a sportsman; he then joined the Grenadier Guards. The two of them were reunited, especially during the Paris Peace Conference of 1919 with this, together with a distinguished war record, paving the way for Menzies to join the Secret Intelligence Service where he excelled; in particular during the Second War World overseeing code-breaking and in liaison with other departments, alongside the work of agents in SOE (the Special Operations Executive) and the Foreign Office. With their life overlaps, Evan was always a target for an approach from Menzies or any one of his henchmen in MI6.

Guy Liddell stands out as another secret agent to feature in the span of Evan's life and he mixed with several of his closest coterie. Guy heard of Evan's adventures first hand from Peter Churchill who, like Evan, was a close boyhood friend. Guy's father held a post at Court in the service of one of Queen Victoria's daughters[1087] so this family background allowed him to come into contact with the same courtiers and Royals as those acquainted with Peter and Evan. Through Evan's mother's Scottish family, with Princess Maud Duff (Lady Southesk) acting as a catalyst, a friendship was formed by Evan with several of the European Royal Princesses and their successors.

In 1931 Evan spent time in Scotland with Princess Helena Victoria[1088] and her sister Princess Marie-Louise, [1089] daughters of Prince and Princess Christian of Schleswig-Holstein. These women counted Guy Liddell as one of their close companions to whom they looked as a chaperone to take them out to private dinners, concerts and Society functions.[1090] A favourite place for Liddell and the Princesses was at the home of one of the lesser known London Society hostesses, Lady Cory, (a fine pianist, separated from her husband, an MP) who held musical evenings at her home at 22, Belgrave Square, attended by many politicians and diplomats. [1091] The Cory family feature in Robin Bryans' autobiographies; they had close links with the Wills family of South Wales[1092] and Lady Cory's estranged husband with whom other notable London figures were entertained.[1093]

Among these too was Cardiff Mayor, Willie Pethybridge, who was "a man in demand for after-dinner speeches in political circles and was an intimate of Lloyd George." [1094]

Beyond giving attention to the two fussy Royal Princesses Helena and Marie-Louise, Guy Liddell lived a double life. He has been named as a

Soviet mole, a fact disputed by others, yet adding clearly about his dealings with the likes of Peter Churchill that he "was extremely careless in the company he kept".[1095]

Liddell's published diaries in the National Archives, Kew[1096] make no reference to Evan Morgan. At the time of Evan's Court Martial in 1943 Liddell's main pre-occupation is over *Operation Mincemeat*, more popularly remembered by the dramatic film *The Man Who Never Was*, a ploy to fool the Germans into believing that the Allied invasion of Europe would be through Italy and not France. [1097]

Since his death, Liddell's reputation has taken a battering. In several books he appears alongside stranger bedfellows who may or may not have been involved in a left-wing conspiracy between the world wars, and in later years, against the interests of this country. Studies of this group of men include the names of Liddell, Peter Churchill and Lord Louis Mountbatten, all cited as homosexuals, with others whose names have entered the great legends of treachery and spying for Russia, including Roger Hollis, Anthony Blunt, Guy Burgess, Kim Philby and Donald Maclean.[1098] These assertions are echoes of threads also set out by Robin Bryans in his books. Two other authors[1099] have repeated Bryans' charges (cited from interviews with him) implicating Mountbatten in all kinds of rogue play. [1100]

Bryans also claims that it was commonplace for Evan to accompany Henry Maxwell on gay sex and pleasure trips to Southern Ireland to Lord Mountbatten's Castle. Bryans highlights that Evan knew Mountbatten from an early age, and although many allegations are made about Mountbatten's homosexuality these have been well enough aired in other books, [1101] besides which at least one of Mountbatten's biographers dismisses suggestions that he had homosexual tendencies.[1102] Other books defend Mountbatten's corner but leave no doubt that Lord Louis and his wife Edwina were agile sexual predators.[1103]

Another duo of writers reveal a trail of debauchery, with Bryans named as the lover of Guy Burgess from 1944 and someone at the centre of knowledge and intrigue in the shady dealings of Anthony Blunt, from spying to cottaging.[1104] It is difficult to take it all seriously, beyond the fact that these sometimes hyped legends began to fester when the retired spy Peter Wright published his memoirs *Spycatcher*[1105] saying there was a fifth man in British Intelligence after the notorious quartet of Burgess, Maclean, Philby and Blunt. Robin Bryans gives himself credit for exposing SIS cover-ups over Blunt and other spies.

The Spanish Civil War: Evan and the Left

Peter, 2nd Viscount Churchill

As well as Evan's left wing friend Nancy Cunard's efforts in war-torn Spain, Peter Churchill was another involved in the anti fascist campaign trail; he collected money for much-needed medical supplies and travelled out to Spain as part of the Spanish Medical Aid Committee. [1106] Peter had succeeded his father as the 2nd Viscount Churchill in 1934. The deceased Viscount was once a favourite at Court, a former Lord Chamberlain and a bully. His fame rested in part from keeping undesirables out of the Royal enclosure at Ascot races and his dedication as Chairman of the Great Western Railway.

The new Viscount was at his peak, described as "tall, blond, full of charm, artistic. [Peter] had worked in films, written revue-sketches and did well on the New York stage." [1107] The flamboyant nobleman once had a lion skin made into a "novel coat". [1108]

When he returned to Britain the storm clouds were blowing in Germany and Spain. Peter chose this as an adventure and a cause to help the fight for freedom in Spain, along with several thousand other Britons who rose up in support of the democratically elected Republican government against the rebel Fascist forces of General Franco. A galaxy of writers and intellectuals also flocked here to claim their part in the liberation, and later write best sellers. [1109]Despite the international support Franco's forces (better trained and equipped) won the day, the General remaining in power for the following three decades.

Evan's half-cousin Esmond Romilly,[1110] (a rebel who, with his brother Giles, [1111]had revolted against school, family and tradition) was also among those who in 1936 enlisted in the International Brigade. He was invalided home, at which point he fell in love with Jessica Mitford [1112] and in an often-mentioned saga they eloped and married.[1113] Esmond was later killed serving in war operations over Germany with the Royal Canadian Air Force in 1941. The Romilly family papers [1114]show some slight contact between the Morgans, Carnegies and the Romilly clan. [1115] Evan's mother was one of the first to buy a hat from Esmond's mother Nellie[1116] after she set herself up as a milliner to London Society women. Nellie saw Evan from time to time and she attended his Memorial Service at Farm Street Church, on 7 May 1949.[1117]

During 1936-8 Evan was engaged in more personal issues to give any thought to his Communist friends and his relative fighting in Spain but he did send a donation of £21 to 'The Bishops' Committee for the Relief of Spanish Distress', who funded medical supplies for the wounded. [1118] Later onboard ship *en route* to the Canaries he encountered a group of Irish soldiers who were part of the Irish Brigade going off to fight in Spain. [1119] His observation on one "fine young fellow" [1120] - that Evan obviously took a shine to - was that "he was far too good to be wasted in that affair." [1121]

Evan and the Right Wingers
Evan's Friends Who Were Well Known to MI5 and MI6

At the end of the 1930s Evan's friend the artist Francis Rose feared for his life. Postcards sent by him to Cecil Beaton care of his solicitor leave no doubt. He stipulates "to be opened only in case of my death or disappearance". [1122] Rose served briefly in the RAF.

Lord William Sempill
The Man Who Once Spied for Japan

Evan's Eton contemporary, William Forbes-Sempill,[1123] provides another intriguing character who knew Evan very well; they were both closely associated with a Catholic body *The Society of St Augustine of Canterbury*.[1124] Evan and Sempill were present at many of the Society's receptions in London between 1926 and 1936.[1125]

Sempill's father John, the 18th Lord Sempill, was a respected ADC to King George V and who lived until 1934. This may have been a factor in the decision not to prosecute William over disclosing aviation secrets to the Japanese government in the 1920s, something that was only revealed after Sempill's death.

Sempill flew his planes throughout UK, Europe and the Far East, touring with his first wife (who died in 1935[1126]). He once tested the etiquette of the Royal Court by suggesting that Highland dress, namely the kilt and jabot, were a more appropriate form of Court dress for a Scotsman than knee breeches and a white tie. [1127]

When the Second World War came Sempill was serving in the Admiralty which gave him access to secret papers and plans. In the years before the war he had been a business consultant to a Japanese company. Suspicions were roused that Sempill was in receipt of money from Japanese sources in exchange for passing them information in the weeks leading up to the attack on Pearl Harbour. Although Sempill was implicated in passing on documents (for a second time) he was merely asked to resign his position.

Right Wing Clubs and Evan

Concurrently with serving non-British interests with his fondness for the Japanese (albeit he was in fact more impressed by their business know-how and aviation technology) Lord Sempill was also associated with *The Right Club*,[1128] taking his place alongside others in the British aristocracy who were unhealthily warm towards the Nazis' principles and at least desired a negotiated peace between Germany and Britain.

A greater number of those who were pro-German were members of the Anglo-German Fellowship which had existed from the mid 1930s to build up friendship between the two nations.[1129]

The Right Club included Lord Redesdale[1130] (who called Herr Hitler 'a right thinking man of irreproachable sincerity and honesty' [1131]) and Evan's half-cousin and fellow old Etonian, Charles, Lord Carnegie (later the 11th Earl of Southesk, who thought himself more a "very loyal and patriotic man" [1132] than a secret dealer working against British interests) and a more distant cousin, Randolph Stewart, the 12th Earl of Galloway. [1133]

Sempill was also a member of *The Link*,[1134] which also represented pro-German interests. He argued tirelessly in the House of Lords in favour of making peace with Adolf Hitler.

Despite the apparent links of such figures as Lord Carnegie, Lord Galloway and others who were related to Evan, examination of the various files released by the Security Services make no mention of Evan being a member of the *Anglo-German Fellowship*, [1135]the Right Club [1136] or *The Link*.[1137]

Spymaster Maxwell Knight made it one of his personal quests to hunt down and smash the more extreme members of *The Right Club* and *The Link*. Several of its members were interned during the Second World War under emergency Regulations rushed through Parliament. [1138] Knight's own account of his successes is detailed in a dossier in the National Archives, which again makes no reference to Evan Morgan.[1139]

In addition there is a entire lack of real substance and justification for inferences made by some commentators about Evan (and also

Princess Olga) having anything other than merely casual associations with a bad brood of dodgy foreigners and a string of wartime spies, including several Royal princesses, some with a scandalous or suspicious past who kept strange bedfellows, and a few who were later identified as working cunningly against Britain, for Germany.

Prince Danylo Skoropadsky

The handsome Prince Danylo Skoropadsky, [1140]son of the deposed Hetman of the Ukraine, [1141]is cited by Robin Bryans as one of Evan's lovers. Both men were devotees of the Russian ballet and saw each other there, but it seems *only* in the company of others. SIS had Prince Danylo's home, telephone line, movements and visitors under close surveillance. [1142]

Such women traitors as Anna Wolkoff [1143] (of White Russian extraction, her father Nicholas [1144] was a retired Admiral of the Tsar) who ran the Russian Tea Rooms in South Kensington[1145] with her father. She was a regular visitor to Germany and knew Rudolf Hess. [1146]

Since the Wolkoff's tearooms "served the finest caviar in London ....keeping visitors well lubricated with vodka"[1147] and since Evan's wife Olga was a White Russian related to the Tsar, it is possible they were acquainted (socially) with the Wolkoffs.

One writer[1148] makes a direct association between Olga and Stella Lonsdale[1149] (a double agent later interned in Britain) whose first husband was Nicolas Sidoroff (son of a White Russian, Prince Dimitri Magaloff). This overlap of the two women is not supported by any SIS or other textual reference and merits the same count as being only of a social glance status.

Whilst these individuals were probably known to Evan and Olga it was from the perchance of meeting them socially and not beyond a level of simply coming into contact with such people in large scale public venues when they were attempting ferociously to attach themselves like leeches to gain a foothold on the tail coat of any notable figure like Evan (and Olga), well placed in moving them around London Society portals.

Evan met all sorts of people by chance. He invited all kinds of people to wine and dine with him in a London hotel, restaurant, club or bar. A few of them received an offer of being spoilt as a weekend house guest at one or more of his colourful parties at Tredegar House. Here Evan assembled people from all walks of life.

The journalist Godfrey Winn, of the *Daily Mirror*, devotes several of his reports of 1936-37 to people tales from Tredegar Park. [1150]

Among the sights to enjoy at Evan's hospitable Welsh pile was a zoo with exotic pets including Alice, a honey bear and Somerset, a boxing kangaroo, as well as exotic birds and reptiles. The appeal of this collection (which was later removed to London Zoo [1151]) may have been of sufficient interest to entice a visit to Evan's sanctuary by animal lover Maxwell Knight.

Robin Bryans records "Evan Tredegar spent much more time with Max Knight of MI5 than he did with Aleister Crowley, for Max and Evan, apart from wanting to keep the wicked Commies in their place, were both deeply involved with zoology, writing books and the occult."[1152]

It is suggested that some guests arrived at Tredegar House unannounced, and remained unnamed and virtually incognito. Among those in this category during the pre-war period may have been the

Austrian Princess Stephane Hohenlohe, [1153] "London's leading Nazi hostess".[1154] A personal friend of Hitler and Goering, their very dear Princess, a "notorious intriguer",[1155] held court from a flat in Mayfair in the late 1930s where she ingratiated herself into the British upper classes, mixing with "the 'Cliveden set', a group centred around the Astors. Evan's friend William Teeling (who was a fellow Tory candidate with Evan in the East End in 1929) mentions the Princess in his memoirs.[1156] She was later interned in the USA and only released after the war was over.[1157]

Evan met members of the Hohenlohe dynasty as far back as his youth before the Great War when he accompanied his father to Cannes and Nice on board the yacht *Liberty*. [1158] One of these friendly chaps that appealed to Evan was a young seventeen-year-old Prince Max Hohenlohe, unmasked by SIS as a "gentleman agent" [1159] during the Second World War. [1160]

Lord Sempill visits Tredegar House

There is evidence demonstrating Evan's friendship too with Lord William Sempill, who (as indicated above) was another spy from the 1920s onwards.

Sempill visited Evan at Tredegar House at least twice in the pre-Second World War period, each time flying and landing his aeroplane at Tredegar Park, to great excitement from the local onlookers. There was no secrecy about the visits; they were mentioned in the *The Times, Court Circular*. Sempill's daughter Ann accompanied her father, perhaps on a mission of her own to explore a marriage plan with Evan. After Lois' death in 1937 Evan had a longing to procreate a son and heir, not least to keep his cousin John Morgan out of inheriting the family titles and Estate.

At one visit in 1938 Sempill was a guest with Evan at nothing more than a meeting of the local Bassaleg branch of the British Legion. Other guests included Lord Luke Annaly[1161] and Henry Maxwell, who were also spending the weekend with Evan at Tredegar House.

There was a threat of war overhanging events. Evan had a high regard for the British Legion and said at the meeting "that he always liked to be thought of by the British Legion. They were joined together in a demonstration of patriotism and love of King and country. " [1162]

Only a short time before, Evan and his deputy land agent and Secretary Captain Harry Ware had taken part in the mobilisation of members of the Legion to serve in the British Legion Volunteer Police Force, between 6 October and 15 October 1938. [1163]

Evan praised the Legion's involvement in being invited by the Germans and Czechs to keep peace in Europe.

He also painted a wonderful picture of almost leaving a half-eaten meal behind to join in on the action, travelling off to London (to swear an oath in a gathering of men at Olympia) and then travel down to the South coast:

"[I] was not allowed to have a batman, and took only what [we] could get in a kit- bag and carried it on [our] backs, [adding] …that his kit included a tin of Keatings[1164] and in the cabin which accommodated four in the ship off Southend
there was a squabble over false teeth and the only glass." [1165]

Evan said he had very proud memories of the "party of 52 Welsh boys who formed a choir and sang for two hours entertaining 500 men."
[1166]

'Mad' Jack Macnamara

Among others known to Evan associated with the widespread number of extreme right wing organisations was Jack Macnamara. [1167] He allegedly appears with Evan on a list of men who met together with a number of high ranking Nazi gays and extremists at a dining club at Bad Weisse near Munich in 1931, as previously mentioned. 'Mad' Jack was also an MP in Parliament in the years overlapping Evan's time as a peer in the House of Lords, as was Peter Churchill who inherited his father's Viscountcy in 1934, the same year as Evan inherited the Tredegar honours.

Macnamara engaged closely with Guy Burgess,[1168] whom he accompanied on a series of sex-tourist trips to pre-war Germany where both of them found the Hitler Youth offered more than just an adoration of the Fuhrer.[1169] Although Macnamara and Burgess had the same taste (as Evan) for young boys and indulged in flagellation there is no evidence that Evan was caught up in their exact same exploits, albeit boys were passed around, for abuse.[1170] Robin Bryans mentions Francis Rose as a further strand in the same gay cell as Macnamara who procured boys for a clergyman named Archdeacon Sharp and for others. [1171]

Within the walls of Parliament, the London theatres, clubs and restaurants, London offered a broad spectrum of different homosexual contacts lined up for Evan but he preferred picking up his own type of rough trade in casual pick-ups; these would often be soldiers near barracks and sailors near the docks. London was awash with easy pickings of such boys and young men of various nationalities, induced by offers of sex for cash or trinkets. There was only at worst the morning after to deal with, and sending the boy off back to his barracks or ship. Evan had a pass key to *The Cavendish Hotel* and this allowed him to act entirely alone. He did not need Macnamara (nor anyone else) to importune boys.

The conclusion is that Evan's presence in the same company as 'Mad' Jack Macnamara (who was killed in action in Italy in 1944) was not of any great or lasting significance beyond the alleged meeting at Bad Weisse in 1931. A file in National Archives on Macnamara shows that Winston Churchill took a close interest in the latter part of Mad Jack's army career after he had personally appealed to Churchill to be allowed to join a fighting regiment. [1172]

James Lonsdale Bryans
The Playboy Spy
Travels in Spain, Germany and the Far East

Evan's boyhood pal James Lonsdale Bryans was an avowed admirer of General Franco, hence Evan ended the 1930s with two of his longest and closest friends in opposing political camps: Lonsdale Bryans on the extreme right, Peter Churchill, on the extreme left.

Like Evan, Lonsdale Bryans was another consumptive. He spent several seasons (for the benefit of his health) in warmer climes including spells in Majorca, in the Balearic Islands. He was living there in 1936 at the outbreak of the Spanish Civil War but soon abandoned this base, influenced by the stampede of other British residents leaving. [1173]

A whirlwind tour [1174] began then for Lonsdale Bryans, travelling three months through the Balkans with several months in Belgium and Luxemburg. He was in Berlin in August-September 1938 and saw Hitler standing up waving in his car *en route* to make one of his rousing speeches at the *Portpalast,* giving the Czechs an ultimatum to accept German occupation of the Sudetenland. A month later this event saw Evan volunteer as a part of the British Legion's initiative over installing a neutral Police force there to bring stability back to the region.

Hitler's increasing menace prompted Lonsdale Bryans to return to Britain but he left a fortnight later for the USA, followed by spending time in the Far East, arriving in Bali in December 1938 where he remained until April 1939.

Meanwhile, as Britain was poised for war, the newly-engaged Evan, Viscount Tredegar, concerned himself with more domestic matters in Newport, South Wales, with several newspaper photographs of him showing Olga off to the rank and file of local civic and sporting clubs. Evan raised morale and for once took an interest in his Welsh lands.

Lonsdale Bryans and Evan seem to have become estranged after visiting Germany in the late 1920s and early 1930s. They had enjoyed time together in Tangier in late 1933 and Lonsdale Bryans maintained regular rooms for himself in London at the *Wellington Club*[1175] and at *Brookes Club* in London's plush St James'. According to Robin Bryans, his namesake, Lonsdale (or "Jim" when referred to by his first name), became a globetrotter; he was well known in the social circles of a number of influential international businessmen. This included Jack Bryans from aviation circles, joint founder of British Continental Airways, [1176] and Sir Hubert Miller,[1177] with whom Lonsdale Bryans often stayed in Venice. Lonsdale Bryans also travelled in the Far East with Jimmy Donahue, [1178] a homosexual, who was a close friend of Wallis Simpson and her husband, the Duke of Windsor.

Lonsdale Bryans had always dreamed of being a diplomat. His health prevented it, his role as an amateur peace mediator from 1939 onwards being his finest hour. During his travels around the globe he was also compiling research for "an extensive work on the anthropological origins and future of the human species." [1179] This was later published as a bizarre and complicated book called *The Curve of Fate: On the Evolution of Man.* [1180]

Evan and Lonsdale Bryans in Bali in 1939

Princess Olga, Evan's Second Wife

Olga and Evan on Honeymoon

In 1939 Evan was mourning the death of Pope Pius XI but his plans to marry Princess Olga, and a wedding trip to the Far East, meant he was cheered by this and the prospect of a rare reunion with his old friend Jim Lonsdale Bryans during the honeymoon tour of islands of the East Indies. On Bali, Lonsdale Bryans was well acquainted with Evan's beach home of *"Soeran Segara"* [1181] and of Evan being referred to there by the name of *Tuan Raja*. [1182]

Lonsdale Bryans: Peacemaker or Troublemaker

James Lonsdale Bryans appears on the official ships passenger lists; arriving back in London on 25 August 1939, he made straight for *Brookes Club*, St James.[1183]

War meant an irresistible chance for the manic, opportunistic Lonsdale Bryans to aim to secure an illustrious place in the history of the world as a peacemaker between Britain and Germany. One good advantage for the would-be spy (whose trade mark was wearing his old Eton school tie) was that he also spoke fluent Italian and German.

Official records show that he first "came to the notice of [SIS] in 1939 when he claimed to be acting on behalf of the [British] Foreign Office and certain members of the aristocracy[1184] in attempting to meet von Ribbentrop[1185] and Hitler to put out peace feelers with Germany". [1186]

The plan, in a nutshell, (agreed by Lord Halifax of the British Foreign Office) was for the amateur spy Lonsdale Bryans to coax Ulrich von Hassell, [1187] the one-time German Ambassador in Italy 1932-1938 and a member of the German Resistance (both Lonsdale Bryans and Evan had met him socially in Rome in the mid 1930s and whose identity is coded in all matters between Lonsdale Bryans and SIS etc as 'Charles') into overthrowing the Fuhrer.

Lonsdale Bryans was successful in tracing the whereabouts of von Hassell; they met together in 1940 in Switzerland, ("a hotbed of Gestapo agents"[1188]) when the somewhat farcical proposal was for a pact between Germany and the British Empire. Germany would control Europe, Britain the rest of the world.

Lonsdale Bryans figures importantly in *The Von Hassell Diaries*[1189] as 'Mr X'.

The plan went cold and Lonsdale Bryans made a fool of himself by demanding to see military leaders and the British Prime Minister to discuss his preparations with von Hassell. None of this stopped Hitler's spies unearthing things and von Hassell was later executed as one of the ringleaders of the July Plot of 1944.

There are several versions of the tale of failure, with Lonsdale Bryans' own account published in 1951 as a book *Blind Victory*.[1190] A Secret Service file on him shows that whilst Lord Halifax (the British Foreign Secretary) was dazzled by Lonsdale's plan, another view from inside the Cabinet from people like Sir Alec Cadogan[1191] was that Lonsdale Bryans was "indiscreet" and he was more of a troublemaker than a peacemaker. After the war there was still a faction within MI5 who deeply distrusted Lonsdale Bryans's motives and integrity. [1192]

Evan and the Home Guard

While Lonsdale Bryans was spinning across occupied Europe Evan languished on the Home Front.

Protecting the Home Front was a vital part of the war effort during the Second World War. Those who became part of what TV portrayed with humour and pathos as *Dad's Army* served their local communities bravely and well.

Evan was far from content serving the war effort with the Home Guard in Monmouthshire. There is a passing reference to his work in the Local Defence Volunteers (LDVs) in a local war history[1193] and a brief passing reference to him speaking in the House of Lords in a debate about LDVs. [1194]

To gasps all round Evan agitated through friends and former colleagues in the War Office to be given any small part of the much bigger, strategic wartime picture, in London, citing his readiness to lead with his past links to the Welsh Guards and playing a leading role in the 17th London (Tower Hamlets Rifles), a regiment (like that of the Monmouthshire) in London's East End where Evan was an Honorary Colonel.[1195] In earlier days he thought nothing of being out overnight, under canvas. [1196]

Evan saw himself as at least the calibre of one of the nation's commanders. However, in reality the army registers listed E F Morgan as only a Second Lieutenant who was released from military service with that lowly officer rank twenty years before, in 1919. Anything else Evan claimed as ranks were merely courtesy ranks customarily given to the local squire or landowner.

There was work for Evan to do in the Home Guard: standards to maintain and exercises to plan and carry out so as to ensure if Hitler invaded South Wales he was met with gallant resistance. After the phoney war of digging and maintaining the local defences with building of shelters and helping to ensure the wartime regulations affecting civilians was superintended, there was everything from the blackout restrictions to attending at fire drills and generally guarding possible enemy targets. Otherwise it was drilling, marching and keeping fit. There was always a new campaign to induce a high degree of readiness to tackle the Hun. Between this there was the nightly parade; many of the exercises were held in Tredegar Park.

One of these that was recorded is "War Weapons Week" at the end of February 1941. Newport's Mayor, Alderman J H Swallow, JP, sent a letter of appreciation and thanks to Evan saying "I should like to express my appreciation of your co-operation in the organisation of last Saturday's parade and the manner in which the Home Guard under your command attended. I should also like to compliment you on the martial bearing and soldierly efficiency of the Home Guards and to ask you to be good enough to convey to the officers and men my sincere thanks for a most inspiring display." [1197]

The career break finally came for Evan in early 1942, when it was announced that "Viscount Tredegar had been officially informed that [he had] relinquished command of a Monmouthshire Battalion of the Home Guard on the grant to him of a commission as a second lieutenant in the Royal Corps of Signals."[1198]

Evan sent a message to express "regret at severing his connection with the Home Guard, with whom he has spent a very happy period."[1199]

Off went Evan to London to his new post. He returned to his old links with the Home Guard after he left the army in 1943, although this period is not reflected in very many public appearances or his personal involvement in parades or local civic functions in Newport or London. He is noticeably missing from the events leading to the standing down of the Home Guard in 1944. He may have spent some time at *Honeywood House* but there hangs a mystery of exactly where Evan was living.

Evan: Gay Martyr?

Evan The Martyr?

Before the stand down of 1944 Evan officially severed his links with the Monmouthshire Home Guard on the grounds of ill-health,[1200] and during a period of closure of Tredegar House his exact whereabouts are unclear. Explanations for this absence range from him being seen taking

241

part in military operations in Holland at the time of the Battle of Arnhem [1201] (almost like a stray member of some 'Dirty Dozen' [1202] brigade), to Evan languishing in a prison cell, as much a victim as Oscar Wilde, after being sent down for committing "unnatural practices ". [1203]

"Evan Morgan (Lord Tredegar) is doing five years for unnatural practices and that young Herbert is in a similar scrape for the same class of depravity. It must have been kept out of the news very well." [1204]

When Evan communicated his regrets to severing his links with the Home Guard in November 1944 saying he could not take part in any further activities due to ill health, was he a guest of the King at Cardiff, Wandsworth or Pentonville prison? If he was, Evan never uttered a single word of being a gay martyr, unlike his hero, Oscar Wilde, who revelled in making speeches from the witness box.

Robin Bryans offers some further clues, explaining how he may have been caught in a compromising situation with Evan at Cardiff Docks, leading to Evan's arrest.

He explains: "the police had to do something so they decided on action more effective than a fine or a binding-over. The police questioned me for hours about my involvement and whether any sexual contact had occurred between Lord Tredegar and me..." [1205]

However, if Evan was incarcerated he did not serve a sentence and must have been released within days, weeks or months of being arrested, after he had been taught a sharp lesson by the police or of his (genuinely) failing health or by intervention from on high. Either way Evan was crushed. He was never the same man or carefree personality ever again.

There were ramifications for others too. Bryans writes "At Evan's downfall, which sparked off a homosexual witch-hunt among the toffs, Robin Chester (who acted for Evan as his lawyer) found himself facing a panic rush of men [1206] who knew Evan".

Filling Some Gaps Between 1944 and 1946

Strange as it seems, about the same time Robin Bryans highlights Evan's participation in providing a "fantastic" [1207] wedding reception for Ruth Crossley[1208] (the sister of an old deceased MP friend, Anthony Crossley[1209]), married to a Polish Military Attache in London, a Lt. Konstanty Scheuhert, [1210] on 9 November 1944, at Brompton Oratory.

Despite this generosity, there is stark evidence of some financial strains on Evan in 1945, with the removal of a good deal of the family silver from Tredegar House for its sale in a London auction house. Although there are reports elsewhere of Evan staging large-scale parties at the war's end, this period from 1945 was the beginning of the end for Evan.

Evan's regular attendance at the bedside of Bosie Douglas also dipped in the last months of the Douglas' life. [1211] There are four letters (from 1945) in the British Library[1212] from Bosie to Evan which largely deal with Bosie's deterioration ("so dreadfully ill again") [1213] and saying thanks for Evan's treats of grapes and chicken: he fondly describes Evan as "the kindest friend I ever had". [1214]

But Bryans says Evan neglected his friend: "Evan no longer brought the best of champagne and his favourite young men to lie at the feet of ageing Lord Alfred Douglas..."[1215]

Bosie died on 20 March 1945 and Evan attended the funeral three days later.[1216] One of the other attendees was the actor Donald Sinden, who writes in his memoirs "Not more than ten of us gathered at his graveside in Crawley as we buried Oscar's 'Rose-lipped youth'." [1217]

Evan arrived last bearing a very large, sprawling wreath and a bunch of flowers. [1218]

Harold Nicolson's Snub of Bosie Douglas

alfred Douglas.

The influential Harold Nicolson always disapproved of Evan's lifestyle. He disappointed Evan over his lacklustre attitude towards financially supporting the call to rescue the decline and poverty during the last years of Bosie Douglas. In the 1940s Evan's campaign (with Marie Stopes and others) to secure a Civil List pension for Bosie became their united crusade. Later Nicolson also declined the invitation to join the committee assembled by Evan and Marie Stopes to push the idea of proclaiming Douglas the greatest sonneteer since Shakespeare. Harold doubted the judgment of the duo's entire proposition, considering it (along with Evelyn Waugh, who had also been approached by Evan[1219]) quite preposterous. [1220]

Both Evan and Nicolson were members of the *Royal Society of Literature* and shared membership of several London Clubs. Occasionally they sought the sanctuary offered for VIPs at the London's *Ritz Hotel*, as a safe place to shelter during the height of the Blitz. Evan had an office nearby (when he was attached as a Major at MI 14) and maintained a bachelor flat at Albany, in Piccadilly. Harold was an MP and worked in Whitehall in the thick of wartime propaganda under Brendan Bracken and Alfred Duff Cooper in the Ministry of Information and he also later lived at Albany. The two shared a cosy chat and a drink until the 'all clear' sounded, then toddled off on their separate ways. Nicolson had become (unlike Evan) a respected homosexual amongst the consortium of other gay and bisexual men in the political establishment. The gay brigade's charm school centred on others (like Evan) that were less discreet but more congenial than Evan, even although this embraced in the grouping some esoteric fellow MPs of Harold including three parliamentarians: Bob Boothby, Tom Driberg and Henry "Chips" Channon,[1221] who also craved the company and sex with underage youths.

Everyone but Evan avoided Francis Rose, who was even less discreet than Evan with his pick ups. After a night spent with rough trade Evan liked taking Rose to breakfast at the *Ritz* and often ran into Nicolson:

"Food rationing at that period of the war had become severe and when a polite young waiter asked if his Lordship would like an egg for breakfast, Evan demanded in his most supercilious and irritating manner that eggs *plural*, and bacon be brought." [1222]

By the end of the Second World War, Evan and Harold Nicolson were finally estranged; they hardly ever met one another again.

Evan Forgets His Script

Old friend Cecil Roberts saw for himself how Evan was a shadow of himself, although Evan was still naughty. The occasion was a Foyle's Literary lunch:

"I took the chair at a Foyle's Lunch to introduce the speaker, Lord Tredegar. He was *mechant,* as so often. He changed his announced subject and bored the audience by reading a lecture he had given elsewhere on Donne the poet. I took Lady [Emerald] Cunard with me.

"What a dreary bore Evan was – and he can be so bright!" was her comment. I scolded him for his behaviour. We could not know that he would die within three years of cancer, at the age of fifty-five. It was a loss; he was a vivid, bizarre personality."[1223]

Chapter 10

Evan's Last Friendships
Evan's disciples

Richard Buckle: Ballet Critic

Dicky Buckle was a talented designer of sets and made his name as a ballet critic and biographer.[1224] Evan saw in the boy a resemblance with Rex Whistler, who had also been an accomplished and stylish décor and costume maker for the ballet. Buckle lodged with Evan in London in 1940 before he went to war; he spent three years of the Second World War serving with the Scots Guards in Italy and from 1943 in Egypt. He caught up with Evan at Chelsea Barracks in March 1943 when Evan was awaiting Court Martial.

When the war finished, and on being demobbed, Buckle renewed his job as a ballet critic and rekindled his old acquaintance with Evan, spending "a few mad weekends… [at Honeywood House] in Surrey..."[1225]

The relationship between them was intimate. When Buckle was not on "hurried trips to Paris on ballet business, weekends in Oxford or

Brighton [or at his] mother's in Norfolk" [1226] he was with Evan at Honeywood during long stretches of 1946 to 1948.

Dicky Buckle with some lady friends

Aleister Crowley's best biographer, John Symonds, records a visit to Honeywood in the summer of 1948: "The eccentric Evan Morgan…invited Freda Harris and me to stay for a weekend with him at Honeywood House… there were several other guests. One of [them] …who seemed to be a permanent guest, was a young male ballet dancer, Tredegar doted on him." [1227] The chances are this is a reference to Dicky Buckle.

A special friendship between Dicky Buckle, Evan and the Conte Tony Mattei [1228] that had begun in the 1930s was another overlap that touched on mutual appreciation and secret love. Like Evan, Tony was a Papal Chamberlain of Cape and Sword.

Shared Friends

The author and Lauretta at Honeywood House, Horsham, by Jean Hugo

Evan welcomed several of Dicky Buckle's relatives and friends into his mother's Surrey home including Lauretta (Laura) Hope -Nicholson[1229] and her husband Jean Hugo, [1230] both fine artists who moved in the very coveted circles alongside the great personalities of 20th Century European art and literature, including Picasso, Dali, Cocteau and Cecil Beaton. Laura had a passion for Russian ballet (Buckle's forte, he secretly loved Laura), she was a member of a eccentric family; her mother and brother Felix[1231] (who was adored by Evan and as a young boy came under Evan's influence;[1232] in later life Felix was a "reclusive aesthete" [1233]) and lived in a house at Tite Street, Chelsea, with links to Oscar Wilde.[1234] Laura's sister Marie-Jaqueline Lancaster wrote a biography of Evan's irritating friend Brian Howard,[1235] another consumptive and another doomed to take his own life after the grief of losing a lover. He is also recalled for being shocked by the level of debauchery at one of Evan's parties that he described as "so stupendously naughty." [1236] Howard (a well known Society prankster) much annoyed Evan's mother Katharine by playing up to her hobby of making birds nests, [1237] by pushing leaves and twigs and branches of trees through the letter box of her London home. Another joke was for

Howard to stand inside a doorway waiting for Evan to pass by and then suddenly surprise him.

Laura Hope-Nicholson became assistant editor of the *Burlington Magazine* and later helped Buckle to produce his Ballet magazine, [1238] which he began producing (financially assisted by Evan) just before going to war.

There was a shared friendship too with Evan and Buckle and a young baronet, Johnnie Philipps. [1239] Buckle spent holidays at the Philipps family pile at Picton Castle[1240] "in the wild extremities of Wales." [1241]

Buckle reveals the hidden truth about Johnnie Philipps (who was another who gave financial support to the rising ballet critic[1242]):

"Philipps [described as "a loveable and witty personality"[1243]] came of an old and rather eccentric Welsh family. He had two castles in Pembrokeshire and a lot of land ...[but] the life of a dilettante was more to his taste than that of a squire, he spent more time at his flat in Albany [Piccadilly] than at remote, romantic Picton..".[1244]

Bachelor Johnnie was doomed to die young: "...he was far from strong, bouts of depression, with days of crazy gaiety. In November 1948, exhausted, he fell asleep and died in his bath." [1245] He was 33. Here is another example (along with other friends) among Evan's circle to die in mysterious or similarly sinister circumstances. The toll of dead friends greatly depressed Evan. Bryans reports that Evan himself contemplated suicide.

A verdict of "Death by Misadventure" [1246] was recorded at the inquest that followed on Philipps, the pronouncement being that the baronet (whose life was depleted by drug addiction) "had a poor heart condition which might have caused faintness and giddiness". [1247]

Olga Tredegar (she used her title of Viscountess Tredegar for the rest of her life) attended Johnnie's memorial service in London[1248] - Evan was abroad on account of his own desperate state of health. Olga was accompanied by her fellow Russian, Prince Nicholas Galitzine, [1249] and Evan's loyal friend Baron George Marochetti.[1250]

Baron George Marochetti

While several of Evan's closest and earliest male friends (like Peter Churchill and James Lonsdale Bryans) saw very much less him, some relationships faded away all together. George Marochetti was one unfailing, endearing figure from his childhood at Windsor Castle, Evan, as boy-Page, George as the small, impressionable son of an artist commissioned to paint several of the Royal courtiers of the era, including Peter Churchill. George ever remained at close quarters for to support Evan *in extremis* (and also shore up Olga) throughout the 1940s. No task was too much for George where Evan was involved, he loved him always and without fault or question.[1251]

Possible Marriage: Evan's Female Admirers Line Up

To Evan's horror his cousin John Morgan (son of Frederic George Morgan, Courtenay's brother) was being fast groomed as the heir to the Tredegar Estates.

James Lees-Milne[1252] describes John as "absurdly pompous and puffed up with his own self- importance."

In September 1946 Evan was buoyed up briefly when he told one friend he was contemplating marriage again.[1253] There were several women in the wings that would have considered Evan's matrimonial terms.

Shane Leslie lamented "Perhaps it was a tragedy that [Evan] had not married Nancy Cunard, seeming so winsomely suited..." [1254]

Besides Nancy Cunard a handful of women, all close to Nancy, admired Evan; well, at least his wit and wealth! Some saw him as a conquest; in Nancy's case it was not about seducing Evan, she merely wished the title of Lady Tredegar but other females thought they could perhaps mother him or tame him and even bed him. One of the latter sort was Wyn Henderson who managed Nancy Cunard's *Hours Press* in Paris and London until the two, equally highly charged assertive women, clashed and parted. Wyn became a figure around Bloomsbury, engaging herself "with notable people, millionaires, surrealist painters, actors and musicians." [1255] She was a close friend of Dylan Thomas, who was often to be found at Wyn's cottage at Polgigga, in Cornwall, a couple of miles from Land's End. Robin Bryans is hostile towards her, commenting "mistress of many [Wyn Henderson] was certainly no friend of Evan Tredegar, one of the millionaires she failed to seduce." [1256]

Lady Hazel Lavery,[1257] second wife of the painter Sir John Lavery, [1258] was a great friend of Nancy's mother Emerald, her "nymph-like beauty contrasting oddly with her Edwardian manner and style of dressing"; [1259] she was another, older woman always full of kindly, maternal advice for Evan. The Laverys were frequent guests of Evan at Phyllis Court, a Regency house near Henley Bridge on the River Thames that had been converted into a riverside club. [1260]

A further hopeful Lady Tredegar was the novelist, and friend of George Orwell, Inez Holden, [1261] who "was said to have talked of marrying"[1262] Evan. Inez had at least something in common for, like Evan, her parents could not agree with each other.[1263] She also had a reputation (like Evan) for gossip "of a high and fantastical category". [1264]

Sadly, despite Evan confiding in a friend that he was "toying with the thought of proposing to Lady Illingsworth", [1265] he never married again, leaving his Uncle Freddie and then cousin John Morgan to succeed. [1266]

Evan's Melancholy

Towards the end of his life Evan was struck hard by melancholy, with one of his weekend visitors recalling years afterwards, "Lord Tredegar was witty, very well read and cynical... he believed that [financially] he had been ruined and knew that he was old." [1267] Evan was still only in his mid-fifties at this time but his last illness had taken a grip.

The death sentence of terminal cancer hanging over him had the effect on hastening his return to the Catholic faith. He spent more time in Ireland where he found some peace and quiet and he wanted to explore Irish citizenship. His excursions to *Castle Monaghan* (the family seat of the Leslies [1268]) and to his favourite spots on the West Coast were spiritually uplifting experiences. Yet, although he still carried his own followers of young men on these trips, he cut a lonely figure walking in the countryside with his constant attachment to his rosary beads providing some comfort and which aided his contemplation.

Of the grim morrow's terrors He reviewed
And with His Father the great pact renewed.

When love hides in a mist
Of passing moods of gloom;
Yet there is ever room
For the sun's return!

Evan Frederic Morgan

Chapter 11

What happened to Evan's Closest Coterie?
Some Sad Endings

Nina Hamnett

Nina Hamnett: Self Portrait

Poor Nina. She met her tragic death in 1956 when she overbalanced accidentally and fell from a window of her Paddington flat. [1269]But was it an accident? Some believed it was a curse beyond the grave from Evan's kindred spirit, the Satanist Aleister Crowley, who had famously sued Nina for libel over her portrayal of his evil Temple of Thelema at Cefalu, Sicily in her book *Laughing Torso*. Nina alleged that Crowley "was supposed to practise Black Magic, and one day a baby was said to have disappeared"[1270] at Thelema, a community that attracted visitors from all parts of the world until it was closed down by the Italian authorities. Nina won the case against her with ease. Crowley (dubbed "the worst man in the world") enjoyed the limelight. An accomplished self-publicist of extremes, Crowley had dabbled in sex and magic rituals his whole life. His denials were a text book tissue of lies. The "Beast 666", "The Master Therion" and "The Master" (three of Crowley's assumed designations) received a priceless wave of publicity and he and his followers rejoiced. However Crowley was made bankrupt in 1935.

Nancy Cunard

Poor Nancy. She met her tragic death in 1965 after a period of mental illness during which she had plunged into irreversible bad physical health and was set on a mission of self destruction. She was found penniless on a Paris street and taken to hospital where she died a few days later.

She was "an alcoholic nymphomaniac" records one reviewer of a book on Nancy. [1271] We learn of the real Nancy from a host of her biographers, that there was more to her than her drink problem and sexual appetite, especially for black jazz musicians and prize fighters. She was the muse of many of the poets, painters and writers of Evan's era.

Peter Churchill

Poor Peter. In his last years he was impoverished and in failing health. He became part of a washed-out old brigade of down-in-their-luck *'has beens'* in Brighton where, at the town's *Bristol Bar,* he held court with friends including the actresses Flora Robson and Hermione Baddeley. To hushed concerns in a variety of establishment circles, Peter was working on a second volume of his memoirs, to add more to all his remembered sins. Alas, it seems the manuscript disappeared or was stolen. Robin Bryans links the crime to the later events of his own run-ins with the authorities. Bryans was working with Peter on this new book project and remarked that the manuscript may have been destroyed to prevent details of Peter's homosexual love affairs and his connections with the Intelligence services being revealed.

In 1964, with the publication of *All My Sins Remembered,* Peter portrays a moving portrait of the last days of the writer and Peter's lover, the enigmatic writer, Malcolm Lowry. [1272] Malcolm drank himself to death in a dingy boarding house.

After the death of Peter's first wife (his mother's companion Katherine) who (like Malcolm) killed herself in 1943, whilst Peter was later in America he met Joan Black whom Peter describes as "beautiful, vulnerable, impossible and fantastically loyal, with a child's clear wisdom and the confused values of a contradictory grown-up; [she] was about the most human person I had ever known in my life."[1273] The couple lived in California, later moving back to London and then they later lived in Sussex. Joan died in 1957, the same year that Peter lost Malcolm Lowry.

Robin Bryans saw Peter his later years and the two of them spent much time together at Rottingdean, with memories to recall about their heyday there with Evan and others.

Peter Spencer, 2nd Viscount Churchill died on 21st December 1973 at the age 83. The title passed to his half-brother.

James Lonsdale Bryans

Poor Jim. Much of the life of James Lonsdale Bryans after the death of Evan is unknown. He was working on an autobiography, which was never published, and he enjoyed painting. Not surprisingly he became an inmate of a house set up "for impoverished gentlefolk living out sad, brave lives under the shadow of Windsor Castle."[1274]

These remarks above are from some brief passing references to Jim in a book called *The Kiss: The Story Of An Obsession* [1275] which reveals, as with Evan's other clique members, another notably harsh final curtain. "Jim Lonsdale Bryans shuffled off to Hellesdon Hospital, near Norwich. He became a victim of senile osteoporosis and senile dementia. He died in the hospital on 25 January 1981 aged eighty-seven, leaving so little that no one bothered to take out a grant of probate." [1276]

Lord George Rodney

Memorial to George, the first Boy Scout

Poor George. Among all those close Eton chums of Evan several of them had died young, including George's younger brother, James. George had married and lived out his life in Canada, where he and his wife Marjorie reared a family and maintained a ranch in Alberta, largely a 1000 acre pig farm. He was the only contemporary of Evan among the Eton coterie of Peter Churchill, James Lonsdale Bryans and Robin Chester[1277] to take a wife and have children. The Rodneys had experienced a generation of hard work and harsh weather, helped by a long line of stray aristocrats and Evan cronies working on the farm.

After Evan's death in 1949, Robin Bryans spent four years in Canada with the Rodneys, lying low. Many of Evan's secrets were expunged during this period; damaging documents and lurid sex photographs were located, seized and destroyed for fear of a backlash from noble, Royal and society contacts of Evan and his circle. Blackmailers were paid off or silenced.

George's memories of Evan were not confined to their Eton days together. Evan had been a visitor to the Rodneys in Canada in the 1920s. The visit still made the hairs on George's head stand up. "You should have seen Evan at the Calgary Stampede". Any sort of adventure roused Evan, but Calgary's combination of wild young horses and wild young cowboys in Stetsons and tight jeans thrilled him more than most things and he found the chuck wagon races in Stampede Week at Calgary much more exciting than accompanying Queen Mary during

Ascot Week. And so did his friend, David, known then as Edward, Prince of Wales." [1278] The Rodneys farmed until retiring in 1960. The couple were leaders of the Boy Scout and Girl Guide movements in Alberta, Lady Marjorie Rodney becoming the first Alberta Provincial Commissioner of the Girl Guides.

Marjorie, Lady Rodney died in 1968. George Bridges Harley Guest Rodney, 8th Baron Rodney, died in 1973.

Memorial to Lord George Rodney

Chapter 12

Epilogue on Robin Bryans

"Hundreds of pages of unstructured rant in which he does not distinguish clearly between what he personally knows and what he has picked up from other sources."

This quote was one man's judgement on *The Dust Has Never Settled*, Robin Bryans' first book of autobiography.

Can the testimony of Robin Bryans be treated seriously? Across his four volumes of autobiography the very many statements that have been examined have thrown up truths, half-truths and untruths. At the end of the day the reader must make up their own mind as to whether some, all or none of it is credible on the basis of both Bryans' account and this appraisal.

Bryans attracted trouble over the last few decades of his life; he became better known for personal attacks on a number of prominent citizens than as his calling as a writer. Something in Bryans' make-up led him to turn against order in his life and he became pre-occupied with exposing (as he saw it) the hypocrisy of many in public office who had led wicked private lives, especially homosexuals who were in the closet.

Much of Bryans' outspoken comments and actions, especially about certain clergymen, literary editors, and judges (many of these individuals are now dead) can be found on the Internet and in a number of publications, already referred to in some of the End Notes section of this book.

Despite Bryans' constant battles against these people, folk who were probably more likely to be guilty as charged rather than innocent lambs, his methods of scorning them through hate mail campaigns and "Letters" to the press usually fell on deaf ears. Bryans used many further dirty tricks and vile acts to bring the villains (as he saw them) to the public's attention. He was not always allowed to be heard, although some factions of the anti- establishment press e.g. *Private Eye Magazine* did heed his cries. But the law came tumbling down on Bryans on several occasions and he went to prison as a result of his own actions, including for contempt of court. He continued to lash out on several people using words, and even with his fists at times. He could be disagreeable, some said mad, a thorn in the flesh of the mighty, whilst others merely shuffled him off as an eccentric. He was subject to numerous gagging orders (writs) by individuals and officialdom.

Bryans strongly believed that Britain was (and he would say still is) in the control of an 'Old Boys network' and that certain allied groups of these cronies in Whitehall, the Universities, the Courts, civil authorities and in Parliament have omnipotence over us all, and some of these factions can ruthlessly and systematically cover things up and have brought down past British governments.

I have stayed clear of this huge minefield and of appraising in detail any of Bryans' later assaults with his barrage of claims against high ranking politicians, clergymen and judges. I think that needs to be the focus of another publication.

Beyond doubt there is very much in the early memoirs, travel and other writings of Robin Bryans (and the titles published under Robert Harbinson) for to enjoy. I warmly recommend that series of books to the reader.

Robin Bryans

APPENDIX 1

PETS OF **LORD TREDEGAR'S SON AND HEIR**

Evan Frederic Morgan 1893-1949

How Some People Saw Evan

Writer J C Squire: The Honeysuckle and the Bee, 1938.

"At Bath we established contact with Evan Morgan, who was at that moment staying in a hotel and whom we found in a vast room of which the

windows were sealed and the floor covered with newspapers because he was travelling with a flock of birds."

Portrait Painter, Augustus John: Letters 1915

'Evan Morgan has joined the Welsh Guards but his figure has to be altered slightly to meet the regulations, so he is now being stretched in various ways.'

Author D J Taylor in his book 'Bright Young People' says:

"Evan Morgan, later Lord Tredegar, at one time a friend of Firbank — Firbank's nickname for him was 'Heaven Organ' "

Novelist, Virginia Woolf: Diary 19 November 1917

Virginia Woolf

'Evan Morgan, a little red absurdity, with a beak of a nose, no chin and a general likeness to a very callow but student Bantam cock, who has run to legs and neck. However he was evidently most carefully prepared to be a poet and an eccentricity, both by his conversation, which aimed at irresponsible brilliance, and lack of reticence and by his clothes, which

must have been copied from the usual Shelley picture. But he was as innocent as a chicken and so foolish that it didn't seem to matter."

Novelist Aldous Huxley: Letter of Aldous Huxley to Juliette Baillot 1917

[Evan]... 'is an adventurous person, a man of action, and he is very salutary in stirring up my contemplative lethargy – with the result we have the greatest fun'

London Magazine, Volume 35.

'Somerset Maugham was in Salzburg, who flirted verbally with Giles [Romilly], and there were some notorious international buggers like [Evan] Lord Tredegar. 'Private faces in public places' would have been Stephen's [Spender's] motto. '

Alan Pryce-Jones, Literary Critic: Memoirs

After being warned by his father *"that there exists a man named Evan Morgan...And [his father continued] I tell you here and now that should you ever find yourself in the same room you are to leave immediately".*

The young Pryce-Jones soon did meet Evan. In his memoirs *The Bonus of Laughter*, he records:

"I was agog. Evan was at that time in his thirties. He was tall and very thin, with odd disarticulated movements, as if preparing to spread wings in flight....his complexion was a little hectic – his voice had a lilt to it. And his speech was often broken by a snort as he took another pinch of snuff."

Various Newspaper etc items:-

"A poet who works very hard is Lieutenant the Hon. Evan Morgan, Lady Tredegar's soldier-poet son. He has just finished one book (Fragments of Verse) and has made up his mind that the next is to be called Stardust.

Of Algiers Evan writes "olive and eucalyptus groves, cacti and aloes, lavender and wild orchids, with mimosa and almond flowering above and asphodel making a carpet beneath......

He has had exciting adventures with hostile Arabs. Once his car was burned in the desert and he narrowly escaped death. When he was disguised as a Moor in Algiers he was detected and flung out of a mosque."

Evan declared in The Daily Express of 6 November 1928 his most exciting moment...

"Driving a car over the Atlas Mountains by night! While in the Sahara I received a message from my mother saying that my house [in Grosvenor Square] had been burned down. Being anxious to return to England with all speed, I took the route over the Atlas. It proved a most exciting trip, as we had a narrow escape of driving over a precipice."

Evan Morgan, Lord Tredegar, reported that Ronald Firbank invariably covered his eyes with his handkerchief when he passed a butcher shop.

And he always skirted Covent Garden in order to avoid the massacre of flowers.

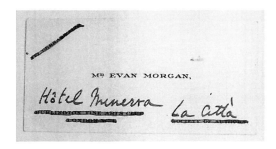

Evan's Temporary Calling Card in Rome c 1922

"And in my dream I heard voices—voices speaking in an unknown tongue. I threw out my arm to stop a fleeting shadow, and suddenly awoke. Upon the sands were six native boys, the eldest was perhaps seventeen. They were playing some game, the rules of which were secret to me. Their clothes were lying in a heap under the reeds, and, bronzed and naked, they played in the sun, leaping into the sea, over rocks, over each other. They wrestled, they rolled in the sand, they buried each other, and swam races through the filmy ripples.

Laughter filled the air—filled my heart; youth reigned supreme, tyrant over a scene of incredible beauty. Close to me the eldest lad, all sinews and muscle, was keeping two younger boys at bay with the shaft of one of the reeds, his white teeth gleaming half with joy, half with determination. It was a real battle. He slipped, fell, and the two leapt upon him. He wrestled. Three lithe bodies tumbled and twisted in the sand, and, with a splash, sought shelter in the blue reflection of the tranquil sky. The ripples licked at the rocks, the quiet images were shattered, and a cry of boyish victory arose.

I closed my eyes, and I fancied I saw the ancient Greeks playing, wrestling, dancing, exercising their limbs on the sands of Corinth, and I knew that I felt the same joy as they : the joy of youth, the joy of impeccable beauty, the joy of unfailing health, of exercise, of classic irresponsibility. I, like them, for a moment realised the perfect aesthetic pleasure given to all time in their superb statuary.

The wondrous beauty of an arm raised to strike, of a leg stretched to spring, of a head thrown back in defence, of a body taut, of a spirit young, and my soul cried "Eureka! I have found it, I have found it!"

Youth by Evan Morgan
Based on a dream!

266

APPENDIX 2

A Few Poems By Evan Frederic Morgan

A Sonnet

Could you deceive me with a show of grace
And hold my hand as cold as death
Could you deceive me with that angels face
And chill my inward heart with icy breath.
Do what you will, deceive me if you wish,
Throw all my thoughts into tormenting flames,
Play me as you would play some silvery fish.
Make me the object of your basest aims
Yet, you can't take from me that chiselled gem
The tranquil water gave me long ago,
Whatever words you use shall not condemn
My thoughts to lethal idleness below.
You are alone all things that God may crave
You are my fort, my canopy, my grave.

Evan Frederic Morgan
Sonnet dedicated to a friend.

THE KNIGHTS TEMPLARS' CAT

Tell me not the tale of the Knights Templars' cat
Which appeared slim and grey and silently sat
High among them for worship sublime.

One man in Paris had heard and had said:
"To the cat or the idol a virgin's bade dead
Had been offered or proffered one time;

In a room in the gloom some seven knights stood,
A Man in the midst with a cat in his hood,
And a name cabalistic and long:

The cat's eyes shed flame, it spread wide a paw
And jumped through the ceiling to be seen no more"-
Thus finished the words of his song.

The cat was a witch or the black Prince of Evil,
The Knights were as black; yet somehow I cavil
Whether really it happened at all.

In Brindisi likewise they have the same tale;
The cat was, I hear, as big as a whale
And appeared in a bonnet and shawl.

Whencever the source, I believe that a cat
Grey, black or brindled, most probably sat
With the knights whilst engaged in their prayers;

For once I served Mass in a convent quite close
To Florence, when I saw a white cat, morose,
Sit and mew on the high altar stairs!

Fiesole

FROM THE EEL AND OTHER POEMS

TO MY MOTHER

There is a love far greater
Than any lover knows,
A love that's purer, straighter
Than any love that grows
For youth and blushing maiden,
For man and wedded wife;
With whiter blossoms laden,
The vital flame of life;
This is the love that mother
Bestows upon her son,
Out-loving any lover
Out-loving anyone.

'Tis sweet as springtime shining
Through mists of April rain,
Its holy love enshrining
The seed of sweetest pain;
The pain which saints and martyrs
Have suffered with a smile,
For which no human barters
Nor thinks to win through guile;
The love-pain of a Being
Who watches from above,
A love that is all-seeing
The inmost soul of love.

THE WRITING ON THE WALL.

A derelict you would call him,
Something sunk and low,
Something to be avoided,
Something that's right below.
He'd fill you more with loathing
Than pity, I would guess,
His dirty, ragged clothing,
His utter wretchedness.
Close by the Thames Embankment
He crawled like wounded fly;
Or mayhap more like spider
That crawls away to die.
Hungry his face, how hungry!
His eyes swam sorrow's sea,
His hands hung grey and nerveless
In unmatched misery.
He crawled 'neath glowing archway,
And slowly scanned their message
Alive with posters' hue,
With lustless eyes of blue.
What message was he reading-
This man half-dead, unfed?
'Twas a message to the people,
"EAT LESS BREAD."

EVAN MORGAN 1917

The Poet – A Riddle

A riddle, he, which many think to solve;
An epigram for wagging tongues to tell;
Round him a thousand magic spheres revolve
Which, knowing him their axis, would rebel,
Yet cannot, since they are a part of him.

Though he may mirror peering face,
Upon his surface they can trace no mark;
Though changing their ungainliness to grace
When he shall speak, their ears no longer hark:
Yet these reflections are a part of him.

Withdrawn alone, he grows a different thing,
Part-bird, part-human, dwelling in the wild;
The blowing winds, the flowing waters sing-
"He has no parent, though he ever child:
We elements have formed the heart of him!"

Villa Mauresgur, Cap Ferrat, Easter. 1927

APPENDIX 3

J.S.5

Extracted from the Principal Registry of the Probate Divorce and Admiralty
Division of the High Court of Justice.
(Decree Absolute for Nullity of Marriage)

IN THE HIGH COURT OF JUSTICE
PROBATE DIVORCE AND ADMIRALTY DIVISION
(DIVORCE)

Before the Honourable   SIR GONNE PILCHER   Knight,

one of the Justices of the High Court,

sitting at the Royal Courts of Justice, Strand, in the County of Middlesex.

On the 27th   day of November   1944.

BETWEEN   OLGA TREDEGAR otherwise Simutovitch (Countess)   Petitioner

and   EVAN FREDERIC TREDEGAR (Viscount)   Respondent

Referring to the Decree made in this Cause on the 20th day of   July 1943

whereby it was ordered that the marriage in fact had and solemnized on the

13th day of March   19 39 at the Marriage Registrars Office at Singapore
between   Olga (Viscountess) Tredegar otherwise Simutovitch then Simutovitch formerly the wife
of George Simutovitch from whom she obtained a divorce   the Petitioner
and   Evan Frederic (Viscount) Tredegar   the Respondent
the Respondent be pronounced and declared to have been and to be absolutely
null and void to all intents and purposes in the law whatsoever by reason

of the incapacity of the Respondent to consummate the marriage

and the said Petitioner be pronounced to have been and to be free from all
Bond of Marriage with the said Respondent unless sufficient cause be shown
to the Court why the said Decree should not be made absolute within six
months from the date of the said Decree—and no such cause having been shown
the Court on application of the said Petitioner by final Decree pronounced
and declared the said marriage to be and to have been absolutely null and
void and that the said Petitioner was and is free from all Bond of Marriage
with the said Respondent.

H.P.O. NORBURY
REGISTRAR.

I Certify that this copy has been
examined with the Original Decree
Absolute of record in this Registry,
and that it is a true copy thereof.

DATED this 12th day of October, 1949

REGISTRAR.

105.B. Bl. x̄α√
(73941) Wt.12296/12 2,000 6/42 A.& O.W.Ltd. Gp.655

The legal document that declares Evan's marriage to
Princess Olga null and void

Honeywood House, Oakwood Hill, Rudgwick. Near Dorking, Surrey

Evan Frederic Morgan died here on 27 April 1949, aged 55

Last Resting Place of Evan Frederic Morgan at Buckfast Abbey

INDEX

Marsh	Edward, Sir		119, 164-5, 213
Martindale	CC, Father		120, 171, 197
Mary	Queen		23, 172, 206-7, 257
Mattei	Conte Tony		248
Maud	Princess	Duff	61, 76, 225
Maugham	Somerset		114, 119, 130, 164, 183, 264
Maxwell	Henry		20, 125, 202-3, 226, 233
McEvoy	Ambrose		128
McGrath	Colonel		16
McGrath	Mrs Rosita		16
Menzies	Stewart		218, 224-5
Messel	Oliver		164-5
Millar	Ella K		69
Miller	Hubert, Sir		236
Mitford	Jessica		228
Mitty	Walter		24
Modigliani	Amedeo		83
Moeran	EJ		84
Monckton	Walter, Sir		149, 211, 217
Montague	Cardie		201
Monteith	Eddy, Hon		102
Montgomery	Hugh		203
Montgomery	Peter		203
Moore	George		135
Morgan	Charles	Sir	44
	Charles Morgan		
Morgan	Robinson		45
Morgan	Charles Rodney		45, 46
Morgan	Courtenay Charles		35-8, 41, 45-6, 49, 59, 67-8, 70, 73, 95, 98-9, 142, 152, 159, 251 Birth, 11,46; death 12,43,46,228,246; marries Lois 17-20; marries Olga 23; Oxford, 36,77-81; prep school 56; See individual subjects- Beda College; black masses; buggery; Eton; Oxford; Paris; Rome; rough trade; sodomy; Vatican
Morgan	Evan Frederic		
Morgan	Freddie, Colonel		39, 45-6, 48, 73
Morgan	Frederic George		43, 46, 251-2
Morgan	George		45
Morgan	Godfrey	The Good	39,40, 41,45-8, 67-8,
	Gwyneth Ericka,		48, 49, 59, 89, 110, 131, 156, 161,
Morgan	Hon.		198-9, 200-1, 213
Morgan	Jane		44, 47
Morgan	John	of Dderw	44

END NOTES

[1] Boris Vasllyevich Anrep (1883-1969). Russian artist and poet – special interest in the art of the mosaic.

[2] Evan Frederic Morgan, (1893-1949) 2nd Viscount (1926 creation), 4th Baron Tredegar, 5th Baronet Morgan.

[3] 13 South Audley Street was described as "an unspoilt Georgian house containing the original decorations in an exception state of preservation, the ceilings being particularly fine examples of the period." See The Times 13 December 1925.

[4] The Della Robbia Pottery was a leading ceramic company. The firm closed down in 1906. The plaque of Gideon was designed by Harold Steward Rathbone in 1900. The Daily Mirror of 28 August 1929 records of Evan's bathroom "looks like a slightly clouded summer sky hangs a Della Robbia plaque..."

[5] These wall coverings at 40 South Street, Mayfair (the matrimonial home to Evan and his first wife Lois Sturt from 1929-1933 (approximately) were brought from Knole, the family seat of Lord Sackville and restored in 1929 on a commission paid by Evan and Lois to Mlle. Zozo Rosen, a famous Polish artist.

[6] Arthur Annesley Ronald Firbank (1886-1926). Known as Ronnie. Author, aesthete and homosexual.

[7] Attributed to Firbank.

[8] Firbank, Ronald. The Flower Beneath The Foot. Grant Richards Ltd (1923).

[9] Alfred Locker had been valet to Evan from the time he was aged 16, he is listed with Captain Harry Ware as accompanying Evan on various holidays abroad in 1936-7. Alfred was succeeded by John York, another seventeen year old who acted as Evan's valet. York sought a new post "with a Bachelor Gentleman as Housekeeper –Valet" in 1939. See The Times 11 August 1939.

[10] This was over a row about an over familiar dedication given by Ronnie to Evan in Firbank's play The Princess Zoubaroff, published by Grant Richards Ltd in 1920. This matter is fully covered later in this book.

[11] Rome's Quirinale Hotel was built in 1865 and remains one of the City's fine hotels. Quironale derives from the god Quirinus. The Quirinale Palace was one of the papal residences of Pope Gregory XIII.

[12] In Ronald Firbank's last letter to his friend Lord Gerard Berners he excuses himself from receiving him at the Hotel Quirinale, in Rome, not on account of his last illness but because the wallpaper was so dreadful.

[13] Winchester, Simon. Their Noble Lordships: Class and Power in Modern Britain. Random House.(1982).

[14] Noel Coward (1899-1973). English playwright, actor and song writer.

[15] Song entitled "I went to a marvellous party" (sometimes referred to as "I've been to a marvellous party") written by Coward in 1938 for the Review Set To Music.

[16] Evan was at London's Dorchester Hotel for a charity function organised by Sir Edward Marsh on 21 July 1937 to raise £30,000 for the Old Vic and Sadler's Wells theatres.

[17] Bryans, Robin. Checkmate: Memoirs of a Political Prisoner. Honeyford Press. (1994).

[18] Robin Bryans comments in his book The Dust Has Never Settled "I knew Evan could switch to a violent dislike of people who were once his close companions."

[19] Throughout the books of Robin Bryans, Evan's sex pick ups are described by this term. Evan sought to pick up rent boys in the street, alleyways, under bridges, the Thames Embankment and in the East End around the docks. Evan rarely used male brothels, although he could also be found in bath houses e.g. Turkish baths.

[20] The writer Richard Rumbold, author of Little Victims (1933) which was condemned by Evan and many Catholics for its portrayal of homosexuality in public schools, wrote in his diary A Message in Code (published after Rumbold's death) that " someone tried to pick me up in a Lyons Corner House when I was 17 or 18."

[21] Roberts, Cecil. The Bright Twenties. Hodder and Stoughton. (1970).

[22] Sir Alan Patrick Herbert (1890-1971). A graduate of New College, Oxford University. He was known as "APH", writer, law reformer and humorist.

[23] The full story of AP Herbert's "triumphant plunge into the complexities of Parliamentary procedure and law making" can be found in his book "The Ayes Have It. The Story of the Marriage Bill." Methuen. (1937)

[24] Winchester, Simon. Their Noble Lordships: Class and Power in Modern Britain. Random House. (1982).

[25] See The Times, 15 July 1937. Evan (with other civic dignitaries) met the King and Queen off their train. The King shortly after arriving inspecting a Guard of Honour of the 1st (Rifles) Battalion, The Monmouthshire Regiment, commanded by Evan, mounted on horseback.

[26] Seymour Leslie says in "The Jerome Connection" p177 "Godfrey Winn told me of the big party Evan Morgan (Tredegar) had given for the royal visit to Wales."

[27] The House of Lords debated the Herbert Divorce Bill on 15 July 1937, and the amendments were passed back to the House of Commons and debated on 30 July 1937.

[28] Herbert was the MP for the University of Oxford 1935 to 1950 - when all the University seats were abolished.

[29] Herbert, A P. "Holy Deadlock." Methuen. (1934).

[30] See Turner, J Neville, Villiams [Editors] "The Happy Couple: Law and Literature." Federation Press. (1994).

[31] The Matrimonial Causes Act, 1857 had allowed a husband to obtain a divorce on the grounds of adultery, but the wife had to prove adultery coupled with incest, bigamy, cruelty or alternatively, rape or an unnatural offence. In 1923 another act put husband and wife on an equal footing. The 1937 change extended the grounds for divorce (and judicial separation) for cruelty, or desertion without cause for three years, or incurable insanity. The change also allowed divorce without proof of adultery.

[32] The Sunday Times, 11 July 1937.

[33] Ibid.

[34] Evan was born in 13 July 1893 at 33, Cadogan Terrace, Chelsea, London.

[35] The Gin Traps (Prohibition) Bill was brought forward on 28 May 1935 and narrowly missed its second reading by 42 votes for to 44 votes against. The gin trap was finally abolished under a 1958 amendment to the Pest Act of 1954.

[36] George Orwell, (1903-1950) novelist and journalist. Real name Eric Arthur Blair.

[37] See Orwell's "Decline of the English Murder." Penguin Books. (First published in Tribune 1946).

[38] Ibid.

[39] The Sunday Times, 11 July 1937.

[40] Henry Havelock Ellis (1859-1939). British Physician and psychologist, co-author with John Addington Symonds (1840-1893) English poet and literary critic of the book Sexual Inversion (1897) the first medical textbook on homosexuality.

[41] Ellis, Havelock. Studies in the Psychology of Sex. Random House (1921).

[42] (Sir) Harold Acton (1904-1994) Writer and dilettante. Lived much of his life in Florence in the Villa La Pietra, which Acton gifted to the New York University. In his Memoirs of an Aesthete he describes his experiences living also in China and Paris.

[43] Norman Douglas (1868-1952) British writer. In 1916 he jumped bail on a charge of indecent assault on a sixteen year old boy. Douglas fled Britain. Although married, Douglas continued to be caught up in gay sex scandals. He lived much of his life in France, Florence, Naples and Capri.

[44] Referred to in an Obituary in The Guardian, 12 February 1952. Two years before Douglas' death "a kind Scots friend on the island [of Capri] offered him hospitality in a large villa, and here it was that he died."

[45] William Lygon (1872-1938) 7th Earl Beauchamp. Left Britain in 1931 after his open secret of chasing men was about to result in his arrest. He was the model for Lord Marchman in Evelyn Waugh's novel Brideshead Revisted. The Earl's son Hugh (1904-1936) – a model for Sebastian in Brideshead – died in a car accident –he was also homosexual. After leaving England Beauchamp rented Gerald Berners' villa in Rome, afterwards wandering the world. He was allowed to return to Britain (with the arrest warrant suspended) at the time of his son Hugh's death. With the accession of King George VI, Beauchamp's lawyer Norman Birkett successfully won a reprieve for the Earl.

[46] Attributed to Mark Amory in the Independent about the 7th Earl's daughter Lady Dorothy Herber-Percy (1912-2001). Repeated in The Sunday Times 25 November 2001. One observer commented on the fact that " The fingers of the [Earl's] footmen serving dinner were said to have been glittering with diamonds"

[47] The warrant on Beauchamp was latterly withdrawn and he was allowed to return to Britain. He was on a world tour when he died in the USA in 1938.

[48] Firbank's gravestone in Rome's Campo Verano Cemetery records that he died "Far Away From His Country".

[49] The unmasking of Earl Beauchamp was done by his brother-in-law, Hugh Grosvenor (1879-1953), the 2nd Duke of Westminster who (for political gain) hounded his "bugger-in-law" out of Britain. The King was appalled to learn that he had made a well known homosexual a Knight of the Garter and asked Beauchamp to retire. The King's comment was "I thought men like that shot themselves".

[50] But the news led to the Earl's sister - who did not know what homosexuality involved - suffering a nervous breakdown. She became a patient at Lady Carnarvon's Nursing Home in Portland Place, London.

[51] Leviticus 18:22 "You shall not lie with a male as with a woman; it is an abomination."

[52] Lois Sturt (1900-1937). Daughter of Humphrey Napier Sturt and Lady Feodorowna Yorke (2nd Baron and Baroness Alington of Crichel).

[53] Napier George Henry Sturt, (1896-1940) 3rd and last Baron Alington. His wife Lady Mary Sibell Ashley-Cooper died in 1936.

[54] Tallulah Bankhead, (1902-1968). American-born actress. One of biographies (which largely comprises a long conversation piece) is Tallulah: Darling of the Gods by Kieran Tunney. Published by Secker and Warberg in 1972. It was said that Tunney reminded Tullulah of her darling Naps.

[55] Made in 1922, a film by J Stuart Blackton starring Lady Diane Manners and Victor McLaglan.

[56] Parker, Derek. Nell Gwyn. Sutton. (2001)

[57] Lois had a four year affair with Reginald Herbert, 15th Earl of Pembroke and Montgomery. Several hundred of Reggie's spicy love letters to Lois are in the National Library of Wales, together with notebooks containing erotic and humorous verse.

[58] South Wales Argus April 1928.

[59] Ibid.

[60] The officiating clergy were the Roman Catholic Bishop of Cardiff and Fathers Martindale, Kerr and Talbot, of Farm Street, London. Father CC Martindale was Evan's close friend and mentor.

[61] Culled from various London newspapers.

[62] One report in the Sunday Times of 15 April 1928 records " The Papal colours of yellow and white are being used for the bridal retinue, though yellow is being interpreted to mean gold.....the bride's train will measure six yards in length, the dress being made on mediaeval lines, and she will wear a veil of old family lace."

[63] Culled from various London newspapers.

[64] Ibid.

[65] They slept away during much of their first year of the marriage whilst a larger house at 40 South Street, Mayfair was built and decorated for them to share, albeit along apartheid lines. When Evan returned from his controversial trip to Canada in the winter of 1929 (when he had made himself unpopular with careless remarks about the absence of any sign of literary works in the country's backwoods) the house was almost completed.

Mlle. Zozo Rosen, the famous Polish artist, was commissioned to restore a set of pictures in grisaille, a set of priceless panels of "The Loves of Cupid and Psyche" painted about 1780, brought from Knole, the family seat of Lord Sackville. Mlle. Rosen in some cases had to redesign the decorations where the original which had been obliterated. A photograph of Rosen carrying out this restoration can be found in The Daily Express for 29 August 1929.

Part of Evan's inspiration for the design was his sojourning in Rome and North Africa and with a touch of glitz from the best of the world's expensive hotels with "a most original cocktail hatch ...hidden behind movable panels in the dining room wall and when the panels are opened an electric sign flashes the words 'The Road To Ruin'."

The inside of the property was exquisite with "one of the most original colour schemes for which a special architect-decorator was called in… [of] royal blue and malachite green" for Evan's bedroom and sitting room. Evan decided on this to best match a gigantic malachite table and collection of vases which were "the gems of [Evan's] vast array of object d'art". He told a reporter "...the table is unique and priceless on account of its size. Oxidized silver sconces provide the lighting, and a flying Cupid hangs above the bed holding a minute reading light". This was a state of divine decadence, representing Evan's fine, discriminating taste and fancy. See Daily Mirror, 4 November 1929.

[66] Herbert, David. Second Son: an autobiography. Owen. (1972).

[67] Henry Maxwell (1909-1996). Life long friend of Evan and a regular house guest at Tredegar House in the 1930s and 1940s.

[68] See As I See Life Daily Mirror, 16 September 1929.

[69] The child was Hon. Mary Anna Sibell Elizabeth Sturt (1929-2010). She married Lt-Commander George Gosselin Marten.

[70] Waugh, Alec. Year to Remember. W H Allen (1975)

[71] Carrington, Dora de Houghton & Garnet David. Carrington: letters and extracts from her diaries. Holt, Rinehart and Winston. (1971).

[72] Harrison, Michael. Rosa. Peter Davies Ltd. (1962).

[73] In Michael Harrison's biography of Rosa Lewis, [Rosa Lewis of the Cavendish, published by Peter Davies Ltd, in 1962], he says "the reign was over by the end of 1931, and we can give it a day - 21st November 1931; the day on which Arthur Jeffress, later a successful dealer in paintings, gave his famous Red-and-White Party in Maud Allan's Regents's Park house….."

[74] Patrick Balfour, (1904-1976). 3rd Baron Kinross. Journalist, historian and homosexual.

[75] The Daily Mirror 3 July 1933.

[76] Ibid.

[77] Ibid.

[78] Ibid.

[79] Arthur Jeffress (1905-1961). Art Collector and Dealer. Committed suicide.

[80] Daily Express 23 November 1931.

[81] Ibid.

[82] See National Archives, Kew file ref J77/3117/5878.

[83] Captain Alexander (Tim) Freeland (1890-1939). His army file is at National Archives Kew, WO 339/ 25549.

[84] Edward George Boulenger (1888-1946). Zoologist. Keeper of the reptile house at London Zoo.

[85] Prince George, Duke of Kent (1902-1942). See Bradford Sarah. Elizabeth: A Biography of Her Majesty the Queen. (2002). Prince George's bisexuality is highlighted, with Lois Sturt cited as one of his mistresses.

[86] Hon. David Alexander Reginald Herbert. (1908-1995). Second son of Lois's lover Reginald Herbert, 15th Earl of Pembroke and Montgomery. David Herbert, a homosexual, was exiled to Tangier after the Second World War where he enjoyed his life as a socialite and an artist.

[87] Herbert, David. Second Son: an autobiography. Owen (1972). This memoir gives a short summary of Lois' affair with Reggie Herbert, including details of the effect it had on Reggie's wife Bee Herbert.

[88] Princess Olga Sergeivna Dolgorouky (1914-1998).Daughter of Prince Serge Dolgorouky (1872-1933) an Equerry to the Romanovs.

[89] Robin Bryans (1928-2005). Writer (his real name Robert Harbinson). Also used the name Robert Bryans.

[90] Bryans, Robin. Checkmate. Honeyford Press. (1994).

[91] See The Times 21 July, 1943.

[92] See Atkinson David and Wilson, Neil, Wales. Lonely Planet (2007)

[93] Frances Stevenson (1888-1972). Private secretary and mistress of David Lloyd George, later his wife and Countess.

[94] Diaries of Frances Stevenson 22 July 1919. Held in Parliamentary Archives.

[95] Percy Bysshe Shelley (1792-1822). One of the great English Romantic poets.

[96] Aubrey Vincent Beardsley (1872-1898). Author and illustrator of erotic images.

[97] From a leader in the Lethbridge Herald, 2 October 1929. A Canadian newspaper reporting on Evan's criticisms about the lack of culture in the pioneering states of Canada. This met with great hostility against Evan in Canada. This article concludes "The heir to the Viscountship of Tredegar may think fondly of the bed of roses in which he was born, but to expect this to be found in new territories is looking for something foreign….The Hon. Evan Morgan has yet to learn to school himself before giving utterance to half-baked impressions…"

[98] A description by Evan's friend, the writer, Aldous Huxley.

[99] Letter in the Tredegar House Archives 1979 from Olga to Curator David Beevers. See also Dart, Monty and Cross William. Aspects of Evan. The Last Viscount Tredegar. Book Midden Publishing (2012).

[100] Dart, Monty and Cross William. Aspects of Evan. The Last Viscount Tredegar. Book Midden Publishing. (2012).

[101] Nicolson, Harold. The development of English biography. L & Virginia Woolf. (1927)

[102] Connolly, Cyril. Enemies of Promise. Routledge and Kegan Paul (1938)

[103] Richard Canning in Introduction to Firbank's early book Vainglory. Penguin (2012).

[104] Evan's mother was Lady Katharine Agnes Blanche Carnegie, (1867-1949). Her half-nephew, Charles Carnegie, 11th Earl of Southesk, wrote to Tredegar House in the 1970s with this information. See Tredegar House files.

[105] Evan's long poem City of Canals (the title of one of his books of verse) charts a failed love affair he had with a Italian youth, in Venice in 1924-5.

[106] Pasolini and Jarman were both homosexual film makers who exploited and combined religious images with sexual rituals.

[107] Bryans, Robin. Let the petals fall. Honeyford Press. (1993).

[108] Attributed to Eddy Sackville-West, 5th Baron Sackville (1901-1965).

[109] Cecil Roberts (1892-1976). Writer and Journalist. Friend of Evan from around 1919.

[110] Roberts, Cecil. The Bright Twenties. Hodder and Stoughton. (1970).

[111] Ibid.

[112] Among Bryans' output are his excellent early memoirs 'Up Spake the Cabin Boy'; 'The Song of Erne'; and 'Ulster: A Journey Through the Six Counties'. He also wrote several dozen travel books.

[113] Sixteen-year-old Robin Bryans came to Wales in 1944 from Belfast, to study at Bible College at Barry. This brought him into contact with the Wills and Stewart families and through them met Evan.

[114] Catherine Elizabeth Stewart born 11 December 1877. Known at Kate or Kitty. She died in 1975. The Stewart family home was "Strathella", High Walls Road, Dinas Powis. Affectionately the same house name was shared by the property of the two spinsters Catherine and her sister Mabel when they lived at "Strathella" in Lavernock Road Penarth, after the death of their parents. Mabel died in 1947.

[115] Bryans, Robin. Blackmail and Whitewash. Honeyford Press. (1996).

[116] Published under Harbinson, Robert. The Protégé. Faber and Faber (1963).

[117] The Dust Has Never Settled. Bryans gives his parents names as Robert and Georgina Bryans, who had three children: Eileen, Margaret and Robin. His violin-playing father died in 1933 when Robin was only four years old.

[118] Cited in An Anthology of Ulster Autobiography edited by Frank Ormsby. Blackstaff. (1987).

[119] See Bryans' book published as Harbinson, Robert. Up Spake The Cabin Boy. Faber. (1961).

[120] Evan's cousin Kate (Kitty) Stewart, daughter of the deceased Rev Henry Holms Stewart (died 1937) and Lady Beatrice Carnegie (died 1934). Beatrice was a half-sister to Evan's mother Katharine. Kitty ran prayer groups with Mabel Wills and Alice Pethybridge, who were Bryans' sponsors at Bible College. Alice Pethybridge was a former Lady Mayoress of Cardiff. The Wills family had help develop Cardiff Docks.

[121] Bryans, Robin. The Dust Has Never Settled. Honeyford Press (1992). Bryans, Robin Let the petals fall. Honeyford Press. (1993). There are two other autobiographical volumes by Bryans in the 1990s. Checkmate. Memoirs of a Political Prisoner. Honeyford Press. (1994), and Blackmail and Whitewash. Honeyford Press. (1996).

[122] Nina Hamnett (1890-1956). Writer, poet and artist. Born Tenby, South Wales. A lifelong friend of Evan. "… one of the most respected women artists in the London avant-garde arts scene." See Grimes, T Collins, J & Baddley, O. Five Women Painters. Lennard Publishing (1991).

[123] In addition to this fact being mentioned by Bryans, there is also a reference to the book Not Behind Lace Curtains and Nina's illustrations for it in Hooker, Dennis. Nina Hamnett: Queen of Bohemia. Constable (1986). Nina was asked p.242 to do "thirteen black and white illustrations and a colour frontispiece for a book by Evan Morgan called Not Behind Lace Curtains, although this was never published."

[124] Leslie, Seymour. The Jerome Connection. John Murray. (1964). Nina completed some 'contemporary' drawings for The Silent Queen. Jonathan Cape. (1927)

[125] See Carey, John. William Golding: Faber and Faber (2009) for Bryans' attack on Charles Monteith, (1921-1995) a senior executive with Faber and Faber. See Kemp, Eric. Shy But Not Retiring: Memoirs. Continuum International Publishing Group (2006) for Bryans' harassment of Bishop Eric Kemp (1915-2009).

NB Robin Bryans (as Robert Harbinson) also took part in a controversial TV programme in 1988 about British Intelligence in the 'After Dark' series.
https://theneedleblog.wordpress.com/2013/05/17/after-dark-british-intelligence/

[126] Robin Bryans died on 11th June 2005. His last home was at 90, Ferrymead Avenue, Greenford, Middlesex UB6 9TN. Bryans names George Henry Balcombe (who owned a half share in the address quoted) as his literary executor. Robin and George co-habited together for several decades, in Brighton and London. Bryans left his estate to the Save the Children charity.

[127] Alec Waugh (1898-1981). Novelist. His most popular book is Loom of Youth.

[128] Waugh, Alec. The Early Years of Alec Waugh. Cassell. (1962)

[129] Courtenay Charles Evan Morgan (1867-1934). 3rd Lord Tredegar. 1st Viscount Tredegar (made in 1926).

[130] According to Dennis Brian in his book Pulitzer: A Life. Wiley (2002). Liberty was owned by Joseph Pulitzer (1847-1911), the American media tycoon. In 1912 it was sold to James Ross, who renamed it Glencairn. Courtenay Morgan restored the name Liberty and owned it until 1920 when it was sold to Sir Robert and Lady Houston who owned it until it was broken up in 1937.

[131] Liberty served as a patrol vessel then a hospital ship in the North Sea and in the Mediterranean Sea in WW1. At the end of the war Courtenay was "awarded OBE .... for valuable services in providing and maintaining the yacht Liberty for use as a hospital ship throughout the war." See National Archives, Kew Ref ADM 337/118.

[132] Whilst parts of Tredegar House date back to medieval days, much of the present building was built between 1664 and 1672. An interesting essay entitled 'An architect for Tredegar House', by Howard Colvin is in Architectural History, 25, (1982) p6-7.

[133] Augustus Edwin John. (1878-1961). Welsh portrait painter and hell raiser.

[134] Evan's friend, the Welsh artist Augustus John puts it succinctly in a letter (in the National Library of Wales)… "his [Evan's] figure has to be altered slightly to meet the regulations, so he is now being stretched in various ways …"

[135] The Times of 18 June, 1915, records: "The Hon. Evan F Morgan, only son of Lord and Lady Tredegar, has received a commission in the Welsh Guards, and joined his regiment at Wellington Barracks last week."

[136] Soldier Poets: Songs of Fighting Men. London. Erskine MacDonald. (1916).

[137] Frederic Courtenay Morgan (1834-1909). Evan's paternal grandfather. Lived at Ruperra Castle until his death. Generally known as Freddie or Fred.

[138] Godfrey Charles Morgan (1831 -1913). Evan's great uncle and Lord Tredegar 1876-1913.

[139] The army careers of Godfrey and Freddie are of some interest; their military achievements became the acid test of Morgan masculinity. After joining the army as Cornet in July 1849, aged just 18, Godfrey Charles Morgan became a Lieutenant by purchase in the 17th Light Dragoons on 31 May 1850 and a Captain in the same regiment by the same process of purchase on 22 April 1853. At Balaclava – in the famous Charge of the Light Brigade by the 17th Lancers - Godfrey is described as the Junior Captain. He led a squadron into the Valley of Death. After that action he was made the Senior Captain. In January 1855, a few months after the battles of Alma, Balaclava and Inkerman, Captain Godfrey Morgan is among the names of those who resigned their Commissions. [See Obituary Godfrey The Times 12 March 1913]. On becoming Lord Tredegar in 1875 a The War Office notice for the Regiments of Yeomanry Cavalry includes "Gloucestershire: Major Godfrey Charles Morgan, Lord Tredegar, is permitted to retain his rank and continue to wear the uniforms of the regiment on retirement." [See The Times 23 June 1875]. A later notice of 9 December 1885 states "MILITIA: Engineers Godfrey Charles, Lord Tredegar, to be Hon. Colonel of the Regiment".

Freddie was transformed from "gent" to a Second Lieutenant in the Rifle Brigade, by purchase, on 11 March 1853. Shortly before his participation in the Battle of Inkerman he was made up to a full Lieutenant. The London Gazette published the War Office List of 8 June 1855 showing in the column of "To be Captains by purchase: " Rifle Bridge Lieutenant Frederick Courtenay Morgan…"

[140] "The Charge of the Light Brigade, the Battle of Balaclava, 15th October 1854, with Godfrey Charles Morgan, 1st Viscount Tredegar, Astride His Horse, 'Sir Briggs'." Painted by John Charlton 1905. On display at Tredegar House. The grave of Godfrey's horse 'Sir Briggs' is also in the grounds of Tredegar Park.

[141] Evan's maternal grandparents were James Carnegie (1827-1905) and Susan Murray (1837-1915). James was a gifted poet and travel writer. Their home was Kinnaird Castle in the Highlands of Scotland, near Brechin. The Carnegies figure in most of the memorable events connected with Scotland and Scottish history. They have Norman roots, taking their name from the area around Carmyllie in Angus. The family who adopted this name however, from an earlier adopted place name of Balinhard. Evan's maternal grandfather Sir James Carnegie took this name for a new Barony from 1869.

[142] Lady Katharine Agnes Blanche Carnegie, (1867-1949). Evan's mother. From 1891 wife of Courtenay Charles Evan Morgan, later 3rd Lord Tredegar. Katharine was Lady Tredegar 1913-1949.

[143] Benkovitz, Miriam J. A Bibliography of Ronald Firbank. Rupert Hart-Davis (1963).

[144] Evidence of this can be found in the Tredegar Estate Archives in the National Library of Wales.

[145] Bryans, Robin. Let the petals fall. Honeyford Press (1993) echoing a remark by the writer/journalist Douglas Goldring in Privileged Persons. Richards Press (1955). " He may be a lord but he is certainly not a gentleman".

[146] John Morgan (1908-1962), Evan's cousin. 6th and last Lord Tredegar.

[147] See Pryce Jones, Alan. The bonus of laughter. Hamish Hamilton. (1987).

[148] Burke John, Burke [Sir] Bernard. A genealogical and heraldic dictionary of the landed gentry of Great Britain. Volume 3. (1850)

[149] Ruperra Castle was built in 1622, burned down in 1783 and restored in 1789. The Castle afforded a refuge to King Charles 1 after the defeat at Naseby. Burned down again whilst occupied by the Military in the Second World War. Now a ruin (privately owned).

[150] Tredegar House was completed in 1672 is set in the beautiful 90 acre (360,000 m²) Tredegar Park. The house is a 17th century Charles II mansion. The earliest surviving part of the building dates back to the early 1500s. For over five hundred years, it was home to the Morgans - later Lords Tredegar - until they left in 1951. The house was then home to St. Joseph's R.C. Girls' School (now a mixed-sex school in Duffryn, Newport) until it was bought by Newport Council in 1974, giving rise to its claim as the grandest council house in Britain! It is now leased to the National Trust.

[151] The Morgan's London town house through the late 19th, early 20th century was at 39 Portman Square. It was sold to help pay off death duties just before the Great War.

[152] Jane Morgan (1731-1797) wife of Charles Gould (1726-1806), the elder son of King Gould of Westminster.

[153] Escott, Margaret. The History of Parliament: Cambridge University Press. (2009). The peerage was granted on 16 April 1859

[154] The first three Morgan baronets (from the 1792 creation of the title) were Charles Gould (later Morgan) (died 1806); his son Charles Gould Morgan (1760 - 1846) and grandson Charles Morgan Robinson Morgan (1792-1875).

[155] Charles Morgan Robinson Morgan (born Gould) (1792-1875). 3rd baronet, first Lord Tredegar. Married Rosamond (Rose) Mundy in 1827. Succeeded his father, Charles Morgan (1760-1846), 2nd baronet.

[156] George Gould Morgan (1794-1845). MP for Brecon 1818-1830.

[157] Charles Octavius Swinnerton Morgan (1803-1888). MP for Monmouthshire from 1841.

[158] Charles Rodney Morgan (1828-1854). Born Ruperra Castle, educated at Eton. Coldstream Guards (Entered 1847, Left 1852). MP for Brecon from 1852 until death. Died at Marseilles, France.

[159] Courtenay's rejection of a political career annoyed his father. This reached a head when Courtenay broke Freddie's record sitting as an MP in Parliament in 1906. The leading sons of each generation of Morgan and even those not cut out for politics had sat in Parliament for generations past. In Wales in British Politics 1868-

1922, published 1980, by Kenneth O Morgan (not a member of the Tredegar family) writes:

"Frederick Courtenay Morgan (Unionist, South Monmouthshire) was the last of a dynasty which had sat intermittently for the county since 1547….."
[160] The Monmouthshire Merlin of 29th January 1854 records: Deaths: On the 14th instant at Marseilles C R Morgan Esq MP for Brecon, eldest son of Sir Charles Morgan, Bart, of Tredegar Park in this country, aged 25 years.
[161] On Charles' brother Godfrey inheriting the title in 1875 a claim against the succession was made (There is a reference to this dispute in letters from Godfrey's sister Mary Anna Morgan (Viscountess Hereford) in the National Library of Wales. It is further claimed that Charles had two illegitimate children to a Catholic woman. In later years after Charles' death these children visited at Tredegar Park. They were eventually paid off.
[162] Freddie Morgan (Colonel F C Morgan (1834-1909) married Charlotte Anne Williamson (1841-1891). Charlotte was the daughter of Charles Alexander Williamson who was of Scottish descent although he was born in the USA. Charlotte's mother was Catharine Harrison. They had a family of two sons and two daughters. Charlotte's death was from heart disease, but she was for many years blind and was scarcely seen in public.
[163] The five sons of Charles Morgan Robinson Morgan and Rosamond Mundy were Charles Rodney, Godfrey, Freddie, George and Arthur John. Mr George (as he was always called) was a whimsical character, straight out of a Dickens novel, who never quite grew up; he suffered from epilepsy. Arthur John suffered from a nervous debility and had a club foot.
[164] Godfrey, Courtenay's uncle, was created a Viscount in his own right in 1906 but this title could not be passed on as Godfrey had no son. So only the Barony of Tredegar (1859) and the Baronetcy (1792) passed to Courtenay after Godfrey's death. Courtenay was himself made a Viscount in 1926; this title passed to Evan in 1934 and ceased in 1949 as he had no son to inherit.
[165] The first three Lady Morgans were Jane Gould Morgan (1731-1797); Margaret Stoney (1770-1808); and Rosamond Mundy (1810-1883). Rosamond was also the first Lady Tredegar (from 1859).
[166] Rosamond (Rose) Mundy (1810 -1883) daughter of General Mundy of Shipley Hall, Derbyshire.
[167] The five Lady Tredegars were respectively Rosamond Mundy (1810-1883, Lady Tredegar from 1859 to 1883); Katharine Agnes Blanche Carnegie (Lady Tredegar from 1913 to 1949); Lois Sturt (1900-1937, Lady Tredegar from 1934 to 1937); Princess Olga Dolgorouky (1914-1998, Lady Tredegar from 1939 to 1998) and Joanna Law Smith (died 2000, Lady Tredegar from 1954 to 2000).
[168] This portrait, Woman in the Green Coat was painted by Augustus John. It is currently on display at Tredegar House.
[169] Katharine's father, James Carnegie had four daughters from his second marriage to place with husbands. In 1885 he was in financial difficulties. He told William Gladstone in a letter

"Like other landowners I find myself brought perilously near to ruin". (See the Gladstone Papers in the British Library, London). By 1890 it was clear that the hand of Courtenay Morgan (who would one day be Lord Tredegar) was a good match for Katharine, at least on paper.

[170] Lady Beatrice Eleanor Paget, (1883-1973) (known as "Bee"), later wife of Reginald Herbert, 15th Earl of Pembroke (1880-1960).

[171] The full story of Gwyneth is in Dart, Monty and Cross William. A Beautiful Nuisance. The Life and Death of the Hon. Gwyneth Ericka Morgan. Book Midden Publishing. (2012).

[172] Bryans, Robin. Let the petals fall. Honeyford Press (1993).

[173] Robin Bryans Author of memoirs The Dust Has Never Settled, (1992) Let the petals Fall (1993). Honeyford Press These books contain numerous references to Evan Morgan.

[174] Bryans, Robin. Let the petals fall. Honeyford Press (1993)

[175] Maurice Harold Macmillan (1894-1986). Conservative politician. Prime Minister of the UK from 1957-1963. Left Eton 1910.

[176] Attributed to the journalist Woodrow Wyatt who disclosed in his diaries that, "on 4 June 1986 he was telephoned by a friend who "told him a very good story about Harold MacMillan being expelled for buggery at Eton". Wyatt replied "it is quite true. J B S Haldane wrote it to me. He was in the same house at Eton". The journalist John Junor reports the same "ancient mythology" that Harold was "expelled from Eton for homosexualism" in his memoir Listening for a Midnight Tram. Chapmans. (1990). In The Macmillans, Heinemann (1992)), p137 Richard Davenport-Hines says simply "Harold was brought home from Eton." As with Evan, no record is held by Eton of the reason Macmillan left the school. Macmillan himself records in his memoirs Winds of Change (1966) that he left Eton on account of illness.

[177] Ronald Arbuthnott Knox (1888-1957). First ordained as an Anglican priest but later became a Roman Catholic. He was a Catholic chaplain at Oxford University from 1926 until 1939. Well known as a broadcaster on BBC Radio. Friend of Evelyn Waugh, who wrote Knox's biography.

[178] See Williams, Charles. Harold Macmillan. Hachette UK. (2012)

[179] Knox developed a sudden and serious illness early in 1957. Macmillan invited him to stay at 10 Downing Street while in London to consult a specialist. The doctor confirmed the verdict of incurable cancer.

[180] Macmillan, Harold. Winds of Change. Macmillian (1966).

[181] Thomas Malcolm Muggeridge (1903-1990) Journalist, broadcaster and author.

[182] Bryans, Robin. Checkmate. Memoirs of a Political Prisoner. Honeyford Press. (1994). Cribbed from the New Statesman.

[183] Ibid.

[184] See Bryans, Robin. Let the petals fall. Honeyford Press, (1993).

[185] Desmond Leslie (1921-2001) youngest son of Evan's Catholic friend, Shane Leslie of Castle Leslie, County Monaghan, Eire.

[186] In Aspects of Evan, Leslie is quoted as saying that In the Manner of the Word was invented by Evan, Knox and H G Wells (another frequent guest of Evan at Tredegar House).

[187] Archibald Philip Primrose, 5th Earl of Rosebery (1847-1929). Attended Eton 1860-1865 and was under the wing there of schoolmaster William Johnston Cory, a suspected pederast.

[188] George Nathaniel Curzon (1859-1925) 1st Marquess Curzon of Kedleston. Whilst at Eton he was a favourite of schoolmaster Oscar Browning, a suspected pederast.

[189] Charles (Chat) Williamson (died 1943) was the son of Selina Morgan (died 1922) and Colonel David Williamson (died 1913). The Colonel was an army contemporary of Selina's wayward bother Charles Rodney Morgan who died in 1854. Selina's other brother Freddie (Evan's paternal grandfather) married David Williamson's sister, Charlotte Anne Williamson. Chat lived in exile in Venice for many years with his young manservant.

[190] Reginald (Reggie) Baliol Brett, (1852-1930) Later 2nd Viscount Esher. Had a 30 year influence at Court. Held the coveted post of Deputy Governor and Constable of Windsor Castle.

[191] The entire story can be gleaned in the book Sodom on the Thames, by Morris B Kaplan. Cornell University Press (2005).

[192] Full details are Lees-Milne: The Enigmatic Edwardian. Life of Reginald, 2nd Viscount Esher. Sidgwick & Jackson Ltd. (1988). See also Kaplan, Morris B. Sodom on the Thames. Cornell University Press. (2005).

[193] See Williams, Charles. Harold MacMillan. Hachette UK. (2012).

[194] William Johnston Cory (1823-1892) resigned from his position as a master at Eton in 1872 under a cloud of suspicion for improper relations with boys, to one of whom he had dedicated *Ionica,* a book of pederastic poetry. He was shortly followed by another master Oscar Browning (1837-1923) who was dismissed in 1875 over his "overly amorous" (but purportedly chaste) relationship with George (later Lord Curzon (1859-1925).

[195] E-mail from M T Phillips, Eton Curator 7 April 2009.

[196] Further details of Evan's interaction with M D Hill are in Aspects of Evan.

[197] James Lonsdale Bryans (1893-1981). Eton chum of Evan and later confidante "keen traveller and Fascist sympathiser. During World War II he aroused the suspicion of both the Foreign Office and MI5 because of his attempts to promote a negotiated end to the war. "

[198] Bryans, Robin. Let the petals fall. Honeyford Press (1993).

[199] Major Victor Albert Francis Charles Spencer, 1st Viscount Churchill (1864-1934).

[200] Bryans, Robin. Let the petals fall. Honeyford Press (1993).

[201] George Bridges Harley Guest Rodney (1891-1973). 8th Lord Rodney.

[202] This statement appears on a plaque unveiled at the Church of Saint Mary the Virgin, Metchosin, Canada in 2007, (by Rodney's daughter) to mark the centenary of the event.

[203] See Jeal. Tim. Baden-Powell. Pimlico.(1991). This book suggests Baden-Powell had possible romantic aspirations upon Corisande which he hoped would lead to

some kind of relationship, fuelled perhaps in part by her having four young boys under his control. Corisande dismissed his interest.

[204] Lady Corisande Evelyn Vere Rodney (nee Guest) (1870-1943).

[205] Hon James Henry Bertie Rodney (1893-1933). Soldier, pilot and adventurer. Killed in a house fire at the Heronry, Whitechurch, in 1933, along with a French nobleman, the Duc de la Tremoille.

[206] Hon (Charles Christian) Simon Rodney (1895-1980) Soldier and later a stockbroker.

[207] George was Patrol Leader of Wolves Patrol; James was in Ravens Patrol; Simon was in Curlews Patrol; William was in Bulls Patrol. There were 20 boys in all at the first camp.

[208] William Francis Rodney (1896-1915). 2nd Lieutenant Rifle Brigade and the Royal Flying Corps. Killed in action 9 May 1915, aged 18.

[209] Lady Wimborne (1847-1927). She was born Cornelia Henrietta Maria Spencer-Churchill, daughter of the 7th Duke of Marlborough. One of her siblings was Randolph Churchill, father of Winston. Described by her husband, Cornelia was "so sweet, so loving and so capable."

[210] Bryans, Robin. Checkmate: Memoirs of a Political Prisoner. Honeyford Press. (1994).

[211] James Lonsdale Bryans (1893-1981). Contemporary of Evan at Eton College.

[212] During Evan's time at prep school in Brighton two women (posing as his aunts) attempted to seize him and take him over to France and hold him for ransom. The kidnapping was foiled by Evan's mother when Evan mentioned the aunts, of whom Katharine had no knowledge.

[213] Herbert William Bryans (1855-1925) artist and draughtsman, he specialised in stained glass windows for churches. Son of a vicar, he spent ten years tea planting in India and wine making in France. He married Laura Richardson. From 1889, back in England he worked for C E Kempe before starting his own business in 1897. His trademark was a running greyhound.

[214] Major Victor Albert Francis Charles Spencer, 1st Viscount Churchill (1864-1934). A Lord in Waiting to Queen Victoria and Edward VII.

[215] Lady Verena Maud Lowther (1865-1938). Her brother was Henry Lowther (1857-1944) 5th Earl of Lonsdale, the famous "Yellow Earl".

[216] Churchill, Viscount. All my sins remembered. An Autobiography. Heinemann: London. (1964)

[217] Ibid.

[218] Peter Spencer Churchill, 2nd Viscount Churchill, died at Brighton on 21 December 1973, aged 83.

[219] Ibid. Peter's father Victor Albert Francis Charles Spencer (1864-1934) had also been a Page of Honour to Queen Victoria.

[220] Courtenay Morgan's army career was erratic. In the 1890s he was precipitated into acting for a General. He was ADC to General Sir Thomas Fraser – in the Home Counties around London - but that posting did not see him safely through the years of the South African (Boer) Wars ahead. There had been an important visit of the Khedive of Egypt in June 1900 and Courtenay was involved in dealing with this.

Fraser saw Courtenay's flaws and sent him packing to South Africa as an officer on the staff there. Courtenay seriously disappointed his father and uncle Godfrey. He served in the Boer War – and whilst wounded he hardly distinguished himself – there were no battle honours on a par with Godfrey's Balaclava charge or Freddie's fierce and bloody hand to hand fighting at Inkerman. Courtenay never reached an army rank beyond Major. His rank of Colonel – in the Monmouthshire Engineers and Militia – as with the other Morgans including his father - who hailed himself as a Colonel – was only an honorary title.

[221] Courtenay was responsible for Colonial Remounts, arriving from the Empire for the Coronation on 22 June, 1902, but the new King fell ill and had an appendectomy – so the Coronation was postponed until 9 August 1902. There were 2,500 colonial troops with 2,200 horses under Courtenay's charge.

[222] Northlands School, Virginia Water, ran by Miss Sophie Weisse. Fuller details are in Dart, Monty and Cross William. A Beautiful Nuisance. Book Midden Publishing (2012).

[223] William Hampton Pethybridge was Lord Mayor of Cardiff in 1924-25. His Lady Mayoress was his spinster sister, Alice Pethybridge, who lived to the age of 103 and died in 1969.

[224]See Dart, Monty and Cross, William. Aspects of Evan. Book Midden Publishing (2012). Baron George Marochetti (who died in 1952) placed In Memoriam notices in The Times for Evan in 1949-1951. This places George (who was only a year younger than Evan) in the company of Evan and Peter at Windsor at the same time.

[225] See The Times, 21 May 1903.

[226] Lady Susan, (an Earl's daughter and Evan's grandmother) spent her early years at Court. Her mother (Lady Catherine Herbert (1814-1886)) was a Lady of the Bedchamber to Queen Victoria. Susan was a child friend of several of Queen Victoria's daughters.

[227] Lionel Fielden (1896-1974) was only three years younger than Evan and there would have been an overlap between them at Eton. A homosexual and friend of E M Forster he writes in his book of memoirs Natural Bent (published in 1960) " When I was at Eton, homosexuality was not only common, it was the general rule."

[228] Attributed to Frank Pakenham, 7th Earl of Longford (1905-2001).

[229] Between 1905 and 1916 the Rev. Hon. Edward Lyttelton (1855-1942)was Eton's headmaster. Son of the 5th Lord Lyttelton, a notable sportsman. Master of College was Aymer Whitworth.

[230] The Princess Louise, (1848-1939). (Louise Caroline Alberta, 4th daughter of Queen Victoria.

[231] John Campbell (1845-1914). Best known as the Marquess of Lorne, later 9th Duke of Argyll.

[232] Rose, Kenneth. Who's Who in the Royal House of Windsor. Crescent Books, New York. (1985)

[233] Ibid.

[234] Maurice Vyner Baliol Brett (1882-1934). 2nd son of Reggie Brett, 2nd Viscount Esher. He edited his father's Journals.

[235] Reginald Lewis Vernon Harcourt (1863-1922). Politician and Cabinet Minister. Nickname of Loulou. Author of An Eton Bibliography. A sexual predator of children. He *may* have taken his own life following the hue and cry that went up on his attempt to seduce 12-year old Edward James (later the art collector and poet). The inquest recorded a verdict of death by misadventure. The Coroner was especially keen to ignore any thought that it was deliberate.

[236] Edward William Frank James (1907-1984). Poet and millionaire. Later the husband of the dancer Tilly Losch, (1903-1975) who attempted to divorce him in 1934 (citing his homosexuality as grounds).

[237] Patrick Jackson (who edited Selections from Harcourt's Journals (to 1895) (published in 2006)) comments in Harcourt's entry in the Oxford Dictionary of National Biography that death by misadventure was recorded "on the basis of post-mortem medical evidence that the heart was extensively diseased and that the overdose would not have been harmful in other circumstances."

[238] Carrington, Dora de, Houghton & Garnet, David. Carrington: letters and extracts from her diaries. Holt, Rinehart and Winston. (1971).

[239] Dorothy Brett (1883-1977) Painter. Dorothy's experience of being touched by Loulou Harcourt made her afraid of men. She later lived a reclusive life in New Mexico.

[240] Horace Brand Farquhar. (1844-1923). First and last Lord Farquhar. Close friend of Edward VII and the Duke of Fife, Farquhar made large sums of money for members of the Royal Family through investment banking. He married the wealthy widow of one of the founders of Scott's Bank (later absorbed by National Westminster Bank). See Montgomery Hyde, H, A Tangled Web. Constable (1986).

[241] See The Times, 1 April 2002. An account of Farquhar's financial skulduggery is in Montgomery Hyde, H, A Tangled Web. Constable (1986). Farquhar embezzled substantial funds as Conservative Party treasurer, with two specific sums of £20,000 and £40,000 being diverted to Lloyd George. A curious feature of the case is Farquhar's Will in which he left large sums to Princess Arthur of Connaught (and her son the Earl of Macduff), and her sister Princess Maud (with a provision should she marry Lord Carnegie, which she did in 1923 (after Farquhar's death). However Farquhar died bankrupt with his debts exceeding the net value of his estate.

[242] Evan's mother's half-brother was Charles Noel Carnegie (1854-1941) the 10th Earl of Southesk. The 10th Earl's eldest son Charles Alexander Bannerman Carnegie (1893-1992) was Lord Carnegie (later 11th Earl of Southesk) who married Princess Maud Duff (1893-1945) daughter of Alexander Duff the 1st Duke of Fife (1840-1912) and Princess Louise, Princess Royal (1867-1931) a daughter of King Edward VII. Lord Carnegie was the same age as Evan and both attended Eton College at the same time. They were lifelong friends as well as half-cousins. Princess Maud's sister Princess Alexandra (1891-1959) married her cousin Prince Arthur of Connaught (1883-1938).

[243] See National Archives, Kew files WORK 19/366 and WORK 19/309. White Lodge is now home of the Royal Ballet School.

[244] Bryans, Robin. Checkmate. Honeyford Press. (1994). NB According to the House notes "The Copeland Spode" dinner service is the most precious; it dates to the 1880s and bears the family crest. An earlier set dates from the 1850s.

[245] An ancient University situated in the Latin Quarter of Paris, France. Peter says in his memoirs All my sins remembered that his Lonsdale grandmother paid for these studies.

[246] This is the "historical Indo-Aryan language, the primary liturgical language of Hinduism and a literary and scholarly language in Buddhism and Jainism."

[247] Aberconway Christabel. A wiser woman A Book of Memories. Hutchinson (1966).

[248] Bryans, Robin. Checkmate: Memoirs of a Political Prisoner. Honeyford Press. (1994).

[249] Ibid.

[250] Ibid.

[251] Robin Bryans describes Chester in Let the petals fall as "Evan's other Etonian friend Robin Chester who had long been Scout master of Toynbee Hall in the East End." He was a partner in the law firm Rankin Ford and Chester of Grays Inn.

[252] Whitaker was an old Etonian, later a Captain in the Grenadier Guards, a close friend of Cecil Beaton.

[253] Bryans, Robin. Let the petals fall. Honeyford Press. (1993).

[254] In 1916 Peter married Kathleen (Katherine) daughter of the Hon. Peter Beaven, formerly Premier of British Columbia, and widow of Captain S Venn Ellis RN. Kathleen Beaven killed herself in Bath, in 1943. She is described by Hugo Vickers in his biography of Gladys, Duchess of Marlborough as "a woman with grey hypnotic eyes."

[255] The Churchills divorced in Scotland in 1927. Peter's father married Christine McRae (1895-1972) who bore him a daughter (Sarah) in 1931 and a son (Victor George Spencer) in 1934, who became the 3rd Viscount Churchill in 1973.

[256] Vickers, Hugo. Gladys: Duchess of Marlborough. Hamish Hamilton (1987).

[257] Internet description paraphrased.

[258] Churchill, Viscount. All my sins remembered. An Autobiography. Heinemann: London. (1964).

[259] Ann Besant (1847-1933). Central figure in the theosophy movement which acquired a large following.

[260] The two daughters of the 1st Viscount Churchill and Verena were (1) Hon. Victoria Ivy Louise Spencer (1897-1946). [Some reports say she died 1949 and others 1968 and 1983] She married in 1920 Captain Hon. Cecil Henry Brassey (1896-1952). (2) Hon. Ursula Spencer (1901-1934), she married Lt Col Alick Frederick Tod.

[261] In his early years Peter had a good relationship with his father but Verena smothered this. He comments in his memoirs All my sins remembered "My father offered me the choice of leaving my mother or being cut off financially, and at the same time he tried to coerce my mother by getting legal control of her money and custody of my two sisters." Peter chose his mother; he was disinherited and hardly spoke to his father ever again.

[262] Churchill, Viscount. All my sins remembered. An Autobiography. Heinemann: London. (1964).

[263] Constance Gwladys Robinson Herbert (1859-1917) Daughter of Sidney Herbert of Lea (Pembroke family of Wilton House) making her a cousin of Evan's grandmother Susan Southesk. Gwladys was first the wife of the 4th Earl of Lowther, (Verena Spencer Churchill's brother) and later married the Marquess of Ripon. She has one daughter Juliet Lowther, later Lady Juliet Duff, the latter was a very close friend of Evan. Gwladys was a hostess and lively personality.

[264] Churchill, Viscount. All my sins remembered. An Autobiography. Heinemann: London. (1964).

[265] In 1916 Verena persuaded Peter to marry a war widow named Katherine Beaven, daughter of a Canadian politician. This was to stop the rumours being spread by Peter's father that Verena was having an affair with Katherine. Peter remained married to Katherine (merely on paper) until she committed suicide in Bath in 1943.

[266] Antonio (Tony) de Gandarillas (1886-after 1940).

[267] Faulks, Sebastian. The Fatal Englishman. Three Short Lives. Vintage Books. (1997).

[268] Christopher (Kit) Wood (1901-1930). English painter.

[269] Churchill, Viscount. All my sins remembered. An Autobiography. Heinemann: London. (1964).

[270] Sir Francis Cyril Rose (1909-1979). Artist and close friend of Evan over many years.

[271] Evan was a long term friend of Tony and Tony's artist wife Carmen Gandarillas. They both attended Evan's Requiem Mass at Farm Street Church, London on Saturday 7 May 1949. See Sunday Times 8 May 1949.

[272] Full details are in Faulks, Sebastian. The Fatal Englishman. Three Short Lives. Vintage Books. (1997).

[273] Christopher Wood killed himself at Salisbury Railway Station on 21 August 1930 at the age of 29. He had a number of illegal drugs in his body system.

[274] See Nichols, Beverley. The Unforgiving Minute. W H Allen (1978). Beverley Nichols (1898-1983) served with Peter in the army during the Great War, in "Secret Service", an office in Whitehall Court. Peter introduced Nichols to the attendees of the Café Royal.

[275] Herbert, David. Second Son: an autobiography. Owen. (1972)

[276] There are a variety of stories about why Peter Churchill left to go to America. One suggestion is that he was declared bankrupt in England, another (which is in his Memoirs) is that he was accused of stealing jewels belonging to Alice Wimborne (his mother's relation). He denied that he stole anything, but Augustus John told him that the story was circulating in London about him being responsible. Peter claims the jewels were found. He adds in All My Sins Remembered "but the story of me as a jewel thief ….was to persist for a very long time."

[277] Hon. Violet Mundy (1860-1943). Courtenay Morgan's sister, wife of Basil St John Mundy (a cousin). A great horsewoman and farmer. The Mundys lived in Thornbury, Gloucestershire. Their only son, Evan's cousin, Lt Freddie Mundy

(1895-1917) was killed in the Great War. Basil Mundy died in 1926. Violet was Courtenay's regular hostess at parties and receptions at Tredegar House.

[278] Hon. Mary Anna Morgan (died 1924). Daughter of the 1st Lord and Lady Tredegar. She married Robert Devereux, 16th Viscount Hereford, in 1863. Robert was mentally unstable and spent 40 years in the Priory Clinic; he died there in 1930. Mary had a large family to rear and fell on her brother Godfrey (2nd Lord Tredegar) for financial help. She repaid this by acting at hostess at functions at Tredegar House.

[279] 1901 Census for Ruperra Castle shows Ella K Millar, Visitor aged 44. Freddie was aged 66 in 1901. In William Beechley's diary referred to in a book called Serving under Ruperra (from local historian, Pat Jones Jenkins) Ella is shown to have a position of authority in the Castle.

[280] Wife's petition for divorce, see papers at National Archives, Kew J77/671/410 and J77/738/2439.

[281] Robin Bryans describes Chester in Let the petals fall as "Evan's other Etonian friend Robin Chester who had long been Scoutmaster of Toynbee Hall in the East End." He was a partner in the law firm Rankin Ford and Chester of Grays Inn.

[282] Bryans, Robin. Checkmate: Memoirs of a Political Prisoner. Honeyford Press. (1994).

[283] Among these was Lord Edward Eugene Fernando Drogo Montagu (1906-1954), Son of the 9th Duke of Manchester. A womaniser, he had been in prison for fraud. A photograph of Edward feeding the pigs at the farm was published in the Daily Mirror in 1929. Other names mentioned among the "students" include Charles Philippe d' Orleans (Duc de Nemours), a member of the French Royal family); Mowbery Howard, Lord Howard of Effingham (1905-1996), whose wife was a target for suspicion by MI5 during the Second World War and Hon. John Stanley, a nephew of Lord Derby. Another contemporary of Evan who fled to farm in Alberta was Hon. Francis Eaton, son of Lord Cheylesmore; he inherited the barony in 1925 and died in 1974 at Happy Valley, Alberta, aged 80. He had two wives, but left no heir.

[284] Major General Sir Hector Archibald MacDonald (1853-1903), known as "Fighting Mac". A notable soldier in the late Victorian period, who shot himself in a hotel in Paris rather than face a court martial involving sexual misconduct with his male servants in Ceylon.

[285] Recent local histories in Newport use this term in describing Octavius. The word had not gained the stigma of being a derogatory term, more a descriptive word to describe the manner and dress of a person.

[286] Hon Selina Maria Morgan (died 1922) was a daughter of the 1st Lord and Lady Tredegar. She married David Williamson of Lawers in 1853. He died in 1913. They had one son Charles (Chat) Williamson (died 1943).

[287] Full details are Lees-Milne: The Enigmatic Edwardian. Life of Reginald, 2nd Viscount Esher. Sidgwick & Jackson Ltd. (1988). See also Kaplan, Morris B. Sodom on the Thames. Cornell University Press. (2005).

[288] There is a photograph from 1906 at a Morgan family wedding at Tredegar House, which features Chat with his mother Selina and his Aunt Mary (Viscountess Herford). Colonel Williamson was unable to attend the event, providing a perfect chance for Chat to see his mother..

[289] Further details about the life of Charles (Chat) Williamson and his antecedents can be found in Bernard Byrom's excellent book Gentlemen of Honour (2010).

[290] Captain Hon. Gerard Philip Montagu Napier Sturt (1893-1918).

[291] Amhurst, Jeffery. Wandering Abroad. Secker & Warburg (1976).

[292] Winifred Selina Sturt (1868-1914), later Lady Winifred Hardinge, was a Lady in Waiting and later a Lady of the Bedchamber to Princess Alexandra, later Queen Alexandra. Winifred's husband was a diplomat, Viceroy of India (1910-1916) and later British Ambassador to France.

[293] Amhurst, Jeffery. Wandering Abroad. Secker & Warburg (1976).

[294] Ibid.

[295] Ibid.

[296] Ibid.

[297] Bankes, Viola and Watkin Pamela. A Kingston Lacy childhood: reminiscences of Viola Bankes. Dovecote Press. (1986)

[298] National Archives Kew, War Diary WO95/3988
" 08.09.14….Miss Bills travelled by ambulance with Hon. G Sturt to St Nazaire to Lady Dudley's Home. He stood the journey well, hit in the region of the spine."

[299] Souhami Diana. Mrs Keppel and her Daughter. Harper Collins UK (1997).

[300] A time line in the Tredegar House Archives cites Evan's 1915 visit to see Gerard at Crichel and suggests this was the first time that Evan met Lois. He would also have seen her earlier than this (although may not have spoken to her) as the families were one time neighbours in London's Portman Square.

[301] In 1915, Gerard became engaged to Honor Dorothy Leigh (1892-1982), daughter of John Blundell Leigh and Lady Rose Nevill. She later married (whilst Gerard was still alive) Merton Beckwith-Smith, who died in a Japanese prisoner of war camp in 1942.

[302] One account in Jeffery Amherst's memoirs Wandering Abroad suggests Gerard died in a hospital in London. Gerard " Critically ill in a London hospital, they sent word to his mother that he was dying and wanted to see her. She sent word that she couldn't come at once as she had an engagement to go to the opera, but would come when it was over. When it was over so was…Gerard. He was dead." The Times of 12 November, 1918, to the contrary, reports that he died at Crichel House. Gerard's father was ill (and in London) at the time. The official death certificate (copy in National Archives file WO 339/ 8161 confirms the death was at Crichel, of the old gunshot wounds sustained four years previously, in 1914, and " Syncope".) Naps was the informant of his brother's death.

[303] See Gerard's army file at National Archives, Kew. The medical reports indicate he was improving but he needed perpetual personal care. He was engaged to Dorothy Leigh, only daughter of John Blundell Leigh, but felt he must always be a burden to her and beseeched her to give him up.

[304] WO 339/ 8161. Exemption / remission of death duties was permitted under the Death Duties (Killed in War) Acts, with time limits applying.

[305] Hon. Guy Edward Colebrooke (1893-1921), heir and only son to Lord Colebrooke. A seasoned traveller in Germany, in 1918 Guy was appointed Secretary to the British Ambassador to Rome. He was also briefly in Paris, whilst Spanish flu raged throughout Europe. Guy served in the war in the RNVR and spent time in the war years in Scandinavia and Russia. He died in a nursing home in London on 19 January 1921. Guy's sister Bridget (1892-1975) had an affair with the Prince of Wales before she married her cousin Lord Victor Paget whose first wife was a showgirl, Olive May.

[306] Edward Arthur Colebrooke (1861-1939), first and last Lord Colebrooke. The barony lapsed with his death. His wife was a member of the Paget (Marquess of Anglesey family).

[307] Guy's mother Alexandra Paget (1865-1944) was granddaughter of Henry William Paget, 1st Marquis of Anglesey. She famously owned a munitions factory in the Great War.

[308] Sir Lancelot Douglas Carnegie (1861-1933). Diplomat and statesman. British Ambassador to Portugal (1925).

[309] Katharine's half-brother was Charles Noel Carnegie (1854-1941), 10th Earl of Southesk. Her brother Lancelot (1861-1933, later Sir Lancelot) was a diplomat and British Ambassador to Portugal. Katharine and Lancelot's nephew (Lord Southesk's eldest son) Charles Alexander Bannerman Carnegie (1893-1992) married in 1923 Princess Maud Alexandra Victoria Georgina Bertha Duff (1893-1945). Charles became the 11th Earl of Southesk. He was a member of the Right Club.

[310] Maurice Richardson in the Times Literary Supplement 7 July 1978 in a book review relating to Philip Purcer's Where is he now? on the poet, artist Edward James.

[311] Thomas Banks Strong (1861-1944).

[312] Gilbert Keith Chesterton (1874-1936). Best known as GK. Writer and poet, with an early fascination for the occult.

[313] Hilaire Belloc (1870-1952). Anglo French writer, poet and historian.

[314] Raymond Rodakowski (1895-1916). Son of Evan's aunt (Katharine's sister Dora Carnegie.)

[315] Cyril Hughes Hartmann. (died 1967). Friend of Raymond Rodakowski at Charterhouse School and Oxford. Regular correspondent of Evan. Requested by Evan in his Will to write his biography. See Aspects of Evan for a closer perspective on their friendship. Hartmann devoted a chapter of his (unpublished) auto-biography to Evan. A copy of this is in the Tredegar House files.

[316] Robert Graves, (1895-1985). Poet. Contemporary and friend of Raymond Rodakowski at Charterhouse School. Features in Graves' classic Goodbye To All That.

[317] According to Raymond's letters another mutual friend of Raymond and Evan was George Patrick Gough (1889-1936), a kinsman of Viscount Gough, and a Captain in the Irish Guards. Gough was at Eton College with Evan.

[318] Lady Ottoline Violet Anne Morrell (1873-1938). Society hostess at Garsington Manor, near Oxford and in London. Along with her husband Philip Edward Morrell (1870-1943, a Liberal party politician) Ottoline acted as a Society host in London and at Garsington Manor, near Oxford. Ottoline had many lovers including several personalities that criss-crossed in Evan's life including the Swedish doctor and animal lover Axel Munthe (1857-1949) and the painter Augustus John. See Aspects of Evan for the interaction between Evan and Axel Munthe, in Sicily.

[319] Bryans, Robin. The Dust Has Never Settled. Honeyford Press (1992).

[320] Nancy Cunard (1896-1965). Socialite, a member of the Cunard shipping family.

[321] Nancy Cunard gathered around her a clique of poets and painters, dubbed her Corrupt Coterie The circle included "Osbert Sitwell, Evan Morgan, Iris Tree, Alvaro "Chile" Guevara, Robert Nichols and Augustus John" – cited in Nancy's Negro: An Anthology.

[322] Gray, Cecil. Musical chairs: Between two stools. Home & Van Thal Ltd. (1948).

[323] Ibid.

[324] Jacob Epstein (1880-1959). American born, British Society and public sculptor.

[325] Philip Arnold Heseltine (1894-1930). Used the pseudonym of Peter Warlock. Contemporary of Evan at Eton and Christ Church, Oxford. Composer and occultist. Committed suicide.

[326] Cecil Gray (1895-1951). Music critic, composer and author. Born Edinburgh. Friend of Philip Heseltine.

[327] Clara Novello Davies (1861-1943). Welsh singer, teacher and conductor. Mother of Ivor Novello.

[328] David Ivor Novello (1893-1951). Composer, singer, actor and homosexual.

[329] Fragments of Autobiography. (By Augustus John) Published in Horizon Magazine 1941.

[330] William Horace de Vere Cole (1881-1936).

[331] Natholie Mamontova Majolier. A member of a Russian émigré family with Imperial links through her mother.

[332] Majolier, Natholie Mamontova. Step-daughter of Imperial Russia. S Apul (1940).

[333] Several of Horace's exploits are mentioned in The Town: Men and Intimacies column of The Sunday Times, 1 February 1931.

[334] George William Frederick FitzGeorge (1892-1960). A Lt. Commander in the navy (retired 1919). Adjudged bankrupt in 1931 "by unjustifiable extravagance". The Times of 25 May 1933 reported he was "living in the Balearic Islands. He had lodged a statement of affairs and had said he was living there because he could not afford to live in England. He was also lacking the fare to London."

[335] See Rose, Francis, Sir. Saying Life: The Memoirs of Sir Francis Rose. Cassell. (1971).

[336] David Herbert Lawrence (1885-1930). Novelist and poet. An occasional visitor to Garsington Manor. Travelled extensively abroad. Women in Love was published in 1920.

[337] According to Mark L Evans in Portraits by Augustus John: family, friends and the famous. National Museum of Wales (1988) "In 1916 Epstein executed a bronze head of Augustus, a cast of which was acquired by Lady Tredegar, whose son

donated it to the National Library (acc.39.390)" of Wales. See also annual report for 1939 of the National Museum of Wales.

[338] William Henry Davies (1871-1940). Welsh poet famous for his Autobiography of a Super-Tramp and his poem Leisure.

[339] John's correspondence is in the National Library of Wales.

[340] Sir Michael De Courcy Fraser Holroyd (born 1935). Leading biographer of his generation. Noted for his work on Augustus John, Lytton Strachey and George Bernard Shaw.

[341] The Sketch, Volume 113, page 87. (1921).

[342] See Camera Magazine, Volume 25, page 152 and Photo-era Magazine, Volumes 46-7 page 287. Karl Tausig was an amateur photographer of New York, a member of that City's Camera Club. Evan's picture brought Tausig the blue ribbon in the grand portrait class at Atlantic City in 1920.

[343] Photo-era Magazine, Volumes 46-7 page 287.

[344] Holroyd. Michael. Augustus John. The New Biography. Vintage (1997).

[345] Gerald Tyrwhitt, (1883-1950). 14th Lord Berners. Composer, diplomat and eccentric.

[346] See Ferris, Paul. Dylan Thomas. A Biography. Athena Books. Paragon House. (1989).

[347] Bryans, Robin. Let the petals fall. Honeyford Press (1993).

[348] Henri Gaudier-Brzeska (1891-1915). French sculptor renowned for his primitive style of carving. Made famous by Ken Russell's Savage Messiah, a film about his life and work. He was killed in the trenches at the age of 23.

[349] Amedeo Modigliani (1884-1920) Italian painter and sculptor who worked mainly in France. Died in Paris. In The Jerome Connection, Seymour Leslie describes Nina as " Modigliani's friend and model."

[350] Madame Marie Vassilieva (1884-1957), Russian Empire painter. See Laughing Torso. Ray Long & Richard R Smith Inc. (1932). Vassilieva made "the most amusing dolls, portraits of people… She made two of Evan Morgan in evening dress, with a white shirt and every detail of his clothes, cuff links, button, shoes, all imitated in an extraordinary ingenious way. "

[351] Princess Eugene Murat (1878-1936) Also known as Violet or Violette, she married one of the Bonapartes. She was sketched by Augustus John, who refers to her in his autobiography Chiaroscuro.

[352] John Augustus. Chiaroscuro. Fragments of Autobiography. Pellegrini & Cudahy. (1952)

[353] Ernest John Moeran (1894-1950). English composer with Irish parentage. His hard drinking with Warlock led to acute alcoholism and bad health.

[354] The London art critic Brian Sewell claims in his autobiography that he is Warlock's son. See Outsider. Always Almost: Never Quite (2 volumes).

[355] Hamnett, Nina. Is She a Lady? A Problem in Autobiography. Alan Wingate. (1955).

[356] Ibid.

[357] John, Augustus. Chiaroscuro. Fragments of Autography. Pellegrini & Cadahy. (1952).

[358] Ibid.

[359] Bryans, Robin. The Dust Has Never Settled. (1992).

[360] Holroyd. Michael. Augustus John. The New Biography. Vintage (1997)

[361] Sir Harold George Nicolson, KCVO, CMG (1886-1968).

[362] A few names are given in Dart, Monty and Cross William, Aspects of Evan. Book Midden Publishing (2012)

[363] See Souhami, Diana. Mrs Keppel and her daughter, St Martins Press (1996). Also Leaska Mitchell A & Phillips [Editors]. Violet to Vita: The Letters of Violet Trefusis to Vita Sackville-West. Mandarin (1990), which cites Harold's "infatuation with Pierre de Lacretelle" (a banker in Constantinople) and an " affair with Edward Molyneux" (1891-1974), a British fashion designer.)

[364] Ibid. The attendees included homosexuals Sir Edward Marsh (1872-1953) and Osbert Sitwell (1892-1969). Also present were the distinguished foreign diplomats Sir Horace Rumbold (1869-1941) and Sir Lois Malet (1864-1936).

[365] Evan's father was Courtenay Charles Evan Morgan (1867-1934), 3rd Lord Tredegar, 1st Viscount (1926 creation). Landowner, sailor, and minor politician. Harold was the youngest of three sons; his father was Arthur Nicolson (1849-1928), created 1st Lord Carnock, 1916. He was a British diplomat who served in Berlin, Peking, Athens, Teheran, Budapest, Constantinople, Tangiers, Madrid (Ambassador) and Saint Petersburg (Ambassador). Evan inherited his father's titles, Harold's elder brother Frederick (1883-1952) became the 2nd Lord Carnock, a notable lawyer, and was unmarried.

[366] A gathering of representatives of most of the nations of the world, to settle the issues from Great War and reach a Peace Treaty. Delegates were summoned to Paris in December 1918 and the formal session began on 18 January 1919. The end game was the treaty of Versailles.

[367] This gave rise to Augustus John recording in one of his letters [held in National Library of Wales, March 1919] "Evan Morgan is busy translating French which he doesn't understand"

[368] One visit to Bath is recorded in The Sunday Times for 21 January 1917. "The Hon. Frederick Morgan visited the Empire Hotel, Bath, during the past week."

[369] Despite his lung problems, Evan smoked cigarettes. This was always an irritation to his father, Courtenay. When at Tredegar House at the same time as his father, Evan had to sneak off to various voids in the house to enjoy a smoke, with comment.

[370] Letter in The Bridgeman Papers in Shropshire Archives Ref 4129/1/1918/20 Evan Morgan to William Bridgeman.

[371] Sir Harold George Nicolson (1886-1968). Civil Servant, diplomat and author.

[372] Vita Sackville-West, Lady Nicolson (1892-1962). Poet and gardener. Known for her lesbian affair with the writer and poet Violet Trefusis (nee Keppel, 1894-1972) and passionate relationship with the novelist Virginia Woolf (1882-1941).

[373] See Dart, Monty and Cross William. A Beautiful Nuisance. Book Midden Publishing (2012).

[374] Huxley, Aldous. Crome Yellow. (1921). A number of online versions of the book are available on the Internet.

[375] Notwithstanding that Vita Sackville-West and Virginia Woolf enjoyed a closeness. Indeed the Nicolsons were on very good terms with Virginia and Leonard Woolf. See Bell, Quentin: Virginia Woolf. Paladon, (1976). Bell records "the book [Orlando, by Virginia Woolf] commemorates Virginia's love for Vita."

[376] See The Manchester Guardian, 5 February 1954.

[377] Letter in The Bridgeman Papers in Shropshire Archives Ref 4129/1/1918/20 Evan Morgan to William Bridgeman.

[378] Ibid.

[379] Ibid.

[380] To "make twins" or "making twins" is a euphemism used by Robin Bryans in his books to describe Evan having sex with men. The phrase was first used by Evan's friend Rosa Lewis, the proprietor of the Cavendish Hotel, London which Evan frequently used for his sexual rendezvous.

[381] Bryans, Robin, Let the petals fall. Honeyford Press (1993).

[382] Lonsdale Bryans. J. Blind Victory. (Secret Communications, Halifax-Hassell). Skeffington and Son Ltd. (1951).

[383] Ibid.

[384] Sassoon was about to be Court Martialled. Evan's Oxford chum the poet Robert Graves wrote to Evan asking him to put a good word in Whitehall circles over Sassoon's stand in throwing his war medals away and refusing to return to fight. A compromise followed whereby Sassoon was sent to a mental hospital for treatment. See also Dart Monty and Cross, William. Aspects of Evan. Book Midden Publishing (2012).

[385] Frances Stevenson (1888-1972). Secretary and mistress of David Lloyd George, later his 2nd wife and Countess.

[386] Frances Stevenson describes Evan's antics and her eventual realisation of him being a degenerate and a liar in her Memoirs The Years That Are Past, also see Campbell, John. If Love Were All, The Story of Frances Stevenson and David Lloyd George. Jonathan Cape (2006).

[387] George Allardice Riddell (1865-1934). Lawyer and Newspaper Magnate. Made a peer in 1920.

[388] See the Lloyd George Papers in the Parliamentary Archives. Letter from Frances Stevenson to H J Creedy (ref LG/F/8/3/35) "the Hon. Evan Morgan's resignation from the Welsh Guards, and Sir C Riddles' (sic) wish to keep Morgan in Paris for Peace Conference work."

[389] William Maxwell "Max" Aitken, Lord Beaverbrook (1879-1964). Newspaper magnate and politician.

[390] See Nicolson, Harold G. Peacemaking 1919: Being Reminiscences of the Paris Peace Conference. Simon Publications. (2001). A reprint of an earlier publication.

[391] See Hyde, Montgomery, H. The Other Love. An Historical and Contemporary Survey of Homosexuality in Britain. Heinemann (1970). "Notable literary-cum-political observers ....are conspicuously silent on the subject of the homosexual tastes of their fellow writers and others in the public eye..." Harold Nicolson is mentioned here. A footnote by Hyde declares "Mr Nigel Nicolson, who edited his

father's diaries, informs me that there are no references to homosexuality in the unpublished portions."

[392] Nicolson's Conference diaries indicate he spent time with the bachelor playwright Edward (Eddie) Knoblock (1874-1945, author of Kismet) who had a flat in Paris. Another of Nicolson's hideaways was with the dress designer Edward Molyneux (1891-1974), a mutual friend of Evan. Edward had a flat in the Rond Point.

[393] From Robin Bryans' memoirs.

[394] This story is revealed in The Journals of Denton Welch. Edited by Michael De-la-Noy. Allison & Busby (1984).

[395] See Bryans, Robin. Blackmail and Whitewash. Honeyford Press (1996).

[396] Carrington, Dora de, Houghton & Garnet David. Carrington: letters and extracts from her diaries. Holt, Rinehart and Winston. (1971). Entry for 2 November 1920. Ralph Partridge (1894-1960) was one of the lesser-known members of the Bloomsbury group.

[397] Cardinal Amette of Paris (1850-1920).

[398] The Tablet, 22 May 1920.

[399] South Wales Argus, 22 May 1920.

[400] These two subjects, of Courtenay's interrogation by the Coal Commission and Alys Bray's involvement in the libel case between Pemberton Billings and Maud Allen - the infamous Cult of the Clitoris - are covered in Dart, Monty and Cross William. A Beautiful Nuisance. Book Midden Publishing (2012).

[401] The Guardian, 20 May 1920.

[402] Firbank, Ronald. The Princess Zoubaroff. Grant Richards Ltd. (1920).

[403] Alan Hollinghurst writes in the Times Literary Supplement on 17 November 2006: "When Siegfried Sassoon pressed [Firbank] for his views on literature and art, the only thing Firbank could find to say was, " I adore italics, don't you?"

[404] See Foreword to Vainglory by Richard Canning. Penguin UK. (2012).

[405] Cited in Horder Mervyn. Ronald Firbank: Memoirs and Critiques. Duckworth (1977).

[406] Books of note in the period 1916-1926 are Caprice, Valmouth, The Flower Beneath the Foot and Prancing Nigger (as known as Sorrow in Sunlight)

[407] Raymond Mortimer's review of Ronald Firbank, a Biography by Miriam J Benkovitz in the Sunday Times, 15 February, 1970.

[408] See Sunday Times 3 March 1957.

[409] From The Diaries of Donald Friend: 1967-1999, published by the National Library of Australia (2001)

[410] See Fletcher, Ifran Kyrle. Ronald Firbank: A Memoir. Duckworth. (1930. Reviewed in the Sunday Times 18 January 1931.

[411] Evan's letter to Dicky Buckle in 1940. Buckle (an aspiring ballet critic whom Evan had befriended) asked Evan for his memories of Firbank.

[412] Ibid.

[413] A well known law firm based in Holborn, London.

[414] Benkovitz, Miriam J. A Bibliography of Ronald Firbank. Rupert Hart-Davis (1963).

[415] Firbank believed in the existence of " special days" in the calendar, which he deemed lucky to publish his books. Grant Richards was further curtailed by this provision.

[416] Benkovitz, Miriam J. A Bibliography of Ronald Firbank. Rupert Hart-Davis (1963).

[417] Ibid.

[418] Ibid.

[419] Ibid.

[420] Richard (Dicky) Buckle (1916-2000). Close friend of Evan from 1930s until death.

[421] See Aspects of Evan for comment on this. Lord Aberdeen actually ceased as Viceroy of Ireland during the Great War.

[422] Benkovitz, Miriam J. A Bibliography of Ronald Firbank. Rupert Hart-Davis (1963).

[423] A full description of Evan's Papal nomination can be found in Aspects of Evan, including details of the research visit to the Vatican Secrets Archives by the Author with Monty Dart. Chamberlain of the Sword and Cape was not so grand a title as it sounds - it was an honorific title given quite freely to aristocrats and other generous donors.

[424] Daily Mirror, 19 December 1923.

[425] Francis Edward Joseph Mostyn (1860-1939), Archbishop of Cardiff from 1921 until his death.

[426] Gasquet was the English Cardinal based in Rome. A scholar and attached to the Vatican Secrets Archives. He befriended Evan during the 1920s.

[427] Attributed to Shane Leslie by Robin Bryans.

[428] Bryans Robin. Let the petals fall. Honeyford Press (1993).

[429] Reference is made in Aspects of Evan to the visit to Beda College in 2009. Refer to Author for further details on this.

[430] Princess Elsie = Princess Mary; Mr Chilleywater = Harold Nicolson; Mrs Chilleywater = Vita Sackville-West; King Geo & Queen Glory = King George V and Queen Mary.

[431] See Aspects of Evan for references to a description of Evan by Donald Friend, the Australian artist, concerning Evan's scandalous reputation on the Island of Bali, Indonesia, where Evan was known as Tuan Raja, after a curious phallic symbol.

Another episode that refers to Evan's phallus is told by Robin Bryans in Blackmail & Whitewash. "An American guest at [Evan's] town house pestered him with a request that he put on his peer's robes had had just worn at the Coronation of George VI, in order that he might make a colour cine-photo. [Evan] consented finally and his guest to take him as he came downstairs. Evan duly appeared in all his regalia, wearing his coronet, ermine cape and crimson robe. Half way down the stairs he opened his robe. He had nothing underneath. The extravaganza on the stately staircase took place not simply to shock the American guest but to show off the size of Evan's penis and his pride in it."

[432] Aleister Crowley (1875-1947). Born Edward Alexander Crowley.

[433] The Daily and Sunday Express used this term and other copied it.

[434] According to John Symonds in The King of the Shadow Realm: Aleister Crowley his life and magic, Duckworth(1989) p125, "No. VII of The Equinox [one of Crowley's publications] which was issued in 1911, contains a full-page reproduction of a drawing by Augustus John of Crowley in a meditative pose with closed eyes. John made three drawings of Crowley, the second about 1912, the third and last in 1946, shortly before Crowley's death. To the Beast's regret John declined to paint his portrait."

[435] John, Augustus. Chiaroscuro. Fragments of Autobiography. Pellegrini & Cudahy. (1952).

[436] Greene, Raymond. Moments of being. Heinemann. (1974).

[437] Ibid.

[438] From articles in the newspaper John Bull, which maintained a campaign against Crowley throughout the early 1920s. Other newspapers joined this campaign, which was at its height in 1923 when the Sunday Express revealed the story of Raoul Loveday (a former Oxford University student) who had died mysteriously at Crowley's Abbey in Cefalu, Sicily. Loveday had died of a drugs overdose but the death had been blown up to include (in the testimony of his wife, an artists' model named Betty May) details of the sex rituals at Cefalu, ruled over by Crowley, and which included drinking animal blood. One man who investigated Raoul's death was an Oxford friend and a doctor, Charles Raymond Greene (1901-1982), and who describes a visit to Cefalu in his memoirs Moments of Being, published by Heinemann in 1974. Greene's judgement was that Betty May had exaggerated her story. "The sinister 'abbey' was a small white bungalow, surrounded by olive trees...as we approached we could hear the laughter of children. They were clean and healthy. And did not seem to have been upset by having been, as John Bull had said, 'forced to witness nameless horrors'" Greene says of his inquiries in the village "Crowley was quite well-liked and certainly not feared.... I was convinced that Raoul had died a natural death and Dr Maggio, an obviously reliable man who had attended him, confirmed this". Crowley was eventually expelled from Sicily by the Italian government in April 1923.

[439] Hamnett, Nina. Laughing Torso. Ray Long & Richard R Smith Inc. (1932)

[440] The dedication dated September 1931 reads "To Harold Nicolson and Douglas Goldring without whose kindness and encouragement I should never have written this book." NB Douglas Goldring (1887-1960) was a writer and prominent member of the 1917 Club, a group of socialists formed by Leonard Woolf, (husband of Virginia). Members included Aldous Huxley, HG Wells and Ramsay MacDonald.

[441] Cefalu is described as forty miles from Palermo, a large village with a railway station.

[442] Hamnett, Nina. Laughing Torso. Ray Long & Richard R Smith Inc. (1932)

[443] Cecil Maitland was a friend of Mary Butts. They both stayed with Crowley at his Abbey at Cefalu, also dubbed the Temple of Thelema in Sicily. According to Nina Hamnett in her memoirs Laughing Torso ".... The climate and the bad food nearly killed Cecil and Mary, and when they came back to Paris they looked like two ghosts and were hardly recognizable."

[444] Ibid.

[445] Ibid.

[446] Ibid.

[447] Mary Butts (1890-1937), Writer. Some-time devotee of Aleister Crowley in his famous temple of Thelema on Sicily which was associated with drug taking and occult rituals.

[448] Butts is credited with working with Crowley on several of his books. She spent 12 weeks at Thelema with her close friend Cecil Maitland.

[449] Butts Mary and Blondel Nathalie. *The Journals of Mary Butts*. Yale University Press. (2000)

[450] Ibid.

[451] Angus Wilson (1913-1991), homosexual and dandy.

[452] Angus Wilson co-authored *For whom the cloche tolls: A scrap-book of the twenties* (1953) with Philippe Jullian (1921-1977, another dandy and biographer of Oscar Wilde), which records "....his friends Mary Butt and Evan Morgan (later an important lord) and Aleister Crowley (a terrible man)." Reflecting on Evan in 1969 Jullian (a French illustrator and aesthete) wrote "Lord Tredegar was witty, very well read and cynical in the manner of those to those to whom everything comes without effort." Vogue Magazine.

[453] See Butts Mary and Blondel Nathalie. *The Journals of Mary Butts*. Yale University Press. (2000) Journal entry for 1927. p262.

[454] Michael Arlen (1895-1956), Armenian, born Dikran Kouyoumdjian, writer and playwright. Roger Wilkes notes in his book Scandal: A scurrilous History of Gossip that "Arlen who was not homosexual...but 'in the climate of the time'....gay".

[455] Forward to Arlen's novel The Green Hat. Capuchin Classics (2008).

[456] Connolly Cyril. The Evening Colonnade. David Bruce & Watson (1973).

[457] Francis Cyril Rose (1909-1979). 4th Baronet. Inherited the title as a small boy. One reference (Rough Guide to Corsica by David Abram) says of Rose's mother: "the son of a wildly beautiful Franco-Spanish arts impresario, Laetitia Rouy, Rose had grown up in Paris knowing Sarah Bernhardt, Jean Cocteau and Isadora Duncan, and had designed sets and costumes for Diaghilev while still in his 20s."

[458] Gertrude Stein (1874-1946). American expatriate author and art collector. Stein saw Rose's work and bought it up. She later met the artist (in 1931) and they became friends.

[459] Wineapple, Brenda. Genet: A Biography of Janet Flanner. University of Nebraska Press, (1992).

[460] Jean Cocteau (1889-1963). French poet, writer and film maker. Mentor/Lover of the bisexual writer Raymond Radiguet (1903-1923).

[461] Rose designed a cookbook for Toklas. Several of his paintings are in the Yale University Art Gallery (Stein-Toklas collection).

[462] Stein, Gertrude, Holbrook Susan, Thomson, Virgil and Dilworth, Thomas: The Letters of Gertrude Stein and Virgil Thomson. Composition As Conversation. Oxford University Press (2009).

[463] Coop, Emmanuel. The Sexual Perspective: Homosexuality and Art in the Last 100 Years in the West. Routledge, (1994).

[464] See Nichols, Beverley. The Unforgiving Minute. W H Allen (1978).

[465] See. Herbert. David. Second Son: an autobiography. Owen. (1972).

[466] Rose, Francis. Saying Life. The Memoirs of Sir Francis Rose. Cassell (1961).

[467] Ibid.

[468] After the Paris Peace Conference Harold Nicolson joined the British Embassy in Berlin in the 1920s and in several other foreign fields, including Teheran, the city where he was born. Nicolson's father Arthur Nicolson was serving in the British delegation in Teheran from 1885 to 1888. Whilst Harold was later serving in Teheran, Vita Sackville-West visited her husband and a description of this is in her book Passenger to Teheran.

[469] Edward Sackville-West, (1901-1965). 5th Baron Sackville. Music critic and writer.

[470] See Firchow Peter Edgerly. Strange Meetings: Anglo-German Literary Encounters from 1910 to 1960. CUA Press (2008)

[471] Ibid.

[472] Ibid.

[473] See file at National Archives, Kew J 77/3117/5878.

[474] See Teeling, William. Corridors of Frustration. Johnson. (1970). Referring to this era " In Germany...one's room was often searched and no one ever knew where were the hidden tape-recorders."

[475] Hamilton. Gerald. The Way it Was With Me. Leslie Frewin. (1969).

[476] Marchesa Luisa Casati (1881-1957) Eccentric Italian Hostess, Socialite, exiled in London where she was financially maintained by the likes of Evan and Naps Alington.

[477] A long way from the likes of Lady Christabel Aberconway, yet it was Christabel who enjoyed challenging Crowley in a contest over whether the power of a magic book she picked up whilst visiting him in London with Cynthia Jebb. Crowley told Christabel to put the book down at once or she would die instantly. She didn't take any notice of him, after which as she survived. Crowley said she was one of the *Elect* and he must read the language of the Angels to her at another meeting, which she accepted. The full tale is in Christabel's autobiography A Wiser Woman: A Book of Memories. Hutchinson & Co (1966). Christabel comments "Poor Aleister, people still believe he had magical powers. I wonder! Anyhow I will undertake that my magic will do down his magic any day and anywhere." She later adds that she thought Crowley "an old fraud".

[478] Louis Umfreville Wilkinson (1881-1966). Novelist, biographer and Man of Letters.

[479] See Bryans, Robin Checkmate. Honeyford Press. (1994). " Aleister Crowley and Evan Tredegar grew so close to Wilkinson that Crowley appointed Wilkinson as one of his executors." Evan "helped [Wilkinson] to become a Fellow of the Royal Society of Literature."

[480] Cited by Howard, Michael. Modern Wicca. Llewellyn Worldwide. (2010).

[481] Gerald Hamilton (1888-1970). Homosexual, hustler in his youth, friend of such rakes as Maundy Gregory and Aleister Crowley. Some texts suggest Hamilton was paid to spy on Crowley.

[482] Mr Norris Changes Trains was published in 1935. Author Christopher Isherwood (1904-1986). Novelist and poet.

[483] John Symonds. (1914-2006). Novelist and biographer. Literary Executive of Aleister Crowley.
[484] See Symonds, John. Conversations with Gerald. Duckworth. (1974).

Clive James reports "At Boca Inferno, on the coast west of Cascais [near Lisbon], there is a stone inscription in Portuguese, referring to Alisteir Crowley [yes, spelt like that] re a 20 day experience, including mock suicide at Sintra with Fernando Pessoa. My Portuguese is not that good! It seemed to indicate, was described as "A Mulher Escarlate" [A Scarlet Woman!], Sept. 1930. "

[485] Dart, Monty and Cross William. Aspects of Evan. The Last Viscount Tredegar. Book Midden Publishing. (2012)

[486] The title given to a BBC Radio Wales programme about the event, in the Past Master series (broadcast 2 January 2011). The author took part in this programme.

[487] A seating plan (unseen by the author, and a request for a copy to verify its veracity by referring it to a Hess historian (who has access to Hess's diaries) was ignored by its custodian. This list apparently shows the expected attendees at the restaurant included Francis Rose, Evan Morgan, James Lonsdale Bryans, Jack Macnamara (1905-1944), Ernst Rohm (1887-1934), Edmund Heines (1897-1934), Rudolf Hess (1894-1987) and Albrecht Haushofer (1903-1945), a friend of Hess, killed by the German military. The Englishmen were all homosexuals, as were Rohm and Heines.

A Hess historian, Mark Bullock, who has access to the diaries of several of the Germans mentioned comments "I have been informed that for the majority of 1930-33 Albrecht Haushofer was rarely in Germany. There were small windows in which he was in Germany but they were very rare occasions, and there are no mentions of Albrecht ever meeting Evan. "

A further remark by Bullock is on note: "Maybe the name on the list was not Rudolf Hess (Rudolf Heß), but rather should read Rudolf Hoss (Rudolf Hoß). It was rumoured that the once time Auschwitz Commander was a rampant homosexual. It was also rumoured that Rohem and Hoss had some kind of interlude(s)!"

[488] In Stephen McCinty's book Camp Z (How British Intelligence Broke Hitler's Deputy) Quercus (2011) he writes about a salacious report (from the Russians) compiled on Rudolf Hess saying "Hess had once belonged to a group of 'hots' (homosexuals) who nicknamed him Black Bertha, a name by which he was referred to behind his back, not only in Munich and Berlin where he was also referred to as 'she' and his wife as 'he'."

[489] Ernst Julius Gunther Rohm (1887-1934). An early Nazi Commander and homosexual. Met his death (on Hitler's orders) in the Night of the Long Knives.

[490] Hess historian Mark Bullock comments in the absence of seeing the document:

"There is nothing to prove or disprove the meeting as fact in the archives. If there was a more precise date then the myth/truth could be established in a matter of hours. Now, this is the clincher. The seating plan/menu needs to be looked at. There will be a few tell-tale signs if it is from the restaurant or not; for instance, is the seating plan headed and bearing the actual date, not just 1931? Are there any folds in the paper? This will prove that the person (Evan) folded the paper up and placed it in his pocket. Now there is another way to spot whether the document is a fake; there is a logo that needs to be on there: if there is no logo it is a fake. Now the biggest question, why would each person at the meeting have an individual seating plan issued to them? Only the Osteria would have the seating plan, drawn up by the host. There would be place cards on the table to show where people were to sit, and the place card would be the only item that Evan would be able to remove.

I don't know if you are aware, but the Osteria seating plans are actually documented. I have had another source check them, and there are no seating plans for the period of 1930 to 1934 that bear Evan's name or his title(s)."

[491] Bryans, Robin. Blackmail and Whitewash. Honeyford Press. (1996).

[492] Between 30 June and 2 July 1934 this was a round up of those in Hitler's regime who posed a threat. Many of those killed were leaders of the Sturmabteilung (SA) and the paramilitary brownshirts.

[493] West, Timothy. Moment Towards the End of the Play. Nick Hern Books. (2001).

[494] See Bryans, Robin. Let the petals fall. Honeyford Press (1993).

[495] Beliner Mittwochsgesellschaft " Secret Berlin Wednesday Society" 1780s Club.

[496] Pastor Martin Niemoller (1892-1984). Anti Nazi theologian and poet.

[497] Bryans, Robin. The Dust Has Never Settled. Honeyford Press (1992). Elsewhere in Checkmate Robin Bryans says that two other people (Princess Despina Karadja and Elizabeth Sprigge) were involved in "some deal for the release of Pastor Niemoller."

[498] Lady Muriel Henrietta Constance Hay (died 2 Jan 1927), married. 3 Jun 1890 Prince Alexander Münster (died 1922), son of Prince Münster, German Ambassador to London, and had issue Count Friedrich zu Münster (1891-1942). Friedrich married Sylvia Fugger von Babenhausen (1892-1949 – they were divorced in 1928.

[499] Hon Agnes Blanche Marie Hay (born 6 Dec 1873; died 13 Dec 1938), married 21 Feb 1903 Baron Herbert Beneckendorff und von Hindeburg (1872-1956), a German diplomat. Agnes was a writer and biographer.

[500] Bryans, Robin. Let the petals fall. Honeyford Press (1993).

[501] George Hay-Drummond, 12th Earl of Kinnoull (1827-1897). A Scottish Earl. The family seat was at Dupplin Castle, Perthshire. His wife (a daughter of the 7th Duke of Beaufort) died in 1895, she bore him ten children. Dupplin Castle and estates were sold in 1911 to Lord Forteviot (the Dewar (Distillers) family). Co-incidentally Caroline Dewar (daughter of the 3rd Lord Forteviot) married Evan's cousin, James Carnegie, the present Duke of Fife, in 1956.

[502] In his book Blind Victory, Lonsdale Bryans refers to dining with Baron Herbert von Hindenburg at the Hotel Bristol in Berlin in August 1930 when the Baron (despite being a Royalist) admitted that national-socialism appeared to be the only

possible alternative to a communist debacle – and, of the two...the lesser evil. [There is no mention of Evan being present.]

[503] See Bryans, Robin. Let the petals fall. Honeyford Press (1993). Edward Frederick Lindley Wood (1881-1959), known as Lord Halifax, was the British Foreign Secretary from 1938 until 1940. Later served as British Ambassador to USA in the Second World War.

[504] Ibid.

[505] Lady Marian Ileene Mabel Cameron (1895-1947) nee Hastings, later Bridges. Former wife of Patrick Keith Cameron and later wife of John Walter Wilson Bridges. Marian was the daughter of the 15th Earl of Huntingdon.

[506] Myrtle Farquharson (1897-1941). From an old Scottish family of Invercauld. Myrtle was killed in the London Blitz on 11 May 1941.

[507] Mentioned in The Singapore Free Press for 21 January 1937.

[508] The Times, 4 December 1936.

[509] Viscount Hastings, (1901-1990). From 1939 the Earl of Huntingdon.

[510] Tallulah Bankhead (1902-1968). American-born daughter of an Alabama politician, known for her husky voice and torrid affairs with several men and women.

[511] Sir Guy Francis William Laking, (1904-1930). Guy was the 3rd and last baronet. His only sister, a spinster, Joan, died in Pretoria, Transvaal on 29 June 1943, aged 43. NB In 2004, a historian named Tor Bomann-Larsen claimed that Princess Maud of Norway artificially used Guy's father's sperm – in a process perfected by Guy's grandfather in 1902. Accordingly the Laking family may have sired the Norwegian Royal Family. See The Times, 15 October 2004.

[512] At the Inquest in Westminster Coroners Court the cause of death was "diabetes, with coma caused by obstruction of the pancreas by a cyst." See Manchester Guardian, 9 August 1930.

[513] Barrow, Andrew. Gossip. Fifty Years of High Society from 1920-1970. Pan Books (1978).

[514] Stern, Keith. Queers in History: The Comprehensive Encyclopedia of His BenBella Books.

[515] Israel, Lee. Miss Tallulah Bankhead. Putnam, (1972). In Tallulah: My Autobiography, Univ. Press of Mississippi (2004) Tallulah records "under any biological classification I must describe his [Laking's] gender as neuter. He lithped."

[516] Quoted in The Manchester Guardian 3 March 2000 in an article entitled "MI5 spied on Tallulah's romp with Eton schoolboys". See also National Archives, Kew file HO 382/9.

[517] Brendan Gill. Tallulah comes to London. The Times, 4 August 1973.

[518] Barrow, Andrew. Gossip. Fifty Years of High Society from 1920-1970. Pan Books (1978).

[519] The Times, 29 December 1951.

[520] Edward (Ned) William [Bootle-Wilbraham], 3rd Earl of Lathom (1895-1930).

[521] Connon, Bryan. Beverley Nichols: a life. Constable, (1991).

[522] See Daily Express, 27 April 2002, pages 52-3 for an article (by Simon Edge) on Lathom at the time a review entitled "Lathom Glitterati" was held to celebrate Lathom's work as an "original and sometimes shocking" playwright.

[523] Rose, Francis [Sir] Saying life: The memoirs of Sir Francis Rose. Cassell. (1961).

[524] Prince Felix Yussupov (1887-1967). A member of the Russian Royal Family, famed as being involved in the assassination of Gregori Rasputin in 1916. According to Robin Bryans in The Dust Has Never Settled "Evan [Morgan] in my mind will always be associated with Peter Churchill and Felix Yussupov".

[525] According to Robin Bryans in Let the petals fall. "Evan had known Dickie Mountbatten from youth." Evan spent weekends (at parties) with the Mountbattens (along with PG (Prince George)) at Adsdean near Portsmouth, (the Mountbatten country estate) where other 'Royals' often stayed. Hollywood actors Douglas Fairbanks and Charlie Chaplin also visited here as did Noel Coward - they may have shared time with Evan here and at Brook House, another Mountbatten residence.

[526] Daily Express, 27 April 2002.

[527] In 1927 Ned married a divorcee Xenia Morison, who died in 1974.

[528] The family previously lived at Lathom Hall, but this building was ravished "after being used as a depot for nurses and grooms in the [Great] war". Ned had the dower house, Blythe Hall renovated.

[529] See Daily Express, 27 April 2002

[530] Lathom was Noel Coward's first patron, providing personal and professional finance and support for the rising young star and backing French impresario Andre Charlot's first Coward revue, London Calling.

[531] The estate was sold in 1924 and with it 40 farms and 4000 acres. Lathom House was demolished except for one wing A biography of Ned entitled Angel Lathom is promised by John Knowles, a Coward and Lathom devotee.

[532] Lord Ivor Spencer Churchill (1898-1956). His mother was the American heiress Consuelo Vanderbilt. A cousin of Winston Churchill, he married in 1947 and had one son. Ivor died of a brain tumour.

[533] Charles Richard John Spencer-Churchill (1871-1934), 9th Duke of Marlborough. Known as "Sunny".

[534] See Pearson, John The Private Lives of Winston Churchill. Simon & Schuster (1991). The book cites Ivor's friend Terence Philip as "what was known as a "society tame cat ..Rumoured to be discreetly homosexual, he enjoyed the company of women, particularly of slightly older women." One of these women was Clementine Churchill.

[535] See Sunday Times, 14 March 1926. (Perth, Australia) (Trove Digitised Archive).

[536] Ibid. The two actresses are named as Pat Kendall and Peggy O'Neill.

[537] The Times, 10 October 1931. A reception of The London Group.

[538] Consuelo Vanderbilt (1877-1964). The Vanderbilts made their millions from railroads. After her divorce from the 9th Duke of Marlborough Consuelo marred Jacques Balsan.

[539] Bryans, Robin. Let the petals fall. Honeyford Press (1993).

[540] The Times 9 April 1914.

[541] Balsan, Consuelo Vanderbilt. The Glitter and the Gold. George Mann. (1973).

[542] Gladys Marie Deacon, (1881-1977), 2nd wife of 'Sunny', 9th Duke of Marlborough. American socialite, born in Paris.

[543] Balsan, Consuelo Vanderbilt. The Glitter and the Gold. George Mann. (1973).

[544] Willis Resa. FDR and Lucy: Lovers and Friends. Routledge, (2012). This book names Consuelo's American lover as Winthrop Rutherford (1862-1944). American Socialite. Curiously Consuelo makes no mention of him in her memoirs The Glitter & the Gold.

[545] CC Martindale (1879-1963), Jesuit author, scholar and Oxford philosopher. Robin Bryans comments "In 1945 I left Bournemouth to visit Evan Tredegar in London and to see his long standing friend and confessor Father CC Martindale. The man I met hardly answered the description given him by a biographer as 'the most brilliant English priest of the century". The unassuming man I first met in Evan's house in South Audley Street had about him an air of tiredness."

[546] Rev Philip Caraman (1911-1998). See Caraman Philip. C C Martindale: A Biography. Longmans (1967). Martindale became a close friend of 'Sunny'. He read the address at the Duke's memorial service at Farm Street Church, in 1934.

[547] Ibid. Campion Hall (founded in 1896) is a house of studies that forms part of the University of Oxford. This is where Evan retreated to in 1925 (after returning from Rome, following the death of sister Gwyneth, and to write "In Pace".) This long poem is reproduced in Dart, Monty and Cross, William, A Beautiful Nuisance. The Life and Death of the Hon. Gwyneth Ericka Morgan. Book Midden Publishing . (2012).

[548] This would have almost certainly have been Cardinal Bourne (1861-1935), Archbishop of Westminster.

[549] Brendan Bracken (1901-1958). 1st Viscount Bracken. Irish born businessman and politician. Avid book collector.

[550] Roberts, Cecil. The Pleasant Years. Hodder and Stoughton (1974).

[551] Bracken was Duff Cooper's successor at the Ministry of Information as Minister, serving there from July 1941 until May 1945.

[552] See Boyle, Andrew. Poor Dear Brendan. Quest for Brendan Bracken. (1974) Hutchinson and Lysaght Charles Edward. Brendan Bracken. Allen Lane. (1979).

[553] Robin Bryans claims in his book Blackmail and Whitewash p125 "all Evan's letters to [Bracken] were burned in the drawing room-room fire during Brendan's lifetime."

[554] Charles Lysaght comments in his biography on Bracken that "In the original [(unpublished]) draft of Cecil Roberts' memoir The Bright Twenties he referred to Bracken's homosexuality which he connected with his mother complex but he later omitted."

[555] Bryans, Robin. Let the petals fall. Honeyford Press. (1993).

[556] Bryans. Robin. Checkmate.Honeyford Press (1994).

[557] Lysaght Charles Edward. Brendan Bracken. Allen Lane. (1979).

[558] Robert Bryans says in his book Blackmail and Whitewash p125 that in 1921 Bracken spent two terms at Rottingdean School. "The red-headed youth loved

country walks and during one of these he chanced to meet Peter Churchill, who later introduced Brendan Bracken to Evan Tredegar".

[559] Bryans, Robin. The Dust has Never Settled. (1992).

[560] Sir Sidney Colvin (1845-1927) Curator, art critic. Lady Frances Colvin (1839-1924). Married late, in 1903. Links to the Fitzwilliam Museum, Cambridge and the British Museum,

[561] Edward Elgar: Letters of a lifetime. Google books (1990) p.373. In some quarters Bracken was thought to be Australian. "I forget whether you have met the young Australian, Bracken, who has become almost like a son or rather a grandson to us. He is coming to tea this afternoon, & bringing Yeats the Irish poet".

[562] Ibid.

[563] Bryans. Robin. Checkmate. Honeyford Press. (1994).

[564] Bryans. Robin. Blackmail and Whitewash. Honeyford Press (1996).

[565] Yeats died in France in 1939. He was temporarily buried, some say in a paupers grave. He was later buried in Ireland in Drumcliffe Churchyard, County Sligo. Bryans charges Evan for not giving any help to Yeats' family in 1939. The feud between the Catholic Evan and the Protestant Yeats centred around a variety of religious and moral issues and the fact that Yeats would not support Evan's quest for greater public recognition of Lord Alfred (Bosie) Douglas, including (after Yeats was dead) a possible Civil List pension. Yeats had also angered Evan because he refused to include any of Lord Alfred Douglas's sonnets when selecting works for a poetry anthology.

[566] Alexander Gavin Henderson (1902-1977). Known as Hendy at Eton, known for his effeminate mannerisms. A socialist, he inherited the title of the 2nd Baron Faringdon in 1934. Served in a field hospital in the Spanish Civil War. He also "lived for three years in India....and travelled from Tibet to Ceylon, from Burma to the North West Frontier..." (see The Times 24 February 1942).

[567] A beautiful house and grounds in Berkshire, built in 1780 with rebuilding in 1936. Paintings and furniture known as the "Briar Rose " are among the best works of art in the Faringdon collection, as well as works by Rembrandt, Murillo and Reynolds. The National Trust took over the house in 1949.

[568] Tom Driberg (1905-1976). Communist and, later, Labour MP. He was also a predatory homosexual.

[569] The relationship between Aleister Crowley and Tom Driberg is to be found in several of the Crowley biographies. They ultimately fell out. Symonds describes Driberg in The Beast 666 as "the traitorous Thomas Driberg, a thoroughly nasty character."

[570] See The Times 2 February 1977.

[571] Boyle, Andrew. Poor, dear Brendan: the quest for Brendan Bracken. Hutchinson (1974)

[572] James (Jim) Louis Garvin (1868-1947). Influential British journalist and newspaper editor, from 1908 he edited The Observer.

[573] Bryans, Robin. Let the petals fall. Honeyford Press (1993).

[574] Attributed by Robin Bryans to Hugh Dalton (1887-1962). Labour politician and statesman.

[575] Princess Dilkusha de Rohan (1899-1978). Had lesbian affairs with a number of notable women, including Poppy Kirk (Maria Annunziata Sartori), and the Russian dancer Catherine Deviller. See Harry Ransom Center. http://research.hrc.utexas.edu:8080/hrcxtf/view?docId=ead/00708.xml

[576] Prince Carlos de Rohan (1895-1931). A scion of an old French family.

[577] Mercedes de Acosta (1893-1968). American poet, playwright and writer. See also Vickers, Hugo. Loving Garbo. The Story of Greta Garbo, Cecil Beaton and Mercedes de Acosta. Jonathan Cape. (1994).

[578] Ibid.

[579] Bryans, Robin. Checkmate. Honeyford Press. (1994).

[580] Robin Bryans makes various references to Otto Mundy, Deputy Director of the Board of Customs and Excise. Mundy was a distant cousin of Evan's. Bryans suggests Mundy's colleagues turned a blind eye to infringements of the regulations on petrol use by several friends of Evan. But Evan's friend, the actor Ivor Novello (who was imprisoned by petrol offences) was made a token "scapegoat".

[581] According to Bryans, writing as Robert Harbinson in his early memoir The Protégé, Mundy's house was Winterfield which "stood on a hill above the Thames at Cookham." Bryans says Mundy was "one of my referees for Caroline College".

[582] In Checkmate Robin Bryans says "Evan Tredegar and Otto Mundy ensured that there were no startling war-shortages at any royal residence, the only scapegoat being Ivor Novello". Bryans adds that Otto "ensured that the best of wines and whisky [impounded by Customs and Excise] found its way to Evan who took it in his Rolls Royce to Queen Mary and other members of the royal family."

[583] From a letter in 1964, mentioned by Robin Bryans in Checkmate (Honeyford Press, 1994) after the death of the broadcaster Bobbie Macdermott, (Robert McDermott Barbour died 1964 aged 52) who, along with Dil and Brendon Bracken, had attempted to find work for James Lonsdale Bryans at the tail end of the Second World War.

[584] The Papers on this, including the correspondence between Evan and Bracken, is in the British Library Manuscripts Division Ref Add 81707

[585] Bryans refers in Checkmate to a political campaign against Bracken which insinuated a compromising involvement with some Boy Scouts. Roberts says his friend, the lawyer Norman Birkett, was involved in an unsuccessful libel case raised by Bracken which he lost, costing him over £5000. This libel was not about a sex scandal. Robin Bryans refers to compromising photographs of Bracken with boys taken at Yew Tree Cottage, Broadstone, Dorset during the time that Bracken represented nearby Bournemouth was as MP. These were taken by a Rodney family connection named Risdon Bennett, an author who lived at the cottage. Rodney family tutor.

[586] Roberts, Cecil. The Pleasant Years. Hodder and Stoughton (1974).

[587] Fielding, Daphne. Mercury Presides. Eyre & Spottiswoode. (1954).

[588] Washington Post, 16 September 1919.

[589] Cited by I F Nicolson in Mystery of Crichel Down, uplifted from Kieran Tunney's Tallulah: Darling of the Gods; An Intimate Portrait.

[590] Sexton, James [Editor] Huxley, Aldous. Selected Letters. Ivan R Dee (2007)

[591] Hastings, Selina. The Secret Lives of Somerset Maugham. John Murray. (2009).

[592] Carrington, Dora de Houghton & Garnet David. Carrington: letters and extracts from her diaries. Holt, Rinehart and Winston. (1971). Entry for 27 August 1929. Letter to Lytton Strachey written at Coombe Bissett, Salisbury.

[593] Jeffery John Archer Amherst (1896-1993), Viscount Holmesdale, the last Earl Amherst from 1927-death. A close friend of Ivor Novello and Noel Coward.

[594] In Tallulah: My Autobiography. Univ. Press of Mississippi (2004), it records that Naps and Tallulah were " together constantly in the winter of '21-'22."

[595] Bret, David: Tallulah Bankhead: A scandalous life. Robson Books. (1998).

[596] Israel, Lee. Miss Tallulah Bankhead. W H Allen / Virgin Books (1972)

[597] Quoted by Robert Gottlieb in The New Yorker, 16 May 2005. DAH-LING: The strange case of Tallulah Bankhead.

[598] Ibid.

[599] Tunney, Kieran. Tallulah Darling of the Gods. E P Dutton & Co Inc. (1973).

[600] Hon Diana Isabel Sturt (born 1884) married Hon. Henry Brougham in 1908, they divorced in 1919. Diana's son later inherited the Brougham peerage.

[601] George Keppel and his wife Alice (mistress of King Edward VII). The Keppels were at 30 Portman Square.

[602] Sonia Rosemary Keppel (later Cubitt, Baroness Ashcombe) (1900-1986) Sister of Violet Keppel, later Trefusis.

[603] There are several anecdotes about Lois Sturt in Sonia Keppel's book The Edwardian daughter. Hamilton (1958)

[604] See Perry, Maria. Chelsea Chicks. Andre Deutsch. (2000).

[605] See Daily Mirror, 20 May 1919. The photograph shows " For Waifs and Strays – The Hon. Lois Sturt will dance at the Palace Theatre ...at a matinee arranged by her mother, Lady Alington, Miss [Catherine] Wendell [later 6th Countess of Carnarvon] will also appear..

[606] San Antonio Light, 3 April 1921.

[607] See Bret, David: Tallulah Bankhead: A scandalous life. Robson Books, (1998) p60: "Tallulah was introduced to the painter Ambrose McEvoy who executed a profile of her glancing at her reflection through a mirror....Shortly afterwards McEvoy died suddenly and the picture was sold by his estate to Anthony de Rothschild for £600."

[608] Daily Mirror, 16 July 1926.

[609] Daily Mirror. 4 January 1928.

[610] Published in The City of Canals and other Poems. Kegan Paul (1929).

[611] Hastings, Selina. The Secret Lives of Somerset Maugham. John Murray. (2009).

[612] Ibid.

[613] Roberts, Cecil. Sunshine and Shadow. Hodder and Stoughton. (1972).

[614] Edwina Mountbatten, Countess of Burma. (1901-1960). Wife of Louis Mountbatten (1900-1979) Lord Louis " had a sexual preference for men".

[615] Roberts, Cecil. Sunshine and Shadow. Hodder and Stoughton. (1972).

[616] The Tablet, 3 July 1926.

[617] Major John 'Johnnie' Bigelow Dodge (1894-1960). Son of Flora Bigelow and Charles Stuart Dodge.

[618] See The New York Times, 28 December 1921.

[619] Dodge was in Tiflis, Georgia, working as a businessman. He was held on trumped up charges and forced to live in poor conditions by the Russians. He was later expelled to Batoum and put on a boat to Constantinople. He made it back to London on 8 October 1922 "a fervent anti-Communist". See Carroll, Tom. The Dodger: The Extraordinary Story of Churchill's Cousin and the Great Escape. Mainstream Publishing (2012).

[620] Johnnie Dodge's mother Flora's second marriage was to Lionel Guest, brother of Corisande Rodney. This makes him a cousin of Winston Churchill as Lionel Guest's mother (Lady Wimborne) was Lady Cornelia Spencer-Churchill.

[621] The Sunday Times of 3 September 1933 reports "The Prince's great friend, the Hon. Evan Morgan". The Prince of Wales had known Evan for many years of family and civic ties. They were in each other company at formal and informal gatherings.

[622] Edward Antony James Bulwer-Lytton, (1903-1933). Viscount Knebworth, son of the 2nd Earl of Lytton. Contested Shoreditch in 1929, later MP for Hitchin. Killed in an air crash.

[623] York Hall (Old Ford Road) Bethnal Green has hosted amateur boxing matches since 1929.

[624] Gordon, Ian and Inglis Simon. Great lengths: the historic indoor swimming pools of Britain. English Heritage. (2009).

[625] Sir Luke William Burke Teeling (1903-1975). Irish born Traveller and Member of Parliament for Brighton, 1944-1969. His memoirs Corridors of Frustration include affectionate references to Evan.

[626] Colonel John Robert Jermain Macnamara (1905-1944). Ft Lt William Teeling MP wrote a tribute in The Times to Macnamara who was killed in action in Italy in 1944. See Chapter 9.

[627] See pgs 56-9 of Teeling, William. Corridors of Frustration. Johnson. (1970).

[628] Teeling, William. Corridors of Frustration. Johnson. (1970).

[629] See Teeling, William. Corridors of Frustration. Johnson. (1970). Pages 34-5. Of Jonnie Dodge's "success next door in Mile End, this was as much due to his mother as anything else. Here really was a dynamic woman, Mrs Lionel Guest, an American and known to everyone as Aunt Flora. She fully entered into the spirit of things."

[630] See Teeling, William. Corridors of Frustration. Johnson. (1970). " Our most colourful and probably most intelligent candidate was Anthony Knebworth.......killed later flying with his auxiliary squadron and England lost the sort of young man we always needed."

[631] Maud [Emerald] Cunard, previously Burke (1872-1948). American born, widow of Sir Bache Cunard, the Cunard shipping line magnate.

[632] Benkovitz, Miriam J. Ronald Firbank: A Biography. Knopf (1969).

[633] Jackson, Stanley. Inside Monte Carlo. W H Allen (1975).

[634] Fielding Daphne. Emerard & Nancy. Lady Cunard and her Daughter. Eyre & Spottiswoode. (1968).

[635] National Archives, Kew. MEPO 38/9.

[636] One of Nancy's campaigns was over the Scottsboro Boys, in the USA. Two white women accused nine black teenagers of rape on 25 March 1931 while riding a freight train as it passed through Jackson County, Alabama. After a series of trials eight of the nine boys were convicted and sentenced to death. No one was executed, the case was fought on for many years by various black and non black organisations, and although the boys were sent to prison the case is now widely considered a miscarriage of justice. Nancy supported the call for justice, distributing literature about the fake charges against the boys in Alabama "where race hatred on the part of the white masters and middle classes is as never before. Conditions are far worse than slavery".

[637] Handwritten letter in file dated 20 February 1932 from Nancy to the Commissioner of Police referring to being stopped by two plain clothes men in Cromer Street, London on 17 February 1932.

[638] Daily Express, 5 July 1933.

[639] This weekend head count included Princess Olga's brother Count Daschkow, who later went to live in the USA. See also Aspects of Evan.

[640] Bedford, John, Duke of. A Silver-Plated Spoon. The Reprint Society of London. (1959).

[641] Ibid.

[642] Ibid.

[643] Victor Cunard was The Times foreign correspondent in Rome 1922-27, Paris 1927-33 and served in the Political Intelligence Department of the Foreign Office, 1941-46. Lived sometime at the Old Rectory, Pertenhall, Bedford. Died in Venice, where he had previously settled on account of an "acute form of rheumatism" contracted in the trenches in the Great War.

[644] Schenkar Joan. Truly Wilde. The Unsettling Story of Dolly Wilde, Oscar's Unusual Niece. Virago (2000) " Cunard (Nancy's witty cousin) was one of many men who proposed marriage to Dolly: he had a lunch date with her on the day of her death, and wrote her obituary for the London Times."

[645] Cecil Roberts (1892-1976), Journalist and writer.

[646] Roberts. Cecil. The Bright Twenties. Hodder and Stoughton. (1970). The Sunday Times review of the book comments "Good glimpses of Churchill and Beaverbrook...Also of Shaw, Brendan Bracken, Guedalla, President Coolidge, Evan Morgan and many more..."

[647] Umberto Nicola Tommaso Giovanni Maria di Savoia, (1904-1983) (Briefly Umberto II King of Italy, 9 May 1946 - 12 June 1946).

[648] Giovanni Dall'Orto in Aldrich, Robert; Wotherspoon. Garry. Who's Who in Contemporary Gay and Lesbian History: From World War II to the Present Day. Routledge. (2001) p452.

[649] Nicolson's fling with the witty Victor Cunard was partly to spite his wife Vita over an argument. The act was much less premeditated than the revenge against Vita later taken in seducing the well-bred Denys Trefusis. Major Denys Robert Trefusis (1890- 1929) was the husband of Violet Keppel a close intimate of Vita, who in turn was sleeping with Violet. But neither Victor nor Denys objected to being shown attention by the attractive frame and interesting mind of Harold.

[650] See The Times 1 September 1960. " HN" records: Victor was " a constant delight" and " his death will leave a gap in many hearts". Not least affected was to spite Vita over an argument, Victor was a witty his cousin Nancy who was seriously mentally ill by 1960. This is described in Anne Chisholm's biography of Nancy Cunard and has neat details of the life long emotional support given by Victor to Nancy.

[651] Violet Trefusis (1894-1972). Writer and socialite.

[652] Hon. Victoria Mary Sackville-West, Lady Nicolson (1892-1962). Writer, poet and gardener. She married Harold Nicolson in 1913.

[653] Jullian Philippe, Phillips, John Nova, Trefusis, Violet Keppel and Sackville-West, Victoria. The other woman: a life of Violet Trefusis. Houghton Miffin. (1976)

[654] Firbank, Ronald. The Flower Beneath The Foot (1923). This book can be downloaded from Internet Archive.

[655] Nicolson, Harold. Some People. Constable. (1927).

[656] Gerald Hugh Tyrwhitt-Wilson (1883-1950), 14th Lord Berners. Writer, composer and artist with houses in Faringdon and Rome.

[657] Concerning the Eccentricities of Cardinal Pirelli, a novel by Firbank published in 1926. According to Violet Trefusis' biographers Philippe Julian and John Nova Phillips this character of a gay Cardinal (who chased choirboys around altars) was inspired by Monsignor Vay de Vaya, a Hungarian prelate and a much travelled Papal envoy.

[658] See Benkovitz, Miriam J. Ronald Firbank A Biography Weidenfeld and Nicolson. (1970) for extracts. Also Dart, Monty and Cross William. Aspects of Evan: The Last Viscount Tredegar. Book Midden Publishing. (2012).

[659] Lady Harriet Jane Firbank (1851-1924).

[660] Aberconway Christabel. A wiser woman A Book of Memories. Hutchinson (1966).

[661] Reginald John "Rex" Whistler (1905-1944). Studied art at the Slade, Chelsea. A intimate of Stephen Tennant and Siegfried Sassoon. His most noted work was for the café at the Tate Gallery, London. He was killed in Normandy by a mortar bomb.

[662] See Daily Mirror, 23 July 1929.

[663] Lady Alexandra Mary Cecilia Paget (1913-1973). Daughter of Charles Paget, 6th Marquess of Anglesey and Lady Marjorie Manners. The nude has pride of place today at Plas Newydd, the seat of the Angleseys, where Whistler's largest painting, a canvas 58 feet by 12 feet can also be seen.

[664] The exact date was 21 August 1939.

[665] See Davenport-Hines, Richard. Ettie: The Intimate Life And Dauntless Spirit of Lady Desborough. Hachette (2012). Ettie was staying at Christabel Aberconway's place at Bodnant, Denbighshire, Wales, with a world famous garden in the Vale of Conway. She records "A heavenly visit... all the Aberconway family plus Norah Lindsay [a landscape gardener of the era], Rex Whistler and three artistic noblemen, Evan Tredegar (whom she thought "quite mad"), Lord Berners and Gerry Wellesley (the future Duke of Wellington)." NB Gerry Wellesley (1885-1972) was the 7th Duke of Wellington and inherited the title in 1943 after the death of the

unmarried 6th Duke (his nephew) who was killed in action in WW2 . Gerry was a married homosexual.

[666] H G Wells (1866-1946). The father of science fiction in Britain. Author of the classics War of the Worlds. The Time Machine and The Invisible Man.

[667] See Gillman Peter and Leni. The Wildest Dream: Mallory His Life and Conflicting Passions. Headline Book Publishing (2000).

[668] One of these was James Hanley's novel Boy (1931) which dealt with homosexuality. [A short novel about a ship's boy who is sexually assaulted by several members of the crew and then (suffering from VD) is murdered by the ship's captain.] See Stone, Wilfred. The Cave and the Mountain: A Study of E.M. Forster, Stanford University Press (1966). E M Forster was author of the homosexual novel Maurice.

[669] Hyde, H. Montgomery. The Other Love. Granada Publishing Ltd. (1972).

[670] See Review in the Daily Mirror, 15 October, 1966, on Christabel Aberconway's memoirs A Wiser Woman: A Book of Memories. Hutchinson & Co. (1966).

[671] Maria's story features in Lockhart, Bruce. Memoirs of a British Agent. Pan Books (2002). There are numerous editions of this book, first published in the 1930s. Sir Bruce Lockhart's dates are 1887-1970.

[672] There are three files in National Archives Kew, ref KV 2/979 -981 covering 1921 to 1952.

[673] See Wikipedia entry. Nicknamed the Red Mata Hari. Moura's dates are 1891-1974. She was an aunt of Nick Clegg, the Liberal Democrat leader, whose recollections of her are on the Internet.

[674] See page 270. Low, Rosemary. A century of parrots. Insignis. (2006). Also referred to in Aspects of Evan: The last Viscount Tredegar (2012).

[675] See Daily Mirror, 12 November 1937.

[676] Driberg, Tom. Ruling Passions. Jonathan Cape. (1977).

[677] See The Times, 12 July 1935 "Technicolor Film Premiere: Becky Sharp". The list of the parties includes "Viscount Tredegar".

[678] Review by David Pryce-Jones in The Tablet, 27 October 1984: Great Larks. Wells, G P. Experiments in Autobiography (2 volumes) and H G Wells in Love. Faber and Faber (1984).

[679] David Pryce-Jones (born 1936). Writer and commentator.

[680] Review by David Pryce-Jones in The Tablet, 27 October 1984: Great Larks. Wells, G P. Experiments in Autobiography (2 volumes) and H G Wells in Love. Faber and Faber (1984).

[681] Mackenzie, NI, Mackenzie, N and Mackenzie J. The life of HG Wells: the time traveller. Hogarth (1987) p.394 " On 1 June 1936, when HG was spending the week-end in South Wales as the guest of Lord Tredegar, a rich coal owner, he wrote to Shaw [George Bernard Shaw, the dramatist] thanking him for a new volume of plays…"

[682] Reproduced in Dart, M and Cross, W. Aspects of Evan: The Last Viscount Tredegar. Book Midden Publishing (2012)

[683] Marks, Howard. Senor Nice: Straight Life from Wales to South America. Random House (2010).

[684] Olga Tredegar (Evan's second wife) makes a point about Evan and Huxley's association being mostly in the 1920s and before.

[685] Huxley, Julian. Memories. Volume 1 page 149. Allen & Unwin. (1970)

[686] Alphonse James Albert Symons (1900-1941), biographer, epicure and dandy - founded the First Edition Club in 1922 – See The Times, 8 December 1922. Cult of the First edition. Symons died aged 40 at a hospital in Colchester on 25 August 1941 – address given as "Brick House, Finchingfield, Essex".

[687] March E and Hassall, C. Ambrosia and Small Beer. The record of a correspondence between Edward Marsh and Christopher Hassall. Longmans (1964).

[688] The Times, 29 August 1941. Obituary by Holbrook Jackson.

[689] In 1937 the First Edition Club had its annual dinner at the Savoy Hotel (NB Company No 225100 First Edition Limited dating from 1927-1948) and published "Letters from Aubrey Beardsley to Leonard Smithers" edited with Introduction and notes by R A Walker. Leonard Charles Smithers (1861-1907) "was a man with an unpleasant disposition, and he was shifty. As a bookseller he dealt in pornography..."

[690] Antiquarian book monthly review. Volume 8, page 435. (1981).

[691] Ibid.

[692] Material supplied to Evan included Wilde texts and 3 "App" and 3 "Res" items for him". See Antiquarian book monthly review. Volume 8, page 435. (1981).

[693] Formed as a joint venture between Symons and M Andre Simon (1877- 1970).

[694] The Book Collector. Volume 56, Issues 1-4. page 71. (2007)

[695] See Hyde, H. Montgomery. Lord Alfred Douglas Methuen. (1984).

[696] Also known as Sir Arthur John Maundy Gregory (1877-1941). He was born in Southampton, the son of a clergyman.

[697] National Archives, Kew ref KV 2/340

[698] Daily Mirror, 22 June 1928.

[699] The Sunday Times of 23 October, 1927 records " The Hon. Evan Morgan is giving a party on Wednesday at the Ambassador Club for the patrons of the Sadlers Wells ball, which is to take place at the club on November 2."

[700] Symons is the subject of a very readable volume by his brother. See Symons. Julian. A J A Symons: His Life & Speculations. Oxford University Press (1986). Julian points out that his brother was not a homosexual. Briefly married, Symons' legacy is undoubtedly his book Quest for Corvo.

[701] This refers to Michael Davidson (1897-1976) whose autobiography The World, The Flesh and Myself (now regarded as a gay classic) begins " This is the life-history of a lover of boys".

[702] Davidson, Michael. The World, The Flesh and Myself. GMP Publishes Ltd. (1985)

[703] Sunday Times, 29 December 1963.

[704] Ibid.

[705] Ibid.

[706] Ibid.

[707] Sir Walter Monckton (1891-1965). Leading advocate and politician. Defended Evan when charged with offences under the Official Secrets Acts in 1943. The full transcript of the case is reproduced in Aspects of Evan.

[708] Sir Russell Facey Wilkinson (died 1968). Royal Physician and medical adviser to Evan and his mother for many years.

[709] Sunday Times, 19 May 1974.

[710] Ibid.

[711] Hamilton. Gerald. The Way it Was With Me. Leslie Frewin. (1969).

[712] Mgr Barlassina, Latin Patriarch of Jerusalem (1872-1947).

[713] The Source of this and the note that follows is The Jewish Telegraphic Agency 30 December 1924.

The interest of the Vatican and the Italian Catholic Union for the Palestine Holy Places and Pilgrimages centers around the Coenaculum.

The allusion to the Coenaculum requires some explanation. The Coenaculum, the traditional scene of the Last Supper, fell into Moslem hands early in the Middle Ages. In the fourteenth century it was recovered by the King of Naples, and the ancient church which formerly stood on the site was replaced by another edifice, which is still in existence.

Shortly after the Ottoman conquest in the sixteenth century, the Coenaculum again passed into Moslem hands, where it has remained ever since. Mainly on the ground that it was recovered for The Christendom by King Robert of Naples, the Italian Government has for some time laid claim to the Coenaculum, the possession of which, it is thought, would add to its prestige in the Near East. This explains the special emphasis which is laid on the Coenaculum in the Italian (Roman) Catholic memorandum. The Italian Government has informed the memorialists that it watches Roman Catholic interests in Palestine with unremitting solicitude, and is doing everything in its power to safeguard them.

[714] In cross-examination Kirby (Secretary to the Patriarch) said Gregory had paid the cheques to him as personal gifts for the use of the mission, but he admitted that they were associated with knighthoods of the Holy Sepulchre, of which the Patriarch was the head.

[715] Some reports refer to her as Marion Rosse and describe her as the wife of a composer–conductor Frederick Rosse and the sum left was £21,000. Her death had been sudden. At lunch on 19 August she was seized with pain and put to bed suffering from sickness and diarrhoea. She decided to make her will, asking Gregory to write it down. It said "Everything I have, if anything happens to me, to be left to Mr J Maundy Gregory to be disposed of as he thinks best and in accordance with what I shall desire." The will was written in pencil by Gregory in the presence of a doctor, who signed as the witness, as did Mrs Rosse's housekeeper. Mrs Rosse recovered, but in the following month she had another illness with the death certificate recording a cerebral haemorrhage and chronic Bright's disease. At the post mortem conducted by Sir Bernard Spilsbury no evidence of Bright's disease was found.

[716] Cullen, Tom. Maundy Gregory, Purveyor of Honours. Bodley Head. (1974).

[717] Inquest held by Igleby Oddie, Coroner at Paddington on 19 July 1934.

[718] John Colin Campbell Davidson (1889-1970) Later Viscount Davidson. Civil Servant and Tory Minister.

[719] See James, Robert Rhodes. Memoirs of a Conservative. J.C.C. Davidson's Memoirs and Papers 1910-37. Weidenfeld and Nicolson. (1969).

[720] See The Times 16 March 1927. An article explains that Lord Tredegar was to give a reception for members of the Central Council on Monday 27 June, 1927.

[721] The Times, 21 September 1927.

[722] See James, Robert Rhodes. Memoirs of a Conservative. J.C.C. Davidson's Memoirs and Papers 1910-37. Weidenfeld and Nicolson. (1969). Davidson told Gregory to accept the charge, then he would be given a light sentence and compensated.

[723] In February 1933 Maundy Gregory was sentenced at Bow Street, London to two months imprisonment in the second division and was fined £50, for having attempted to obtain £10,000 from a naval officer for trying to procure him a title.

[724] National Archives, Kew file KV2/ 340 reveals a document from 1946 which states "He [Gregory] was transferred in October 1940 from either the Bordeaux area or Brittany area Camps. Whilst [at a camp] at St Denis he was a very sick man, fussy, erratic and secretive. Most of the time he was an inmate of the Camp Infirmary, being later send to the Duval de Grace Military Hospital [Paris] where he died.." The date of his death is recorded as 3 October 1941. Gregory is buried at the Cemetery, Ivry in the name Maundy Gregory. His address in Paris before the war was 8, Rue de Anjou.

[725] See Wilson, Colin and Wilson, Damon. Scandal! Virgin Books. (2007).

[726] Andrew Cook author of Cash for Honours: The True Life of Maundy Gregory. History Publishing Group (2008) says The Council of the Anglo-Ukrainian Committee was formed in November 1931. This body ran until 1934. Originally Gregory was chairman with Lords Southborough, Strathspey and Ffrench, Brigadier-General Horwood and Korostovetz. The honorary secretary and treasurer was Louis Tufnell, who worked with Gregory on the Whitehall Gazette. Gregory introduced Korostovetz to wealthy supporters of the Hetman but his frauds were suspected, he was sidelined and a new Committee formed.
http://www.ukrainiansintheuk.info/eng/01/aucomm1931-e.htm

[727] The Times of 1 March 1935 announces the creation of an Anglo-Ukrainian Committee in London "to protect the interests of the Ukrainian peoples." The leading lights were Lord Dickinson and Lord Noel Baker.

[728] Bryans, Robin. Checkmate. Honeyford Press. (1994). Bryans adds that Hitler hoped that Prince Paul Skoropadsky's young son, Prince Danylo, would lead Ukrainian exiles in Hitler's army against the Soviet troops in the Ukraine. Danylo fled to the UK. He later toured the USA and Canada, raising money to help to restore his family to power.

[729] Behind the scenes a negotiated settlement was reached between Tufnell and the Hetman's representatives, and no action was taken against Tufnell for embezzlement.

[730] E-mail from Paul Busby a former Tredegar House guide) to Monty Dart dated 18 December 2012, copied to the author since it refers to the book Aspects of Evan, published on 10 December 2012.

[731] Bryans, Robin. The Dust Has Never Settled. Honeyford. (1992).

[732] Richard William John Nugent Rumbold (1913-1961). Author of three gay classics: Little Victims (1933); My father's son (1958) and A message in code (1964).

[733] Rumbold Richard. Little Victims. Fortune Press. (1933).

[734] Richard Aldington in the Eveing Standard.

[735] Ralph Straus in the Sunday Times, 12 March 1932.

[736] Ibid.

[737] Douglas Murray's biography Lord Alfred Douglas. Sceptre/ Hodder and Stoughton (2000) cites a letter from Bosie describing Rumbold as "a ghastly and pretentious undergraduate".

[738] The Colemans were sheep farmers in West Sussex, Evan knew them well. According to Douglas Murray, Rumbold first introduced the Colemans to Bosie. (see Murray p323) The Colemans spearheaded the campaign to restore Bosie's reputation and were Bosie's literary executors. Edward died in 1993, Shelia in 2001.

[739] Rumbold records in his diary for 20 March, 1945 "heard today that poor Bosie is dead. Teddy (Edward Colman) rang me up."

[740] Douglas Murray's biography of Bosie is recommended for references to Evan and Olga's visits to see Bosie.

[741] There is some dispute about whether Evan's chest and lung disease was actually diagnosed as full blown TB, a disease that was treated by the patient being isolated on account of it being infectious. All that can be said is that he was affected by a hereditary lung ailment, passed down on both sides of his family.

[742] Rumbold's father was Charles E A L Rumbold, a Captain of the Royal Yacht Squadron and an author of books on yachting, with a connection to Sir Horace Rumbold who was a notable British diplomat, well known to Harold Nicolson.

[743] Rumbold records this in A Message in Code – his diary for 5 December 1957: "Suicide of my sister. Failure of humanity on my part." Elsewhere he records her as Mrs Puigcerver.

[744] This had been forced on Ronnie Knox by his Archbishop. It is a marked omission that Rumbold is not listed in the index to Evelyn Waugh's biography of Knox, published in 1959. The reference to Little Victims is an ode written by Knox during his student days. Evan (who barely knew Waugh) is not mentioned in the book either. Waugh was Knox's literary executor.

[745] Rumbold's diary reveals a long, close relationship with Harold Nicolson, especially in London. "I went to see Harold, and breathed again the fine rare atmosphere of his mind" (Diary 12 October 1944). This link may have been fostered by Nicolson's knowledge of Richard Rumbold's uncle Horace who was (like Nicolson) a diplomat. Horace Rumbold (1869-1941) was Nicolson's boss as British Ambassador in Berlin 1928-1933.

[746] Bryans, Robin. Blackmail and Whitewash. Honeyford Press (1996).

[747] Rumbold's diary for 2 June 1943 records "I go tomorrow to the Cotswold Sanatorium, Gloucester, for about a month's rest." He returned there on 27 August 1943 for another month's bed rest.

[748] Roberts, Cecil. Sunshine and Shadow. Hodder and Stougton. (1972).

[749] Cecil Roberts refers in his book The Bright Twenties, which contains a good biographical sketch of Evan, that as an illustration (from 1938) of Evan going to "considerable trouble to be kind" he drove some American ladies (lunching with Roberts) off in his Rolls-Royce to Christ Church, Oxford where he showed them around. "The great dining-hall was closed. He had it opened. He seemed to know the name and history of every portrait on its walls. Then he took us to the library in Peckwater Quad. It was closed. Again he had it opened."

[750] Rumbold's body was brought back to England and buried in the Anglican church of Watton-on-Stone Hertfordshire.

[751] Bryans, Robin. Let the petals fall. Honeyford Press. (1993).

[752] Ibid. NB The reference to the macaw, Blue Boy as being vicious is inconsistent with another reference to the bird making friends on sight (Sunday Times 26 May 1935 refers). But it is also recorded that Blue Boy terrified Evan's friends (Source Tredegar Lectures).

[753] Leslie, Seymour. The Jerome Connection. John Murray. (1964).

[754] Alistair Hugh Graham (1904-?), Welsh recluse, now deceased. Solid back-up for Graham's relationship with Evan is lacking. This may be another embroidered yarn.

[755] Bryans, Robin. Let the petals fall. Honeyford Press. (1993).

[756] The Court Circular in The Times of 8 February 1932 records "Viscount Tredegar, accompanied by the Hon. Mrs Evan Morgan, Mrs Peter Gurney [Avis Morgan], Dr Forsyth, and Major Corbet has sailed in the ss Orford for Ceylon.."

[757] See The Times 8 February, 1932.

[758] The Court Circular in The Times of 5 March 1932 records "the Hon. Evan Morgan has returned to London from Bath."

[759] The Times, Saturday 17 September 1932. The Court Circular also records "The Duke and Duchess of York will arrive in London on Monday from Scotland.."

[760] See Cecil Roberts' The Bright Twenties, Hodder & Stoughton (1974) pages 95-104. Roberts found Evan outside the Café Royal, ill (or drunk), took him home to Grosvenor Square and put him safely to bed.

[761] Roberts Cecil. The Bright Twenties. Hodder & Stoughton (1974).

[762] Squire, Sir John Collings, (1884-1958). Poet, writer and literary editor.

[763] Squire, Sir John Collings. The Honeysuckle and the bee, Dutton (1938).

[764] The patter from Peter included variations and repetition of such words and phrases as " Titty, titty; Cunty, cunty; Show a cock, Show a cock; and Nice big cocky, nice big cocky."

[765] Winifred Graham was the literary name for the writer Mrs Theodore John Cory (1873-1950). She is the author of many dozens of books.

[766] See Graham, Winifred. Observations: Casual and Intimate. Skeffington and Son Ltd. (1947).

336

[767] This anecdote is cited by Rosemary Low in Century of Parrots, Insignia Publications. (2006) and is one mentioned by the writer Maurice Richardson (1907-1978) in the Times Literary Supplement on 7 July 1978 in a book review on a book about Edward James. Richardson (a friend of Brian Howard) adds that Blue Boy had a "terrifying habit of seizing your ear in its beak. If you shrank away, it nipped". However the foundation for several other tales seems to originate *only* from the guides at Tredegar House, well known for embellishing stories about Evan.

[768] Ibid.

[769] Low, Rosemary. Century of Parrots Insignia Publications. (2006).

[770] Ibid.

[771] Ibid.

[772] A photograph on display at Tredegar House of Evan with a small group of visiting dignitaries is cited by guides as a snapshot of these visitors' reaction to Blue Boy's bad language but the ladies and gentleman in the picture may just have been horrified by having their photo taken or Blue Boy performing some trick. None of the servant's recollections examined or later testimonies in letters from Evan's friends mention Blue Boy's profane language.

[773] Ibid.

[774] See Pryce Jones, Alan. The bonus of laughter. Hamish Hamilton. (1987).

[775] Huxley, Julian. Memories. Allen & Unwin. (1970)

[776] Sunday Times, 26 May 1935. Interview with Evan at the time his Gin Traps Bill was before the House of Lords for consideration.

[777] Eric Buchanan, son of Jack Buchanan. Eric was employed from c1934 until two years before war broke out. He worked under Mr Bill Pitt, who was in overall charge of the menagerie. This story comes from the Servants files in Tredegar House, based on transcriptions from the 1970s.

[778] See the Sunday Times 26 May 1935. This article tells us that the South American crested magpie was brought back from a trip with Prince Paul of Greece to the West Indies.

[779] Sunday Times 26 May 1935

[780] Daily Express 10 June 1927.

[781] Ibid.

[782] Daily Express 7 February, 1928.

[783] Ibid.

[784] Oliver Hilary Sambourne Messel (1904-1978). His nephew was Tony Armstrong-Jones, Lord Snowdon. Messell was an artist, set and stage designer. Studied at the Slade at the same time as Rex Whistler. A homosexual, there are references to Messel in Anne De Courcy's biography of Lord Snowdon, Cecil Beaton's diaries, Dicky Buckle's book and reviews and Cecil Roberts' autobiographies. A large collection of Messel's work is deposited in the Victoria and Albert Museum, London.

[785] Victor William (Peter) Watson (1908-1956). Art Collector and patron of the arts who encouraged Lucien Freud and Francis Bacon. Lived for a while in Paris where he also supported new artist talent. He funded the magazine Horizon and founded

the Institute of Contemporary Arts. Adored by Cecil Beaton. Watson was "found mysteriously drowned in his bath" in London. Peter's father George Watson (of Maypole Dairies fame) paid £30,000 to Maundy Gregory. In 1932 the executors of George Watson sued him for the return of the money the deceased had paid for a baronetcy he never received.

[786] Denham Fouts (1914-1948). Male whore, with a string of lovers who knew Evan including Gore Vidal and Prince Paul of Greece. See also Dart, Monty and Cross, William. Aspects of Evan. Book Midden Publishing (2012).

[787] The Times, 5 December, 1932.

[788] Ibid. Philip Guedalla (1889-1944). In the same mould as Lytton Strachey, Guedalla challenged the reputation of his subjects which included biographies of Lord Palmerston and the Duke of Wellington.

[789] Ibid.

[790] See The Times, 2 December 1938.

[791] See Aspects of Evan for several of these anecdotes taken from Aberconway, Christabel: A wiser woman A Book of Memories. Hutchinson (1966). Rafaelle, Duchess of Leinster. So brief a Dream. W H Allen (1973) Marsh, Edward and Hassell, Christopher:Ambrosa and Small beer. Longmans (1964).

[792] Yale University Library, Alan Pryce Jones, Papers GEN MSS 513. See Box 15, Folder 831. In addition to this the collection at Yale contains other correspondence from Evan, Cyril Hughes Hartmann's essay " Evan Morgan" (Box 44, Folder 2011), the typescripts of poems written by Evan 1926-33 (Box 44, Folder 2016), a photograph of Evan (marked Corsica 1932) (Box 46, Folder 2061), a " portrait of unidentified subject. Pen and Ink, by Evan Morgan (Box 63, Folder 2372).

[793] Dorothy Cecil Wynter Warren (1896-1954). Hostess and owner of the Warren Gallery in Maddox Street, London. She features prominently in the biographies of D H Lawrence as she mounted an exhibition of Lawrence's paintings in 1928-29.

[794] Cathleen Nesbitt (1888-1982). British character actress.

[795] Sir Charles Otto Desmond MacCarthy (1877-1952). Journalist and critic. MacCarthy had a regular column in the Sunday Times.

[796] See the Daily Mirror, 28 March 1927. Today's Broadcasting 7(pm) Mr Desmond MacCarthy: Literary Criticism. 8.30(pm) (approximately) "a reading of his own poems by the Hon. Evan Morgan, assisted by Dorothy Warren."

[797] Alfred Noyes (1880-1958). Poet and Catholic convert.

[798] Noyes married his second wife Mary Angela Mayne in 1927.

[799] Morgan, Evan. The Eel and other Poems. Kegan Paul (1926).

[800] Frederick Charles Loveday (known as Raoul) died 16 February 1923.

[801] Noyes, Alfred. Two Worlds for Memory. Lippincott. (1953). The whereabouts of this portrait is unknown.

[802] Daily Express, 20 October 1930.

[803] Sissinghurst, a ruined Tudor castle in Kent which the Nicolsons bought in 1930. The gardens were transformed into an English showpiece. Vita worked with the garden designer Nora Lindsay (1873-1948) to achieve the prefect landscape.

[804] One want to be diplomat named Valentine Lawford records in his memoirs Bound for Diplomacy John Murray (1963). "The news that Harold Nicolson was to

deliver a lecture at Cambridge on the Diplomatic Career at the end of November, 1931, caused a spasm too."

[805] The Times of 12 April 1935 records that the Anchor-Donaldson liner Letitia ran aground off Cape Papas, in the Gulf of Patras, Greece. Those on board among the lecturer-guides were the homosexual Hugh Walpole (1884-1941), a novelist and art collector, and Harold Nicolson.

[806] Edward Frederic Benson (1867-1940). English writer and homosexual. Lived on the Isle of Capri with John Ellingham Brooks, a painter and translater, although married, who died in 1929.

[807] Mosley, Leonard. Castlerosse. A Barker. (1956). Additional names listed are Lord Carlyle, Lady Oxford, Sir Philip Sassoon, Lord and Lady Weymouth, Mrs Edwin Montagu, Lord Stanley and Mrs Euan Wallace.

[808] Ibid.

[809] Susan Ottilia de Rodakoski-Rivers (died 1968) (known as Suki). She married her half cousin Commander Hon, Alexander Bannerman Carnegie (son of the 10th Earl of the Southesk), in 1919.

[810] Daily Express, 15 June 1929.

[811] Daily Mirror, 15 July 1927.

[812] Ernest Frederic Graham Thesiger (1879-1961). Actor, with aristocratic links. Best known in horror movies, especially James Whale's film Bride of Frankenstein (1935).

[813] Aberconway, Christabel. A Wiser Woman. A Book of Memories. Hutchinson & Co. (1966).

[814] William Allen Jowitt, (1885-1957). 1st and last Earl Jowitt. Lord High Chancellor in Clement Atlee's Labour government 1945-1951.

[815] The Argus (Melborne) 11 September 1937.

[816] The Times, 18 November 1938.

[817] Costello, John. The Mask of Treachery. Collins (1988). John Costello died in 1995, aged 52.

[818] Carter, Miranda. Anthony Blunt. His Lives. Pan Macmillan. (2002).

[819] The Royal Archives, Windsor Castle have no record of Evan being appointed to any such post in the Royal Household. Queen Mary was aware of Evan's collection of Chinese ceramics and in particular of possessing some rare examples of jade, something she collected too. She may have seen this unofficially at Evan's home at South Street or South Audley Street since the Queen had a habit of gate crashing. Beyond that Evan had contributed in small part to making a miniature book available for the Queen's Dolls House, held in the Royal Collection.

[820] Bryans, Robin. Let the petals fall. Honeyford Press. (1993).

[821] Lady Mary Bridget Parsons (1907-1972). Sister of the 6th Earl of Rosse. Her obituary in The Times of 17 February 1972 said "She never married, largely because she perceived in others, more sharply than their virtues, the degree to which they fell short of the perfection she sought."

[822] Fielding, Daphne. Emerald and Nancy: Lady Cunard and her daughter. Eyre & Spottiswoode. (1968).

[823] Bryans. Robin. Let the petals fall. Honeyford Press. (1993).

[824] Costello, John. The Mask of Treachery. Collins (1988). According to Costello the homosexual networking [among the Royals] that operated in the glittering pre-war London circle …revolved around Edward, the Prince of Wales, his younger brother, George, the Duke of Kent, the Queen's brother, David Bowes Lyon and their cousin Lord Louis Mountbatten."

[825] Princess Marina of Greece and Denmark, (1906- 1968) later Duchess of Kent.

[826] Private source, name withheld, contact the author for further details.

[827] A Sunderland Flying Boat (Flight W4026) in which the Prince was travelling crashed into a remote hilltop on 25 August 1942.

[828] Picknell, L, Prince, C and Prior, S. Double Standards. The Rudolf Hess Cover-up. Sphere; New Ed Edition (2002).

[829] Lees-Milne, James. Ancestral Voices. Faber and Faber. (1984). Entry for 25 August 1942).

[830] Lees-Milne, James. Ancestral Voices. Faber and Faber. (1984). Entry for 29 August 1942).

[831] See Picknell, L, Prince, C and Prior, S. Double Standards. The Rudolf Hess Cover-up. Sphere; New Ed Edition (2002). This controversial book list the members of the crew who lost their lives, including three members of the staff of the Duke of Kent: Lt John Arthur Lowther, RNVR, the Duke's private secretary, grandson and heir of Viscount Ullswater; P/O Hon. Michael Strutt, son of Lord Belper and Leading Aircraftman John Hales, the Duke's Batman.

Double Standards challenges much of the story of Rudolf Hess's flight to Britain in 1941 and implicates a member of the Royal Family as being aware of the mission; this disturbed a lot of people.

The premise of the book is that "Hess flew to Britain with Hitler's full knowledge and acquiescence. A substantial peace party existed in Britain in 1941, including most of the aristocracy and the Royal Family, a senior member of which was actually waiting for Hess to arrive. The prisoner known as 'Hess' who died in Spandau prison was probably a brain-washed double. The fate of the real Hess was inextricably linked to the mysterious death of the King's brother, the Duke of Kent, in a plane crash in Scotland in 1942. [Finally that] Winston Churchill manipulated the imprisonment of the real Hess to influence Hitler and change Britain's fortunes."

[832] Cathleen Mann (1896-1959). Artist, trained at the Slade. 2nd wife of the 11th Marquess of Queensbury.

[833] The reference to a portable altar is almost certainly an embroidered element from Evan or one of his followers.

[834] Amory, Mark. Lord Berners. The Last Eccentric. Pimlico. (1999).

[835] One instance of this is featured by The Tablet of 8 December 1928 when Evan and Lois were both present at a reception organised by the Duchess of Norfolk " in aid of the Million Pound Fund of the Guild of Our Lady of Ransom" :

"The Hon. Evan Morgan said that the very name of the appeal, in any other country than our own, would be sufficient to put it to bed. But the name should not be allowed to frighten any English Catholic who realized what our forefathers had suffered during the penal times right down to the year 1829. He would remind them that in one year of the reign of James I fines amounting to four million pounds (according to the present value of money) were paid by a mere handful of Catholics for refusal to attend Protestant worship."

[836] The 1930 Conference of the Catholic Young Men's Society was held at Newport. Evan was one of the principal speakers to the 200 delegates. He later repeated his support at a function at Olympia where about 1500 people attended. See The Tablet 14 June 1930.

[837] One story is told that Evan had his own special seating area at St David's Church to pray and take Mass. This area was roped off. On the death of his friend Archbishop Mostyn in 1939, Evan was not well received by his successor, Archbishop Michael Joseph McGrath (1882-1961). NB the Ship's bell of the Courtenay's steam yacht Liberty is held at St David's Church, a new building erected in the 1960s.

Father Maloney was a sympathetic ear for Evan. One man (now in his 80s and who has memories of the "hard faced caretaker (Emily Sutherland) and groundsman at Tredegar House in Evan's era "who thought nothing of taking a shot at trespassers", told the author that when he returned safely from the army in the post-war period, Maloney was so pleased he had survived that he warmly embraced him. As a younger member of Maloney's orbit, he recalled Maloney was "a touchy-feely type".

Maloney is remembered with affection by local Newport writer David (Dai) Jones: "I remember Father Maloney (later Canon) from late '40's -'70's; in fact he married my wife Jill and I in 1964 on the opening day of the then new St David's Church. We had the reception in the old church which was adjacent. (You know the type of thing. Someone smashes a cup and everyone looks under the table to see who it belonged to). He worked tirelessly to raise funds for the said church and lived a very frugal life. I would like to think that the Morgans at least afforded him some sustenance".

His Parish included Maesglas, the partially developed Gaer Estate and St Brides as far down as St Mellons. This included the POW camp at St Brides and he served Mass at three different locations (inc. PoWs) every Sunday. He walked everywhere, even to Cardiff once a fortnight for his ecumenical meetings with the Archbishop. He served the Church and Parish unselfishly until his death. As kids he would put the fear of God into us (excuse awful pun). He had a glass eye, lost playing hurling, and a broad Irish accent which no one could understand."

[838] For many years Vernon Morgan (a former member of the staff of Newport Council and whose office was based for a time inside Tredegar House) carried out a series of surveys. This work (supplemented by maps and drawings) shows a number of unexplained and unexplored voids within the buildings and inside the main house. Was one of these Evan's Magick Room?

[839] David Freeman and David Beevers, the former Curators at Tredegar House from the 1970s, made contact with a number of Evan's surviving relatives and friends, including Evan's second wife Olga (who was living in retirement on the Island of Guernsey), Evan's half-cousin, Charles, 11th Earl of Southesk, Henry Maxwell (one of those chosen by Evan to write his biography) and Tony Mattei (the 2nd Marshese Conte) whose close friendship with Evan went from the late 1920s onwards. Each offered some recollections and memories of Evan and Tredegar House. See Aspects of Evan.

[840] When Firbank took Evan off to the British Museum to see his supposed likeness, the arch-riddler Firbank did not point to the statue of Ramases II but to a sarcophagus in which lay an age-emaciated figure "a fanciful reproduction of myself", as Evan out it.

[841] In 1918 Warlock spent two months on a desolate island off the West coast of Ireland. He met WB Yeats in Dublin in April 1918. He became a fan of Yeats's poetry, especially his early verse with it's old Celtic and lyrical qualities. This inspired Warlock's work The Curlew (1920-1922).

[842] Heseltine, Nigel. A Memoir of Philip Heseltine, Thames Publishing. London (1992). In the reference to the writers and artists who met together at the Café Royal Heseltine lists among others Jacob Epstein (sculptor), Wyndham Lewis (painter), Evan and Aleister Crowley. There is no other corroboration for Evan meeting Crowley before Nina Hamnett's introductions in Paris in the 1920s.

[843] Wilson, Elizabeth. Bohemians: The Glamorous Outcasts. Tauris Parke. (2002).

[844] The composer Sir William Walton (1902-1983) records, in his recollections in an interview in The Sunday Times of 25 March 1962, an abiding memory of Warlock's drinking: " Heseltine, yes, Peter Warlock – I went down to stay with him once; but the *drinking* – I couldn't keep up."

[845] See Wilson, Elizabeth. Bohemians: The Glamorous Outcasts. Tauris Parke. (2002). A very good summary of Warlock and many others in the Café Royal clique.

[846] Published by Winthrop Rogers with nine copies between May 1920 and March 1921 edited by Warlock. Rogers then decided to withdraw funding. According to Barry Smith (in his book on Warlock) Evan offered to buy out Rogers for £200 on Warlock's behalf but this offer came to nothing. Nigel Heseltine (son of Peter Warlock) records in his very readable A Memoir of Philip Heseltine, Thames Publishing, London (1992): "Evan Morgan (later Lord Tredegar) bought out Winthrop Rogers for £200 which sum, however, he omitted to pay, so that the Sackbut remained dormant until February 1921."

One reviewer said of the Sackbut "Generally controversial, the Sackbut was highly regarded by many and especially those who wished to see the "establishment" in the field of British music taken to task. It was Heseltine's pleasure to be one of, if not

THE most vociferous critics of his time and history shows that his eloquent and learned use of the English language was used to its fullest degree."

[847] For further information on Warlock (also known as Philip Heseltine) see Smith Barry. Peter Warlock: the life of Philip Heseltine. Oxford University Press. (1994)

[848] Heseltine, Nigel. A Memoir of Philip Heseltine, Thames Publishing. London (1992).

[849] This is from the final scene of Mozart's opera Don Giovanni, in which the statue of the Commendatore arrives to have supper with Don Giovanni. The full line the Commendatore sings is, "Don Giovanni! a cenar teco m'invitasti! e son venuto! ("Don Giovanni! By thee invited, Here behold me as thou directed").

[850] Heseltine, Nigel. A Memoir of Philip Heseltine, Thames Publishing. London (1992).

[851] This is an interesting review (from 1932) by B.E.C. Davis of Evan's "Some Aspects of Mysticism in Verse," "straightforward, fearless expression, simple diction of genuine mystical poetry", as contrasted with "the wool-gathering of a lazy poetaster, inert, flabby, vague and fruitless", sometimes mistaken for it. Mr. Morgan's specimen of his own poetry is welcome, but we question whether many readers will concur unreservedly with the statement that "mysticism is inbred in every poet or he is no poet at all."

[852] In 1920 Evan produced a book in verse entitled Psyche: An Unfinished Fragment.

[853] Robin Bryans wrote to Tredegar House in the 1990s enclosing cuttings of reviews of Evan's paintings - seen by the art world of Paris in the 1920s.

[854] Bryans, Robin. The Dust Has Never Settled. Honeyford Press (1992).

[855] Summers, Montague. Witchcraft and Black Magic. Dover Publications (2000)

[856] Guiley, Rosemary. The Encyclopedia of Witches, Witchcraft and Wicca. Infobase Publishing (2008).

[857] Black Magic is Not a Myth by Aleister Crowley in The London Sunday Dispatch 2 July 1933.

[858] Victor Neuberg (1883-1940) Poet and writer and sex slave to Aleister Crowley. He later suffered severe mental health problems and abandoned Crowley. Peter Warlock put several of his poems to music. Neuberg published some of the early works of Dylan Thomas.

[859] Eileen J Garrett (1893-1970) Medium and author.

[860] Garrett, Elieen. Many voices: the autobiography of a medium. Putnam. (1968) See also Richardson, Alan, Aleister Crowley and Dion Fortune: The Logos of the Aeon and the Shakti of the Age. Llewellyn Worldwide (2009).

[861] Taken from The Beastly Life of a Man Called Crowley by Frater Achad Osher 583.

[862] Magic is Not a Myth by Aleister Crowley in The London Sunday Dispatch 2 July 1933.

[863] The Diaries of Donald Friend: 1967-1999, published by the National Library of Australia (2001)

[864] Ibid.

[865] Bryans. Robin. The Dust Has Never Settled. Honeyford Press. (1992),

[866] Auden, W H. Forewords and Afterwords. Faber and Faber (1973) and Auden in the New Yorker Magazine.

[867] Vernon Charles Wills (1900-1964). Lived at 107 Richmond Road, Cardiff. Died Whitchurch Hospital, Glamorgan, 1 November 1964.

[868] Bryans. Robin. Let the petals fall. Honeyford Press. (1993).

[869] Bryans, Robin. Blackmail and Whitewash. Honeyford Press. (1996)

[870] http://en.wikipedia.org/wiki/Tantra

[871] Bryans, Robin. Blackmail and Whitewash. Honeyford Press. (1996).

[872] Ibid.

[873] Ibid

[874] Ibid.

[875] http://www.stwulfrans.org.uk/history/history.php

[876] Bryans, Robin. The Dust Has Never Settled. Honeyford Press (1992).

[877] Robin Bryans' partner, George Balcombe lived at The Welkin, Rottingdean where the garden led directly onto the Sussex Downs.

[878] Bryans, Robin. Blackmail and Whitewash. Honeyford Press (1996).

[879] Bryans, Robin. The Dust Has Never Settled. Honeyford Press (1992).

[880] Ibid.

[881] Ibid.

[882] From Robert Ziegler's Satanism, Magic and Mysticism in Fin-de-siecle France. Palgrave Macmillan. (2012).

[883] Bryans, Robin. Blackmail and Whitewash. Honeyford Press. (1996)

[884] Crowley had already established homosexual sex magick rituals as a higher degree or part of what he deemed Ordo Templi Orientis – his Order of the Temple of the East.

[885] Bryans, Robin. The Dust Has Never Settled. Honeyford Press (1992).

[886] Channon, Sir Henry. Chips: The Diaries of Sir Henry Channon. Edited by Robert Rhodes James. Weidenfeld & Nicolson. (1967).

[887] Bryan, Robin. Blackmail and Whitewash. Honeyford Press (1996).

[888] Robin Bryans writes in Blackmail and Whitewash p 129 "Evan in my mind will always be associated with Peter Churchill and Felix Yussupov". Prince Felix Felixovich Yusupov (1887-1967), Russian born bisexual who was almost certainly involved in the scheme to murder Rasputin, the mad monk. Evan and Felix met a few times in London and Paris.

[889] Philippe Jullian: Fresh Remembrance of Oscar Wilde, from Vogue, 1 November 1969.

[890] Bryans. Robin. Blackmail and Whitewash. Honeyford Press (1996).

[891] A 12th century monastery which passed from Augustinians to Franciscans in the 16th century.

[892] Bryans. Robin. Blackmail and Whitewash. Honeyford Press. (1996).

[893] Gabriele D'Annunzi (1863-1938). Writer and Poet. Extreme right wing Italian: a rival with Mussolini. Evan learned of him from the Marchesa Luisa Casati (one of D'Annenzi's former lovers).

[894] Bryans. Robin. Blackmail and Whitewash. Honeyford Press (1996).

[895] According to Bryans " Meg Jenkins was said to have had polymastia [an additional nipple] to an excessive degree and these supernumerary nipples were seen at her public examination before being immersed in one of Llanover's wells to determine her guilt or innocence of witchcraft".

[896] Bedford, John, Duke of. A Silver-Plated Spoon. The Reprint Society of London. (1959).

[897] This was Crowley's motto and greeting.

[898] Carrington, Dora de Houghton & Garnet David. Carrington: letters and extracts from her diaries. Holt, Rinehart and Winston. (1971). Entry for 18 September 1929.

[899] See Booth Martin. A Magick Life: A biography of Aleister Crowley. Hodder. (2000).

[900] Dennis Wheatley (1897-1977). British writer, especially well known for his novels on the occult and black magic.

[901] Wheatley, Dennis. The Time Has Come: The Memoirs of Dennis Wheatley. Drink and Ink, 1919-1977. Hutchinson. (1979).

[902] Reference is made by Bryans to the suicide of the actress Ione de Forest (mistress of Crowley's former slave Victor Neuberg) as being attributed to Crowley. Another of Crowley's associates, Norman Mudd was so affected by Crowley's powers he drowned himself. A still more terrifying tale was an occasion in Paris when Crowley (with his son MacAliester) attempted to invoke the spirit of Pan. The ritual went badly wrong and resulted in MacAliester's death. Crowley could not explain what happened and ended up in a mental institution. http://radicalrog.hubpages.com/hub/ALEISTER-CROWLEY-AND-THE-PARIS-INCIDENT-AN-OCCULT-MYSTERY

[903] Bryans. Robin. Checkmate. Honeyford Press. (1994).

[904] Ibid.

[905] Bryans, Robin. The Dust Has Never Settled. Honeyford Press. (1992)

[906] William Hampton Pethybridge, born Cornwall - son of William Ford Pethybridge. The family are on the 1911 Census at 162 Richmond Road, Cardiff, William is aged 43, single and a Solicitor.

[907] William Hampton Pethybridge of 104 Ninian Road, Cardiff died 19 April 1944 at 30a, Cowbridge road, Cardiff. Left Estate valued at £20,694.

[908] The Times of 26 November 1892 lists William Hampton Pethybridge as having been successful in The Law Society's Final Examination held on 8 and 9 November 1892.

[909] The Times of 27 August 1969 contains a short tribute to Alice Pethybridge who had died at the age of 103.

[910] A link between on of the wives of the Marquess of Queensbury and the Pethybridge/ Wills is described by Robin Bryans.

[911] Robin Bryans writes in Checkmate about William Pethybridge being implicated in a scandal over a Protestant Monastery in Barry: There was much rejoicing when "Rev. Dr Matthew abandoned the Church of Rome and set up a Protestant monastery in Barry, which, it seems had hardly opened before it was forcibly closed again after Alderman Willie Pethybridge of Cardiff City Hall was found doing to the boys there what his friend, Lord Alfred Douglas, had done to him less than

twenty years before. However, worse threatened to come in 1930, for the corruption of Willie Pethybridge, and his City of Dreadful Knights faced the horrors of exposure with the tactless death of Sir George Watson, Lord of the Manor of Sulhamstead Abbots who paid £30,000 for his baronetcy. ...George had paid out .to Maundy Gregory but died before receiving the summons to Buckingham Palace. For Sir George to have paid out such a lot for an honour he did not get because he died was too much for his executors, who instructed lawyers to retrieve the large sums already handed over to the Liberal party funds..."

[912] Despite the assertions made by Robin Bryans, the author's research has not established that William Pethybridge was sexually corrupted by Bosie Douglas or that Pethybridge acted for Maundy Gregory (as legal advisor) in the Cash for Honours scandal or in the Anglo-Ukrainian Committee.

[913] Sir Harry George Handover. Twelve times Mayor of Paddington 1911- 1935.

[914] Bryans. Robin. Checkmate. Honeyford Press. (1994).

[915] Sir Percy Alfred Harris. (1876-1952) Liberal Party Politician.

[916] Bryans, Robin. Blackmail and Whitewash. Honeyford Press (1996).

[917] Taken from The Beastly Life of a Man Called Crowley by Frater Achad Osher 583.

[918] Crowley met such individuals as the author Ian Fleming. It was during the Second World War that Fleming, (who worked for the Department of Naval Intelligence), hatched a scheme to have Crowley interrogate the 'captured' Nazi leader Rudolf Hess about 'occult' matters. [This must have been after May 1941] Crowley actually accepted his offer but Fleming's superiors decided that it was not a good idea and they vetoed the overall plan. Ian Fleming's biographer, John Pearson, wrote in 1966: "It is a pity that this had to be one of Fleming's bright ideas which never came off: understandably, there was hilarity in the department at the idea of the Great Beast 666 doing his bit for Britain." In March of 1952 when Ian Fleming wrote his first James Bond novel titled Casino Royale, he looked for someone on whom he could base his arch-villain. He needed an evil figure so he dredged up his past images of his old friend Aleister Crowley. After all, Fleming "always knew a good villain when he saw one." He decided to give his villain the name Le Chiffre." (Cribbed from The Beastly Life of a Man Called Crowley).

[919] MI8 was the cover designation for the Radio Security Service (RSS) which was absorbed by MI6 from May 1941. Ralph Mansfield, Lord Sandhurst (1892-1964 was leading the research strategy in MI8. See also Pidgeon, Geoffrey. The Secret Wireless War. Arundel Books. (2008). NB This reference in referring to Evan as being a part of MI8 is contained in Kaczynski, Richard. Perdurabo: The Life of Aleister Crowley. North Atlantic Books. (2010). A further likely inexactitude can be found in several books on the history of MI5/MI6 describing Evan as a "Falconer" and participating in covert activities in the South Coast of England.

[920] Grant, R G. MI5 MI6 Britain's Security and Secret Intelligence Services. See page 65 (which is not indexed under Lord Tredegar). It is also the claimed by Grant that Evan was imprisoned in The Tower of London "for revealing details of his secret employment to a fellow peer."

[921] West, Nigel. MI5: British Security Service Operations, 1909-1945. Stein and Day (1982).

[922] Popular Mechanics . May 1957. Hearst Magazines.

[923] See South Wales Argus, 12 January 1942, which has a photograph of Evan with a caption 'Corps of Signals: Viscount Tredegar a Second Lieutenant', saying that Evan "has relinquished command of a Monmouthshire Battalion of the Home Guard on the grant to him of a commission …. in the Royal Corps of Signals."

[924] This discredits other references from Evan worshippers (referred to in Aspects of Evan) that he was let off a court martial by the intervention of MI5. Evan went into the Royal Masonic Military Hospital, Ravenscourt Park in London for an operation on his knee and then returned to Wales, to Tredegar House to recuperate. See The Times 22 May 1943.

[925] Letter in the South Wales Argus, November 1944.

[926] A C Diaries. Binder 8. H.8.. 65-70. With comments by Richard Kaczyski or Gerald Yorke.

[927] Monty Dart (who is Guide at Tredegar House comments, "The Oak Room is probably the rather dark room known as the Master's Bedchamber. It is next door to the Cow Bathroom."

[928] According to John Symonds in The Beast 666: The Life of Aleister Crowley. The Pindar Press (1997) (which also refers to the Crowley visit to Tredegar House) "Robert Arthur Talbot Gascoyne Cecil, third Marquis of Salisbury (1830-1903), Conservative prime minister and a pillar of the establishment, was not by any stretch of the imagination Aleister Crowley's old patron."

[929] Probably [Marguerite] Frieda Harris (1877-1962), Occult Magician. She is best known for her artistic design of Crowley's Thoth tarot deck.

[930] Emily Sutherland, MS Landers (1894-1980) Evan's Secretary. Known as "Mother".

[931] Wife of a cousin of Evan. The Forestier-Walkers married into the Morgans in the 19th century.

[932] According to John Symonds in p559 of The King of the Shadow Realm (which also refers to the Crowley visit to Tredegar House) "From an earlier reference (20 July 1931) to 'The Eye of Horus', it seems that Crowley used this term for the anus". Another text suggests this term refers to anal intercourse (buggery):

"Oh, how superior is the Eye of Horus to the Mouth of Isis!" Diary 1913 about a boy showered with "foaming seed": "While the other in his orgasm receives the waters." "Let it be no sin to us to have buggered the virile bum." "While the priest thrusts his thyrsus between boyish buttocks, all is accomplished; come Holy Dove!"

http://bluepyramid.tripod.com/index/id4.html. "The Equinox" IV;2, Maine 1998, 405.

http://www.parareligion.ch/sunrise/xi.htm

[933] See Aspects of Evan for details of Crowley's visit to Tredegar House.

[934] According to the biography on Amazon.com of the David Conway ("a genuine mystic") "Mr James" was a local farmer in mid Wales whom Conway came to know as a young boy. James was the boy's "chief mentor, introducing him to the basic principles of magic".

[935] Conway, David. Magic Without Mirrors. Logious Publishing (2011).

[936] From Aleister Crowley's unpublished diary for 1943.

[937] These are Crowley's own exact words from his diary.

[938] A description by one contributor to the BBC Radio Wales programme Meeting at Munich that Crowley recorded that the room was the "Largest (the biggest) and best equipped Magick Room he'd ever seen" is exposed as utterly false and fabricated.

[939] In Witch Hunts in the Western World, p96, Brian Paviac refers to "The followers of the Devil had allegedly once even held a Black Mass in his own bedroom."

[940] Bedford, John, Duke of. A Silver-Plated Spoon. The Reprint Society of London. (1959). At Honeywood House Rafaelle, Duchess of Leinster refers in her memoirs to guests being taken to see Evan's private Chapel on the first floor with his collection of rare ivory figures. See Aspects of Evan.

[941] Courtenay would never have allowed Catholic symbols in the house. Evan made several changes to the inside of the house to suit himself after he became Viscount Tredegar.

[942] According to Gordon Cadden, Chess historian, Crowley was a leading player in the Hastings Chess Club. The Crowley Diaries for 1941-1944 indicate that The Great Beast and Evan played chess together once in a while.

[943] No reference exists to support a wild claim made by some that Crowley was asked to perform a ritual spell to inflict a dire consequence upon Evan's Commanding Officer at the time of Evan's Court Martial, a few weeks before. This is a wholly false and mischievous claim. In the BBC Radio Wales programme Meeting at Munich the contributor of this fiction states "Evan wanted to do a cursing ritual on his commanding officer Lt Colonel Parks..." This testimony goes on to say that Crowley "left [Evan to it] before any harm could be done." and that "Bizarrely Lt Colonel Parks is taken seriously ill and almost dies..." The perpetrators of this nonsense shoot themselves in the foot; there was a Lt Colonel A B Parkes, OBE, TD, who was the Commanding Officer of the 30th Battalion, the Middlesex Regiment on the Court Martial panel. The other Lt Colonel Norman Parkes, was the prosecuting Counsel from the Judge Advocate's Department. Neither man was Evan's Commanding Officer.

[944] Augustus John refers in Chiaroscuro: Fragments of Autobiography to Crowley's "sustained exhibition of verbal effervescence.....by nothing more recondite than a bottle of brandy...."

[945] Quoted in Bizarre Magazine, May 2001 page 97.

[946] According to Robin Bryans "a woman was burnt as a witch near Tredegar in the late seventeenth century".

[947] Howard Michael. The Occult War. Secret Agents, Magicians and Hitler. http://www.the-cauldron.org.uk/Resources/Occult%20War.pdf

[948] The written testimony of Olga Tredegar, Henry Maxwell, Tony Mattai and Desmond Leslie (who all lived / visited Tredegar House regularly in the 1930s and 1940s) make no reference to the Magick Room or Evan's Black Masses.

[949] Bryans, Robin. Blackmail and Whitewash. Honeyford Press (1996).

[950] Monty Dart has made a search of many local Welsh (and other) sources without tracing a reference to Meg Jenkins to corroborate Bryans' assertions.

[951] Augusta Hall, Lady Llanover (1802-1896). Youngest daughter of Benjamin Waddington of Nottinghamshire. She married Benjamin Hall in 1826. (He gave his name to the Westminster Clock, Big Ben, and died in a gun accident in 1867). Lady Llanover's daughter Mrs Herbert lived at Llanover until at least 1911.

[952] One appreciation web site on Lady Augusta Llanover says "There was little distinctly Welsh about the clothes that Augusta based her version of Welsh national dress on, and much the same was worn by country women in England around this time too. Although black beaver hats had been worn by Welsh women from the end of the eighteenth century, the tall 'chimney hats' of the archetypal Welsh lady were a Victorian invention. Augusta was so excited by her idea of Welsh national dress that she required all her maids to wear it at work. She even built a woollen mill in the grounds of Llanover House to produce the native cloth out of which the costume was made, giving a much needed boost to local Welsh industry."
http://womenshistorynetwork.org/blog/?tag=lady-llanover

[953] In Tom Driberg's biography by Frances Wheen reference is made to a sale by Tom of Book of Law presented to him by Crowley, inscribed To True Thomas of the Eidon Hills with all best wishes from Boleskine and Alertariff .

[954] Howard Michael. The Occult War. Secret Agents, Magicians and Hitler.
http://www.the-cauldron.org.uk/Resources/Occult%20War.pdf

[955] Symonds, John. The Beast 666: The Life of Aleister Crowley. The Pindar Press (1997).

[956] David Conway says in Secret Wisdom: The Occult Universe Explored. Jonathan Cape Ltd (1987) that Crowley " liked to call himself, the Master Therion, alias the Great Beast of Revelation, [and] the number 666.."

[957] Crowley, Aleister. The Eternal sun.
http://www2.arnes.si/~uljfarh3/david/iao.html

[958] Greene Raymond. Moments of being. Heinemann. (1974). Attributed by Greene to the journalist Cassandra, who had first dubbed Aleister Crowley The Wickedest Man in the World. David Conway also refers to this in Magic Without Mirrors (and quotes from the Hymn to Pan). He attributes the performance to Louis Wilkinson (1881-1966), he was one of Crowley's executors.

[959] Another description of the dozen or so that attended Crowley's funeral (several accounts say it was at Brighton Crematorium) include this one from Eillen Garrrett – the medium in her autobiography: "an odd mixture of crumpled raincoats, coughs, bright scarves, a lack of haircuts and the indefinable spoor of Charlotte Street and Soho." Louis Wilkinson (an old friend of Crowley and one of Crowley's executors) is named elsewhere as delivering Hymn to Pan, the Collects and Anthems and selected passages from the Book of the Law.

[960] See Sunday Times, 13 August 2000.

[961] Symonds John. The King of the shadow real: Aleister Crowley, his life and magic. Duckworth. (1989).

[962] Some references (originate from the licence taken on Evan tales by former guides at Tredegar House) substitute " Black Hand" for " Black Circle".

[963] Howard Michael. The Occult War. Secret Agents, Magicians and Hitler. http://www.the-cauldron.org.uk/Resources/Occult%20War.pdf

[964] Howard Michael. The Occult War. Secret Agents, Magicians and Hitler. http://www.the-cauldron.org.uk/Resources/Occult%20War.pdf

[965] Bryans, Robin. Let the petals fall. Honeyford Press (1993).

[966] Bryans. Robin. The Dust Has Never Settled. Honeyford Press (1992).

[967] Referred to by a former guide at Tredegar House in a talk about Evan Morgan to The Friends of Tredegar House on 10 April 2013, attended by the Author.

[968] In Rome in 1921 pilgrims both English and Italian celebrated the centenary of Keats' death in Rome, on 23 February, 1821. On the 100th anniversary of Shelley's death on 8 July 1922, the British Ambassador, the Mayor of Rome, and members of the Keats and Shelley Association gathered at the Protestant cemetery, where Shelley's ashes are buried, to lay wreaths. This tribute included attendance by members of the British colony in Rome.

[969] Shane Leslie, full name Sir John Randolph Leslie (1885-1971). Irish-born diplomat and writer. Cousin of Winston Churchill.

[970] Cardinal Gasquet – Francis Aiden (1846-1929). English Cardinal in Rome at the Vatican. He was attached to the Vatican Secret Archives.

[971] Leslie, Shane. Long shadows. Murray (1966).

[972] Symons inscribed The Quest for Corvo "To Shane Leslie". The reprint of the book by the Folio Society in 1952 (reissued 1992) contains a Introduction by Norman Birkett and a Memoir by Shane Leslie.

[973] This can be found on Y-Tube.

[974] Symons inscribed The Quest for Corvo "To Shane Leslie". The reprint of the book by the Folio Society in 1952 (reissued 1992) contains a Introduction by Norman Birkett and a Memoir by Shane Leslie.

[975] Leslie, Shane. The passing chapter. Cassel (1934).

[976] Rauchbauer, Otto. Shane Leslie Sublime Failure. Lilliput Press Ltd. (2009) The book merely includes a reference to the home of Evan Morgan, Viscount Tredegar as one of the "Catholic Houses" that Leslie often visited.

[977] Bryans, Robin. The Dust Has Never Settled. Honeyford Press (1992).

[978] Ibid.

[979] Lady Beatrice Carnegie (1852-1934) Wife of Rev Henry Holmes Stewart.

[980] Rev. Henry Holmes Stewart (1847-1937).

[981] The earliest records show that the Church goes back to at least 1200. It was restored in the 19th century.

[982] Bryans. Robin. Let the petals fall. Honeyford Press. (1993).

[983] The Times of 19 May 1945 records this death intimation "On May 16 1945 at Edward's Nursing Home, West Malvern, Canon John Lonsdale Bryans, aged 92."

[984] Bryans. Robin. The Dust Has Never Settled. Honeyford Press (1992).

[985] Ibid.

[986] According to Robin Bryans "... in 1898 seven young men left Belfast to found the Egypt General Mission." It was an interdenominational Christian mission.

[987] Ibid.

[988] Ibid.

[989] I am indebted to a member of the Carnegie family for transcribing one of Raymond Rodakowski's letters from 1916, describing a row between Gwyneth and her mother (referred to as Aunt K) '24th July 1916. 'Gwyneth is absolutely fed up with Aunt K. after a row. Hope things are better now as awful pity if another incident occurred.'

[990] The Sunday Times of 31 May 1925 carries a report of Gwyneth's funeral at Putney Vale Cemetery. Several additional names of mourners appear in the report excluded from those previously seen. "Miss Eileen Plunkett": possibly Hon. Eileen Hermione Plunket (born 1896), daughter of the William Lee Plunket, 5th Baron Plunket of Newton. There is a reference to "the Honourable Eileen Plunkett" in biographies of the colourful lesbian Radcliffe Hall and Virginia Nicholson's Singled Out: Two Million Women Survived Without Men After the First World War. Eileen was an ambulance driver in the Great War, she later married. The Sunday Times report also gives one of Gwyneth's mourners as "Miss L Laws (her devoted maid)".

[991] John. Augustus. Chiaroscuro. Fragments of Autobiography. Pellegrini & Company (1952).

[992] Bryans, Robin. The Dust Has Never Settled. Honeyford Press. (1992).

[993] Bryans. Robin. Let the petals fall. Honeyford Press. (1993).

[994] Rosita Forbes (1890-1967). Explorer and travel writer. Henry Maxwell recalls that Rosita visited Tredegar House.

[995] Henry Herbert, 6th Earl of Carnarvon (1898-1987).

[996] Barbara Hutton (1912-1979). Seven times married, riches to rags Woolworth department store heiress. Known as a lover of drugs, drink and playboys.

[997] Forbes. Rosita. Appointment with destiny. E P Dutton & Co. (1946).

[998] Princess Mary Brenda de Chimay (nee Hamilton) (1897-). Wife of Prince Alphonse de Chimay.

[999] Forbes. Rosita. Appointment with destiny. E P Dutton & Co. (1946).

[1000] Henry Maxwell was a friend of Evan's for many years in the 1930s and 1940s. He was named in Evan's last Will and Testament (along with Cyril Hughes Hartmann) as being Evan's choice to write his biography. Maxwell recalled this in 1979, writing to David Beevers (Tredegar House Curator).

[1001] Ibid.

[1002] Ibid.

[1003] The BBC were required to launch several enquiries into the activities of Sir Jimmy Savile, a deceased TV disc jockey, after a documentary and press reports alleged that he had committed sexual offences against children and young women over many decades, with many individuals in the BBC (and elsewhere) turning a blind eye to the abuse.

[1004] See Henry Maxwell's letter to David Beevers at Tredegar House Archives, 1979.

[1005] Bryans, Robin. Checkmate. Honeyford Press (1994).

[1006] Ibid.

[1007] Prince Birabongse Bhanudej Bhanubandh (1914-1985). Best known as Prince Bira of Siam. (Thailand) Motoring racing star in Formula One and Grand Prix races. Also a talented artist.

[1008] Prince Chula Chakrabongse (1908-1963). Cousin of Prince Bira. Author and Motor racing team star.

[1009] The Catholic Herald of 2 July 1971 carries an obituary of Mgr. Hugh Montgomery, who died at the age of 75. He is described as "Secretary of the British Legation to the Holy Sec from 1933-36."

[1010] A series of books from an American author Ms Randy Engel entitled the Rite of Sodomy make startling suggestions about homosexuality in the Vatican in the period that straddles Evan's links with Rome. These damning indictments from the 1930s implicate a Mgr Montina (who was later Pope Paul VI). It is inferred that Montina "had a homosexual affair with English Charge d'affaires, Hugh Montgomery (who later became a Catholic priest), brother of homosexual Peter Montgomery, partner to Cambridge spy Anthony Blunt." Montina also met Evan during this same era and there are references to Evan in Engel. http://newengelpublishing.com/ Robin Bryans says that "facing the media after his exposure as a Soviet spy, Blunt's Cambridge friend Peter Montgomery was certified insane."

[1011] Maxwell is the author of The Book of Words, published by Martin Secker in 1939.

[1012] Maxwell was co-author (with Prince Chula of Siam) of Wheels At Speed (1946).

[1013] Bryans, Robin. Checkmate. Honeyford Press (1994).

[1014] Luis Fernando de Orleans y Borbon. (1888-1945). Infante of Spain. In 1924 he was expelled from France and stripped of all royal privileges on account of trading in illegal drugs.

[1015] Referred to by Robin Bryans in Checkmate. Honeyford Press (1994). Uplifted from Saying life by Sir Francis Rose.

[1016] Two short other anecdotes from Alan Carnegie Stewart
"Evan or Evan's father, I'm not sure which, didn't like wrinkles on his sheets. When making his bed four housemaids were required to hold a corner of the bed sheet each, to make it as tight as a drum. Evan liked to walk around the house naked, and would ring a bell to alert the servants to keep out of sight. I remember that it was jolly cold in Tredegar House!"

[1017] Gogarty, O. St J. As I was Going Down Sackville Street. Rich & Cowan London (1937).

[1018] Bryans, Robin. The Dust Has Never Settled. Honeyford Press (1992).

[1019] Leslie, Seymour. The Jerome Connection. John Murray. (1964).

[1020] Williams, Guy St John (Ed). The Renvyle Letters. Gogarty Family Correspondence, 1939-1957. Daletta Press (2000).

[1021] Williams, Guy St John (Ed). The Renvyle Letters. Gogarty Family Correspondence, 1939-1957. Daletta Press (2000). p191. Letter dated July 25, 1948, from Desmond to "Doctor" Gogarty.

[1022] Bryans, Robin. Checkmate. Honeyford Press (1994).

[1023] See Caitlin, George [Sir] For God's sake Go. Smythe (1972) p135. "One memorable occasion he [Rose] had prevailed upon Queen Mary to visit his Cheyne Walk studio. Wicked fellows with a misplaced sense of humour were aware of this. In a room above the studio they awaited the solemn moment with pails of water. Her Majesty having arrived and been centrally seated, and Sir Francis have begun to display his wares, all was thrown into embarrassed confusion by drippings from the ceiling which increased in volume. I was never told whether Queen Mary's sense of humour rose to the occasion – she was a stern lady, with a long knobbed umbrella which she was capable of using – but that Sir Francis himself was thrown into a condition of near panic, I do know". The perpetrator of this leaking prank was Evan Morgan (says Robin Bryans).

[1024] Bryans. Robin. Checkmate. Honeyford Press. (1994).

[1025] Ibid.

[1026] Ibid.

[1027] Ibid.

[1028] Ibid.

[1029] The case provoked the journalist J R Ackerley (1896-1967) (himself a homosexual) to write to The Spectator on 20 November 1942. (The Spectator was one of the few publications of the time that was prepared to print the word homosexual.). Ackerley's brave protest was to point to the barbarity of the sentences and highlight that "during the course of the legal proceedings .... one youth of nineteen committed suicide on the railways lines and two others attempted unsuccessfully to do away with themselves by hanging and poison, to avoid the shame of exposure". Only The News of the World reported details about the case on 3 August and 8 November 1942. See also Braybrooke Neville [editor] The Letters of J R Ackerley. Duckworth. (1975) and Parker, Peter. Ackerley. The Life of J R Ackerley. The Noonday Press.(1989).

[1030] Bryans. Robin. Checkmate. Honeyford Press. (1994).

[1031] The full story of Dennis Parry is told in Gibbard. Noel. Taught to serve. The History of Barry and Bryntirion Colleges. Evangelical Press of Wales. (1996). Dennis Parry was brought up in South Norwood, London, the youngest of a family of six, and lost his mother when he was very young. He was converted as a Christian in 1937 and worked as a shop assistant. When war broke out in 1939 Dennis took his stand as a conscientious objector.

[1032] In the autumn of 1942 sixteen year old Ian Paisley enrolled in the Barry School of Evangelism. He was allowed into the school on a personal favour to his father, Kyle Paisley, a close friend of the Principal Rev SB Fidler.

[1033] Bryans. Robin. Checkmate. Honeyford Press (1994).

[1034] Bryans, Robin. The Dust Has Never Settled. Honeyford Press. (1992).

[1035] Dennis Parry was killed with his wife Nora and children Andrew and Grace in the Congo in December 1964. He was said to be from South Norwood, Surrey. In the Martyrs Memorial Free Presbyterian Church in Belfast there is a plaque in memory of Dennis Parry.

[1036] Bryans, Robin. The Dust Has Never Settled. Honeyford Press. (1992).

[1037] Ibid.

[1038] Authors R G Grant (MI5 MI6) and Nigel West (MI5: British Security Service Operations, 1909-1945) claim that Evan was held in the Tower of London awaiting his Court Martial.

[1039] Hon. Patrick Kinnaird (1898-1948). Relative by marriage to Buckle, he was the son of the 11th Lord Kinnaird.

[1040] Buckle, Richard. The Adventures of a Ballet Critic. Cresset Press (1953).

[1041] Russell Facey Wilkinson (1889-1968), KCVO, MRCS, LRCP. Society and Royal physician. He had advised Katharine and Evan on medical matters for several decades.

[1042] Letter in the Parliamentary Archives from Evan to Frances Stevenson, written at Rottingdean.

[1043] This comment appears in Stevenson's draft notes (held in the Parliamentary Archives). Asquith was Liberal Prime Minister from 1908 to 1916. Edward Marsh (1872-1953) was private secretary to several Cabinet Ministers, a man of letters and a homosexual, well known to Evan.

[1044] William Randolph Hearst (1863-1951). American newspaper magnate.

[1045] Marion Cecillia Douras (1897-1961). American Actress and mistress of William Randolph Hearst.

[1046] A home (parts of it are from the 12th Century) bought by William Hearst in the Vale of Glamorgan in the mid 1920s. The house and garden parties held there were large scale events with film stars, politicians and London Society's movers and shakers. In the summer of 1925 Richard E Pennoyer sold St Dunstan's to William Hearst, who spent about £250,000 restoring and modernising before putting it back on the market in 1938. The building opened as Atlantic College, in 1962.

[1047] At least one of these courier bags is held by the Tredegar House Collection.

[1048] Uplifted from Norwich, John Julius. [Editor] The Duff Cooper Diaries. 1915-1951. Orion Books. (2006).

[1049] John Frost (1784-1877). In 1835 he was Mayor Newport and a champion for universal suffrage. In 1839 led the Newport Rising, a march on the Westgate Hotel protesting about political corruption and came up against government soldiers. The battle resulted in over 20 deaths, Frost as one of the organisers was arrested, tried and sentenced to death for high treason. This was later commuted to transportation to Australia. Frost was released and returned to Britain (to Bristol) in 1856. There are several memorials to the Chartists is Newport, notably outside the Westgate Hotel. John Frost Square in Newport is named after him.

[1050] Maxwell Knight (1900-1968). Worked for MI5 from 1925 until 1956. Ran Section B5(b) of MI5 during the Second World War.

[1051] Miller, Joan. One Girl's War. Brandon Books. Dublin. 1986. Miller, (personal secretary and favourite of Knight), was one of Knight's agents who infiltrated members of the so-called Fascist sympathisers in the Right Club.

[1052] Guy Maynard Liddell (1892-1958). Trained as a musician in Germany, later won the Military Cross in the Great War. He was a rising star in Scotland Yard (Special Branch) and later the Foreign Office. Worked for MI5 from 1931 and rose to a Senior Intelligence Officer, but passed over to head the department. Liddell was a close friend of Guy Burgess and caught up as a possible Fifth Man in the

Cambridge Spies Scandal. He was later cleared. The Liddell Diaries (covering each day of the Second World War) are at National Archives, Kew and have been abridged by Nigel West.

[1053] Major General Sir Stewart Menzies (1890-1968). Head of MI6 during and after the Second World War. Known as 'C'. At Eton College in the period to 1909.

[1054] See Wheen, Francis. Tom Driberg, his life and indiscretions. Chatto & Windus (1990). In 1941 Anthony Blunt (at the time an officer in MI5) who despised Driberg leaked inside the Communist Party that Driberg was an SIS informer. This unmasking (Blunt was only named later as Driberg's enemy) resulted in Driberg being expelled from the Communist Party. See also Tom Driberg's book Ruling Passions.

[1055] Lonsdale Bryans' personal file maintained by SIS – National Archives, Kew Ref KV 2/2839- contains a detailed picture of where he was between 1928 and 1939. Some of his overseas haunts include possible overlaps with Evan. However, Evan is not mentioned. This calendar of dates includes Lonsdale Bryans staying for 3 months at Schloss Deineberg in the Hartz Mountains with the Munsters in 1928 (see also Chapter 5). Other places mentioned include Berlin (1930-1), Italy, West Indies (1932-3), Tangier (1936), Dutch East Indies (1938) and Bali (1939). An absence of any reference in this list to Evan is odd and leans towards either Evan being expunged or this is evidence that he and Lonsdale Bryans were not as close and involved as Robin Bryans infers in his books.

[1056] See Masters, A. The Man Who Was M. The life of Maxwell Knight. Grafton Books. (1986).

[1057] Cited in various books as the name given to the proposal involving Ian Fleming, Dennis Wheatley with Maxwell Knight (Head of MI5's B5(b)) to use Aleister Crowley in the war effort against Germany and Russia. According to David Conway in Magic without Mirrors Crowley was stood down after Rudolf Hess landed in Scotland in May 1941. A further element is described in various texts as revolving around Crowley performing a ritual in Ashdown Forest, Sussex, with some Canadian soldiers to enticed Hess to fly to Britain.

[1058] See Churton, Tobias. Aleister Crowley The Biography. Spiritual Revolutionary, Romantic Explorer, Occult Master – and Spy. Watkins Publishing (2012), which refers to p 384 " Declassified material associates Swiss astrologer Louis de Wohl with a plot to lure Hess to Britain."

[1059] See Masters, A. The Man Who Was M. The life of Maxwell Knight. Grafton Books. (1986),p126-9.

[1060] Irving, David . Hess: the missing years 1941-1945. Grafton (1989)

[1061] Churton, Tobias. Aleister Crowley: The Biography. Spiritual Revolutionary, Romantic Explorer, Occult Master-and Spy. Watkins Publishing. (2012)

[1062] Ibid.

[1063] Information from Hess historian, Mark Bullock, who comments "Hess's use of the Horn name was nothing new. It was his alias, and the interesting thing is that in the early 1930's (1930-32) Hess travelled far and wide on the passport that he had obtained for the alias. The idea of the alias was two fold. Firstly, it was to ensure that Hess travels could go untracked. Secondly, it diverted unwanted attention. The passport has long since disappeared, but I have spoken to a former SS officer who knew of the existence of the Hess/Horn escapades. He informed me that, when Hess assumed the identity of Horn, he would also assume a disguise. His usual preference was a pair of glasses, bushy wig and moustache."

[1064] http://www.hrp.org.uk/Resources/Prisoners.pdf NB Ronnie and Reggie (the Kray twins, notorious South London gangsters) were briefly held there for a few days in 1952, for failing to report for national service.

[1065] Hess historian Mark Bullock comments "Hess was never a PoW, as if he had been he would have been sent back to Germany due to his mental health. There is still a quandary as to his official status while in captivity in the UK, some historians seem to think that he was a PoW, others that he was a Political Prisoner. In reality he was neither, and was actually held for his own safety in the end."

[1066] A brand new building, a County Mental hospital opened in June 1939. It was requisitioned by the military as a War Emergency Hospital.

[1067] See Double Standards: The Rudolf Hess Cover-Up by Lynn Picknell, Clive Prince and Stephen Prior. Sphere; New Ed Edition (2002), which says "On 25 June 1942 Hess was moved again. This time his home was Maindiff Court, just outside Abergavenny in Wales where – officially at least – he was to remain until being taken to Germany to stand trial at Nuremberg in October 1945." Hess historian Mark Bullock comments "He [Hess] was moved on the 25 June but did not arrive at Maindiff Court until the 26 June. A number of historians and conspiracy theorists have tried to say that this was due to some secret meeting etc. In reality, it was due to complications on the route, and the guards of Hess chose to stay at an RAF station (RAF Worcester) the night.

[1068] The author recommends McGinty, Stephen. Camp Z. How British Intelligence Broke Hitler's Deputy. Quercus books. (2011).

[1069] http://www.the-cauldron.org.uk/Resources/Occult%20War.pdf

[1070] Bryans, Robin. The Dust Has Never Settled. Honeyford Press (1992).

[1071] Some material is due for release by National Archives, Kew in 20107 and some in 2035.

[1072] Colville, John. The Fringes of Power. Downing Street Diaries 1939-1955. Hodder and Stoughton (1985) Entry for 13 May 1941. NB A forthcoming biography by Mark Peel using both official files and the Duke of Hamilton's own private papers "takes issue with conspiracy theorists. While not disputing his [the Duke's] naivety in attempting to reach an accommodation with Nazi Germany long after the cause had become helpless, he firmly exonerates him of any pro-fascist sympathies and collusion with the enemy".

[1073] Attributed by Sir John Colville (No 10 insider) to Sir Alec Cadogan (a Foreign Office diplomat). Entry in The Fringes of Power. Downing Street Diaries 1939-1955, for 14 May 1941.

[1074] King's Counsellor: Abdication and War – The Diaries of Sir Alan Lascelles. Weidenfeld and Nicolson (2006). Entry for 26 May 1943.

[1075] An e-mail to the author on 11 April 2013 from Mark Bullock, writer and Hess historian.

[1076] See Daily Mail, 1 September 1943. This is also referred to by Picknell and Co in Double Standards to which is added "Abergavenny newspapers made no mention of Hess until it announced his move to Nuremberg." Hess historian Mark Bullock comments that this breach "was ....due to the first Junior Guards Officer [who was a key part of Hess's personal protection], which led to his replacement with a few hours of the story breaking."

[1077] There are several texts from authors on Hess that refer to the visits by Walther Thurnheer. Bryans slips in the suggestion that Dil de Rohan (on the Swiss desk of the Ministry of Information, under Brendon Bracken) " wanted to know if any trace of amnesia could be found when Hess was confronted with friends who had known him in Germany". Sir Francis Rose is mentioned as one who had known Hess in the 1930s.

[1078] Bryans, Robin. Blackmail and Whitewash. Honeyford Press (1996).

[1079] An e-mail to the author on 25 April 2013 from Mark Bullock, writer and Hess historian.

[1080] An e-mail to the author on 15 January 2013 from Steve Barber, Newport writer and historian. Hess historian Mark Bullock comments "The Pioneer Corps were responsible for Hess's overall guarding at Maindiff Court but his personal protection was actually due to the RAMC and a Junior Guards Officer, along with about 10 Coldstream Guardsmen and NCOs."

[1081] An e-mail to the author on 7 January 2013 from Mark Bullock, writer and Hess historian asks "I am currently writing a book on the late Rudolf Hess and his life and death. During my research I have come across references that Hess was a regular dinner guest of the late Evan Morgan 2nd Viscount of Tredegar. I have seen that Evan Morgan was Court Martialled for breaching the Official Secrets Act in 1943. During the course of your research have you come across any documents that relate to the link of Rudolf Hess and Evan Morgan?"

[1082] Hess historian Mark Bullock comments "The files in Zurich were the Hess family files and also the Swiss Ambassador's files from London, along with his [Hess's] Red Cross file (that remains closed, unless you are accompanied by a member of the Hess family.)."

[1083] An e-mail to the author on 11 April 2013 from Mark Bullock, writer and historian. [It begs the question whether the person spreading Evan untruths was Robin Bryans, someone who was well known to SIS.].

[1084] Ibid. This is based in part in an article in Western Mail & South Wales News of 26 June 1941, entitled "Welsh Link With Rudolf Hess".

[1085] Examination made on the author's behalf into the servants files held by Tredegar House Archives.

[1086] See Howard, Philip. Myths of the school of schools. The Times, 18 May 1990.

[1087] Guy Liddell's father, Captain Augustus Frederick Liddell (1852-1929) held the post of Gentleman–at-Arms, Comptroller and Treasurer to Prince and Princess Christian of Schleswig-Holstein. The Princess was the 3rd daughter of Queen Victoria.

[1088] Princess Helena Victoria Schleswig-Holstein (1870-1948). Unmarried.

[1089]Princess Marie-Louise Schleswig-Holstein (1872-1956). Married briefly to a homosexual, the marriage was annulled.

[1090] See Deacon Richard. The Greatest Treason. The Bizarre Story of Hollis, Liddell and Mountbatten. Century. (1989).

[1091] Lady Jane Ann Gordon Cory (MS Lethbridge). (1865- 1947), pianist and embroider. Wife of Sir Clifford Cory (1859-1941) a Welsh coal owner (Cory Brothers Ltd) and Liberal politician. Lived at Llantarnam Abbey. The couple separated early in their marriage. The Lethbridges were connected to the Wills family of Cardiff. Robin Bryans writes "Mabel Wills was delighted when a relation of Rector Lethbridge of St Stephen's Launceston called Anne Lethbridge married Sir Clifford Cory whose father, John Cory, had presented to Cardiff the great Memorial Hall".

[1092] In the 1880s two Wills brothers married two Cory sisters to unit two shipbuilding families who left Cornwall for industrial South Wales.

[1093] In The Dust Has Never Settled. Robin Bryans says "Mabel Wills and her Cory in-laws started many evangelical institutes in Wales such as the Christian Alliance of Women and Girls in 1896. The patrons met in the ancient Llantarnam Abbey where Sir Clifford Cory MP presided over Hunt Balls [and] royal polo matches.

[1094] Bryans, Robin. Checkmate. Honeyford Press. (1994) Bryans says Willie Pethybridge was Annie Lethbridge's true love, but he was homosexual, adding "for many years [Willie] ran Liberal affairs in Cardiff where he became Lord Mayor in 1924. If Willie knew about Lloyd George's affairs with women, the Prime Minister knew Willie was homosexual, filling Lady Cory's parties with his favourites".

[1095] Attributed to Andrew Boyle, Author of The Climate of Treason. See The Guardian 6 February 1980.

[1096] See National Archives, Kew Files KV4/ 185 to KV4/196.

[1097] See National Archives, Kew, File KV 4/191.

[1098] See Deacon Richard. The Greatest Treason. The Bizarre Story of Hollis, Liddell and Mountbatten. Century. (1989). Deacon makes assertions about the close friendship between Liddell and Kim Philby and Guy Burgess in The Guardian of 30 May 1979 saying that Liddell, the respected Deputy Director of MI5 " lived to regret the connection" with these men. The writer Andrew Boyce (citing a death bed confession by writer Goronwy Rees) claims that Liddell waited 10 days before telling his bosses of the likely defection of Burgess and Maclean in 1951. See The Observer 20 January 1980.

[1099] These two books are John Costello's Mask of Treachery. Collins. (1988) and Mike and Jacqui Welham's The Crabb Enigma. Matador. (2010).

[1100] Bryans claims that Mountbatten, Anthony Blunt and other prominent men were implicated in the Kincora children's home scandal in Northern Ireland in which boys were sexually abused. http://ukpaedos-exposed.com/cover-ups/kincora-boys-home/

Other facts are cited by Bryans with riddles over several men associated with Rev Ian Paisley, including relatives of Paisley. One other particular man, John McKeague (a prominent Ulster loyalist shot dead by the INLA in 1982), is cited as someone who was ready to spill the beans on people in high places being involved in systematic child abuse. All these allegations lack evidence of substance. A letter written by Bryans to the London Evening Standard about Mountbatten and others and the Kincora affair is published on the Internet. http://theneedleblog.wordpress.com/2013/04/08/robin-bryans-letter/

[1101] See Mike and Jacqui Welham's The Crabb Enigma. Matador. (2010), which (based on an interview with Bryans) identifies Mountbatten's relationship with a long-term lover Peter Murphy and overlaps with an outline of some of Tom Driberg's sex adventures. See also Hoey, Brian. Mountbatten: The Private Story: Sidgwick & Jackson (1994).

[1102] Ziegler, Philip. Mountbatten: The Official Biography. Orion (New Edition) (2001)

[1103] See Hoey, Brian, Mountbatten: The Private Story. The History Press (2008). A startling revelation in Paul Pender's The Butler Did It (Mainstream Publishing 2012) suggests Sir Walter Scott-Elliot (1895-1977), who was murdered by his Butler, was one of Mountbatten's male lovers.

[1104] Penrose Barrie and Freeman Simon. Conspiracy of Silence. The Secret Life of Anthony Blunt. Grafton Books (1986).

[1105] Wright, Peter and Greengrass, Paul. Spycatcher: The candid Autobiography of a Senior Intelligence Officer. Heinemann. (1987).

[1106] http://www.spartacus.schoolnet.co.uk/SPspencerP.htm

[1107] Daily Express, 4 January 1934.

[1108] Daily Mirror, 20 March 1933.

[1109] Ernest Hemingway's novel For Whom The Bell Tolls (1941) and George Orwell's Homage to Catalonia (1938) are based on their experiences of the Spanish Civil War.

[1110] Esmond Marcus David Romilly (1918-1941). Left wing anti-fascist, his grandmother was Lady Arabella Carnegie, half sister to Katharine (Evan's mother). Arabella married Samuel Henry Romilly, their son Bertram, married Nellie Hozier (sister of Winston Churchill's wife Clementine). See also Ingram, Kevin. Rebel: The Short Life of Esmond Romilly. George Weidenfeld & Nicolson. (1985).

[1111] Giles Romilly (died 1967, aged 50, in USA). Journalist and Author.

[1112] Jessica Freeland Mitford (1917-1996). Writer and political activist. Married to Esmond Romilly 1937-1941, when widowed. Her second husband was a lawyer Robert Truhart.

[1113] Jessica Mitford's obituary in The Times of 25 July 1996 says "she and Romilly eloped, first to France and then over the border to Spain. ....eventually family opposition crumbled" They married and moved to New York. There was one daughter, Constancia ('Dinky').

[1114] The papers of the Romilly Family of Huntington Park, Kington, Herefordshire are held in Herefordshire Record Office; access is by permission only from the surviving children of Giles Romilly.

[1115] Address books of Nellie Hozier list Evan and his aunt Lady Helena (Nellie) Carnegie.

[1116] Nellie Hozier (1880-1955). Mrs Bertram Romilly from 1915.

[1117] The Times, 9 May 1949.

[1118] See The Tablet, 2 July 1938.

[1119] See Dart, Monty and Cross, William. Aspects of Evan. The Last Viscount Tredegar. Book Midden Publishing. (2012). This refers to a letter in the University of Limerick from Evan in the Robert Stradling Collection. Ref P/13, item 58.

[1120] Ibid.

[1121] Ibid.

[1122]

http://janus.lib.cam.ac.uk/db/node.xsp?id=EAD%2FGBR%2F0275%2FBeaton%2FA1%2F456

This comprises 28 letters and 4 postcards sent to Cecil Beaton from 1939 until 1971.

[1123] William Francis Forbes-Sempill (1893-1965), 19th Lord Sempill. Aviator and industrial spy.

[1124] An organisation that continues today for the promotion and advancement of the Catholic faith in England and Wales. Its central purpose is to raise funds for maintaining the cost and upkeep of the Archbishop's House, the official residence of the Archbishop of Westminster.

[1125] The Times carries a record of these receptions often held at the Archbishop of Westminster's House, with senior figures of Britain's Catholic faith coming together. The 1926 reception (see The Times 22 July 1926) refers to a reception held on 20 July 1926 with Cardinal Bourne (Archbishop of Westminster). Further reportage (including reference to Evan and Sempill) are in back copies of The Tablet, the international Catholic weekly newspaper.

[1126] Lord Sempill remarried in 1941 to Cecilia Alice Dunbar Kilburn.

[1127] The Sunday Times, 16 May 1937.

[1128] The Right Club was a secret society comprising upper and middle classes who wanted to see peace with Hitler. They considered themselves patriots and loyal to Britain. The names of members was recorded in a book called 'The Red Book'. The membership has been published in book form by Robin Saikia.

[1129] See file KV 5/3 in National Archives, Kew.

[1130] David Bertram Ogilvy Freeland-Mitford, (1878-1958) 2nd Baron Redesdale. Father of the famous Mitford girls.

[1131] Quoted by Amos William. The originals: who's really who in fiction. Cape. (1985) and in the excellent books by Richard Griffiths on the Right Club. See Patriotism perverted: Captain Ramsay, the Right Club and English anti-semitism 1939-40 Constable. (1998) and Fellow travellers of the Right: British enthusiasts for Nazi Germany, 19933-9. Constable (1980).

[1132] Cited by Saikia, Robin. The Red Book. The Membership List of the Right Club 1939. Foxley Books
(2010). Lord Carnegie usually denied any knowledge of the Right Club but recalled its founder, Captain Archibald Maule Ramsey (a Tory MP), describing him as "a very loyal, patriotic man". This also sums up Carnegie.

[1133] Randolph Algernon Ronald Stewart (1892-1978), 12th Earl of Galloway. Fellow Officer with Lord Carnegie in the Scots Guards and Carnegie's best man when he married Princess Maud. There was a family link by marriage between the Carnegies and the Stewarts. When Randolph was heir to the Earldom he was introduced to Gwyneth Morgan, at the time she was a debutante. There was no romantic spark between them. Subsequently the Great War came and Randolph was a long stay prisoner of war in Germany.

[1134] An independent non-party organisation to promote Anglo-German friendship. Very pro-Nazi views.

[1135] See file KV5/3 in National Archives, Kew.

[1136] There are numerous KV files at National Archives, Kew on members of the Right Club interned during the Second World War.

[1137] There are numerous KV files at National Archives, Kew on members of The Link during the Second World War.

[1138] Regulation 18B of the Defence (General) Regulations 1939 an Emergency Measure passed by Parliament that year permitted the Home Secretary to intern people if he had "reasonable cause" to believe that they had "hostile associations".

[1139] See file KV 4/227 in National Archives Kew, being "Report on the work of M/S (agents) during the Second World War. The wartime history of M/S section, its personnel, philosophy and some of its operations, written by Maxwell Knight. M/S operations discussed include those of Percy Glading, the Anna Wolkoff/Tyler Kent and Molly Hiscox/Norah Briscoe cases and Werner Osterwald."

[1140] Danylo Skoropadski (1906-1957). See National Archives Kew files KV 2/661 and KV 2/662. No reference had been found in these files to Evan Morgan. On 23 February 1957 Prince Danylo was killed in London on the eve of his marriage, probably by the KGB; Russia feared the restoration of Danylo at Hetman in the Ukraine.

[1141] See files KV2/661 and KV 882 in National Archives. Kew, Danylo's father was Pavlo (Paul) Skoropadski, (1873-1945), Hetman of the Ukraine 1917-8. Danylo trained as an aircraft design engineer. According to Robin Bryans Danylo visited Llanover Castle South Wales, where he met Evan.

[1142] See National Archives, Kew file KV 2/662.

[1143] Anna Nikolayevna Wolkova (known as Anna de Wolkoff). (1902-1973). Leading member of the Right Club. There are four files in National Archives covering 1938-1949. KV2/840, KV2/841, KV2/ 843 and KV2/843.

[1144] See National Archives, Kew file KV2/2258.

[1145] The tearooms were situated at 57, Harrington Road, London SW7.

[1146] In 1915 Nicholas Wolkoff, a Russian Naval Attache was received by King George V at Buckingham Palace. He was later promoted to Admiral; after the fall of the Tsar he came to London. His daughter Anna became a naturalised British subject. She was first a successful dressmaker – her clients included Wallis Simpson. During the 1930s the Wolkoffs were "fiercely anti-Communist, but also anti-semitic and pro-German". With these credentials Anna joined The Link and was also a member of The Right Club. She was suspected of passing secrets to the Germans. Using his secretary Joan Miller to befriend Anna, sending her on visits to the Russian tearoom, B5(b)'s Maxwell Knight successfully infiltrated The Right Club. This soon established Anna's association with Tyler Kent, a cipher clerk in the American Embassy in London, and revealed the activities of Archibald Ramsay, his wife Ismay and others in passing telegrams leaked to the Nazis from Tyler between the Americans and British. In 1940 Anna and Tyler (whose diplomatic immunity was waived by American Ambassador Joseph Kennedy) were arrested, charged and sent to prison. Anna was released from prison in 1947 (her father died soon afterwards) and she later died in a car crash in Spain.

[1147] See The Sunday Times, 26 December 2004.

[1148] In Matthew Sweet's The West End Front: The Wartime Secrets of London's Grand Hotels. Faber & Faber. (2011) Sweet writes, p 243 "She [Stella] gossiped with Olga Tredegar, a White Russian émigré who married Evan, Lord Tredegar…"

[1149] Stella Edith Lonsdale (1913 - 1994).

http://www.conscript-heroes.com/Art%20Stella%20Lonsdale.html

See also National Archives, reference KV 2/734.

[1150] Daily Mirror, Column Personality Parade. 16 November 1936 and 13 July 1937.

[1151] Evan's birds and other pets were removed to London Zoo during the Second World War.

[1152] Bryans, Robin. The Dust Has Never Settled. Honeyford Press (1992).

[1153] Stephanie Juliana Princess Hohenlohe –Waldenberg- Schilling (1891-1972). Born Vienna Stephanie Richter, she married an Austrian Prince. She met Hitler in 1933 and intimate of Lord Rothermere, publisher of the Daily Mail.

[1154] National Archives, Kew files KV2/1696 and KV 2/1697.

[1155] National Archives papers (1943) refer to Stephanie as follows: "This woman is a notorious intriguer who had in the past extremely close connections with the Nazi leaders. She must still be regarded as a highly dangerous person". W T Caulfield E 2b.

[1156] See Teeling, William. Corridors of Frustration. Johnson. (1970).

[1157] See National Archives files KV2/1696 and KV 2/ 1697.

[1158] See The Times 30 March, 8 April and 9 April 1914. The Hohenlohes were prominent in Nice, Cannes and throughout the resorts of the Riviera.

[1159] National Archives, Kew file KV 2/3289.

[1160] Prince Max Hohenloche- Langenburg, (1897-1968), a friend of Goering, was said to be used as a gentleman agent by Admiral Canaris and as a special informant by others. See National Archives Kew file KV2/3289. Max (and his son Alfonso (1924-2003)) were among the jet set of Marbella after the war.

[1161] Luke Henry [White] (1885-1970) 4th Baron Annaly. MC JP. A Soldier in the Great War. He later served as a Pilot Officer in the RAFVR,

[1162] South Wales Argus, 7 November, 1938.

[1163] A short-lived police force established in response to the outcome of the Munich agreement. Sir Frederick Maurice, the President of the British Legion, offered the services of members to act as a police force in the Sudetenland. 1200 men were selected at Olympia (from 10,000 volunteers). The force was sworn in as special constables and sent to Tilbury where they boarded the SS Naldera and another ship. On 13 October before the ships sailed the International Commission meeting at Berlin decided they were not needed. The force was therefore disbanded. See also The Times 13 September 1938 – 15 October 1938.

[1164] Keatings Powder was for killing bugs and beetles.

[1165] South Wales Argus 7 November, 1938.

[1166] Ibid.

[1167] Colonel John Robert Jermain Macnamara (1905-1944) MP for Chelmsford 1935-1944. Pro-German. Arranged gay sex trips with Guy Burgess in Germany in the 1930s. Killed in action in Italy.

[1168] In the mid 1930s Guy Burgess was based in Tory Central office and went to work for Macnamara.

[1169] An article in The Sunday Times of 8 October 1967 records "One of his [Burgess's] assignments for Macnamara was to convoy a group of pro-Fascist schoolboys, the Britannia Youth, to a Nuremberg Rally."

[1170] According to Tom E Mahl in Espionage's Most Wanted, Potomac Books (2003), Burgess was sexually entangled with Edouard Pfeiffer, a paedophile, who passed secrets to Britain about French government matters. Pfeiffer was also " an officer of the French Boy Scouts organisation, which gave him much opportunity in this regard....Burgess found himself in a male brothel in Paris as he and other high notables danced around a young naked boy tied to a post, whipping him."

[1171] See Bryans, Robin. The Dust Has Never Settled. Honeyford Press. (1992).

[1172] See National Archives, Kew file CAB 120/809. Colonel J B J MacNamara.

[1173] Lonsdale Bryans' personal file at National Archives, KV 2/2839 (maintained by SIS) includes a calendar of his movements "1936 " Majorca just in time for Spanish Civil War. First experience of revolution...but ten days quite enough. Leave after first rush exodus abated for Gibraltar and Tangier, whence to Malta and Tripoli, returning home in December."

[1174] Based on the calendar of Lonsdale Bryans' movements in file KV 2/2839.

[1175] The Ships Passenger Lists show that Lonsdale Bryans arrived back in Southampton on 4 November 1933 (from off the Baloeran, having boarded ship at Tangier). The forty-year old Bryans gives his address as Wellington Club, London. There is no mention of his profession. In 1933 Lonsdale Bryans' widowed mother, Mrs Herbert Bryans was living at Bradford Priory, Wilts.

[1176] British Continental Airways was founded by Frederick Farey-Jones, Grahame Mackinnon and Jack Bryans; it amalgamated in 1936 with British Airways and afterwards continued as BCA under Sir Percy Grahame Mackinnon. See Flightglobal Archive for page from Flight Magazine 29 October 1936.

[1177] Sir Charles John Hubert Miller (1858- 1940). Last Lord of the Manor of Froyle. Army Officer and Traveller. Spent the winter months in Venice where he had a home.

[1178] James Paul Donahue, Jr. (1915-1966). Heir to the Woolworth estate and New York socialite. See Wilson, Christopher. Dancing with the devil. St Martin's Press. (2001)

[1179] Bryans, Robin. Checkmate. Honeyford Press (1994).

[1180] Bryans, James Lonsdale. The Curve of Fate. Andrew Dakers. (1941). Synopsis "Man-Ape to The Man-God: this is an exploration of the evolution of man and addresses the age old questions What are we? Where are we? and Why are we? It centres around the philosophy that evolutionary time and change move in inverse ratio and in formulating this theory the author explores the whole field of human speculation, from mathematics to metaphysics, from ancient wisdom to modern science, from traditional mysticism to an intense individual inward vision."

[1181] "Soeran Segara", Dutch East Indies is listed by Evan in The Catholic who's who and yearbook for 1941.

[1182] The Diaries of Donald Friend: 1967-1999, published by the National Library of Australia (2001) record recollections of Evan by the Balinese, of him having a house on the beach and that "The dimensions of his cock and many of his doings have become folklore."

[1183] Passenger Lists online via National Archives, Kew. Lonsdale Bryans arrived back in London from Japan on 25 August 1939.

[1184] National Archives, Kew file KV2/ 2839 indicates that Lonsdale Bryans had the ear of several peers, including Lord Brocket and Arthur Ronald Nall Nall-Cain (1904-1967), a notorious friend of Hitler and Von Ribbentrop, who worked for a negotiated peace settlement with Germany. Another Nazi sympathiser (and Eton and Oxford crony of Evan and Lonsdale Bryans) who supported the quest was Walter, the 8th Duke of Buccleuch (1894-1973). Lonsdale Bryans also tried to get his old bachelor friend Sir Hubert Miller (with whom he had spent holidays in his Venetian palazzo) to put a word in the right ear in government. Miller died in 1940, aged 82. Several other men were approached for help who were at Eton with Lonsdale Bryans and Evan, including John Jestyn (Lord)Llewellin (1893-1957) and Oliver Lyttelton (later Viscount Chandos, 1893-1972).

[1185] Ulrich Friedrich Wilhelm Jochim von Ribbentrop (1893-1946). German Ambassador to Britain 1936-38. Foreign Minister in Nazi Germany from 1938 to 1945. Hanged after the Nuremberg Trials.

[1186] See National Archives, Kew file KV 2/2839.

[1187] Ulrich von Hassell (1881-1944). Diplomat and member of the German Resistance against Hitler.

[1188] Lonsdale Bryans. James. Blind Victory. Skeffington & Son Ltd. (1951).

[1189] Von Hassell, Ambassador. The von Hassell Diaries 1938-1944: The Story of the Forces Against Hitler Inside Germany. Doubleday & Company (1947).

[1190] Lonsdale Bryans. James. Blind Victory. Skeffington & Son Ltd. (1951).

[1191] Sir Alexander George Montagu Cadogan (1884-1968). Diplomat, Diarist and Civil Servant, Permanent Under Secretary for Foreign Affairs 1938 to 1946.

[1192]C1954: A letter, dated 22 February, from Brigadier Harker (Acting Director General, MI5) to Sir Alexander Cadogan (Permanent Undersecretary at the FO) who was pro-Churchill. He is warned about James Lonsdale Bryans who has the backing of the Duke of Buccleuch as an emissary of Lord Halifax. MI5 say that Bryans is "indiscreet" and Rab Butler should not have confidence in him. C2785G covers seven pages of A4. Dated 15 March 1941 it starts with a report to Sir A. Cadogan from MI5. The report was also seen by others including Strang and Sargent of the FO's Central and Southern Depts. (They were also involved in propaganda at the FO and also worked for the Political Warfare Executive, sending propaganda into Germany with the Gustav Siegfried Eins radio station). The report states that James Lonsdale Bryans has returned from Lisbon. He knows a Danish citizen called Ole Erik Anderson who worked as a courier for the Germans.

Anderson was captured and interned in Britain. When caught he had documents from Bryans on his person. MI5 interviewed Bryans and found him very pro-Hitler. He was supposed to be meeting the anti-Hitler faction in Germany. He in fact wants to meet Hitler and it is not known if he has. MI5 had observed Bryans with Lords Lymington and Brocket (both pro-NS). Anderson had a letter from Bryans to a German publisher to publish his book. This offer was turned down by the publisher. Anderson had the names of Lord Lymington and Drummond Wolfe as supporters of a peace movement in Britain. He claimed to know Ribbentrop and Hengel (Ribbentrop's father in law) well. Anderson was also found with the names of the Duke of Buccleuch and Lord Brocket. Bryans had written a letter to an Italian friend D. Pirzio Biroli of Civitavecchia who was also pro-Hitler. The MI5 reports state that James Lonsdale Bryans is not to be trusted. There is also a FO Central Dept handwritten report from 22 March 1941 about Lonsdale Bryans. It advises warning people about him. They cannot have Bryans locked up because of his Foreign office contacts. Notes were written by Rab Butler, A. Cadogan and Frank Roberts of Central Dept. amongst others. Bryans was not to be issued with an exit permit. The last note was written on 4 April and recommends that Bryans be "strictly watched". The last page is a letter dated 7 April from Sir A. Cadogan to Brigadier Harker of MI5. It states that they cannot lock up Lonsdale Bryans because of his friendship with Lord Halifax but requests that MI5 keep him under surveillance and check his mail. (Later that month Harker was sacked as Acting D G). Source: Monty Dart uplifted from Ancestry web site.

[1193] See National Archives, Kew, file WO199/3356. 2nd (Newport) Bn Monmouthshire HG.

[1194] House of Lords Debate 11 July 1940 on Local Defence Volunteers. At the time Evan said that he was "speaking as an L.D.V. who has seen active service in the particular part of the country from which I come — for we have received visits from the enemy for a fortnight past …"

The late Terry Underwood's book 'Time to Remember, Time to Forget' The Story of Newport in the War Years, (1996) (page 5) advises that prior to July 1940 that the Cleveland Oil Depot, on Newport's Corporation Road was bombed. No fatalities. Then things kicked off in a big way shortly afterwards – with 46 people being killed in the town between Sept 13th 1940 and July 1st 1941.

[1195] See file WO32/18642 in National Archives. Kew regarding the name change from the 17 London Regt (Poplar and Stepney Rifles) to 17 London Regt (Tower Hamlets Rifles). (1926).

[1196] The Times of 7 August 1930 reports "The 17th London Regiment (Tower Hamlets Rifles) under canvas at Oxney Farm, Borden, were inspected yesterday by their honorary colonel, the Hon Evan Morgan….. The Hon. Evan Morgan remained under canvas with the battalion for the night, and will go out with them on manoeuvres today."

[1197] Saturday Weekly Argus 1 March 1941.

[1198] South Wales Argus, Monday 12 January, 1942.

[1199] Ibid.

[1200] The evidence for this is in a article in the South Wales Argus from November 1944.

[1201] Renowned military engagement centred in and around the Dutch towns of Arnhem, Oosterbeek, Wolfheze and Driel and surrounding parts between 17-26 September 1944. Part of Operation Market Garden. The 1976 film A Bridge Too Far, directed by Richard Attenborough, is based on the event. The remark about Evan being a part of the 21 Regiment in Holland in 1944 was made at a talk given by a former Tredegar House guide at the Friends of Tredegar House on 10 April 2013.

[1202] A film from 1967 where a group of convicted men take part in a daring but deadly WW2 exploit to gain their freedom.

[1203] Williams, Guy St John (Ed). The Renvyle Letters. Gogarty Family Correspondence, 1939-1957. Daletta Press (2000).

[1204] Williams, Guy St John (Ed). The Renvyle Letters. Gogarty Family Correspondence, 1939-1957. Daletta Press (2000). A letter dated 2 October 1944 from Oliver Gogarty to Nin. The informant of this startling revelation on Evan is "a Mrs Aherne, who was Lady Patricia Moore (1912-1947), daughter of the 10th Earl and Countess of Drogheda. The "young Herbert" mentioned is almost certainly Hon. David Herbert (1908-1995), second son of Reggie, 15th Earl of Pembroke. After the Second World War David Herbert lived (and thrived there an iconic gay settler, artist and socialite) in Tangier.

There is an extraordinary co-incidence to consider when Lady Patricia Moore's history is considered. Her previous husband was Captain (later Major) Sir Herbert Paul Latham (1905-1955), an MP (for Whitby and Scarborough), who was court martialled in 1941 and sentenced to two years imprisonment for "ten charges of disgraceful conduct of an improper kind while on active service and one of attempting to commit suicide" (See Cornishman 2 October 1941). Latham was some time the lover of Evan's friend, Eddy Sackville-West.

[1205] Bryans, Robin. Blackmail and Whitewash. Honeyford Press (1996).

[1206] Ibid.

[1207] Bryans, Robin. The Dust Has Never Settled. Honeyford Press. (1992).

[1208] Ruth Irwin Crossley (1909-) Daughter of Sir Kenneth Irwin, 2nd Baronet.

[1209] Anthony Crommelin Crossley (1903-1939). Conservative MP throughout the 1930s. Killed in a flying accident. Evan knew Crossley whose personal/ parliamentary life overlapped with the bisexual millionaire MP, Ronald Tree (1897-1976) and Mad Jack Macnamara. See Ronald Tree's Memoirs When the Moon was High: Memoirs of peace and war 1897-1942. Macmillan (1975).

[1210] Konstanty Scheunert, (died 1970). Assistant Military Attache at the Polish Embassy in London. Later lived with his wife Ruth at Irish Rath, Linaskea, Northern Ireland. Known as 'Kot'.

[1211] Evan was saddened by Bosie's deterioration. Evan remarked to a friend (Philippe Jullian, French author and illustrator) about Bosie's last months "Essentially he's a washed poet, nothing more." It may well have been that Evan was unable to visit Bosie in late 1944-early 1945 as Evan was held in prison.

[1212] British Library Manuscripts Division Ref Add 81707.

[1213] Ibid. Letter dated 12 March 1945.

[1214] Ibid. Letter dated 15 February 1945.

[1215] Robin Bryans adds in The Dust Has Never Settled that Edward Coleman wrote of an earlier period of Evan's visits that "He [Evan] was indeed a good friend to Bosie and came frequently to see him with succulent titbits to tempt his failing appetite, and often brought with him a somewhat strange entourage of youthful admirers whom Bosie enjoyed immensely."

[1216] See The Times 24 March 1945. The funeral was at the Franciscan Friary, Crawley, Sussex.

[1217] Sinden Donald. A Touch of the Memoirs. Hodder and Stoughton. (1982).

[1218] Robin Bryans comments "Like myself, Henry Maxwell also declined to go to Bosie's funeral and the Coleman wake"

[1219] See Evelyn Waugh's diary for 26 April 1946. Also cited in The New Oxford Book of Literary Anecdotes. Oxford University Press. (2006).

[1220] Wilson John Howard. Evelyn Waugh: 1924-1966. Fairleigh Dickinson Univ Press. (1996).

[1221] Bob Boothby (1900-1986); Tom Driberg (1905-1976) ; Henry Chips Channon (1897-1958). The autobiographies and biographies of these three men describe the difficulty for gay men conducting their secrets lives whilst in the public domain. Chips Channon was one of the notable diarists of his time. To his great credit, Bob Boothby was one of the leading protagonists in favour of a commission to examine the law relating to homosexuality and his public statements were made on the subject from 1954 onwards; this campaign for change led to the eventual change in the law in 1967.

[1222] Bryans, Robin. Blackmail and Whitewash. Honeyford Press (1996).

[1223] Roberts, Cecil. Sunshine and Shadow. Hodder and Stoughton. (1972).

[1224] Buckle produced biographies of Jacob Epstein (1963), Nijinsky (1975), Diaghilev (1984) and George Balanchine (1988). He was one of the founders of the Theatre Museum in London.

[1225] Buckle, Richard. The Adventures of a Ballet Critic. Cresset Press (1953).

[1226] Ibid.

[1227] Symonds, John. The King of Shadow Realm. Aleister Crowley his life and magic. Duckworth (1989). By the time of Symond's visit in the summer of 1948, Crowley was dead.

[1228] The Marchese Anthony Mattei (1902 - 1992) head of an old Maltese family. Tony lived in Hove and contributed his memories of Evan to Tredegar House Archives in the late 1970s.

[1229] Mary Lauretta Jaqueline Desiree Valentine Esme Hope-Nicholson (1919-2005). Artist. Usually known as Laura. Richard Buckle adored her.

[1230] Jean Hugo. (1894-1984) French Painter, illustrator and theatre designer. Great grandson of the writer Victor Hugo.

[1231] Charles Felix Otho Victor Gabriel John Adrian Hope-Nicholson. (1921-1990). Known as Felix. Robin Bryans describes him as " The Squire of Chelsea".

[1232] Bryans, Robin. Let the petals fall. Honeyford Press (1994). There is evidence that Evan was first introduced to Felix through Lord Alfred Douglas, who was a close friend of Hedley Hope-Nicholson (1888-1969), father of Felix and Laura.

[1233] The Sunday Times, 30 December 1990.

[1234] Wilde lived at 34 Tite Street, Chelsea and at other flats here. His two sons lived here in the 1920s and were painted by Laura Hope-Nicolson. Tite Street was the home of other Evan–known residents: Peter Warlock lived at No30 (formerly 12A) and committed suicide here in 1930. Augustus John lived at No 33 from 1940 until 1958.

[1235] Brian Christian de Claiborne Howard (1905-1958) See Lancaster, Marie-Jaqueline. Brian Howard. Portrait of a Failure. Timewell Press Ltd (2005). Lancaster was a secretary in the War Office during the 1940s and observed Howard in the regular company of Guy Burgess and Dylan Thomas at the Gargoyle Club, a place also frequented by Evan.

[1236] "I went to the most horrible party given by Evan Morgan, which began at the Eiffel Tower and ended at somebody's bedroom at Prince's hotel in Jermyn Street. I rushed out, clutching my remaining bits of virtue – bundled them into a taxi, and trundled home. I've never seen anything so stupendously naughty, even in Oxford! Never again – as I value my reputation." Cited by Marie-Jaqueline Lancaster in Portrait of a Failure.

[1237] See Roberts, Cecil. The Bright Twenties. Hodder and Stoughton. (1970), pages 100-1 has a wonderful description of Katharine's hobby of making nests to aid her crippling arthritis.

[1238] The material on Lauretta used here comes from an Obituary (by her sister Marie-Jaqueline) in The Independent for 18 February 2005.

[1239] Sir John Erasmus Gwynne Alexander Philipps (1915-1948). Succeeded his father in 1938. He was High Sheriff of Pembrokeshire.

[1240] Picton Castle, Siebech, Pembrokeshire, West Wales.

[1241] Buckle, Richard. The Adventures of a Ballet Critic. Cresset Press (1953).

[1242] Buckle comments in his memoirs…. "He [Johnnie Philipps] put up several hundred pounds for Ballet [Buckle's magazine] with great benevolence and amusement, and would probably have done more.."

[1243] From a tribute to Philipps in The Times of 30 November 1948 by 'H.N.H.'.

[1244] Buckle, Richard. The Adventures of a Ballet Critic. Cresset Press (1953).

[1245] Ibid.

[1246] See The Times of 30 November 1948.

[1247] Ibid.

[1248] See the Times 8 December 1948. The memorial service was held at St George's Hanover Square, conducted by the Archdeacon of Hampstead.

[1249] Prince Nicholas Vladimirovitch Galitzine (1914-1999). White Russian descent, he came over to Britain with Olga in 1919 on board HMS Marlborough. A right winger (he was a member of The Right Club) he later emigrated to Canada. See obituary in The Times 20 May 1999.

[1250] Baron George Marochetti (died 1952), Journalist, diplomat and wine agent.

[1251] For two years on the anniversary of Evan's death Marochetti placed an In Memoriam notice in The Times: " Tredegar, Viscount Evan, 27 April 1949. In loving memory of dear Evan, so sadly missed. BM." The notices ended when Marochetti died in 1952, aged 58.

[1252] James Lees-Milne (1908-1997). Best known for his close associations as a diary writer and the work done restoring old houses on behalf of the National Trust.

[1253] See Lowndes Marie Belloc and Lowndes Susan. Diaries and letters of Marie Belloc Lowndes, 1911-1947, Chatto & Windus. (1971). Entry for 22 September 1946 "He [Evan] is toying with the thought of proposing marriage to Lady Illingworth..."

[1254] Leslie, Shane. Long Shadows. Murray. (1966).

[1255] Mortimer, John. Clinging to the Wreckage. Penguin Books. (2010) Famous barrister and writer Mortimer adds of Wyn " She had been a close friend of Havelock Ellis, who taught her to pee standing up, an art she often used to practise as we staggered out of the White Hart [pub] at closing time..."

[1256] Bryans, Robin. The Dust Has Never Settled. Honeyford Press (1992).

[1257] Lady Hazel Lavery (1886-1935). American born, Irish republican sympathiser.

[1258] Sir John Lavery (1856-1941). Portrait Painter.

[1259] Fielding. Daphne. Emerald and Nancy. Eyre & Spottiswoode. (1968).

[1260] Cecil Roberts was another guest of Evan's at Phyllis Court. Roberts describes a "ludicrous experience" with Evan in Sunshine and Shadow. Hodder and Stoughton, (1972). Evan introduced Roberts to a young man he called Andre Maurois. [French Author, (1885-1961)]. The man explained to Roberts "This is terrible! Lord Tredegar persists in introducing me as Andre Maurois, I am not Andre Maurois, I am Paul Morand" [another French author (1888-1976)].

[1261] Inez Holden (1906-1974). Novelist and short story writer and bohemian adventurer. Anthony Powell says of her in Messengers of day "a torrential talker, an accomplished mimic, her gossip of a high and fantastical category".

[1262] London Magazine, Volume 14, page 92 (1974).

[1263] The London Magazine, Volume 33, Issues 7-12, page 29, (1993), says "When speaking of her childhood the novelist Inez Holden sometimes used to say she came from a bad home....her mother and father quarrelled incessantly..."

[1264] Powell, Anthony. Messengers of day. Google Books. (1978).

[1265] See Lowndes Marie Belloc and Lowndes Susan. Diaries and Letters of Marie Belloc. 1911-1947. Chatto & Windus (1973) entry for 22 September 1946. Lady Illingsworth was a member of the Wilberforce family, she died in 1986.

[1266] The immediate heir to the Morgan legacies was Evan's uncle Freddie who was nearly 80. Freddie succeeded as the next Lord Tredegar but for tax cover renounced his ownership of the Estates, which passed to John. In turn on his father's death in 1954, John became the 6th and last Lord Tredegar. He died in 1962.

[1267] Philippe Jullian Fresh Remembrance of Oscar Wilde, from Vogue, 1 November 1969.

[1268] Castle Leslie, Glaslough, County Monaghan, Eire.

[1269] An interesting appraisal of Nina and Crowley (and Nina's death) can be found in David Conway's Magic without Mirrors LOGIOS (2011) pages 197-201. Another commentary by Frank Mort in Cultures of Consumption says Nina "was [by the 1950s] a chronic alcoholic....penniless and incontinent and was often to be seen demanding drinks in Soho pubs."

[1270] Hamnett, Nina. Laughing Torso. Ray Long & Richard R Smith Inc. (1932).

[1271] Burkhart, Charles. Herman and Nancy and Ivy. Victor Gollancz. (1977).

[1272] Malcolm Lowry (1909-1957). Writer best known for his novel Under The Volcano.

[1273] Churchill, Viscount. All my sins remembered. An Autobiography. Heinemann: London. (1964).

[1274] Vickers, Hugo. The Kiss. The Story of an Obsession. Hamish Hamilton. (1996).

[1275] Ibid.

[1276] Ibid.

[1277] The author has been unable to trace what happened in the end to the lawyer, Robin Chester. Any information would be most welcome.

[1278] Bryans, Robin. Blackmail and Whitewash. Honeyford Press (1996).

THANKS AND ACKNOWLEDGEMENTS

The author graciously acknowledges the various authors of material quoted in the text and End Notes and their respective publishers and copyright holders. Such quotes used have been kept modest and incidental. Care has been taken *not* to exceed the spirit of the copyright principles laid down in the respective *"Permissions and Fair Dealing"* guidelines in terms of the limits under the criteria for *" the purposes of criticism or review"*.

He particularly wishes to thank Steve Barber, Robin Bryans, Mark Bullock, Bernard Byrom, Monty and Tom Dart, Dai Jones, Annie Parker and Les Case, all the past Curators at Tredegar House, Newport, Newport City Council, staff of the National Trust at Tredegar House and anyone else consulted in the research process.

Considerable thanks are also owed to the staff of Newport Reference Library, The British Library, the Vatican Secret Archives and other repositories used by the author to compile this book.

Among the public records to acknowledge is the material in Crown Copyright extracted from National Archives, Kew.

Any errors in the text etc are the author's and his alone. He welcomes corrections, with sources and any additional data to include in any future reprints of the book. He thanks also Newspaper Archive.com, Abe Books, Amazon Books, Google Books, the National Library of Wales. Finally, he records considerable thanks to his wife Perry and their family and apologies for all the disruption, by necessity, compiling a book creates by day and night.

About The Author William Cross

William Cross (Will) spent 28 years as a Civil Servant, in London. He took early retirement in July 2005 to concentrate on writing and research. His roots are Scottish; his family origins are in Erskine, Renfrewshire and Kilmaronock, Loch Lomondside. Will was brought up in a small coal-mining village in Lanarkshire. After schooldays in Scotland he studied at the Universities of London and Southampton. He now lives in Wales. A Fellow of the Society of Antiquaries of Scotland since 1984, he regularly lectures on Scottish history topics and the Morgan Women of Tredegar House. Will is a Member of the Society of Authors. He is married with two grown up sons and two grandchildren. Contact Will by email: williecross@aol.com

Aspects of Evan is still available
e-mail williecross@aol.com

Other Titles from Book Midden Publishing

These titles are written by William Cross

The Life and Secrets of Almina Carnarvon: A Candid Biography of Almina, 5th Countess of Carnarvon. 3rd Edition.
ISBN 9781905914081

Lady Carnarvon's Nursing Homes: Nursing the Privileged in Wartime and Peace.
ISBN 9781905914036

The Dustbin Case: Dennistoun versus Dennistoun ISBN 9781905914043

Lordy! Tutankhamun's Patron As A Young Man. ISBN 9781905914050

These titles are written by Monty Dart and William Cross

A Beautiful Nuisance by Monty Dart and William Cross.
ISBN 9781905914104

Aspects of Evan by Monty Dart and William Cross
ISBN 9781905914159

Other Titles

Daphne's Story: The Long Journey from the Red Brick Building by Daphne Condon.
ISBN 9781905914128

Steaming Light: by Bernard Pearson.
ISBN 9781905914135

Who Killed Dripping Lewis? By Monty Dart
ISBN 9781905914199

Forthcoming Titles from Book Midden Publishing

The Court Martial of Evan, Viscount Tredegar by Monty Dart and William Cross.
ISBN 9781905914142

The Five Lady Tredegars By Monty Dart and William Cross.
ISBN 9781905914203

The Abergavenny Witch Hunt of 1942: A full account of a case of the persecution of over 20 gay men in 1942. By William Cross.
ISBN 9781905914227

To Seanie, With Love. By Greggorie Douglas and William Cross.
ISBN 9781905914166

Catherine and Tilly: Porchey Carnarvon's Two Duped Wives. The Tragic Tales of the Sixth Countesses of Carnarvon.
ISBN 9781905914258

Contact Book Midden by e-mail williecross@aol.com

Not Behind Lace Curtains

The Hidden World of Evan, Viscount Tredegar

Si deus nobiscum quis contra nos,

"If God is with us, then who is against us".

Eadem, Edam Sequentur

The Gods were sitting dreaming at a pool;
A spider trapped a fly, a bird, a bee,
A knave with specious arguments, a fool;
One raised his head and murmured, " Yes, I see !"
Whilst one with drowsy eyelids gazed around
And mumbled something low about a noise.
Another languid pointed to the ground :
" Those children should not play with dangerous toys."
The eldest yawned and stretched himself and said :
"Always it was the same, and still must be;
Give each his wants, and his contentment's dead.
Forthwith he rushes into mutiny !
Since first the day was severed from the night
Was ever heard the same unceasing cry,
Justice and Freedom, Liberty and Right!
Yet unto these whoever cometh night ?
Defeats and victories all must pass away,
Each leaves its little mark upon the hour :
And the hours fading follow with the day,
Alone Eternity doth keep its power."

Evan Morgan 1919